T4-AHW-687

The Condition of Education 2016

MAY 2016

Grace Kena
William Hussar
Joel McFarland
Cristobal de Brey
Lauren Musu-Gillette
National Center for Education Statistics

Xiaolei Wang
Jijun Zhang
Amy Rathbun
Sidney Wilkinson-Flicker
Melissa Diliberti
American Institutes for Research

Amy Barmer
Farrah Bullock Mann
Erin Dunlop Velez
RTI International

Thomas Nachazel
Senior Editor
Wyatt Smith
Mark Ossolinski
Editors
American Institutes for Research

NCES 2016-144
U.S. DEPARTMENT OF EDUCATION

U.S. Department of Education
John B. King, Jr.
Secretary

Institute of Education Sciences
Ruth Neild
Deputy Director for Policy and Research
Delegated Duties of the Director

National Center for Education Statistics
Peggy G. Carr
Acting Commissioner

The National Center for Education Statistics (NCES) is the primary federal entity for collecting, analyzing, and reporting data related to education in the United States and other nations. It fulfills a congressional mandate to collect, collate, analyze, and report full and complete statistics on the condition of education in the United States; conduct and publish reports and specialized analyses of the meaning and significance of such statistics; assist state and local education agencies in improving their statistical systems; and review and report on education activities in foreign countries.

NCES activities are designed to address high-priority education data needs; provide consistent, reliable, complete, and accurate indicators of education status and trends; and report timely, useful, and high-quality data to the U.S. Department of Education, the Congress, the states, other education policymakers, practitioners, data users, and the general public. Unless specifically noted all information contained herein is in the public domain.

We strive to make our products available in a variety of formats and in language that is appropriate to a variety of audiences. You, as our customer, are the best judge of our success in communicating information effectively. If you have any comments or suggestions about this or any other NCES product or report, we would like to hear from you. Please direct your comments to

> NCES, IES, U.S. Department of Education
> Potomac Center Plaza
> 550 12th Street SW
> Washington, DC 20202

May 2016

The NCES Home Page address is http://nces.ed.gov.
The NCES Publications and Products address is http://nces.ed.gov/pubsearch.

This report was prepared with assistance from the American Institutes for Research under Contract No. ED-IES-12-D-0002. Mention of trade names, commercial products, or organizations does not imply endorsement by the U.S. Government.

Suggested Citation
Kena, G., Hussar W., McFarland J., de Brey C., Musu-Gillette, L., Wang, X., Zhang, J., Rathbun, A., Wilkinson-Flicker, S., Diliberti M., Barmer, A., Bullock Mann, F., and Dunlop Velez, E. (2016). *The Condition of Education 2016* (NCES 2016-144). U.S. Department of Education, National Center for Education Statistics. Washington, DC. Retrieved [date] from http://nces.ed.gov/pubsearch.

Content Contact
Grace Kena
(202) 245-6135
grace.kena@ed.gov

ISBN: 978-1-59888-845-4

A Letter From the
Commissioner of the
National Center for Education Statistics

May 2016

Congress has required that the National Center for Education Statistics (NCES) produce an annual report to policymakers about the progress of education in the United States. *The Condition of Education 2016* presents 43 key indicators on important topics and trends in U.S. education. These indicators focus on population characteristics, such as educational attainment and economic outcomes; participation in education at all levels; and several contextual aspects of education, including international comparisons, at both the elementary and secondary education level and the postsecondary education level. The three Spotlight indicators for the 2016 report provide a more in-depth look at some of the data. Supplemental indicators, which help to provide a fuller picture of the state of American education, are available online.

The Condition includes an At a Glance section, which allows readers to quickly make comparisons within and across indicators, and a Highlights section, which captures a key finding or set of findings from each indicator. The report contains a Reader's Guide, Glossary, and a Guide to Data Sources that provide additional information to help place the indicators in context. In addition, each indicator references the data tables that were used to produce the indicator, most of which are in the *Digest of Education Statistics*.

This year's *Condition* shows that 91 percent of young adults ages 25 to 29 had a high school diploma or its equivalent in 2015, and that 36 percent had a bachelor's or higher degree. Median earnings continued to be higher for 25- to 34-year-olds with higher levels of education in 2014, and in 2015, the employment rate was generally higher for those with higher levels of education.

Student enrollment patterns in preprimary and K–12 education have varied over time. The percentages of 3- and 4-year-olds enrolled in preprimary programs in 2014 (43 and 66 percent, respectively) were higher than the percentages enrolled in 1990 (33 and 56 percent, respectively), but these percentages have not changed much in recent years. In the fall of 2013, total public school enrollment was at 50.0 million students, an increase of 3 percent from the fall of 2003. During this period, the number of White students enrolled in public elementary and secondary schools decreased from 28.4 million to 25.2 million, and the percentage of students who were White decreased from 59 to 50 percent. The percentage of White students in public schools is projected to continue to decline as the enrollments of Hispanic students and Asian/Pacific Islander students increase. In addition, over 2.5 million students were enrolled in charter schools in the fall of 2013; enrollment in these schools has increased from the fall of 2003, when it was just under 1 million students.

Students who are English language learners (ELL) are making up a growing share of public school students. In 2013–14, Spanish, Arabic, and Chinese were the most common languages spoken by ELL students. Another aspect of the landscape of schools is the percentage of schools that are considered high poverty. In the fall of 2013, high-poverty schools accounted for 25 percent of all public schools. In that year, 24 percent of traditional public schools were high poverty, compared with 39 percent of charter schools. In terms of school climate and safety, rates of school crime against students have declined significantly over the last two decades. Schools have also implemented more safety and security procedures in recent years.

Letter From the Commissioner

According to the National Assessment of Educational Progress, or NAEP, mathematics and reading scores for both 4th- and 8th-graders were higher in 2015 than in the early 1990s, when the earliest assessments were conducted. However, the 2015 average mathematics scores in grades 4 and 8 were 1 and 2 points lower, respectively, than the 2013 average mathematics scores. The 2015 average reading score for 4th-graders was not significantly different from the score in 2013, and the 2015 score for 8th-graders was 2 points lower than the score in 2013. At grade 12, the average mathematics score was lower in 2015 than in 2013, and the average reading score did not significantly differ between the two years. Of particular note is that in both mathematics and reading, the lowest performing 12th-grade students—those performing at the 10th and 25th percentiles—had lower scores in 2015 than in 2013.

In school year 2013–14, some 82 percent of public high school students graduated with a regular diploma. This rate is the highest it has ever been. Sixty-eight percent of 2014 high school completers enrolled in college the following fall: 44 percent went to 4-year institutions and 25 percent went to 2-year institutions. Meanwhile, the status dropout rate, or the percentage of 16- to 24-year-olds who are not enrolled in school and do not have a high school credential, declined from 10.9 percent in 2000 to 6.5 percent in 2014.

We are pleased to present to you *The Condition of Education 2016*. As new data are released, the indicators will be updated on *The Condition of Education* website and on the *Condition* mobile website. NCES also produces a wide range of reports and data as well as other tools and products designed to help keep policymakers and the American public informed about trends and conditions in U.S. education.

Peggy G. Carr, Ph.D.
Acting Commissioner
National Center for Education Statistics

Reader's Guide

The Condition of Education contains indicators on the state of education in the United States and abroad. This report is available on the National Center for Education Statistics (NCES) website, as a full PDF, as individual indicator PDFs, and on the NCES mobile website. All reference tables are hyperlinked within the PDF and HTML versions, as are the sources for each of the graphics. The reference tables can be found in other NCES publications—primarily the *Digest of Education Statistics*.

Data Sources and Estimates

The data in these indicators were obtained from many different sources—including students and teachers, state education agencies, local elementary and secondary schools, and colleges and universities—using surveys and compilations of administrative records. Users should be cautious when comparing data from different sources. Differences in aspects such as procedures, timing, question phrasing, and interviewer training can affect the comparability of results across data sources.

Most indicators in *The Condition of Education* summarize data from surveys conducted by NCES or by the Census Bureau with support from NCES. Brief descriptions of the major NCES surveys used in these indicators can be found in the Guide to Sources. More detailed descriptions can be obtained on the NCES website under "Surveys and Programs."

The Guide to Sources also includes information on non-NCES sources used to develop indicators, such as the Census Bureau's American Community Survey (ACS) and Current Population Survey (CPS). For further details on the ACS, see http://www.census.gov/acs/www/. For further details on the CPS, see http://www.census.gov/cps/.

Data for *Condition of Education* indicators are obtained from two types of surveys: universe surveys and sample surveys. In universe surveys, information is collected from every member of the population. For example, in a survey regarding certain expenditures of public elementary and secondary schools, data would be obtained from each school district in the United States. When data from an entire population are available, estimates of the total population or a subpopulation are made by simply summing the units in the population or subpopulation. As a result, there is no sampling error, and observed differences are reported as true.

Since universe surveys are often expensive and time consuming, many surveys collect data from a sample of the population of interest (sample survey). For example, the National Assessment of Educational Progress (NAEP) assesses a representative sample of students rather than the entire population of students. When a sample survey is used, statistical uncertainty is introduced, because the data come from only a portion of the entire population. This statistical uncertainty must be considered when reporting estimates and making comparisons. For more information, please see the section on standard errors below.

Various types of statistics derived from universe and sample surveys are reported in *The Condition of Education*. Many indicators report the size of a population or a subpopulation, and often the size of a subpopulation is expressed as a percentage of the total population. In addition, the average (or *mean*) value of some characteristic of the population or subpopulation may be reported. The average is obtained by summing the values for all members of the population and dividing the sum by the size of the population. An example is the annual average salaries of full-time instructional faculty at degree-granting postsecondary institutions. Another measure that is sometimes used is the *median*. The median is the midpoint value of a characteristic at or above which 50 percent of the population is estimated to fall, and at or below which 50 percent of the population is estimated to fall. An example is the median annual earnings of young adults who are full-time, full-year wage and salary workers.

Standard Errors

Using estimates calculated from data based on a sample of the population requires consideration of several factors before the estimates become meaningful. When using data from a sample, some *margin of error* will always be present in estimations of characteristics of the total population or subpopulation because the data are available from only a portion of the total population. Consequently, data from samples can provide only an approximation of the true or actual value. The margin of error of an estimate, or the range of potential true or actual values, depends on several factors such as the amount of variation in the responses, the size and representativeness of the sample, and the size of the subgroup for which the estimate is computed. The magnitude of this margin of error is measured by what statisticians call the "standard error" of an estimate. Larger standard errors typically mean that the estimate is less accurate, while smaller standard errors typically indicate that the estimate is more accurate.

When data from sample surveys are reported, the standard error is calculated for each estimate. The standard errors for all estimated totals, means, medians, or percentages are reported in the reference tables.

In order to caution the reader when interpreting findings in the indicators, estimates from sample surveys are flagged with a "!" when the standard error is between 30 and 50 percent of the estimate, and suppressed with a "‡" when the standard error is 50 percent of the estimate or greater.

Data Analysis and Interpretation

When estimates are from a sample, caution is warranted when drawing conclusions about whether one estimate is different in comparison to another; about whether a time series of estimates is increasing, decreasing, or staying the same; or about whether two variables are associated. Although one estimate may appear to be larger than another, a statistical test may find that the apparent difference between them is not measurable due to the uncertainty around the estimates. In this case, the estimates will be described as having *no measurable difference*, meaning that the difference between them is not statistically significant.

Whether differences in means or percentages are statistically significant can be determined using the standard errors of the estimates. In the indicators in *The Condition of Education* and other reports produced by NCES, when differences are statistically significant, the probability that the difference occurred by chance is less than 5 percent, according to NCES standards.

For all indicators that report estimates based on samples, differences between estimates (including increases and decreases) are stated only when they are statistically significant. To determine whether differences reported are statistically significant, two-tailed t tests at the .05 level are typically used. The t test formula for determining statistical significance is adjusted when the samples being compared are dependent. The t test formula is not adjusted for multiple comparisons, with the exception of statistical tests conducted using the NAEP Data Explorer. When the variables to be tested are postulated to form a trend over time, the relationship may be tested using linear regression or ANOVA trend analyses instead of a series of t tests. Indicators that use other methods of statistical comparison include a separate technical notes section. For more information on data analysis at NCES, please see the NCES Statistical Standards, Standard 5-1, available at http://nces.ed.gov/statprog/2012/pdf/Chapter5.pdf.

Multivariate analyses, such as ordinary least squares (OLS) regression models, provide information on whether the relationship between an independent variable and an outcome measure (such as group differences in the outcome measure) persists, after taking into account other variables, such as student, family, and school characteristics. For *The Condition of Education* indicators that include a regression analysis, multiple categorical or continuous independent variables are entered simultaneously. A significant regression coefficient indicates an association between the dependent (outcome) variable and the independent variable, after controlling for other independent variables included in the regression model.

Data presented in the indicators typically do not investigate more complex hypotheses or support causal inferences. We encourage readers who are interested in more complex questions and in-depth analysis to explore other NCES resources, including publications, online data tools, and public- and restricted-use datasets at http://nces.ed.gov.

A number of considerations influence the ultimate selection of the data years to feature in the indicators. To make analyses as timely as possible, the latest year of available data is shown. The choice of comparison years is often also based on the need to show the earliest available survey year, as in the case of the NAEP and the international assessment surveys. In the case of surveys with long time frames, such as surveys measuring enrollment, a decade's beginning year (e.g., 1980 or 1990) often starts the trend line. In the figures and tables of the indicators, intervening years are selected in increments in order to show the general trend. The narrative for the indicators typically compares the most current year's data with those from the initial year and then with those from a more recent period. Where applicable, the narrative may also note years in which the data begin to diverge from previous trends.

Rounding and Other Considerations

All calculations within the indicators in this report are based on unrounded estimates. Therefore, the reader may find that a calculation, such as a difference or a percentage change, cited in the text or figure may not be identical to the calculation obtained by using the rounded values shown in the accompanying tables. Although values reported in the reference tables are generally rounded to one decimal place (e.g., 76.5 percent), values reported in each indicator are generally rounded to whole numbers (with any value of 0.50 or above rounded to the next highest whole number). Due to rounding, cumulative percentages may sometimes equal 99 or 101 percent rather than 100 percent.

Race and Ethnicity

The Office of Management and Budget (OMB) is responsible for the standards that govern the categories used to collect and present federal data on race and ethnicity. The OMB revised the guidelines on racial/ethnic categories used by the federal government in October 1997, with a January 2003 deadline for implementation. The revised standards require a minimum of these five categories for data on race: American Indian or Alaska Native, Asian, Black or African American, Native Hawaiian or Other Pacific Islander, and White. The standards also require the collection of data on ethnicity categories, at a minimum, Hispanic or Latino and Not Hispanic or Latino. It is important to note that Hispanic origin is an ethnicity rather than a race, and therefore persons of Hispanic origin may be of any race. Origin can be viewed as the heritage, nationality group, lineage, or country of birth of the person or the person's parents or ancestors before their arrival in the United States. The race categories White, Black, Asian, Native Hawaiian or Other Pacific Islander, and American Indian or Alaska Native, as presented in these indicators, exclude persons of Hispanic origin unless noted otherwise.

The categories are defined as follows:

- *American Indian or Alaska Native:* A person having origins in any of the original peoples of North and South America (including Central America) and maintaining tribal affiliation or community attachment.

- *Asian:* A person having origins in any of the original peoples of the Far East, Southeast Asia, or the Indian subcontinent, including, for example, Cambodia, China, India, Japan, Korea, Malaysia, Pakistan, the Philippine Islands, Thailand, and Vietnam.

- *Black or African American:* A person having origins in any of the black racial groups of Africa.

- *Native Hawaiian or Other Pacific Islander:* A person having origins in any of the original peoples of Hawaii, Guam, Samoa, or other Pacific Islands.

- *White:* A person having origins in any of the original peoples of Europe, the Middle East, or North Africa.

- *Hispanic or Latino:* A person of Mexican, Puerto Rican, Cuban, South or Central American, or other Spanish culture or origin, regardless of race.

Within these indicators, some of the category labels have been shortened in the text, tables, and figures for ease of reference. American Indian or Alaska Native is denoted as American Indian/Alaska Native (except when separate estimates are available for American Indians alone or Alaska Natives alone); Black or African American is shortened to Black; and Hispanic or Latino is shortened to Hispanic. Native Hawaiian or Other Pacific Islander is shortened to Pacific Islander.

The indicators in this report draw from a number of different data sources. Many are federal surveys that collect data using the OMB standards for racial/ethnic classification described above; however, some sources have not fully adopted the standards, and some indicators include data collected prior to the adoption of the OMB standards. This report focuses on the six categories that are the most common among the various data sources used: White, Black, Hispanic, Asian, Pacific Islander, and American Indian/Alaska Native. Asians and Pacific Islanders are combined into one category in indicators for which the data were not collected separately for the two groups.

Some of the surveys from which data are presented in these indicators give respondents the option of selecting either an "other" race category, a "Two or more races" or "multiracial" category, or both. Where possible, indicators present data on the "Two or more races" category; however, in some cases this category may not be separately shown because the information was not collected or due to other data issues. In general, the "other" category is not separately shown. Any comparisons made between persons of one racial/ethnic group to "all other racial/ethnic groups" include only the racial/ethnic groups shown in the indicator. In some surveys, respondents are not given the option to select more than one race. In these surveys, respondents of Two or more races must select a single race category. Any comparisons between data from surveys that give the option to select more than one race and surveys that do not offer such an option should take into account the fact that there is a potential for bias if members of one racial group are more likely than members of the others to identify themselves as "Two or more races."[1] For postsecondary data, foreign students are counted separately and are therefore not included in any racial/ethnic category.

The American Community Survey (ACS), conducted by the U.S. Census Bureau, collects information regarding specific racial/ethnic ancestry. Selected indicators include Hispanic ancestry subgroups (such as Mexican, Puerto Rican, Cuban, Dominican, Salvadoran, Other Central American, and South American) and Asian ancestry subgroups (such as Asian Indian, Chinese, Filipino, Japanese, Korean, and Vietnamese). In addition, selected indicators include "Two or more races" subgroups (such as White and Black, White and Asian, and White and American Indian/Alaska Native).

For more information on the ACS, see the <u>Guide to Sources</u>. For more information on race/ethnicity, see the <u>Glossary</u>.

Limitations of the Data

The relatively small sizes of the American Indian/Alaska Native and Pacific Islander populations pose many measurement difficulties when conducting statistical analyses. Even in larger surveys, the numbers of American Indians/Alaska Natives and Pacific Islanders included in a sample are often small. Researchers studying data on these two populations often face small sample sizes that reduce the reliability of results. Survey data for

---

[1] Such bias was found by a National Center for Health Statistics study that examined race/ethnicity responses to the 2000 Census. This study found, for example, that as the percentage of multiple-race respondents in a county increased, the likelihood of respondents stating Black as their primary race increased among Black/White respondents but decreased among American Indian or Alaska Native/Black respondents. See Parker, J. et al. (2004). Bridging Between Two Standards for Collecting Information on Race and Ethnicity: An Application to Census 2000 and Vital Rates. *Public Health Reports, 119*(2): 192–205. Available through <u>http://www.pubmedcentral.nih.gov/articlerender.fcgi?artid=1497618</u>.

American Indians/Alaska Natives often have somewhat higher standard errors than data for other racial/ethnic groups. Due to large standard errors, differences that seem substantial are often not statistically significant and, therefore, not cited in the text.

Data on American Indians/Alaska Natives are often subject to inaccuracies that can result from respondents self-identifying their race/ethnicity. According to research on the collection of race/ethnicity data conducted by the Bureau of Labor Statistics in 1995, the categorization of American Indian and Alaska Native is the least stable self-identification. The racial/ethnic categories presented to a respondent, and the way in which the question is asked, can influence the response, especially for individuals who consider themselves as being of mixed race or ethnicity. These data limitations should be kept in mind when reading this report.

As mentioned above, Asians and Pacific Islanders are combined into one category in indicators for which the data were not collected separately for the two groups. The combined category can sometimes mask significant differences between subgroups. For example, prior to 2011, the National Assessment of Educational Progress (NAEP) collected data that did not allow for separate reporting of estimates for Asians and Pacific Islanders. Information from *Digest of Education Statistics, 2015* (table 101.20), based on the Census Bureau Current Population Reports, indicates that 96 percent of all Asian/Pacific Islander 5- to 24-year-olds are Asian. This combined category for Asians/Pacific Islanders is more representative of Asians than Pacific Islanders.

Symbols

In accordance with the NCES Statistical Standards, many tables in this volume use a series of symbols to alert the reader to special statistical notes. These symbols, and their meanings, are as follows:

— Not available.

† Not applicable.

Rounds to zero.

! Interpret data with caution. The coefficient of variation (CV) for this estimate is between 30 and 50 percent.

‡ Reporting standards not met. Either there are too few cases for a reliable estimate or the coefficient of variation (CV) for this estimate is 50 percent or greater.

* $p < .05$ Significance level.

Contents

Contents

Chapter 1. Population Characteristics 35

Attainment

Economic Outcomes

Contents

Contents

Contents

Postsecondary

Chapter 3. Elementary and Secondary Education 113

School Characteristics and Climate

Contents

Contents

Contents

Student Effort, Persistence, and Progress

Transition to College

Contents

Chapter 4. Postsecondary Education 211

Postsecondary Environments and Characteristics

Programs, Courses, and Completions

Contents

Finance and Resources

Contents

This page intentionally left blank.

The Condition of Education 2016 At a Glance

More information is available at nces.ed.gov/programs/coe.

Population Characteristics

Educational Attainment of Young Adults	2014	2015	Change between years
Percentage of 25- to 29-year-olds with selected levels of educational attainment			
High school completion or higher	91%	91%	
Associate's or higher degree	44%	46%	
Bachelor's or higher degree	34%	36%	
Master's or higher degree	8%	9%	▲

International Educational Attainment	2012	2014	
Percentage of the population 25 to 34 years old who completed high school			
United States	89%	90%	
Organization for Economic Cooperation and Development (OECD) countries	82%	83%	▲
Percentage of the population 25 to 34 years old who attained a postsecondary degree			
United States	44%	46%	▲
OECD countries	39%	41%	▲

Annual Earnings of Young Adults	2013	2014	
Median annual earnings for 25- to 34-year-olds[1]			
Total	$40,600	$40,000	▼
With less than high school completion	$24,300	$25,000	
Who completed high school as highest level	$30,500	$30,000	▼
Who attained a bachelor's or higher degree	$50,800	$52,000	

Employment and Unemployment Rates by Educational Attainment	2014	2015	
Unemployment rates of 20- to 24-year-olds			
Total	15%	12%	▼
With less than high school completion	25%	20%	
Who completed high school as highest level	19%	16%	▼
Who attained a bachelor's or higher degree	7%	5%	

See notes at end of table.

LEGEND: ▲ = Higher,   ▼ = Lower,   Blank = Not measurably different

Family Characteristics of School-Age Children	2009	2014	Change between years
Highest level of education attained by parents of 5- to 17-year-olds			
Percentage whose parents' highest level of education was less than high school	11.2%	10.8%	▼
Percentage whose parents' highest level of education was a bachelor's or higher degree	35.2%	38.1%	▲
	2013	2014	
Percentage of 5- to 17-year-old children in families living in poverty	20.7%	20.3%	▼

Participation in Education

Enrollment Trends by Age	2013	2014	Change between years
Percentage of persons enrolled in school			
3- and 4-year-olds	55%	54%	
5- and 6-year-olds	94%	93%	
7- to 13-year-olds	98%	98%	
14- and 15-year-olds	98%	98%	
16- and 17-year-olds	94%	93%	
18- and 19-year-olds	67%	68%	
20- to 24-year-olds	39%	38%	
25- to 29-year-olds	13%	13%	
30- to 34-year-olds	7%	6%	
Preschool and Kindergarten Enrollment	**2013**	**2014**	
Percentage of children enrolled in preprimary education			
3-year-olds	42%	43%	
4-year-olds	68%	66%	
5-year-olds	84%	85%	
Public School Enrollment	**2012–13**	**2013–14**	
Number of students enrolled in public schools	49.77 million	50.04 million	▲
Prekindergarten through grade 8	35.02 million	35.25 million	▲
Grades 9 through 12	14.75 million	14.79 million	▲

See notes at end of table.

LEGEND: ▲ = Higher, ▼ = Lower, Blank = Not measurably different

Charter School Enrollment	2012–13	2013–14	Change between years
Number of students enrolled in public charter schools	2.3 million	2.5 million	▲
Percentage of public school students enrolled in charter schools	4.6%	5.1%	▲
Number of public charter schools	6,100	6,500	▲
Percentage of public schools that are charter schools	6.2%	6.6%	▲
Private School Enrollment	**2011–12**	**2013–14**	
Total number of students enrolled in private schools (Prekindergarten through grade 12)	5.3 million	5.4 million	▲
Prekindergarten through grade 8	4.0 million	4.1 million	▲
Grades 9 through 12	1.3 million	1.3 million	
Percentage of all students enrolled in private schools (Prekindergarten through grade 12)	9.6%	9.7%	▲
Racial/Ethnic Enrollment in Public Schools	**Fall 2012**	**Fall 2013**	
Percentage of public school students (Prekindergarten through grade 12)			
White	51.0%	50.3%	▼
Black	15.7%	15.6%	▼
Hispanic	24.3%	24.9%	▲
Asian/Pacific Islander	5.1%	5.2%	▲
American Indian/Alaska Native	1.1%	1.0%	▼
Two or more races	2.8%	3.0%	▲
English Language Learners in Public Schools	**2012–13**	**2013–14**	
Percentage of public school students who are English language learners	9.2%	9.3%	▲
Children and Youth with Disabilities	**2012–13**	**2013–14**	
Number of public school students ages 3–21 receiving special education services	6.4 million	6.5 million	▲
Percentage of public school students ages 3–21 receiving special education services	12.92%	12.92%	▼ [2]
Undergraduate Enrollment	**Fall 2013**	**Fall 2014**	
Total enrollment	17.47 million	17.29 million	▼
Full-time enrollment	10.94 million	10.78 million	▼
Part-time enrollment	6.54 million	6.51 million	▼
Percentage enrolled in any distance education course	26%	28%	▲
Percentage enrolled exclusively in distance education	11%	12%	▲

See notes at end of table.

LEGEND: ▲ = Higher, ▼ = Lower, Blank = Not measurably different

Postbaccalaureate Enrollment	Fall 2013	Fall 2014	Change between years
Total enrollment	2.90 million	2.91 million	▲
Full-time enrollment	1.66 million	1.67 million	▲
Part-time enrollment	1.24 million	1.24 million	▲ [2]
Percentage enrolled in any distance education course	31%	33%	▲
Percentage enrolled exclusively in distance education	23%	25%	▲

Elementary and Secondary Education

Characteristics of Traditional Public and Public Charter Schools	2012–13	2013–14	Change between years
Traditional public schools			
Total number of traditional public schools	92,375	91,806	▼
Percentage of traditional public schools			
With more than 50% White enrollment	60.4%	59.8%	▼
With more than 50% Black enrollment	9.3%	9.1%	▼
With more than 50% Hispanic enrollment	14.9%	15.3%	▲
Public charter schools			
Total number of public charter schools	6,079	6,465	▲
Percentage of public charter schools			
With more than 50% White enrollment	36.6%	35.8%	▼
With more than 50% Black enrollment	24.9%	24.4%	▼
With more than 50% Hispanic enrollment	22.6%	23.4%	▲

Concentration of Public School Students Eligible for Free or Reduced-Price Lunch	2011–12	2012–13	
Percentage of students attending high-poverty public schools[3]	19%	24%	▲

School Crime and Safety	2013	2014	
Nonfatal victimization rate per 1,000 students			
Victimization occurred at school	55	33	▼
Victimization occurred away from school	30	24	

Teachers and Pupil/Teacher Ratios	Fall 2012	Fall 2013	
Number of public school teachers	3.11 million	3.11 million	▲ [2]
Pupil/teacher ratio at public schools	16.0	16.1	▲
Number of private school teachers	431,000	441,000	▲
Pupil/teacher ratio at private schools	12.4	12.2	▼

See notes at end of table.

LEGEND: ▲ = Higher, ▼ = Lower, Blank = Not measurably different

Public School Revenue Sources[1]	2011–12	2012–13	Change between years
Total revenues	$622 billion	$618 billion	▼
Federal sources	$63 billion	$57 billion	▼
State sources	$280 billion	$279 billion	▼
Local sources	$279 billion	$281 billion	▲
Public School Expenditures[1]	**2011–12**	**2012–13**	
Total expenditures	$626 billion	$620 billion	▼
Current expenditures per student	$11,074	$11,011	▼

Education Expenditures by Country (2012)	U.S.	OECD	Difference between the U.S. and OECD
Expenditure per full-time-equivalent (FTE) student			
Elementary and secondary education	$11,700	$9,000	▲
Postsecondary education	$26,600	$14,800	▲

Reading Performance	2013	2015	Change between years
Percentage of students who scored at or above *Proficient*[4]			
4th-grade students	35%	36%	
8th-grade students	36%	34%	▼
12th-grade students	38%	37%	
Mathematics Performance	**2013**	**2015**	
Percentage of students who scored at or above *Proficient*[4]			
4th-grade students	42%	40%	▼
8th-grade students	35%	33%	▼
12th-grade students	26%	25%	

See notes at end of table.

LEGEND: ▲ = Higher, ▼ = Lower, Blank = Not measurably different

International Assessments	U.S. average score	International average score	Difference between the U.S. average and the international average
Program for International Student Assessment (2012)			
Mathematics literacy of 15-year-olds	481	494	▼
Trends in International Mathematics and Science Study (2011)			
Mathematics scores of 4th-grade students	541	500	▲
Mathematics scores of 8th-grade students	509	500	▲
Science scores of 4th-grade students	544	500	▲
Science scores of 8th-grade students	525	500	▲
Progress in International Reading Literacy Study (2011)			
Reading literacy of 4th-grade students	556	500	▲

High School Coursetaking	2005	2009	Change between years
Percentage of high school graduates who took selected mathematics courses			
Algebra II/trigonometry	71%	76%	▲
Analysis/precalculus	29%	35%	▲
Percentage of high school graduates who took selected science courses			
Biology and chemistry	64%	68%	▲
Biology, chemistry, and physics	27%	30%	▲

Public High School Graduation Rates	2011–12	2012–13	
Number of graduates with a regular diploma	3.1 million	3.2 million	▲
Averaged Freshman Graduation Rate (AFGR)[5]	81%	82%	▲
	2012–13	2013–14	
Adjusted Cohort Graduation Rate (ACGR)[6]	81%	82%	▲

See notes at end of table.

LEGEND: ▲ = Higher, ▼ = Lower, Blank = Not measurably different

Status Dropout Rates	2013	2014	Change between years
Percentage of 16- to 24-year-olds not enrolled in school who have not completed high school	7%	7%	
Young Adults Neither Enrolled in School nor Working	**2014**	**2015**	
Percentage of 20- to 24-year-olds neither enrolled in school nor working			
Total	19%	17%	▼
With less than high school completion	46%	41%	
High school completion	31%	28%	
Some college, no bachelor's degree	10%	9%	
Bachelor's or higher degree	9%	8%	
Immediate College Enrollment Rate	**2013**	**2014**	
Percentage of recent high school graduates enrolled in college	66%	68%	
2-year institutions	24%	25%	
4-year institutions	42%	44%	
College Participation Rates	**2013**	**2014**	
College participation rates for 18- to 24-year-olds			
Total, all students	40%	40%	
Male	37%	37%	
Female	43%	43%	
White	42%	42%	
Black	34%	33%	
Hispanic	34%	35%	
Asian	62%	65%	
Pacific Islander	33%	41%	
American Indian/Alaska Native	32%	35%	
Two or more races	45%	32%	▼

See notes at end of table.

LEGEND: ▲ = Higher, ▼ = Lower, Blank = Not measurably different

Postsecondary Education

Characteristics of Degree-Granting Postsecondary Institutions	2013–14	2014–15	Change between years
Total number of degree-granting institutions with first-year undergraduates	4,294	4,207	▼
Number of 4-year institutions with first-year undergraduates	2,634	2,603	▼
Number of 2-year institutions with first-year undergraduates	1,660	1,604	▼
Characteristics of Postsecondary Students	**Fall 2013**	**Fall 2014**	
Total undergraduate enrollment	17.47 million	17.29 million	▼
4-year institutions			
Total enrollment	10.51 million	10.58 million	▲
Number enrolled full time	8.11 million	8.12 million	▲
Percentage enrolled full time	77.2%	76.8%	▼
2-year institutions			
Total enrollment	6.97 million	6.71 million	▼
Number enrolled full time	2.83 million	2.66 million	▼
Percentage enrolled full time	40.7%	39.6%	▼
Characteristics of Postsecondary Faculty	**Fall 2011**	**Fall 2013**	
Number of full-time instructional faculty	762,100	791,400	▲
Number of part-time instructional faculty	762,400	752,700	▼
	2013–14	**2014–15**	
Average salary for full-time instructional faculty at public institutions[1,7]	$75,800	$77,000	▲
Average salary for full-time instructional faculty at private nonprofit institutions[1,7]	$87,400	$88,200	▲
Average salary for full-time instructional faculty at private for-profit institutions[1,7]	$51,100	$49,900	▼
Undergraduate Degree Fields	**2012–13**	**2013–14**	
Number of bachelor's degrees awarded			
Business	360,900	358,100	▼
Health professions and related programs	181,100	198,800	▲
Social sciences and history	177,800	173,100	▼
Graduate Degree Fields	**2012–13**	**2013–14**	
Number of master's degrees awarded			
Business	188,600	189,300	▲
Education	164,700	154,600	▼
Health professions and related programs	90,900	97,400	▲

See notes at end of table.

LEGEND: ▲ = Higher, ▼ = Lower, Blank = Not measurably different

Undergraduate Retention and Graduation Rates	2012–13	2013–14	Change between years
4-year institutions			
Retention rate of first-time undergraduates	79.6%	80.5%	▲
Graduation rate (within 6 years of starting program) of first-time, full-time undergraduates	59.4%	59.6%	▲
2-year institutions			
Retention rate of first-time undergraduates	60.0%	60.7%	▲
Graduation rate (within 3 years of starting program) of first-time, full-time undergraduates	29.4%	27.9%	▼
Degrees Conferred by Public and Private Institutions	**2012–13**	**2013–14**	
Number of degrees/certificates conferred by postsecondary institutions			
Certificates	967,214	969,353	▲
Associate's degrees	1,007,427	1,003,364	▼
Bachelor's degrees	1,840,381	1,869,814	▲
Master's degrees	751,718	754,475	▲
Doctor's degrees	175,026	177,580	▲
Price of Attending an Undergraduate Institution[1]	**2012–13**	**2013–14**	
Average net price at 4-year institutions			
Public, in-state	$12,930	$12,750	▼
Private nonprofit	$24,620	$24,690	▲
Private for-profit	$22,000	$21,000	▼
Loans for Undergraduate Students[1]	**2013–14**	**2014–15**	
Average tuition and fees	$11,200	$11,500	▲
	2012–13	**2013–14**	
Average student loan amount	$7,058	$7,063	▲
Sources of Financial Aid	**2012–13**	**2013–14**	
Percentage of students receiving any financial aid at 4-year institutions	85.0%	85.1%	▲
Percentage of students receiving any financial aid at 2-year institutions	78.3%	78.4%	▲
Postsecondary Institution Revenues[1]	**2012–13**	**2013–14**	
Revenue from tuition and fees per FTE student			
Public institutions	$6,461	$6,639	▲
Private nonprofit institutions	$20,010	$20,293	▲
Private for-profit institutions	$16,252	$19,480	▲

See notes at end of table.

LEGEND:　▲ = Higher,　▼ = Lower,　Blank = Not measurably different

Postsecondary Institution Expenses[1]	2012–13	2013–14	Change between years
Instruction expenses per FTE student			
Public institutions	$7,870	$8,070	▲
Private nonprofit institutions	$16,552	$17,003	▲
Private for-profit institutions	$3,921	$5,266	▲

LEGEND: ▲ = Higher, ▼ = Lower, Blank = Not measurably different

[1] Data are reported in constant 2014–15 dollars, based on the Consumer Price Index (CPI).

[2] Despite appearances, the unrounded estimates are significantly different.

[3] A high-poverty school is defined as a public school where more than 75 percent of the students are eligible for free or reduced-price lunch.

[4] Proficient represents solid academic performance. Students reaching this level have demonstrated competency over challenging subject matter.

[5] The Averaged Freshman Graduation Rate (AFGR) is the number of high school diplomas awarded expressed as a percentage of the estimated freshman class 4 years earlier.

[6] The Adjusted Cohort Graduation Rate (ACGR) uses detailed student-level data to determine the percentage of students who graduate within 4 years of starting 9th grade for the first time.

[7] Data are for full-time faculty on 9-month contracts in degree-granting postsecondary institutions.

NOTE: All calculations within the At a Glance are based on unrounded numbers. Race categories exclude persons of Hispanic ethnicity.

SOURCE: The Condition of Education 2016.

Highlights From *The Condition of Education 2016*

Spotlights

Kindergartners' Approaches to Learning, Family Socioeconomic Status, and Early Academic Gains

First-time kindergartners who demonstrated positive approaches to learning behaviors more frequently in the fall of kindergarten tended to make greater gains in reading, mathematics, and science between kindergarten and second grade. For each additional point in students' fall kindergarten approaches to learning score, average gains from kindergarten to second grade were 3.4 points higher for reading, 1.9 points higher for mathematics, and 1.3 points higher for science. The positive relationships between initial approaches to learning behaviors and academic gains in reading, mathematics, and science were larger for students from lower socioeconomic status (SES) households than for students from higher SES households.

Differences in Postsecondary Enrollment Among Recent High School Completers

In fall 2013, among fall 2009 ninth-graders who had completed high school, three-quarters were enrolled at postsecondary institutions: some 14 percent were taking postsecondary classes only and were not enrolled in a degree program, 3 percent were enrolled in occupational certificate programs, 25 percent were enrolled in associate's degree programs, and 32 percent were enrolled in bachelor's degree programs. The remaining 25 percent were not enrolled in a postsecondary institution at all.

Post-Bachelor's Employment Outcomes by Sex and Race/Ethnicity

While 86 percent of all young adults ages 25–34 with a bachelor's or higher degree were employed in 2014, differences in employment outcomes were observed by sex and race/ethnicity. For example, female full-time, year-round workers earned less than their male colleagues in nearly all of the occupation groups examined and for every employment sector (e.g., private for-profit, private nonprofit, government). Black young adults who worked full time, year round also earned less than their White peers in a majority of the occupations analyzed.

Population Characteristics

ATTAINMENT

Educational Attainment of Young Adults

In 2015, some 36 percent of 25- to 29-year-olds had attained a bachelor's or higher degree. The percentage of White 25- to 29-year-olds who had attained this level of education increased from 1995 to 2015, as the size of the White-Black gap in the attainment of a bachelor's or higher degree widened from 13 to 22 percentage points and the size of the White-Hispanic gap widened from 20 to 27 percentage points.

International Educational Attainment

The OECD average percentage of the adult population with a postsecondary degree increased by 11 percentage points between 2001 and 2014, from 22 to 33 percent. During the same period, the percentage of U.S. adults with a postsecondary degree increased by 7 percentage points, from 37 to 44 percent.

$ ECONOMIC OUTCOMES

Annual Earnings of Young Adults

In 2014, the median earnings of young adults with a bachelor's degree ($49,900) were 66 percent higher than the median earnings of young adult high school completers ($30,000). The median earnings of young adult high school completers were 20 percent higher than the median earnings of those without a high school credential ($25,000).

Employment and Unemployment Rates by Educational Attainment

The employment rate was higher for people with higher levels of educational attainment than for those with lower levels of educational attainment. For example, among 20- to 24-year-olds in 2015, the employment rate was 89 percent for those with a bachelor's or higher degree and 51 percent for those who did not complete high school.

DEMOGRAPHICS

Family Characteristics of School-Age Children

In 2014, approximately 20 percent of school-age children were in families living in poverty. The percentage of school-age children living in poverty ranged across the United States from 12 percent in Maryland to 29 percent in Mississippi.

Participation in Education

ALL AGES

Enrollment Trends by Age

In 2014, some 93 percent of 5- to 6-year-olds and 98 percent of 7- to 13-year-olds were enrolled in elementary or secondary school. In that same year, 68 percent of 18- to 19-year-olds and 38 percent of 20- to 24-year-olds were enrolled in a secondary school or postsecondary institution. For all age groups from 3 to 34, total school enrollment rates were not measurably different in 2014 than they were in 2013.

PREPRIMARY

Preschool and Kindergarten Enrollment

In 2014, the overall percentage of 3- to 5-year-olds enrolled in preschool programs was higher for children whose parents had a graduate or professional degree (49 percent), as compared to those whose parents had a bachelor's degree (43 percent), an associate's degree (38 percent), some college (35 percent), a high school credential (32 percent), and less than a high school credential (28 percent).

ELEMENTARY/SECONDARY

Public School Enrollment

Between school year 2013–14 and 2025–26, total public school enrollment in preK through grade 12 is projected to increase by 3 percent (from 50.0 million to 51.4 million students), with changes across states ranging from an increase of 39 percent in the District of Columbia to a decrease of 15 percent in New Hampshire.

Charter School Enrollment

Between school years 2003–04 and 2013–14, overall public charter school enrollment increased from 0.8 million to 2.5 million. During this period, the percentage of public school students who attended charter schools increased from 1.6 to 5.1 percent.

Private School Enrollment

Private school enrollment in prekindergarten (preK) through grade 12 increased from 5.9 million students in 1995–96 to 6.3 million in 2001–02, and then declined to 5.4 million in 2013–14.

Racial/Ethnic Enrollment in Public Schools

Between fall 2003 and fall 2013, the number of White students enrolled in public elementary and secondary schools decreased from 28.4 million to 25.2 million, and the percentage who were White decreased from 59 to 50 percent. In contrast, the number of Hispanic students enrolled increased from 9.0 million to 12.5 million, and the percentage who were Hispanic increased from 19 to 25 percent.

English Language Learners in Public Schools

The percentage of public school students in the United States who were English language learners (ELL) was higher in school year 2013–14 (9.3 percent) than in 2003–04 (8.8 percent) and 2012–13 (9.2 percent). In 2013–14, five of the six states with the highest percentages of ELL students in their public schools were located in the West.

Children and Youth with Disabilities

In 2013–14, the number of children and youth ages 3–21 receiving special education services was 6.5 million, or about 13 percent of all public school students. Among students receiving special education services, 35 percent had specific learning disabilities.

POSTSECONDARY

Undergraduate Enrollment

Total undergraduate enrollment in degree-granting postsecondary institutions increased 31 percent from 13.2 million in 2000 to 17.3 million in 2014. By 2025, total undergraduate enrollment is projected to increase to 19.8 million students.

Postbaccalaureate Enrollment

Total enrollment in postbaccalaureate degree programs was 2.9 million students in fall 2014. Between 2014 and 2025, postbaccalaureate enrollment is projected to increase by 21 percent, to 3.5 million students.

Elementary and Secondary Education

 ## SCHOOL CHARACTERISTICS AND CLIMATE

Characteristics of Traditional Public and Public Charter Schools

High-poverty schools, in which more than 75 percent of the students qualify for free or reduced-price lunch under the National School Lunch Program, accounted for 25 percent of all public schools in 2013–14. In that year, 24 percent of traditional public schools were high-poverty, compared with 39 percent of charter schools.

Concentration of Public School Students Eligible for Free or Reduced-Price Lunch

In school year 2012–13, higher percentages of Black, Hispanic, and American Indian/Alaska Native students attended high-poverty public schools than did Pacific Islander students, students of Two or more races, Asian students, and White students (ordered by descending percentages).

School Crime and Safety

Through nearly two decades of decline, the rate of nonfatal victimization of 12- to 18-year-old students at school fell from 181 victimizations per 1,000 students in 1992 to 33 per 1,000 students in 2014. The rate of nonfatal victimization of these students occurring away from school also declined from 173 to 24 victimizations per 1,000 students during the same period.

TEACHERS AND STAFF

Teachers and Pupil/Teacher Ratios

Of the 6.2 million staff members in public elementary and secondary schools in fall 2013, half (3.1 million) were teachers. The pupil/teacher ratio in public schools declined from 15.9 in 2003 to 15.3 in 2008. In the years after 2008, the pupil/teacher ratio rose, reaching 16.1 in 2013.

FINANCE

Public School Revenue Sources

From school years 2002–03 through 2012–13, total elementary and secondary public school revenues increased from $572 billion to $618 billion (in constant dollars). From 2011–12 through 2012–13, total revenues for public elementary and secondary schools decreased by $4 billion, or 1 percent.

Public School Expenditures

Current expenditures per student in public elementary and secondary schools increased by 5 percent overall between 2002–03 and 2012–13; however, expenditures per student peaked in 2008–09 at $11,621 and decreased each year since then, after adjusting for inflation. The amount for 2012–13 ($11,011) was less than 1 percent lower than the amount for 2011–12 ($11,074).

Education Expenditures by Country

In 2012, the United States spent $11,700 per full-time-equivalent (FTE) student on elementary/secondary education, which was 31 percent higher than the OECD average of $9,000. At the postsecondary level, the United States spent $26,600 per FTE student, which was 79 percent higher than the OECD average of $14,800.

ASSESSMENTS

Reading Performance

While the 2015 average 4th-grade reading score was not measurably different from the 2013 score, the average 8th-grade score was lower in 2015 than in 2013, according to data from the National Assessment of Educational Progress. At grade 12, the average reading score in 2015 was not measurably different from that in 2013.

Mathematics Performance

The average 4th- and 8th-grade mathematics scores in 2015 were lower than the scores in 2013 but were higher than the scores in 1990, according to data from the National Assessment of Educational Progress. At grade 12, the average mathematics score in 2015 was lower than the score in 2013, but not measurably different from the score in 2005.

International Assessments

Among 15-year-old students, 29 education systems had higher average scores than the United States in mathematics literacy, 22 had higher average scores in science literacy, and 19 had higher average scores in reading literacy, according to the 2012 Program for International Student Assessment (PISA).

STUDENT EFFORT, PERSISTENCE, AND PROGRESS

High School Coursetaking

The percentages of high school graduates who had taken mathematics courses in algebra I, geometry, algebra II/ trigonometry, analysis/precalculus, statistics/probability, and calculus increased from 1990 to 2009. The percentages of high school graduates who had taken science courses in chemistry and physics also increased between 1990 and 2009.

Public High School Graduation Rates

In school year 2013–14, the adjusted cohort graduation rate (ACGR) for public high schools rose to an all-time high of 82 percent. This indicates that approximately 4 out of 5 students graduated with a regular high school diploma within 4 years of the first time they started 9th grade. Asian/Pacific Islander students had the highest ACGR (89 percent), followed by White (87 percent), Hispanic (76 percent), Black (73 percent), and American Indian/Alaska Native (70 percent) students.

Status Dropout Rates

The status dropout rate decreased from 12.1 percent in 1990 to 6.5 percent in 2014, with most of the decline occurring since 2000. From 1990 to 2014, the Hispanic status dropout rate decreased by 21.8 percentage points, while the Black and White status dropout rates decreased by 5.8 and 3.7 percentage points, respectively. Nevertheless, in 2014 the Hispanic status dropout rate (10.6 percent) remained higher than the White (5.2 percent) and Black (7.4 percent) status dropout rates.

Young Adults Neither Enrolled in School nor Working

In 2015, some 13 percent of young adults ages 18 to 19 and 17 percent of young adults ages 20 to 24 were neither enrolled in school nor working. In 2015, the percentage of young adults ages 18 to 19 neither enrolled in school nor working was higher for those from poor families (26 percent) than for their peers from nonpoor families (10 percent). The same pattern was observed for young adults ages 20 to 24 (31 percent for those from poor families versus 14 percent for those from nonpoor families).

→ TRANSITION TO COLLEGE

Immediate College Enrollment Rate

The immediate college enrollment rate for high school completers increased from 60 percent in 1990 to 68 percent in 2014. The rate in 2014 for those from high-income families (81 percent) was nearly 29 percentage points higher than the rate for those from low-income families (52 percent). The 2014 gap between those from high- and low-income families did not measurably differ from the corresponding gap in 1990.

College Participation Rates

Although the college enrollment rate increased between 2004 and 2014 for Hispanic young adults (25 vs. 35 percent), it did not measurably differ between 2004 and 2014 for young adults who were White, Black, Asian, Pacific Islander, American Indian/Alaska Native, and of Two or more races.

Postsecondary Education

POSTSECONDARY ENVIRONMENTS AND CHARACTERISTICS

Characteristics of Degree-Granting Postsecondary Institutions

In 2014–15, some 29 percent of 4-year institutions had open admissions policies (accepted all applicants), an additional 28 percent accepted three-quarters or more of their applicants, 30 percent accepted from one-half to less than three-quarters of their applicants, and 13 percent accepted less than one-half of their applicants.

Characteristics of Postsecondary Students

Some 10.6 million undergraduate students attended 4-year institutions in fall 2014, while 6.7 million attended 2-year institutions. Some 77 percent of undergraduate students at 4-year institutions attended full time, compared with 40 percent at 2-year institutions.

Characteristics of Postsecondary Faculty

From fall 1993 to fall 2013, the number of full-time faculty at degree-granting postsecondary institutions increased by 45 percent, while the number of part-time faculty increased by 104 percent. As a result of the faster increase in the number of part-time faculty, the percentage of all faculty who were part time increased from 40 to 49 percent during this period.

PROGRAMS, COURSES, AND COMPLETIONS

Undergraduate Degree Fields

From 2003–04 to 2013–14, the number of associate's degrees conferred increased by 51 percent, from 665,300 to over 1 million, and the number of bachelor's degrees conferred increased by 34 percent, from 1.4 million to 1.9 million.

Graduate Degree Fields

Between academic years 2003–04 and 2013–14, the number of master's degrees conferred increased by 34 percent, from 564,300 to 754,500, and the number of doctor's degrees conferred increased by 41 percent, from 126,100 to 177,600.

Undergraduate Retention and Graduation Rates

About 60 percent of students who began seeking a bachelor's degree at a 4-year institution in fall 2008 completed that degree within 6 years; the graduation rate was higher for females than males (62 percent vs. 57 percent).

Degrees Conferred by Public and Private Institutions

The number of postsecondary degrees conferred at each degree level increased between 2003–04 and 2013–14. The number of certificates below the associate's degree level awarded during this period increased by 41 percent, the number of associate's degrees increased by 51 percent, the number of bachelor's degrees increased by 34 percent, the number of master's degrees increased by 34 percent, and the number of doctor's degrees increased by 41 percent.

FINANCE AND RESOURCES

Price of Attending an Undergraduate Institution

The average net price of attendance (total cost minus grant and scholarship aid) for first-time, full-time students in 2013–14 (in constant 2014–15 dollars) was $12,750 at 4-year public institutions, $24,690 at 4-year private nonprofit institutions, and $21,000 at 4-year private for-profit institutions.

Loans for Undergraduate Students

In 2013–14, the average annual student loan amount of $7,100 was 23 percent higher than the average of $5,700 in 2005–06 (in constant 2014–15 dollars). For undergraduate students ages 18 to 24 in their 4th year of college or above, the average cumulative amount borrowed was $26,400 in 2011–12.

Sources of Financial Aid

The percentage of first-time, full-time undergraduate students at 4-year degree-granting postsecondary institutions receiving financial aid was higher in 2013–14 (85 percent) than in 2008–09 (82 percent).

Postsecondary Institution Revenues

Between 2008–09 and 2013–14, revenues from tuition and fees per full-time-equivalent (FTE) student increased by 17 percent at public institutions (from $5,681 to $6,639, in constant 2014–15 dollars) and by 6 percent at private nonprofit institutions (from $19,206 to $20,293). At private for-profit institutions, revenues from tuition and fees per FTE student were 34 percent higher in 2013–14 than in 2008–09 ($19,480 vs. $14,515).

Postsecondary Institution Expenses

In 2013–14, instruction expenses per full-time-equivalent (FTE) student (in constant 2014–15 dollars) was the largest expense category at public institutions ($8,070) and private nonprofit institutions ($17,003). At private forprofit institutions, instruction expenses per FTE student was the second largest expense category ($5,266).

This page intentionally left blank.

This chapter of *The Condition of Education* features spotlight indicators on selected issues of current policy interest.

This chapter's indicators, as well as spotlight indicators and special analyses from previous editions, are available at *The Condition of Education* website: http://nces.ed.gov/programs/coe.

Spotlights

Kindergartners' Approaches to Learning, Family Socioeconomic Status, and Early Academic Gains

First-time kindergartners who demonstrated positive approaches to learning behaviors more frequently in the fall of kindergarten tended to make greater gains in reading, mathematics, and science between kindergarten and second grade. For each additional point in students' fall kindergarten approaches to learning score, average gains from kindergarten to second grade were 3.4 points higher for reading, 1.9 points higher for mathematics, and 1.3 points higher for science. The positive relationships between initial approaches to learning behaviors and academic gains in reading, mathematics, and science were larger for students from lower socioeconomic status (SES) households than for students from higher SES households.

At kindergarten entry, children differ not only in their cognitive knowledge and skills but also in their approaches to learning behaviors, such as their ability to pay attention in class, follow classroom rules, complete tasks independently, and show eagerness to learn.[1] In the early years, even before formal schooling begins, children from socioeconomically disadvantaged households typically have less access to resources that have been associated with learning, such as books and educational toys in their homes and quality preschool settings, than do students from more socioeconomically advantaged households.[2] As these children enter school, they tend to exhibit positive approaches to learning behaviors less often than students from more socioeconomically advantaged households.[3] Research suggests that children who demonstrate positive approaches to learning behaviors more frequently perform better academically, on average, in the early grades than students who demonstrate these behaviors less frequently.[4] This Spotlight analysis extends findings from *The Condition of Education 2015* Spotlight Kindergartners' Approaches to Learning Behaviors and Academic Outcomes to describe associations between the approaches to learning behaviors of first-time kindergartners in the fall of kindergarten and their academic gains in reading, mathematics, and science from kindergarten through the spring of second grade for students from different family socioeconomic status (SES) backgrounds.[5]

In the Early Childhood Longitudinal Study, Kindergarten Class of 2010–11 (ECLS-K:2011), teachers of kindergarten students rated their students on seven approaches to learning behaviors: paying attention in class, persisting in completing tasks, showing eagerness to learn new things, working independently, adapting easily to changes in routine, keeping belongings organized, and following classroom rules. Teachers assigned a rating of 1 (never), 2 (sometimes), 3 (often), or 4 (very often) for each of the seven items during the fall kindergarten round of the ECLS-K:2011. Following data collection, an average of the seven ratings was calculated to represent a composite score for each child's fall kindergarten approaches to learning behaviors.[6]

Information on family SES was collected through parental reports of parent/guardian educational attainment, occupations, and household income in the kindergarten year. In addition, trained ECLS-K:2011 assessors conducted one-on-one adaptive testing through computer-assisted personal interviews with children in reading and mathematics in the fall and spring of kindergarten,[7] first grade, and second grade. Science was assessed in the spring of kindergarten and in the fall and spring of first grade and second grade. More details on the family SES and academic assessment components included in the analysis can be found in the Technical Notes section of this Spotlight.

Figure 1. Average approaches to learning scores of first-time kindergartners, by family socioeconomic status (SES):
Fall 2010

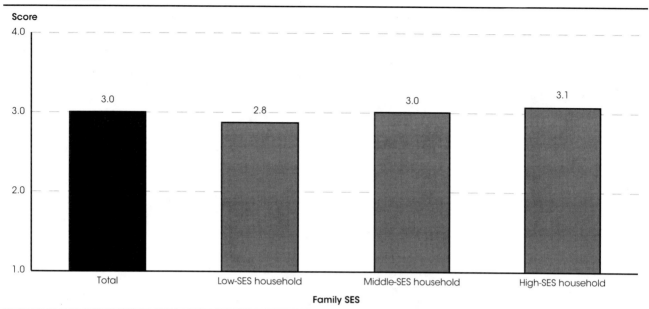

NOTE: The approaches to learning scale is based on teachers' reports on how often students exhibit positive learning behaviors in seven areas: attentiveness, task persistence, eagerness to learn, learning independence, ability to adapt easily to changes in routine, organization, and ability to follow classroom rules. Possible scores on the scale range from 1 to 4, with higher scores indicating that a child exhibits positive learning behaviors more often. Socioeconomic status (SES) was measured by a composite score based on parental education and occupations and household income in the child's kindergarten year. Kindergartners living in households in the highest 20 percent of the SES scale were identified as kindergartners from high-SES households, those living in households in the middle 60 percent of the SES scale were identified as kindergartners from middle-SES households, and those living in households in the lowest 20 percent of the SES scale were identified as kindergartners from low-SES households. Estimates weighted by W6C6P_6T0. Estimates pertain to a sample of children who were enrolled in kindergarten for the first time in the 2010–11 school year. Most of the children were in second grade in 2012–13, but 6 percent were in first grade or other grades (e.g., third grade, ungraded classrooms).
SOURCE: U.S. Department of Education, National Center for Education Statistics, Early Childhood Longitudinal Study, Kindergarten Class of 2010–11 (ECLS-K:2011), Kindergarten–Second Grade Restricted-Use Data File. See *Digest of Education Statistics 2015*, table 220.45.

In the fall 2010 kindergarten data collection, the average approaches to learning score for first-time kindergartners was 3.0, indicating that they "often" demonstrated positive approaches to learning behaviors. Overall, 26 percent of first-time kindergartners were rated by their teachers in the fall of kindergarten as demonstrating positive approaches to learning behaviors "very often" (average rating of 4), 49 percent were rated as demonstrating them "often" (average rating of 3), 24 percent were rated as demonstrating them "sometimes" (average rating of 2), and 1 percent were rated as "never" demonstrating them (average rating of 1).[8] Students from low-SES households tended to have lower fall kindergarten approaches to learning scores (2.8) than students from middle-SES (3.0) and high-SES households (3.1).

Figure 2. Average reading scale scores of fall 2010 first-time kindergartners, by frequency of positive approaches to learning behaviors in fall of kindergarten and time of assessment: Fall 2010 through spring 2013

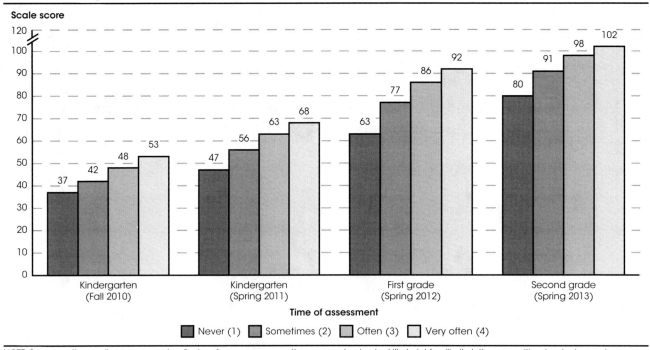

NOTE: Scores on the reading assessments reflect performance on questions measuring basic skills (print familiarity, letter recognition, beginning and ending sounds, rhyming words, and word recognition); vocabulary knowledge; and reading comprehension, including identifying information specifically stated in text (e.g., definitions, facts, and supporting details), making complex inferences from texts, and considering the text objectively and judging its appropriateness and quality. Possible scores for the reading assessment range from 0 to 120. Frequency of positive approaches to learning behaviors is derived from kindergartners' fall 2010 approaches to learning scores. The approaches to learning scale is based on teachers' reports on how often students exhibit positive learning behaviors in seven areas: attentiveness, task persistence, eagerness to learn, learning independence, ability to adapt easily to changes in routine, organization, and ability to follow classroom rules. Possible scores on the scale range from 1 to 4, with higher scores indicating that a child exhibits positive learning behaviors more often. Fall 2010 approaches to learning scores were categorized into the anchor points on the original scale by rounding the average score to the nearest whole number. Estimates differ from previously published figures because reading scale scores were recalculated to represent the kindergarten through second-grade assessment item pools, and weights were adjusted to account for survey nonresponse at each data collection wave. Estimates weighted by W6C6P_6T0. Estimates pertain to a sample of children who were enrolled in kindergarten for the first time in the 2010–11 school year. Most of the children were in second grade in 2012–13, but 6 percent were in first grade or other grades (e.g., third grade, ungraded classrooms).
SOURCE: U.S. Department of Education, National Center for Education Statistics, Early Childhood Longitudinal Study, Kindergarten Class of 2010–11 (ECLS-K:2011), Kindergarten–Second Grade Restricted-Use Data File. See *Digest of Education Statistics 2015*, table 220.40.

Results from the previous Spotlight on kindergartners' approaches to learning behaviors and academic outcomes indicated that the frequency of positive approaches to learning behaviors for first-time kindergartners (or their average approaches to learning rating) in the fall of kindergarten was positively associated with their reading, mathematics, and science scores in the spring of kindergarten and the spring of first grade. The same pattern was observed in the spring of 2013, when most of the ECLS-K:2011 students were enrolled in second grade. Students who had an average rating of "never" on the approaches to learning scale in the fall of kindergarten

had the lowest reading, mathematics, and science scores in the spring of second grade, and students who had an average rating of "very often" in the fall of kindergarten had the highest scores in these subjects in the spring of second grade. For example, students who were rated by teachers as "never" demonstrating positive approaches to learning behaviors in the fall of kindergarten had an average spring second-grade reading score of 80 points, compared with an average score of 91 points for those with a rating of "sometimes," 98 points for those with a rating of "often," and 102 points for those with a rating of "very often."

Figure 3.   Average mathematics scale scores of fall 2010 first-time kindergartners, by frequency of positive approaches to learning behaviors in fall of kindergarten and time of assessment: Fall 2010 through spring 2013

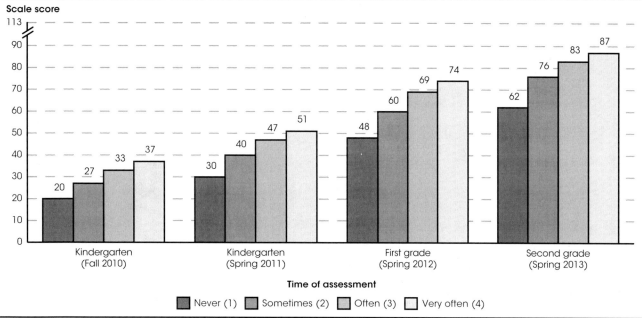

NOTE: Scores on the mathematics assessments reflect performance on questions on number sense, properties, and operations; measurement; geometry and spatial sense; data analysis, statistics, and probability; and prealgebra skills such as identification of patterns. Possible scores for the mathematics assessment range from 0 to 113. Frequency of positive approaches to learning behaviors is derived from kindergartners' fall 2010 approaches to learning scores. The approaches to learning scale is based on teachers' reports on how often students exhibit positive learning behaviors in seven areas: attentiveness, task persistence, eagerness to learn, learning independence, ability to adapt easily to changes in routine, organization, and ability to follow classroom rules. Possible scores on the scale range from 1 to 4, with higher scores indicating that a child exhibits positive learning behaviors more often. Fall 2010 approaches to learning scores were categorized into the anchor points on the original scale by rounding the average score to the nearest whole number. Estimates differ from previously published figures because mathematics scale scores were recalculated to represent the kindergarten through second-grade assessment item pools, and weights were adjusted to account for survey nonresponse at each data collection wave. Estimates weighted by W6C6P_6T0. Estimates pertain to a sample of children who were enrolled in kindergarten for the first time in the 2010–11 school year. Most of the children were in second grade in 2012–13, but 6 percent were in first grade or other grades (e.g., third grade, ungraded classrooms).
SOURCE: U.S. Department of Education, National Center for Education Statistics, Early Childhood Longitudinal Study, Kindergarten Class of 2010–11 (ECLS-K:2011), Kindergarten–Second Grade Restricted-Use Data File. See *Digest of Education Statistics 2015*, table 220.40.

As in the previous Spotlight, first-time kindergartners who received an average approaches to learning rating of "never" in the fall of kindergarten not only scored the lowest on the reading, mathematics, and science assessments at each assessment time point, but their scores at subsequent assessment time points did not catch up to the previous assessment time point scores of peers who had received an approaches to learning rating of

"very often" in the fall of kindergarten. For example, in mathematics, students with an approaches to learning rating of "very often" in the fall of kindergarten had an average score of 74 points in the spring of first grade, whereas students with an approaches to learning rating of "never" in the fall of kindergarten had an average score of 62 points in the spring of second grade.

Figure 4. Average science scale scores of fall 2010 first-time kindergartners, by family socioeconomic status (SES) and time of assessment: Spring 2011 through spring 2013

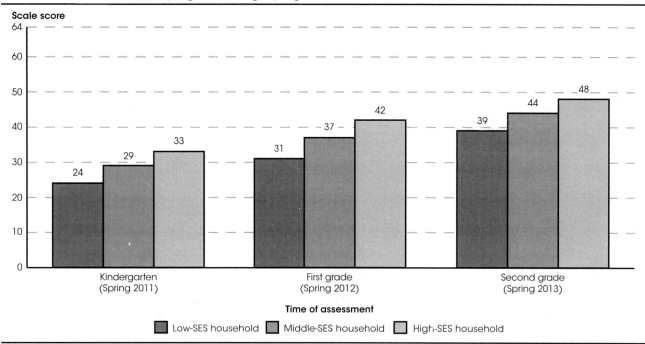

NOTE: Scores on the science assessments reflect performance on questions on physical sciences, life sciences, environmental sciences, and scientific inquiry. Possible scores for the science assessment range from 0 to 64. Science was first assessed in the spring of kindergarten. Socioeconomic status (SES) was measured by a composite score based on parental education and occupations and household income in the child's kindergarten year. Kindergartners living in households in the highest 20 percent of the SES scale were identified as kindergartners from high-SES households, those living in households in the middle 60 percent of the SES scale were identified as kindergartners from middle-SES households, and those living in households in the lowest 20 percent of the SES scale were identified as kindergartners from low-SES households. Estimates differ from previously published figures because science scale scores were recalculated to represent the kindergarten through second-grade assessment item pools, and weights were adjusted to account for survey nonresponse at each data collection wave. Estimates weighted by W6C6P_6T0. Estimates pertain to a sample of children who were enrolled in kindergarten for the first time in the 2010–11 school year. Most of the children were in second grade in 2012–13, but 6 percent were in first grade or other grades (e.g., third grade, ungraded classrooms).
SOURCE: U.S. Department of Education, National Center for Education Statistics, Early Childhood Longitudinal Study, Kindergarten Class of 2010–11 (ECLS-K:2011), Kindergarten–Second Grade Restricted-Use Data File. See *Digest of Education Statistics 2015*, table 220.40.

With respect to family SES, students from households with the lowest SES in the fall of kindergarten had the lowest reading, mathematics, and science scores in kindergarten through second grade, while those from households with the highest SES had the highest scores in all three subjects during this period. For example, in the spring of kindergarten students from low-SES households had an average science score of 24 points, compared with average science scores of 29 points for students from middle-SES households and 33 points for students from high-SES households. In the spring of second grade, students from low-SES households still had the lowest average science score (39 points) when compared with students from middle-SES households (44 points) and high-SES households (48 points).

Given that reading, mathematics, and science scores varied at different assessment time points both for students with different fall kindergarten approaches

to learning scores and for students from different SES households, multivariate analyses were conducted to explore students' academic gains from kindergarten to second grade in relation to their initial approaches to learning scores and family SES. Two sets of ordinary least squares (OLS) regression analyses were conducted. For both sets, gains in children's reading, mathematics, and science scores from the initial kindergarten assessment to the spring second-grade assessment were the outcome measures. The gains scores were calculated as the difference between the spring second-grade score and the initial kindergarten score (fall for reading and mathematics; spring for science). All regression analyses of gain scores also controlled for children's initial assessment scores because gains made at different points on the Item Response Theory (IRT) scale score have qualitatively different interpretations.[9] More details on the regression methodology and IRT scale interpretation can be found in the Technical Notes section of this Spotlight.

Table 1. Estimated coefficients from ordinary least squares (OLS) regressions of reading, mathematics, and science kindergarten through second-grade gains, by fall kindergarten approaches to learning scores and family socioeconomic status (SES): Fall 2010 through spring 2013

	Kindergarten through second-grade gain scores					
	Reading[1]		Mathematics[2]		Science[3]	
	Model 1	Model 2	Model 1	Model 2	Model 1	Model 2
Variable	Coefficient (s.e.)	Coefficient (s.e.)	Coefficient (s.e.)	Coefficient (s.e.)	Coefficient (s.e.)	Coefficient (s.e.)
Intercept	60.99* (0.877)	56.43* (1.358)	50.52* (1.104)	45.63* (2.305)	18.57* (0.640)	17.28* (0.964)
Initial kindergarten score[4]	-0.53* (0.015)	-0.53* (0.015)	-0.28* (0.016)	-0.28* (0.016)	-0.30* (0.016)	-0.30* (0.016)
Fall kindergarten approaches to learning score[5]	3.39* (0.268)	5.01* (0.434)	1.92* (0.247)	3.66* (0.702)	1.34* (0.123)	1.80* (0.284)
Family SES[6]						
Middle-SES household	4.04* (0.420)	8.98* (1.619)	2.56* (0.481)	7.92* (2.393)	1.22* (0.241)	2.55* (0.968)
High-SES household	5.78* (0.496)	14.81* (1.873)	3.63* (0.551)	13.28* (2.802)	2.43* (0.284)	5.27* (1.102)
Interaction of SES and approaches to learning score						
Middle-SES household		-1.76* (0.506)		-1.91* (0.760)		-0.47 (0.326)
High-SES household		-3.05* (0.558)		-3.26* (0.857)		-0.95* (0.342)

* $p < 0.05$.
[1] Reflects performance on questions measuring basic skills (print familiarity, letter recognition, beginning and ending sounds, rhyming words, and word recognition); vocabulary knowledge; and reading comprehension, including identifying information specifically stated in text (e.g., definitions, facts, and supporting details), making complex inferences from texts, and considering the text objectively and judging its appropriateness and quality. Possible scores for the reading assessment range from 0 to 120.
[2] Reflects performance on questions on number sense, properties, and operations; measurement; geometry and spatial sense; data analysis, statistics, and probability (measured with a set of simple questions assessing children's ability to read a graph); and prealgebra skills such as identification of patterns. Possible scores for the mathematics assessment range from 0 to 113.
[3] Science was not assessed in the fall of kindergarten. Reflects performance on questions on physical sciences, life sciences, environmental sciences, and scientific inquiry. Possible scores for the science assessment range from 0 to 64.
[4] Initial reading and mathematics scores are from fall kindergarten; initial science scores are from spring kindergarten.
[5] The approaches to learning scale is based on teachers' reports on how often students exhibit positive learning behaviors in seven areas: attentiveness, task persistence, eagerness to learn, learning independence, ability to adapt easily to changes in routine, organization, and ability to follow classroom rules. Possible scores on the scale range from 1 to 4, with higher scores indicating that a child exhibits positive learning behaviors more often.
[6] Socioeconomic status (SES) was measured by a composite score based on parental education and occupations and household income in the child's kindergarten year. The reference category for the regression model is the low-SES household group. Kindergartners living in households in the highest 20 percent of the SES scale were identified as kindergartners from high-SES households, those living in households in the middle 60 percent of the SES scale were identified as kindergartners from middle-SES households, and those living in households in the lowest 20 percent of the SES scale were identified as kindergartners from low-SES households.
NOTE: Estimates weighted by W6C6P_6T0. Estimates pertain to a sample of children who were enrolled in kindergarten for the first time in the 2010–11 school year. Most of the children were in second grade in 2012–13, but 6 percent were in first grade or other grades (e.g., third grade, ungraded classrooms).
SOURCE: U.S. Department of Education, National Center for Education Statistics, Early Childhood Longitudinal Study, Kindergarten Class of 2010–11 (ECLS-K:2011), Kindergarten–Second Grade Restricted-Use Data File.

The first set of regression analyses (table 1, model 1) included the fall kindergarten approaches to learning scores and kindergarten family SES as independent predictors of children's academic gains. Regressions of students' gains in reading, mathematics, and science from kindergarten to the spring of second grade indicated that students who demonstrated positive approaches to learning behaviors more frequently in the fall of kindergarten tended to make greater gains in all three subjects in their first three years of school after accounting for initial assessment scores and family SES. For each additional point in students' fall kindergarten approaches to learning scores, average gains from kindergarten to second grade were 3.4 points higher for reading, 1.9 points higher for mathematics, and 1.3 points higher for science. For example, on average a student with a fall kindergarten approaches to learning score of 4 (very often) would gain 10.2 points[10] more in reading than a similar student with a fall kindergarten approaches to learning score of 1 (never).

Results from this regression set also indicated that family SES in kindergarten was positively associated with

students' gains between kindergarten and second grade in reading, mathematics, and science. For example, for students with the same fall kindergarten approaches to learning score, those from high-SES households would gain on average 5.8 points more in reading, 3.6 points more in mathematics, and 2.4 points more in science than students from low-SES households.

The second set of regression analyses (table 1, model 2) included an interaction variable of family SES and the fall kindergarten approaches to learning score, in addition to the variables included in the first set of regressions. Interaction variables are used to explore whether the relationship between two variables, such as the approaches to learning score and reading gains, differ across levels of a third variable, such as family SES. Significant interaction coefficients indicate that the relationships between initial approaches to learning scores and gains in reading, mathematics, and science from kindergarten to second grade differed for students from different family SES backgrounds.

Figure 5.   Average fall kindergarten to spring second-grade reading gain scores associated with fall kindergarten approaches to learning scores, by family socioeconomic status (SES): Fall 2010 through spring 2013

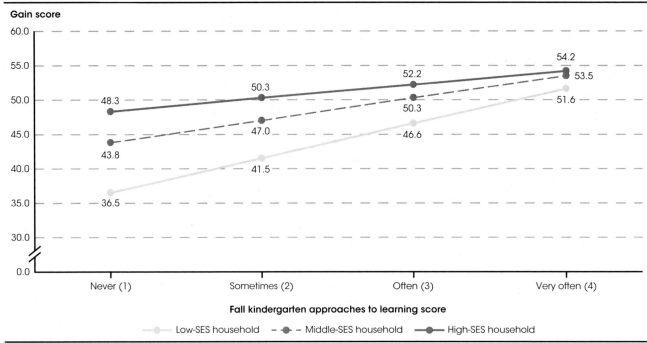

NOTE: Figure estimates are based on the average fall kindergarten reading score of 47.4. The approaches to learning scale is based on teachers' reports on how often students exhibit positive learning behaviors in seven areas: attentiveness, task persistence, eagerness to learn, learning independence, ability to adapt easily to changes in routine, organization, and ability to follow classroom rules. Possible scores on the scale range from 1 to 4, with higher scores indicating that a child exhibits positive learning behaviors more often. Scores on the reading assessment reflect performance on questions measuring basic skills (print familiarity, letter recognition, beginning and ending sounds, rhyming words, and word recognition); vocabulary knowledge; and reading comprehension, including identifying information specifically stated in text (e.g., definitions, facts, and supporting details), making complex inferences from texts, and considering the text objectively and judging its appropriateness and quality. Possible scores for the reading assessment range from 0 to 120. Socioeconomic status (SES) was measured by a composite score based on parental education and occupations and household income in the child's kindergarten year. Kindergartners living in households in the highest 20 percent of the SES scale were identified as kindergartners from high-SES households, those living in households in the middle 60 percent of the SES scale were identified as kindergartners from middle-SES households, and those living in households in the lowest 20 percent of the SES scale were identified as kindergartners from low-SES households. Estimates weighted by W6C6P_6T0. Estimates pertain to a sample of children who were enrolled in kindergarten for the first time in the 2010–11 school year. Most of the children were in second grade in 2012–13, but 6 percent were in first grade or other grades (e.g., third grade, ungraded classrooms).
SOURCE: U.S. Department of Education, National Center for Education Statistics, Early Childhood Longitudinal Study, Kindergarten Class of 2010–11 (ECLS-K:2011), Kindergarten–Second Grade Restricted-Use Data File.

Findings from the second set of regression analyses showed negative interaction effects between fall kindergarten approaches to learning scores and family SES (table 1, model 2). A negative interaction means that the academic gains associated with fall kindergarten approaches to learning scores in reading, mathematics, and (to an extent) science are largest for children from low-SES households and smaller for children from middle- and high-SES households. In reading, for example, each additional point on the fall kindergarten approaches to learning score is associated with a 5.0-point gain increase, on average, for students from low-SES households, while it is associated with a 3.2-point gain increase for students from middle-SES households and a 2.0-point gain increase for students from high-SES households.[11] The larger gain increase associated with the fall kindergarten approaches to learning score for students from low-SES households decreases the gap in the reading gains between students from households with different SES levels.

Among students whose average rating was "never (1)" on the fall kindergarten approaches to learning scale and who had the average fall kindergarten reading score of 47.4 points, for example, students from low-SES households would have an average reading gain of 36.5 points, students from middle-SES households would have an average gain of 43.8 points, and students from high-SES households would have an average gain of 48.3 points.[12] In contrast, among students with an average score of "very often (4)" on the fall kindergarten approaches to learning scale and the average fall kindergarten reading score (47.4 points), students from low-SES households would have an average reading gain of 51.6 points, students from middle-SES households would have an average gain of 53.5 points, and students from high-SES households would have an average gain of 54.2 points. The gap in reading gain scores between students from high-SES and low-SES households who had the same fall kindergarten reading score decreases from 11.8 points for students with the lowest fall kindergarten approaches to learning score to 2.6 points for students with the highest approaches to learning score.

Figure 6. Average fall kindergarten to spring second-grade mathematics gain scores associated with fall kindergarten approaches to learning scores, by family socioeconomic status (SES): Fall 2010 through spring 2013

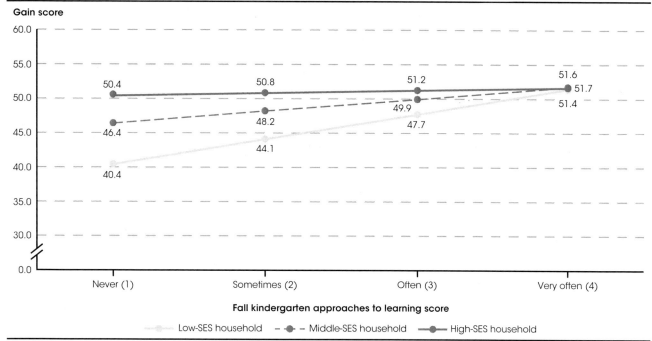

NOTE: Figure estimates are based on the average fall kindergarten mathematics score of 32.3. The approaches to learning scale is based on teachers' reports on how often students exhibit positive learning behaviors in seven areas: attentiveness, task persistence, eagerness to learn, learning independence, ability to adapt easily to changes in routine, organization, and ability to follow classroom rules. Possible scores on the scale range from 1 to 4, with higher scores indicating that a child exhibits positive learning behaviors more often. Scores on the mathematics assessments reflect performance on questions on number sense, properties, and operations; measurement; geometry and spatial sense; data analysis, statistics, and probability; and prealgebra skills such as identification of patterns. Possible scores for the mathematics assessment range from 0 to 113. Socioeconomic status (SES) was measured by a composite score based on parental education and occupations and household income in the child's kindergarten year. Kindergartners living in households in the highest 20 percent of the SES scale were identified as kindergartners from high-SES households, those living in households in the middle 60 percent of the SES scale were identified as kindergartners from middle-SES households, and those living in households in the lowest 20 percent of the SES scale were identified as kindergartners from low-SES households. Estimates weighted by W6C6P_6T0. Estimates pertain to a sample of children who were enrolled in kindergarten for the first time in the 2010–11 school year. Most of the children were in second grade in 2012–13, but 6 percent were in first grade or other grades (e.g., third grade, ungraded classrooms).
SOURCE: U.S. Department of Education, National Center for Education Statistics, Early Childhood Longitudinal Study, Kindergarten Class of 2010–11 (ECLS-K:2011), Kindergarten–Second Grade Restricted-Use Data File.

In mathematics, the positive relationship between approaches to learning behaviors and gains was also largest for children from low-SES households. Each additional point on the fall kindergarten approaches to learning score results in a 3.7-point mathematics gain increase for students from low-SES households, while it results in a 1.8-point gain increase for kindergartners from middle-SES households and a 0.4-point gain increase for students from high-SES households.

Among students whose average rating was "never (1)" on the fall kindergarten approaches to learning scale and who had the average fall kindergarten mathematics score of 32.3 points, for example, students from low-SES households would have an average mathematics gain of 40.4 points, students from middle-SES households would have an average gain of 46.4 points, and students

from high-SES households would have an average gain of 50.4 points. In contrast, among students with an average score of "very often (4)" on the fall kindergarten approaches to learning scale and the average fall kindergarten mathematics score (32.3 points), students from low-SES households would have an average mathematics gain of 51.4 points, students from middle-SES households would have an average gain of 51.7 points, and students from high-SES households would have an average gain of 51.6 points. The gap in mathematics gain scores between students from high-SES and low-SES households who had the same fall kindergarten mathematics score decreases from 10.0 points for students with the lowest fall kindergarten approaches to learning score to 0.2 points for students with the highest approaches to learning score.

Figure 7.   Average spring kindergarten to spring second-grade science gain scores associated with fall kindergarten approaches to learning scores, by family socioeconomic status (SES): Spring 2011 through spring 2013

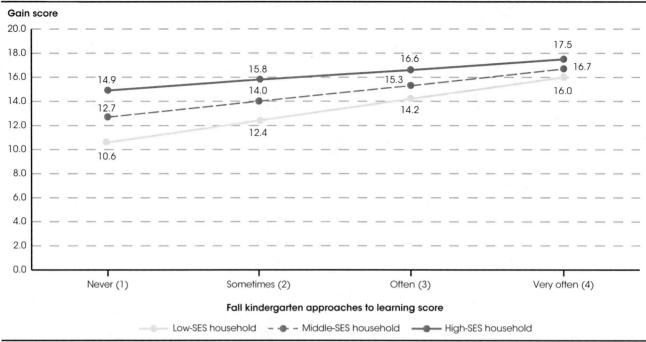

NOTE: Figure estimates are based on the average spring kindergarten science score of 28.6. The approaches to learning scale is based on teachers' reports on how often students exhibit positive learning behaviors in seven areas: attentiveness, task persistence, eagerness to learn, learning independence, ability to adapt easily to changes in routine, organization, and ability to follow classroom rules. Possible scores on the scale range from 1 to 4, with higher scores indicating that a child exhibits positive learning behaviors more often. Scores on the science assessments reflect performance on questions on physical sciences, life sciences, environmental sciences, and scientific inquiry. Possible scores for the science assessment range from 0 to 64. Socioeconomic status (SES) was measured by a composite score based on parental education and occupations and household income in the child's kindergarten year. Kindergartners living in households in the highest 20 percent of the SES scale were identified as kindergartners from high-SES households, those living in households in the middle 60 percent of the SES scale were identified as kindergartners from middle-SES households, and those living in households in the lowest 20 percent of the SES scale were identified as kindergartners from low-SES households. Estimates pertain to a sample of children who were enrolled in kindergarten for the first time in the 2010–11 school year. Most of the children were in second grade in 2012–13, but 6 percent were in first grade or other grades (e.g., third grade, ungraded classrooms).
SOURCE: U.S. Department of Education, National Center for Education Statistics, Early Childhood Longitudinal Study, Kindergarten Class of 2010–11 (ECLS-K:2011), Kindergarten–Second Grade Restricted-Use Data File.

In science, the positive relationship between fall kindergarten approaches to learning scores and gains was larger for students from low-SES households than for students from high-SES households; however, no significant interaction was found for students from middle-SES households, indicating that the relationships between approaches to learning scores and science gains were not measurably different for children from low- and middle-SES backgrounds. Each additional point on the fall kindergarten approaches to learning score results in a 1.8-point science gain increase for students from low-SES households and a 0.8-point science gain increase for students from high-SES households.

Among students whose average rating was "never (1)" on the fall kindergarten approaches to learning scale and who had the average spring kindergarten science

score of 28.6 points, for example, students from low-SES households would have an average science gain of 10.6 points and students from high-SES households would have an average science gain of 14.9 points. In contrast, among students with an average score of "very often (4)" on the fall kindergarten approaches to learning scale and the average spring kindergarten science score (28.6 points), students from low-SES households would have an average science gain of 16.0 points and students from high-SES households would have an average gain of 17.5 points. The gap in science gain scores between students from high-SES and low-SES households who had the same spring kindergarten science score decreases from 4.3 points for students with the lowest fall kindergarten approaches to learning score to 1.5 points for students with the highest approaches to learning score.

Technical Notes

This Spotlight uses bivariate and multivariate analyses of data from the Early Childhood Longitudinal Study, Kindergarten Class of 2010–11 (ECLS-K:2011) to explore relationships between approaches to learning behaviors, academic gains, and family SES. For the first section of the Spotlight, average reading, mathematics, and science second-grade scores are compared by fall kindergarten approaches to learning categories using analysis of variance (ANOVA) procedures and post hoc t test comparisons, tested for statistical significance at the .05 level with False Discovery Rate (FDR) adjustment. For the second section, two sets of ordinary least squares (OLS) regression analyses were conducted. For both sets of regression analyses, gains in children's reading, mathematics, and science scores from the initial kindergarten assessment to the spring second-grade assessment are the outcome measures. The reading and mathematics gain scores were calculated as the difference between the spring second-grade score and the fall kindergarten score, while the science gain score was calculated as the difference between the spring second-grade score and the spring kindergarten score. Following the recommendation outlined in the ECLS-K:2011 Kindergarten–Second Grade Data File user's manual, both sets of regression analyses of gain scores controlled for children's initial assessment scores (i.e., fall kindergarten scores for reading and mathematics, and spring kindergarten scores for science) because gains made at different points on the item response theory (IRT) scale score have qualitatively different interpretations.[13] Children who made gains toward the lower end of the scale, for example in skills such as identifying letters and associating letters with sounds, are learning different skills than children who made gains at the higher end of the scale, for example those who have gone from reading single words to reading sentences, although their gains in number of scale score points may be the same. Comparison of gains in scale score points is most meaningful for groups that started with similar initial status. One way to account for children's initial status is to include a prior round assessment score as a control variable in an analytic model.

In addition to initial assessment scores as controls, the first set of regression analyses includes the continuous measure of fall kindergarten approaches to learning scores and the three-category kindergarten family SES variable as the independent variables. Built on the first set of models, the second set of analyses includes the interaction variables of family SES categories and the continuous fall kindergarten approaches to learning score. Interaction variables are used to explore whether the relationship between two variables, such as approaches to learning score and reading gains, differs across levels of a third variable, such as family SES. To test for interactions, new terms are added to the regression in which the approaches to learning and family SES group designation are multiplied. Significant interaction coefficients in the second set of models would indicate that the relationships

between initial approaches to learning scores and gains in reading, mathematics, and science from kindergarten to second grade differed for students from different family SES backgrounds. For all regression analyses, the low-SES household group is the reference category.

The reading assessment included questions measuring basic skills (print familiarity, letter recognition, beginning and ending sounds, rhyming words, and word recognition), vocabulary knowledge, and reading comprehension. The reading comprehension questions asked the child to identify information specifically stated in the text (e.g., definitions, facts, supporting details) and to make inferences about the text. The math assessment was designed to measure skills in conceptual knowledge, procedural knowledge, and problem solving. The assessment consisted of questions on number sense, properties, and operations; measurement; geometry and spatial sense; data analysis, statistics, and probability; and patterns, algebra, and functions. The science assessment included questions on physical sciences, life sciences, environmental sciences, and scientific inquiry.

Broad-based scores using the full set of items administered in the kindergarten through second-grade assessments in reading, math, and science were calculated using IRT procedures. The IRT-based overall scale score for each content domain is an estimate of the number of items a child would have answered correctly in each data collection round if he or she had been administered all of the questions that had been included in the assessments for that domain in kindergarten, first grade, and second grade. The ECLS-K:2011 employed a two-stage adaptive assessment (in reading and mathematics in kindergarten and in reading, mathematics, and science in first and second grade) in which children were individually administered a set of items appropriate to their demonstrated ability level rather than all of the items in the assessment. Although this procedure resulted in children being administered different sets of items, there was a subset of items that all children received (the items in the routing tests, plus a set of items common across the different second-stage forms). These common items were used to calculate scores for all children on the same scale. IRT also was used to calculate scores for all children on the same scale for the science assessment fielded in the spring of kindergarten even though that assessment was not two-stage. In that assessment, the assortment of items a child received was not dependent upon routing to a second stage, but instead on omissions by the child or the discontinuation of the administration of the assessment. In those cases, IRT was used to estimate the probability that a child would have provided a correct response when no response was available.

Information on family SES was collected through parental reports of parent/guardian educational attainment, occupational prestige levels, and household income in the kindergarten year. Occupational prestige level was based on information collected about the type of business or industry in which the parent worked, the parent's job title, and the most important activities or duties the parent did for the job. For this Spotlight, kindergartners living in households in the highest 20 percent of the SES scale were identified as being from high-SES households, those in households in the middle 60 percent of the SES scale were identified as being from middle-SES households, and those in households in the lowest 20 percent of the SES scale were identified as being from low-SES households.

More information about the ECLS-K:2011 is available at http://nces.ed.gov/ecls/kindergarten2011.asp.

Endnotes:

[1] See *The Condition of Education 2015* Spotlight indicator <u>Kindergartners' Approaches to Learning Behaviors and Academic Outcomes</u> and Zill, N., and West, J. (2001). *Entering Kindergarten: A Portrait of American Children When They Begin School: Findings From The Condition of Education 2000* (NCES 2001-035). National Center for Education Statistics, Institute of Education Sciences, U.S. Department of Education. Washington, DC.

[2] Arnold, D.H., and Doctoroff, G.L. (2003). The Early Education of Socioeconomically Disadvantaged Children. *Annual Review of Psychology, 54*: 517–545.

[3] Ladd, G.W., Birch, S.H., and Buhs, E.S. (1999). Child.en's Social and Scholastic Lives in Kindergarten: Related Spheres of Influence? *Child Development, 70*(6): 1373–1400. Zill, N., and West, J. (2001). *Entering Kindergarten: A Portrait of American Children When They Begin School: Findings From The Condition of Education 2000* (NCES 2001-035). National Center for Education Statistics, Institute of Education Sciences, U.S. Department of Education. Washington, DC.

[4] See *The Condition of Education 2015* Spotlight indicator <u>Kindergartners' Approaches to Learning Behaviors and Academic Outcomes</u> and Entwisle, D.R., and Alexander, K.L. (1998). Facilitating the Transition to First Grade: The Nature of Transition and Research on Factors Affecting It. *The Elementary School Journal, 98*(4): 351–364.

[5] Fall 2011 first-grade and fall 2012 second-grade scores are excluded from the discussion because data were collected from a representative subsample (and not the full sample) of ECLS-K:2011 students at those time periods.

[6] The reliability coefficient for the approaches to learning scale was 0.91 in the fall of kindergarten (Tourangeau et al. 2015); this coefficient is a measure of the internal consistency of the scale.

[7] This Spotlight builds on an analysis of children who were first-time kindergartners in the fall of 2010. Although the discussion makes reference to later rounds of data collection by the grade the majority of children are expected to be in (that is, the modal grade for children who were first-time kindergartners in the fall 2010–11 school year), children are included in subsequent data collections regardless of their actual grade level.

[8] For average reading, mathematics, and science score comparisons across approaches to learning categories in this Spotlight, kindergartners' average scores on the approaches to learning scale in the fall of kindergarten were rounded to the nearest whole number (following the initial calculations with unrounded numbers) so that students could be grouped into the original categories represented by the four-point scale. For example, a student with an average score of 2.4 would be categorized into the "sometimes" (value of 2) group.

[9] Tourangeau, K., Nord, C., Lê, T., Wallner-Allen, K., Vaden-Kiernan, N., Blaker, L., and Najarian, M. (2015). *Early Childhood Longitudinal Study, Kindergarten Class of 2010–11 (ECLS-K:2011) User's Manual for the ECLS-K:2011 Kindergarten–Second Grade Data File and Electronic Codebook, Restricted Version* (NCES 2015-049). U.S. Department of Education. Washington, DC: National Center for Education Statistics.

[10] To calculate the change in gain score associated with the fall kindergarten approaches to learning rating, a student's approaches to learning score is multiplied by the unstandardized regression coefficient for fall kindergarten approaches to learning. For instance, the change in reading gain score for a student with a fall kindergarten approaches to learning score of 4 would be calculated as 4 x 3.39 = 13.56 point increase in gain score, while the change in gain score for a student with an approaches to learning score of 1 would be 1 x 3.39 = 3.39 point increase. The difference in the gain score increase would equal 10.17 (i.e., 13.56 points - 3.39 points), or 10.2 points.

[11] Students from low-SES households had an average increase in their reading gain score of 5.0 points, based on the 5.01 coefficient for the fall kindergarten approaches to learning score, while students from middle-SES households had an average gain increase of 3.2 points (5.01 - 1.76 interaction effect) and students from high-SES households had an average gain increase of 2.0 points (5.01 - 3.05 interaction effect) (based on unrounded numbers in formula).

[12] Estimated gain scores are calculated as the sum of five components: (1) the intercept coefficient, (2) the average initial kindergarten score multiplied by the initial kindergarten score coefficient, (3) the student's approaches to learning score multiplied by the fall kindergarten approaches to learning rating coefficient, (4) the student's family SES coefficient, and (5) the student's approaches to learning score multiplied by the interaction coefficient that corresponds to the student's family SES. For instance, the kindergarten through second-grade reading gain score for a student with the initial reading score of 47.4 points and a fall kindergarten approaches to learning score of 1 from a high-SES household would be: 56.43 + [(47.42 x (-0.53)] + (1 x 5.01) + (14.81) + [(1 x (-3.05)] = 48.30 (based on unrounded numbers in formula).

[13] Tourangeau, K., Nord, C., Lê, T., Wallner-Allen, K., Vaden-Kiernan, N., Blaker, L., and Najarian, M. (2015). *Early Childhood Longitudinal Study, Kindergarten Class of 2010–11 (ECLS-K:2011) User's Manual for the ECLS-K:2011 Kindergarten–Second Grade Data File and Electronic Codebook, Restricted Version* (NCES 2015-049). U.S. Department of Education. Washington, DC: National Center for Education Statistics.

Reference tables: *Digest of Education Statistics 2015,* tables 220.40 and 220.45

Related indicators: Preschool and Kindergarten Enrollment, Kindergarten Entry Status: On-Time, Delayed-Entry, and Repeating Kindergartners [*The Condition of Education 2013 Spotlight*], Kindergartners' Approaches to Learning Behaviors and Academic Outcomes [*The Condition of Education 2015 Spotlight*]

Glossary: Household, Socioeconomic status (SES)

Differences in Postsecondary Enrollment Among Recent High School Completers

In fall 2013, among fall 2009 ninth-graders who had completed high school, three-quarters were enrolled at postsecondary institutions: some 14 percent were taking postsecondary classes only and were not enrolled in a degree program, 3 percent were enrolled in occupational certificate programs, 25 percent were enrolled in associate's degree programs, and 32 percent were enrolled in bachelor's degree programs. The remaining 25 percent were not enrolled in a postsecondary institution at all.

The attainment of postsecondary education credentials is associated with enhanced employment opportunities and increased earning potential. Both the financial returns and the nonfinancial returns (such as its positive effects on preventive health care use) are evidence of the importance of postsecondary education to the well-being of individuals and the society as a whole.[1,2] In addition, recent results from the Program for the International Assessment of Adult Competencies (PIAAC) allow for direct comparisons of a person's knowledge and skills with the person's level of education. PIAAC data indicate that among young adults ages 16–34, the higher the level of education completed, the larger the percentages of young adults at the top proficiency levels in the domains of literacy, numeracy, and problem-solving in technology-rich environments, and the smaller the percentages at the bottom proficiency levels.[3,4]

This Spotlight focuses on differences in the postsecondary enrollment status of recent high school completers (specifically, whether they are enrolled, and if they are enrolled, whether they are taking classes only or are enrolled in an occupational certificate, associate's degree, or bachelor's degree program). The Spotlight examines how other variables, such as student demographics, socioeconomic status (SES), high school academic characteristics (i.e., mathematics coursetaking and grade point average [GPA]), and student expectations are related to students' postsecondary enrollment status. This Spotlight focuses on fall 2009 ninth-graders who graduated from high school by September 2013.[5] Data were obtained from the High School Longitudinal Study of 2009 (HSLS:09) and its follow-up studies.[6] HSLS:09 followed a nationally representative cohort of students who were in the 9th grade in fall 2009 and surveyed them again in spring 2012 as well as the last half of 2013, after most students had graduated from high school. Data from the HSLS:09 and its follow-up studies provide a unique opportunity for researchers to investigate the pathways into postsecondary education, as well as the educational and social factors that are associated with students' choice of schooling after high school.

Figure 1.   Percentage distribution of fall 2009 ninth-graders who had completed high school, by fall 2013 postsecondary enrollment status: 2013

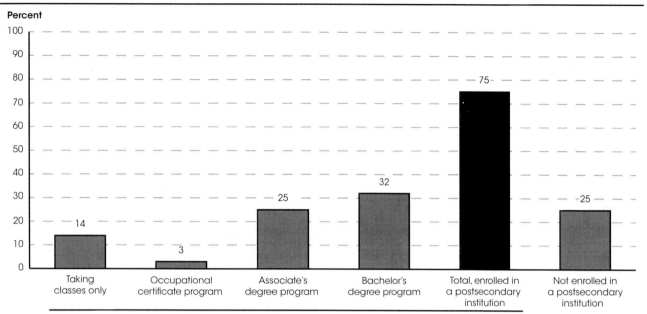

NOTE: Detail may not sum to totals because of rounding.
SOURCE: U.S. Department of Education, National Center for Education Statistics, High School Longitudinal Study of 2009 (HSLS:09), Base-Year, First Follow-up, 2013 Update, and High School Transcripts Restricted-Use Data File. See *Digest of Education Statistics 2015*, table 302.43.

In fall 2013, among fall 2009 ninth-graders who had completed high school, three-quarters were enrolled at postsecondary institutions: 14 percent were taking postsecondary classes without being enrolled in a particular program, 3 percent were enrolled in occupational certificate programs, 25 percent were enrolled in associate's degree programs, and 32 percent were enrolled in bachelor's degree programs. The remaining 25 percent were not enrolled in a postsecondary institution at all.

Figure 2. Percentage distribution of fall 2009 ninth-graders who had completed high school, by fall 2013 postsecondary enrollment status and sex: 2013

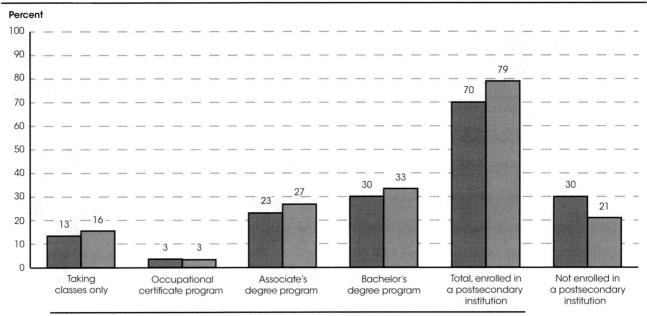

NOTE: Detail may not sum to totals because of rounding. Although rounded numbers are displayed, the figures are based on unrounded estimates.
SOURCE: U.S. Department of Education, National Center for Education Statistics, High School Longitudinal Study of 2009 (HSLS:09), Base-Year, First Follow-up, 2013 Update, and High School Transcripts Restricted-Use Data File. See *Digest of Education Statistics 2015*, table 302.43.

Postsecondary enrollment status differed by individual and family characteristics, including sex, race, and SES. Some 70 percent of male students were enrolled in a postsecondary institution, compared with 79 percent of female students. Enrollment was higher for female than for male students in bachelor's degree programs (33 vs. 30 percent) and associate's degree programs (27 vs. 23 percent). The percentages of males and females enrolled in occupational certificate programs; however, were not measurably different.

Figure 3. Percentage distribution of fall 2009 ninth-graders who had completed high school, by fall 2013 postsecondary enrollment status and race/ethnicity: 2013

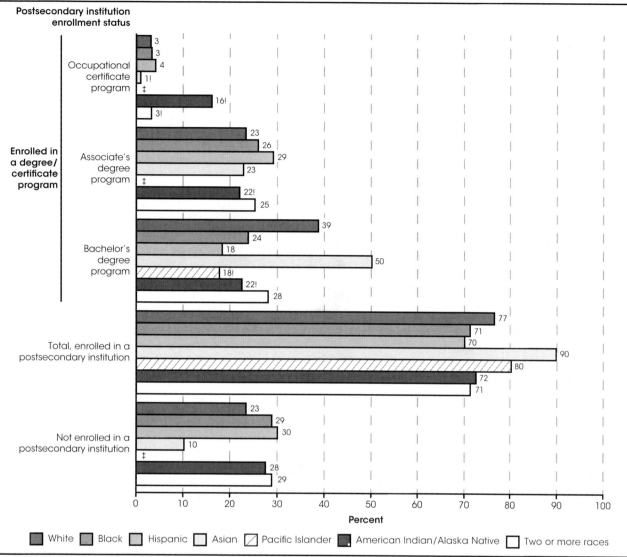

! Interpret data with caution. The coefficient of variation (CV) for this estimate is between 30 and 50 percent.
‡ Reporting standards not met. Either there are too few cases for a reliable estimate or the coefficient of variation (CV) is 50 percent or greater.
NOTE: Total enrolled in a postsecondary institution includes students who were taking classes only, although they are not shown separately in the figure. Detail may not sum to totals because of rounding. Race categories exclude persons of Hispanic ethnicity. Although rounded numbers are displayed, the figures are based on unrounded estimates.
SOURCE: U.S. Department of Education, National Center for Education Statistics, High School Longitudinal Study of 2009 (HSLS:09), Base-Year, First Follow-up, 2013 Update, and High School Transcripts Restricted-Use Data File. See *Digest of Education Statistics 2015*, table 302.43.

Among fall 2009 ninth-graders who had completed high school, postsecondary enrollment status differed by race/ethnicity. The findings for overall postsecondary enrollment are similar to those for enrollment in bachelor's degree programs. Enrollment in bachelor's degree programs was highest for Asian students: 50 percent of these students were enrolled in fall 2013. Enrollment in these programs was also higher for White students (39 percent) than for students of Two or more races (28 percent), Black students (24 percent), Hispanic students (18 percent), and Pacific Islander students (18 percent). For associate's degree programs, the percentage of Hispanic students (29 percent) enrolled in these programs was higher than the percentages of their White and Asian counterparts (23 percent each). The findings for students in occupational certificate

programs were the opposite of those for bachelor's degree students. The percentage of students enrolled in an occupational certificate program was lower for Asian students (1 percent) than for American Indian/Alaska Native students (16 percent), Hispanic students (4 percent), White students (3 percent), Black students (3 percent), and students of Two or more races (3 percent). In addition, higher percentages of Hispanic students (30 percent), Black students (29 percent), and students of Two or more races (29 percent) were not enrolled in a postsecondary institution, compared with the percentages of White (23 percent) and Asian (10 percent) students. The percentage of American Indian/Alaska Native students (28 percent) who were not enrolled in a postsecondary institution was also higher than that of Asian students.

Figure 4.   Percentage distribution of fall 2009 ninth-graders who had completed high school, by fall 2013 postsecondary enrollment status and socioeconomic status (SES): 2013

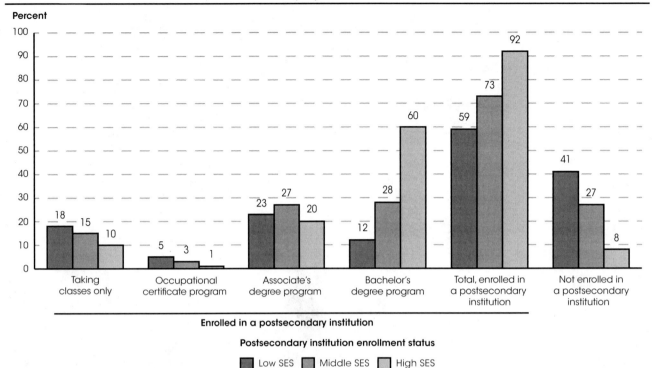

NOTE: SES was measured by a composite score based on parental education and occupations, family income, and school urbanicity in the student's 11th-grade year. The weighted SES distribution (weighted by W2STUDENT) was divided into five equal groups. Low SES corresponds to the lowest one-fifth of the population, and high SES corresponds to the highest one-fifth of the population. The three fifths in the middle were combined to form the middle SES category. Detail may not sum to totals because of rounding.
SOURCE: U.S. Department of Education, National Center for Education Statistics, High School Longitudinal Study of 2009 (HSLS:09), Base-Year, First Follow-up, 2013 Update, and High School Transcripts Restricted-Use Data File. See *Digest of Education Statistics 2015*, table 302.43.

Students from families with a low SES are less likely than those from families with a higher SES to obtain higher levels of postsecondary education.[7] In this Spotlight, postsecondary enrollment status also differed by SES, and the findings for overall postsecondary enrollment are similar to those for enrollment in bachelor's degree programs. The percentage of high-SES students enrolled in a bachelor's degree program was more than twice as high as the percentage of middle-SES students enrolled in a bachelor's degree program (60 vs. 28 percent), and both percentages were higher than the percentage of low-SES students (12 percent) enrolled in a bachelor's degree program. The pattern for enrollment in associate's degree programs was different: the percentage enrolled in

an associate's degree program was higher for middle-SES students (27 percent) than for low- and high-SES students (23 and 20 percent, respectively). Turning to enrollment in occupational certificate programs, these findings were the opposite of those observed for bachelor's degree students. The percentage enrolled in an occupational certificate program was highest for low-SES students (5 percent) and lowest for high-SES students (1 percent). Similarly, a higher percentage of low-SES students (41 percent) than of middle-SES students (27 percent) were not enrolled in a postsecondary institution, and both percentages were larger than the percentage of high-SES students (8 percent) who were not enrolled in a postsecondary institution.

Figure 5.   Percentage distribution of fall 2009 ninth-graders who had completed high school, by fall 2013 postsecondary enrollment status and highest mathematics course completed in high school: 2013

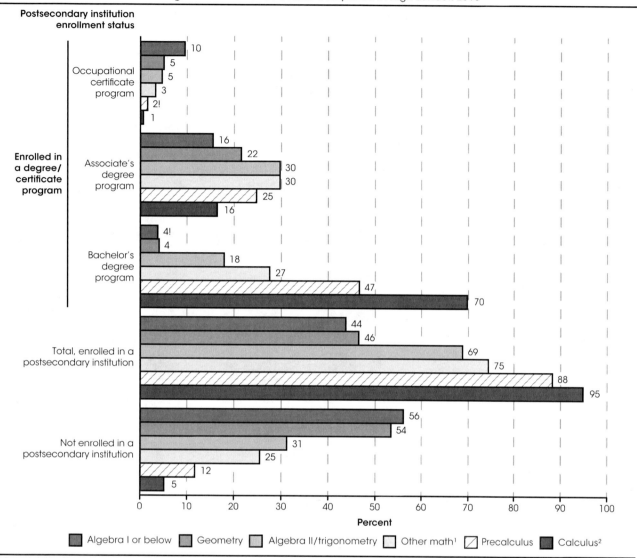

! Interpret data with caution. The coefficient of variation (CV) for this estimate is between 30 and 50 percent.
[1]Includes integrated math, algebra III, probability and statistics, and non-calculus Advanced Placement (AP) or International Baccalaureate (IB) courses.
[2]Includes AP/IB calculus.
NOTE: Total enrolled in a postsecondary institution includes students who were taking classes only, although they are not shown separately in the figure. Detail may not sum to totals because of rounding. Although rounded numbers are displayed, the figures are based on unrounded estimates.
SOURCE: U.S. Department of Education, National Center for Education Statistics, High School Longitudinal Study of 2009 (HSLS:09), Base-Year, First Follow-up, 2013 Update, and High School Transcripts Restricted-Use Data File. See *Digest of Education Statistics 2015*, table 302.43.

Students' high school academic characteristics, such as mathematics coursetaking and GPA in high school are strong predictors of students' success in postsecondary education.[8,9] Postsecondary enrollment status also differed in this analysis by mathematics coursetaking and GPA. Enrollment in postsecondary institutions, overall, as well as enrollment in bachelor's degree programs specifically was highest for students with higher levels of high school math coursetaking.[10] The majority of students whose highest mathematics course was calculus (70 percent) enrolled in a bachelor's degree program in fall 2013. This percentage was also higher for students whose highest level of mathematics was precalculus (47 percent) than for students whose highest level was

other math (27 percent) and algebra II or trigonometry (18 percent); the percentage was lowest for students who completed their highest mathematics course in lower-level courses such as algebra I or below (4 percent) and geometry (4 percent). Enrollment in associate's degree programs was higher for those who completed mid-level mathematics courses such as algebra II or trigonometry (30 percent) and other math (30 percent) than for those who completed both higher levels of mathematics courses (such as calculus [16 percent] and precalculus [25 percent]) and lower levels of mathematics courses (such as algebra I or below [16 percent] and geometry [22 percent]). Overall coursetaking patterns were similar for students who were enrolled in an occupational certificate program and those who were not enrolled in a postsecondary institution. For example, more than half of students whose highest mathematics course was algebra I or below (56 percent) and students whose highest mathematics course was geometry (54 percent) were not enrolled in a postsecondary institution, compared with 5 percent of students whose highest mathematics course was calculus. Additionally, 10 percent of students whose highest mathematics course was algebra I or below were enrolled in occupational certificate programs, compared with 1 percent of students whose highest mathematics course was calculus.

Figure 6. Average overall grade point average (GPA) earned in high school of fall 2009 ninth-graders who had completed high school, by students' fall 2013 postsecondary institution enrollment status: 2013

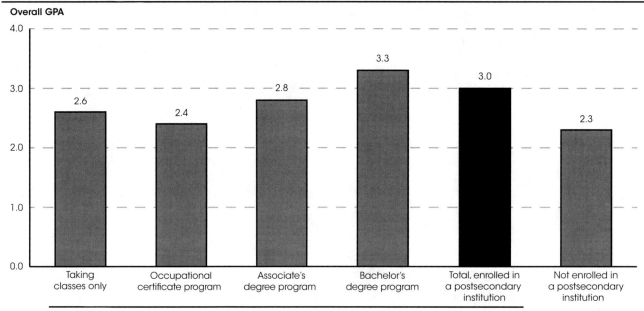

NOTE: GPA ranges from 0 to 4.
SOURCE: U.S. Department of Education, National Center for Education Statistics, High School Longitudinal Study of 2009 (HSLS:09), Base-Year, First Follow-up, 2013 Update, and High School Transcripts Restricted-Use Data File. See *Digest of Education Statistics 2015*, table 302.43.

The average high school GPA was 2.8 for fall 2009 ninth-graders who had completed high school by 2013. Among students who were enrolled in a postsecondary degree or certificate program, the average high school GPA was highest for students who were enrolled in a bachelor's degree program (3.3) and lowest for those who were enrolled in an occupational certificate program (2.4). The average high school GPA of students who were not enrolled in a postsecondary institution (2.3) was lower than the average GPAs of students who were in a bachelor's degree program, students who were in an associate's degree program (2.8), and students who were taking classes only (2.6). But, it was not measurably different from the average GPA of students who were enrolled in an occupational certificate program (2.4).

Students' educational expectations have been shown to relate to their eventual educational attainment.[11] HSLS:09 collected data on ninth-graders' educational expectations in fall 2009: some 15 percent of these students expected to complete high school or less, 7 percent expected to complete some college, 17 percent expected to complete a bachelor's degree, and 39 percent expected to complete a graduate or professional degree (see High School Longitudinal Study of 2009, table 1). In addition, 22 percent of these students did not know what level of education they would complete.

Figure 7. Percentage distribution of fall 2009 ninth-graders who had completed high school, by fall 2013 postsecondary enrollment status and expected levels of educational attainment at 9th grade: 2013

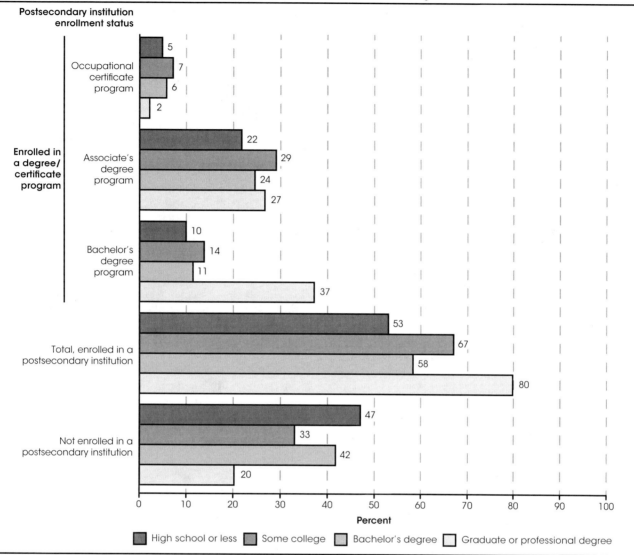

NOTE: Total enrolled in a postsecondary institution includes students who were taking classes only, although they are not shown separately in the figure. Detail may not sum to totals because of rounding. Although rounded numbers are displayed, the figures are based on unrounded estimates.
SOURCE: U.S. Department of Education, National Center for Education Statistics, High School Longitudinal Study of 2009 (HSLS:09), Base-Year, First Follow-up, 2013 Update, and High School Transcripts Restricted-Use Data File. See *Digest of Education Statistics 2015*, table 302.43.

In this analysis, students' educational expectations were associated with their postsecondary enrollment status, and the findings for overall postsecondary enrollment were similar to those for enrollment in bachelor's degree programs. Students whose 9th-grade educational expectations were a graduate or professional degree were enrolled in bachelor's degree programs by 2013 at a higher rate (37 percent) than students whose 9th-grade educational expectations were high school or less (10 percent), a bachelor's degree (11 percent), or some college (14 percent). In contrast, students whose

educational expectations at 9th grade were a graduate or professional degree were enrolled in occupational certificate programs at a lower rate (2 percent) than students whose educational expectations at 9th grade were high school or less (5 percent), a bachelor's degree (6 percent), or some college (7 percent). In addition, 47 percent of students whose educational expectations at 9th grade were high school or less were not enrolled in a postsecondary institution by 2013 versus 20 percent of students whose expectations at 9th grade were a graduate or professional degree.

Endnotes:

[1] Baum, S., Ma, J., and Payea, K. (2013). *Education Pays 2013: The Benefits of Higher Education for Individuals and Society* (Trends in Higher Education Series Report). New York: The College Board. Retrieved from https://trends.collegeboard.org/sites/default/files/education-pays-2013-full-report.pdf.

[2] Fletcher, J.M., and Frisvold, D.E. (2009). Higher Education and Health Investments: Does More Schooling Affect Preventive Health Care Use? *Journal of Human Capital, 3*(2), 144–176. Retrieved from http://doi.org/10.1086/645090.

[3] Rampey, B.D., Finnegan, R., Goodman, M., Mohadjer, L., Krenzke, T., Hogan, J., and Provasnik, S. (2016). *Skills of U.S. Unemployed, Young, and Older Adults in Sharper Focus: Results From the Program for the International Assessment of Adult Competencies (PIAAC) 2012/2014: First Look* (NCES 2016-039). U.S. Department of Education. Washington, DC: National Center for Education Statistics. Retrieved March 22, 2016, from http://nces.ed.gov/pubs2016/2016039.pdf.

[4] Zinshteyn, M. (2016, March 11). Americans With Bachelor Degrees Lag Behind Other Nations in Labor Skills. *The Rundown* [News blog]. PBS NewsHour. Retrieved from http://www.pbs.org/newshour/rundown/americans-with-bachelor-degrees-lag-behind-other-nations-in-labor-skills/.

[5] The population of interest for this Spotlight is recent high school completers, or fall 2009 ninth-graders who graduated from high school by September 2013. For ease of reference in the text, this group will also be referred to as "students."

[6] High School Longitudinal Study of 2009 (HSLS:09), Base-Year, First Follow-up, 2013 Update, and High School Transcripts Restricted-Use Data File.

[7] Long, B.T. (2007). The Contributions of Economics to the Study of College Access and Success. *Teachers College Record, 109*(10): 2367–2443.

[8] Hiss, W., and Franks, V.W. (2014). *Defining Promise: Optional Standardized Testing Policies in American College and University Admissions.* Arlington, VA: The National Association for College Admission Counseling (NACAC). Retrieved from http://www.nacacnet.org/research/research-data/nacac-research/Documents/DefiningPromise.pdf.

[9] Levine, P.B., and Zimmerman, D.J. (1995). The Benefit of Additional High-School Math and Science Classes for Young Men and Women. *Journal of Business and Economic Statistics, 13*(2): 137–149.

[10] The math sequence is as follows: below algebra I, algebra I (combined here), geometry, algebra II/trigonometry, other math, precalculus, and calculus. Other math includes courses such as integrated math, algebra III, probability and statistics, and non-calculus Advanced Placement (AP) or International Baccalaureate (IB) courses.

[11] Jacob, B.A., and Wilder, T. (2011). Educational Expectations and Attainment. In G.J. Duncan and R.J. Murnane (Eds.), *Whither Opportunity? Rising Inequality and the Uncertain Life Chances of Low-Income Children.* New York, NY: Russell Sage Press.

Reference tables: *Digest of Education Statistics 2015,* table 302.43; High School Longitudinal Study of 2009 table 1 at https://nces.ed.gov/surveys/hsls09/tables/educationalexpectations2009_01.asp

Related indicators: Educational Attainment of Young Adults, Undergraduate Enrollment, Immediate Transition to College, Postsecondary Attainment: Differences by Socioeconomic Status [*The Condition of Education 2015 Spotlight*]

Glossary: Associate's degree, Bachelor's degree, Certificate, College, Educational attainment, Enrollment, High school completer, Postsecondary education, Racial/ethnic group, Socioeconomic status (SES)

This page intentionally left blank.

Post-Bachelor's Employment Outcomes by Sex and Race/Ethnicity

While 86 percent of all young adults ages 25–34 with a bachelor's or higher degree were employed in 2014, differences in employment outcomes were observed by sex and race/ethnicity. For example, female full-time, year-round workers earned less than their male colleagues in nearly all of the occupation groups examined and for every employment sector (e.g., private for-profit, private nonprofit, government). Black young adults who worked full time, year round also earned less than their White peers in a majority of the occupations analyzed.

On average, individuals with at least a bachelor's degree earn more and have lower rates of unemployment than their less educated peers, although the benefits of higher education can also vary based on individual characteristics such as sex, race/ethnicity, occupation, field of study, and level of degree.[1] For instance, on average, males ages 25–34 who worked full time, year round[2] and possessed at least a bachelor's degree earned over $9,000 more than their female counterparts in 2014 (see *Digest of Education Statistics 2015*, table 505.15). Asian young adults with at least a bachelor's degree who worked full-time, year-round earned an average of over $20,000 more than their Black peers. One factor contributing to the Asian-Black earnings gap is that 20 percent of Asian young adults with

a bachelor's degree or higher were employed in computer and mathematical occupations, one of the top paying job groups examined, compared to 5 percent of Black young adults. This Spotlight, using the latest data from the Census Bureau's American Community Survey (ACS), identifies disparities such as these among bachelor's degree holders by examining employment status, occupation, and employment sector[3] by sex and race/ethnicity. Further research with ACS and other data sources is needed to measure the degree to which the differences observed in occupational and earnings outcomes are related to individual preferences, undergraduate or graduate field of study, family structure, child care responsibilities, "undermatching,"[4] discrimination, or other factors.

Figure 1. Percentage distribution of 25- to 34-year-old bachelor's or higher degree recipients, by sex, race/ethnicity, and employment status: 2014

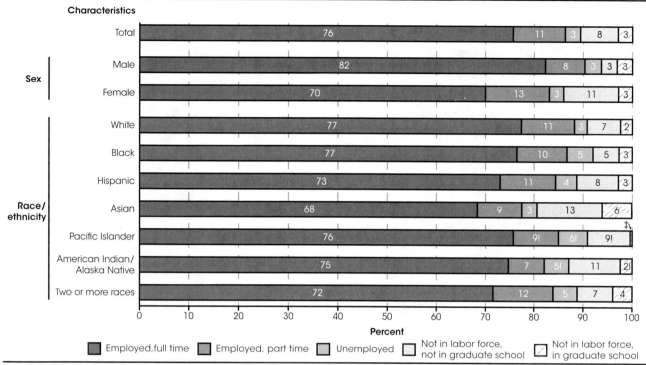

! Interpret data with caution. The coefficient of variation (CV) for this estimate is between 30 and 50 percent.
‡ Reporting standards not met. Either there are too few cases for a reliable estimate or the coefficient of variation (CV) for this estimate is 50 percent or greater.
NOTE: Estimates are for the entire population of civilian 25- to 34-year-old bachelor's degree holders including persons living in households and persons living in group quarters (such as college residence halls, residential treatment centers, and correctional facilities). Detail may not sum to totals because of rounding. Total includes other racial/ethnic groups not separately shown. Race categories exclude persons of Hispanic ethnicity. Although rounded numbers are displayed, the figures are based on unrounded estimates.
SOURCE: U.S. Department of Commerce, Census Bureau, American Community Survey (ACS), 2014. See *Digest of Education Statistics 2015*, table 505.15.

In 2014, some 86 percent of all young adults ages 25–34 with a bachelor's or higher degree were employed, 3 percent were unemployed, and 11 percent were not in the labor force (NILF).[5] However, these percentages varied by sex and race/ethnicity. For example, in 2014 a higher percentage of male than female young adults were employed (90 vs. 83 percent). In addition, a higher percentage of females were employed part time[6] (13 percent) than their male peers (8 percent). The percentage of those who were NILF was also higher for females than males (14 vs. 6 percent). For males, the 6 percent included 3 percent who were enrolled in graduate school and 3 percent who were not enrolled. For females, the 14 percent included 3 percent who were enrolled in graduate school and 11 percent who were not enrolled in graduate school.

The employment percentage for those with a bachelor's or higher degree was higher for White young adults

(88 percent) than young adults who were Black (87 percent), Hispanic (84 percent), of Two or more races (84 percent), American Indian/Alaska Native (82 percent), and Asian (78 percent). A higher percentage of Hispanic (11 percent), White (11 percent), and Black young adults (10 percent) held part-time employment than Asian young adults (9 percent). In terms of unemployment, a lower percentage of White and Asian young adults were unemployed (both 3 percent) than Black (5 percent) and Hispanic young adults (4 percent). Asian young adults had a higher NILF rate (19 percent) than young adults who were Hispanic (11 percent), of Two or more races (11 percent), White (9 percent), and Black (8 percent). The percentage classified as NILF who were attending graduate school was higher for Asian young adults (6 percent) than for Hispanic (3 percent), Black (3 percent), and White (2 percent) young adults.

Figure 2. Median earnings and percentage distribution of 25- to 34-year-old bachelor's or higher degree recipients who were employed, by major occupation group: 2014

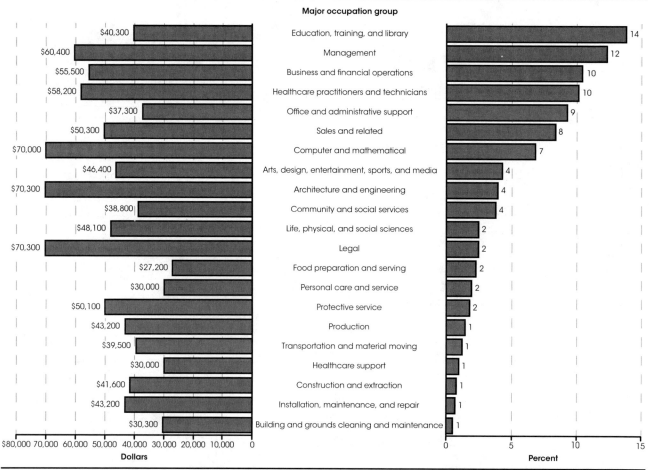

NOTE: Percentage distribution estimates are for the entire population of employed civilian 25- to 34-year-old bachelor's or higher degree holders including persons living in households and persons living in group quarters (such as college residence halls, residential treatment centers, and correctional facilities). Estimates for median earnings are for those who worked full time, year round. Excludes Farming, fishing, and forestry and Military-specific occupation groups, whose shares of employed bachelor's degree recipients are negligible. Detail may not sum to totals because of rounding. Although rounded numbers are displayed, the figures are based on unrounded estimates.
SOURCE: U.S. Department of Commerce, Census Bureau, American Community Survey (ACS), 2014. See *Digest of Education Statistics 2015*, table 505.15.

About 4 out of 5 (83 percent) employed young adults ages 25–34 with a bachelor's or higher degree worked in one of the 10 largest occupation groups in 2014. These groups, along with the percentages constituting them, were as follows: education, training, and library (hereinafter, "education"), 14 percent; management, 12 percent; business and financial operations, 10 percent; healthcare practitioners and technicians (hereinafter, "healthcare"), 10 percent; office and administrative support (hereinafter, "office support"), 9 percent; sales and related (hereinafter, "sales"), 8 percent; computer and mathematical (hereinafter, "computer/mathematical"), 7 percent; arts, design, entertainment, sports, and media (hereinafter, "arts and media"), 4 percent; architecture

and engineering, 4 percent; and community and social services, 4 percent.

Median earnings of young adults ages 25–34 who were employed in the 10 largest occupations full time, year round were higher for those working in architecture and engineering ($70,300) and computer/mathematical occupations ($70,000) than those in the remaining eight most common occupations. Median earnings in these occupations were as follows: management ($60,400), healthcare ($58,200), business and financial operations ($55,500), sales ($50,300), arts and media ($46,400), education ($40,300), community and social services ($38,800), and office support ($37,300).

Figure 3.   Percentage of 25- to 34-year-old bachelor's or higher degree recipients who were employed in the 10 largest major occupation groups, by sex and race/ethnicity: 2014

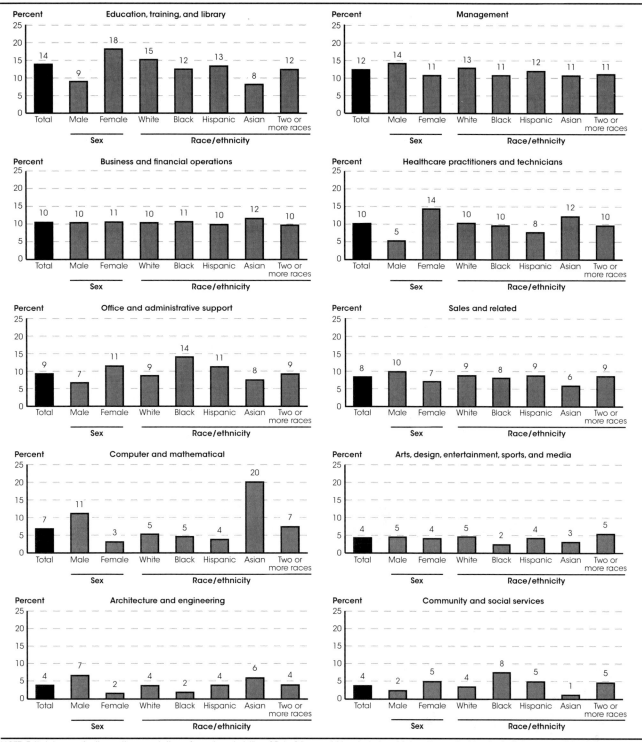

NOTE: Estimates are for the entire population of employed civilian 25- to 34-year-old bachelor's or higher degree holders including persons living in households and persons living in group quarters (such as college residence halls, residential treatment centers, and correctional facilities). Totals include other racial/ethnic groups not separately shown. Race categories exclude persons of Hispanic ethnicity. Although rounded numbers are displayed, the figures are based on unrounded estimates.
SOURCE: U.S. Department of Commerce, Census Bureau, American Community Survey (ACS), 2014. See *Digest of Education Statistics 2015*, table 505.15.

Figure 4. Median earnings of 25- to 34-year-old bachelor's or higher degree recipients who worked full time, year round in the 10 largest major occupation groups, by sex and race/ethnicity: 2014

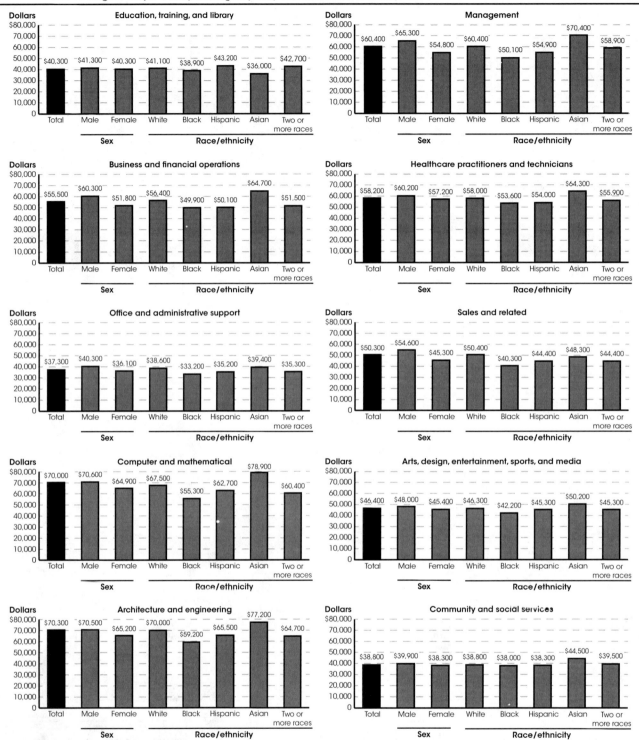

NOTE: Estimates are for the entire population of civilian 25- to 34-year-old bachelor's or higher degree holders who worked full time, year round including persons living in households and persons living in group quarters (such as college residence halls, residential treatment centers, and correctional facilities). Totals include other racial/ethnic groups not separately shown. Race categories exclude persons of Hispanic ethnicity.
SOURCE: U.S. Department of Commerce, Census Bureau, American Community Survey (ACS), 2014. See *Digest of Education Statistics 2015*, table 505.15.

Concerning employment in these occupations, a higher percentage of females ages 25–34 than males held occupations in education (18 vs. 9 percent), healthcare (14 vs. 5 percent), office support (11 vs. 7 percent), and community and social services (5 vs. 2 percent). Conversely, a higher percentage of males than females held positions in computer/mathematical occupations (11 vs. 3 percent), architecture and engineering (7 vs. 2 percent), management (14 vs. 11 percent), sales (10 vs. 7 percent), and arts and media (5 vs. 4 percent). Females who worked full-time, year-round earned less than males in all of the 10 largest occupations except education and arts and media, where the male-female differences in earnings were not measurably different. For instance, median earnings for males in management were $65,300, whereas median earnings for their female peers were $54,800.

There were also notable differences in the percentages of racial/ethnic groups working in various occupations. For instance, the percentage of those with at least a bachelor's degree working in office support (the lowest paying occupation among the 10 examined) was higher for Black young adults (14 percent) than young adults who were Hispanic (11 percent), of Two or more races (9 percent), White (9 percent), and Asian (8 percent). Also, there was a higher percentage of Black young adults (8 percent) in community and social services than those who were Hispanic (5 percent), of Two or more races (5 percent), White (4 percent), and Asian (1 percent). The percentage of Asian young adults who were employed in education (8 percent) was lower than the percentages of young adults in this occupation group who were White (15 percent), Hispanic (13 percent), Black (12 percent), and of Two or

more races (12 percent). Conversely, the percentage of Asian young adults employed in healthcare (12 percent) was higher than the percentage in this occupation group who were White (10 percent), of Two or more races (10 percent), Black (10 percent), and Hispanic (8 percent). Also, the percentage of Asian young adults in high-paying computer/mathematical occupations (20 percent) was higher than the corresponding percentages of young adults in these occupations who were of Two or more races (7 percent), White (5 percent), Black (5 percent), and Hispanic (4 percent). Similarly, the percentage of Asian young adults (6 percent) working in architecture and engineering, another top-paying occupation, was higher than the corresponding percentages of young adults who were of Two or more races (4 percent), Hispanic (4 percent), White (4 percent), and Black (2 percent) working in these occupations.

Hispanic young adults ages 25–34 who worked full time, year round in education had median earnings of $43,200, higher than the earnings of their counterparts in all other racial/ethnic groups[7] except those of Two or more races, whose earnings were not measurably different. Asian and White young adults both had higher earnings than their Black and Hispanic peers in management, business and financial operations, and office support. In management, for instance, Asian young adults had the highest median earnings ($70,400), followed by White ($60,400), Hispanic ($54,900), and Black young adults ($50,100). Black young adults employed in computer/mathematical occupations and architecture and engineering earned less than their White counterparts.

Figure 5. Percentage distribution of 25- to 34-year-old bachelor's or higher degree recipients who were employed, by sex, race/ethnicity, and employment sector: 2014

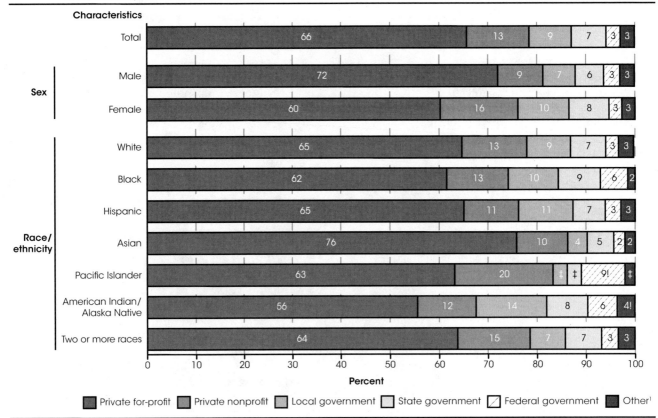

! Interpret data with caution. The coefficient of variation (CV) for this estimate is between 30 and 50 percent.
‡ Reporting standards not met. Either there are too few cases for a reliable estimate or the coefficient of variation (CV) for this estimate is 50 percent or greater.
[1] Includes unpaid family members and self-employed individuals with nonincorporated businesses.
NOTE: Estimates are for the entire population of employed civilian 25- to 34-year-old bachelor's degree holders, including persons living in households and persons living in group quarters (such as college residence halls, residential treatment centers, and correctional facilities). Detail may not sum to totals because of rounding. Total includes other racial/ethnic groups not separately shown. Race categories exclude persons of Hispanic ethnicity. Although rounded numbers are displayed, the figures are based on unrounded estimates.
SOURCE: U.S. Department of Commerce, Census Bureau, American Community Survey (ACS), 2014. See *Digest of Education Statistics 2015*, table 505.15.

Figure 6. Median earnings of 25- to 34-year-old bachelor's or higher degree recipients who worked full time, year round, by selected employment sector, sex, and race/ethnicity: 2014

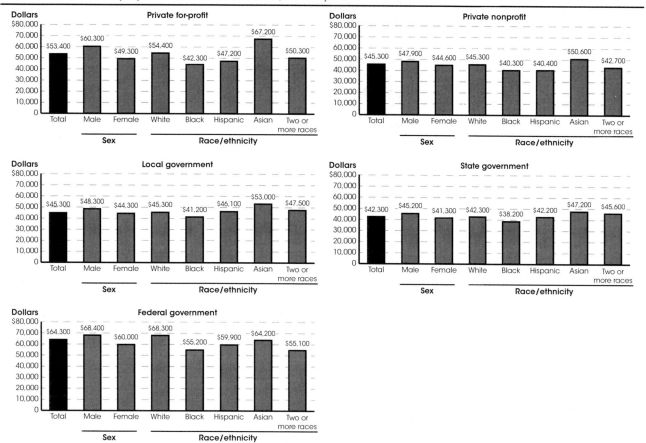

NOTE: Estimates are for the entire population of civilian 25- to 34-year-old bachelor's or higher degree holders who worked full time, year round including persons living in households and persons living in group quarters (such as college residence halls, residential treatment centers, and correctional facilities). Totals include other racial/ethnic groups not separately shown. Race categories exclude persons of Hispanic ethnicity.
SOURCE: U.S. Department of Commerce, Census Bureau, American Community Survey (ACS), 2014. See *Digest of Education Statistics 2015*, table 505.15.

The private for-profit sector employed the highest percentage (66 percent) of workers ages 25–34 with a bachelor's or higher degree, followed by the private nonprofit sector (13 percent), local government (9 percent), state government (7 percent), and the federal government (3 percent). Full-time, year-round workers in the federal government had higher median earnings ($64,300) than employees in the private for-profit ($53,400), private nonprofit, local government (both $45,300), and state government ($42,300) sectors.

A higher percentage of male than female young adults ages 25–34 worked in the private for-profit sector (72 and 60 percent, respectively), while a higher percentage of females than males were employed in the private nonprofit sector and in state and local governments. Females also earned less than their male colleagues in each employment sector observed. For instance, females in the private for-

profit sector earned $11,000 less than their male peers ($49,300 vs. $60,300).

The percentage of employed Asian young adults ages 25–34 with a bachelor's or higher degree working in the private for-profit sector (76 percent) was higher than that of Hispanic (65 percent), White (65 percent), and Black (62 percent) young adults. Conversely, a higher percentage of Black young adults were employed in federal and state governments (6 and 9 percent, respectively) than of White, Hispanic, and Asian young adults. In the private for-profit sector, Asian young adults who worked full-time, year-round earned the most ($67,200), followed by White ($54,400), Hispanic ($47,200), and Black ($42,300) young adults. Black young adults also earned less than their White peers in the private nonprofit sector as well as in all three levels of government.

Endnotes:
[1] See Annual Earnings of Young Adults, Employment Rates and Unemployment Rates by Educational Attainment, Employment Outcomes of Bachelor's Degree Recipients.
[2] Median earnings by occupation and employment sector are restricted to full-time, year-round workers. Full-time, year-round workers are those who worked at least 35 hours per week for the past year.
[3] Employment sector refers to the Census Bureau's "class of worker" classification which categorizes people according to the type of ownership of their employing organization. Assigning class of worker categories is, in most cases, independent of industry and occupation. In this indicator, employment sector includes private for-profit, private nonprofit, local, state, and federal government, and other.
[4] "Undermatching" is a term usually used to describe students attending less-competitive colleges than

their academic credentials warrant. In this context, "undermatching" refers to a similar concept in the labor market: candidates accepting or settling for positions that pay lower than their qualifications allow.
[5] This category consists mainly of students, homemakers, seasonal workers interviewed in an off season who were not looking for work, institutionalized people, and people doing only incidental unpaid family work (less than 15 hours during the reference week).
[6] Part-time work is defined as less than 35 hours per week.
[7] A comparison between Hispanic and Pacific Islander young adults is not possible since reporting standards were not met for the latter group.

Reference tables: *Digest of Education Statistics 2015,* table 505.15
Related indicators: Educational Attainment of Young Adults, Annual Earnings of Young Adults, Employment and Unemployment Rates by Educational Attainment

Glossary: Bachelor's degree, Employment status, Median earnings, Racial/ethnic group

This page intentionally left blank.

The indicators in this chapter of *The Condition of Education* report on educational attainment and economic outcomes for the United States as a whole. The level of education attained by an individual has implications for his or her median earnings and other labor outcomes, such as unemployment. Comparisons at the national level to other industrialized nations provide insight into our global competitiveness. In addition, this chapter contains indicators on key demographic characteristics, such as poverty.

This chapter's indicators, as well as additional indicators on population characteristics, are available at *The Condition of Education* website: http://nces.ed.gov/programs/coe.

Chapter 1

Population Characteristics

Educational Attainment of Young Adults

In 2015, some 36 percent of 25- to 29-year-olds had attained a bachelor's or higher degree. The percentage of White 25- to 29-year-olds who had attained this level of education increased from 1995 to 2015, as the size of the White-Black gap in the attainment of a bachelor's or higher degree widened from 13 to 22 percentage points and the size of the White-Hispanic gap widened from 20 to 27 percentage points.

Educational attainment refers to the highest level of education completed (e.g., a high school diploma or equivalency certificate, an associate's degree, a bachelor's degree, or a master's degree). Between 1995 and 2015, educational attainment rates among 25- to 29-year-olds increased. The percentage who had received at least a high school diploma or its equivalent increased from 87 to 91 percent, with most of the change occurring between 2005 and 2015. The percentage who had completed an associate's or higher degree increased from 33 percent in 1995 to 46 percent in 2015. Similarly, the percentage who had completed a bachelor's or higher degree increased from 25 percent in 1995 to 36 percent in 2015, and the percentage who had completed a master's or higher degree increased from 5 percent in 1995 to 9 percent in 2015.

Figure 1. Percentage of 25- to 29-year-olds who completed a bachelor's or higher degree, by sex: Selected years, 1995–2015

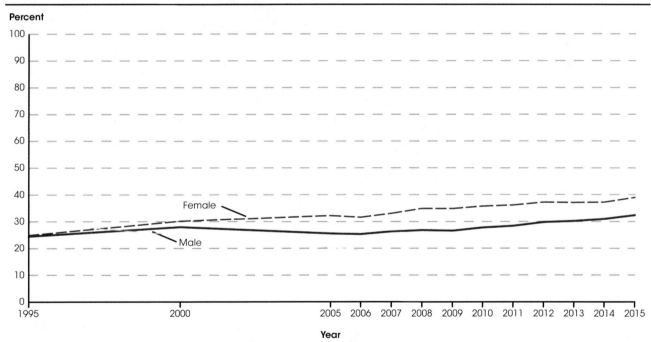

SOURCE: U.S. Department of Commerce, Census Bureau, Current Population Survey (CPS), Annual Social and Economic Supplement, selected years, 1995–2015. See *Digest of Education Statistics 2015*, table 104.20.

Since 2000, attainment rates among 25- to 29-year-olds have generally been higher for females than for males at each education level. Postsecondary degree attainment rates have increased more rapidly for females than for males since 1995. This pattern was observed across all levels of postsecondary education. For example, in 1995 the percentages of males and females who had completed an associate's or higher degree were not measurably different, but in 2015 some 50 percent of females had completed an associate's or higher degree, compared with 41 percent of males. Similarly, in 1995 the percentages of male and female 25- to 29-year-olds who had completed a bachelor's or higher degree were not measurably different, but in 2015 the percentage of females (39 percent) who had attained this level of education was 7 percentage points higher than the percentage of males doing so (32 percent).

Figure 2. Percentage of 25- to 29-year-olds who completed at least a high school diploma or its equivalent, by race/ethnicity: Selected years, 1995–2015

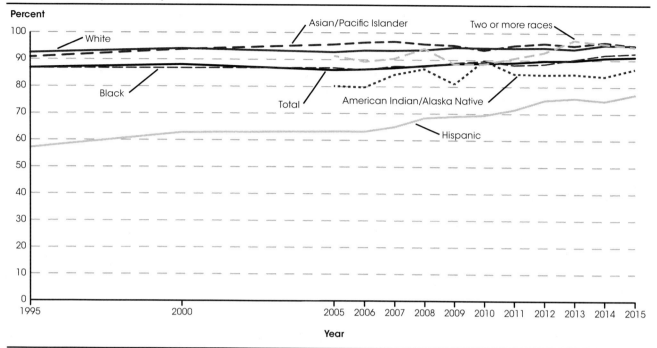

NOTE: Race categories exclude persons of Hispanic ethnicity. Prior to 2005, separate data on persons of Two or more races were not available; data for American Indians/Alaska Natives are not shown prior to 2005.
SOURCE: U.S. Department of Commerce, Census Bureau, Current Population Survey (CPS), Annual Social and Economic Supplement, selected years, 1995–2015. See *Digest of Education Statistics 2015*, table 104.20.

Between 1995 and 2015, the percentage of 25- to 29-year-olds who had completed at least a high school diploma or its equivalent increased for those who were White (from 92 to 95 percent), Black (from 87 to 93 percent), and Hispanic (from 57 to 77 percent). For those who were Hispanic, most of the change over this period (i.e., 14 percentage points out of the total 20 percentage point change) occurred between 2005 and 2015. The percentage of Asian/Pacific Islander 25- to 29-year-olds who had completed at least a high school diploma or its equivalent in 2015 (95 percent) was not measurably different from the percentage who had attained this education level in 1995. In 2015, some 87 percent of American Indians/Alaska Natives and 95 percent of persons of Two or more races had completed at least a

high school diploma or its equivalent; neither percentage was measurably different from its 2005 counterpart.[1]

Between 1995 and 2015, the percentage of White 25- to 29-year-olds who had attained at least a high school diploma or its equivalent remained higher than the percentages of Hispanic and Black 25- to 29-year-olds who had attained this education level. Over this period, the size of the White-Hispanic attainment gap at this education level narrowed from 35 to 18 percentage points, primarily due to an increase in percentage of Hispanic 25- to 29-year-olds who had completed at least a high school diploma. In contrast, the White-Black gap at this education level in 2015 (3 percentage points) did not differ measurably from the gap in 1995.

Figure 3. Percentage of 25- to 29-year-olds who completed an associate's or higher degree, by race/ethnicity: 1995–2015

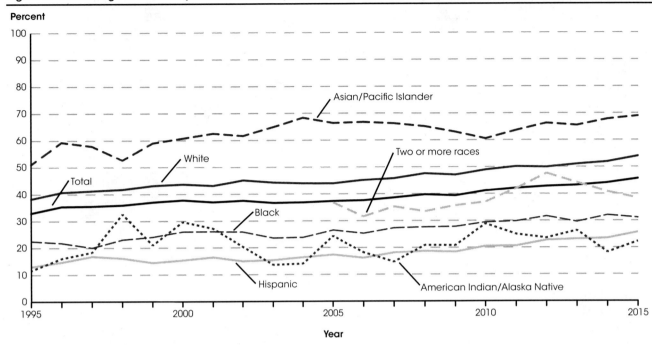

NOTE: Race categories exclude persons of Hispanic ethnicity. Prior to 2005, separate data on persons of Two or more races were not available.
SOURCE: U.S. Department of Commerce, Census Bureau, Current Population Survey (CPS), Annual Social and Economic Supplement, 1995–2015. See *Digest of Education Statistics 2015*, table 104.65.

From 1995 to 2015, the percentage of 25- to 29-year-olds who had attained an associate's or higher degree increased for those who were White (from 38 to 54 percent), Black (from 22 to 31 percent), Hispanic (from 13 to 26 percent), and Asian/Pacific Islander (from 51 to 69 percent). Neither the percentage of American Indians/Alaska Natives (22 percent) nor the percentage of persons of Two or more races (38 percent) who had attained an associate's or higher degree in 2015 were measurably different from the corresponding percentages in 2005. Between 1995 and 2015, the gap between White and Black 25- to 29-year-olds who had attained an associate's or higher degree widened from 16 to 23 percentage points, primarily due to an increase in the percentage of White 25- to 29-year-olds who had attained this level of education. The White-Hispanic gap at this education level did not change measurably over this period; in 2015, the gap was 28 percentage points.

Figure 4.   Percentage of 25- to 29-year-olds who completed a bachelor's or higher degree, by race/ethnicity: Selected years, 1995–2015

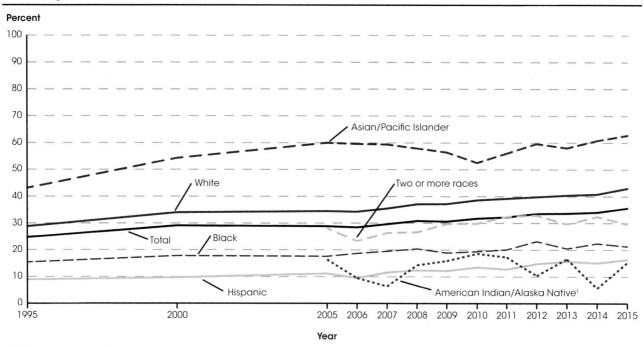

[1] Interpret data for 2006, 2007, and 2014 with caution. The coefficients of variation (CVs) for these estimates are between 30 and 50 percent.
NOTE: Race categories exclude persons of Hispanic ethnicity. Prior to 2005, separate data on persons of Two or more races were not available; data for American Indians/Alaska Natives are not shown prior to 2005.
SOURCE: U.S. Department of Commerce, Census Bureau, Current Population Survey (CPS), Annual Social and Economic Supplement, selected years, 1995–2015. See *Digest of Education Statistics 2015*, table 104.20.

From 1995 to 2015, the percentage of 25- to 29-year-olds who had attained a bachelor's or higher degree increased for those who were White (from 29 to 43 percent), Black (from 15 to 21 percent), Hispanic (from 9 to 16 percent), and Asian/Pacific Islander (from 43 to 63 percent). The 2015 percentages of American Indians/Alaska Natives (15 percent) and of persons of Two or more races (30 percent) who had attained a bachelor's or higher degree were not measurably different from their 2005 counterparts. Over the period from 1995 to 2015, the gap between White and Black 25- to 29-year-olds who had attained a bachelor's or higher degree widened from 13 to 22 percentage points, and the gap between White and Hispanic 25- to 29-year-olds at this level widened from 20 to 27 percentage points.

From 1995 to 2015, the percentage of 25- to 29-year-olds who had attained a master's or higher degree increased for those who were White (from 5 to 10 percent), Black (from 2 to 5 percent), Hispanic (from 2 to 3 percent), and Asian/Pacific Islander (from 11 to 22 percent). The gap between the percentages of White and Hispanic 25- to 29-year-olds who had attained a master's or higher degree widened from 4 to 7 percentage points from 1995 to 2015. In contrast, the gap between the percentages of White and Black 25- to 29-year-olds who had attained this education level in 2015 (5 percentage points) was not measurably different from the gap in 1995.

Endnotes:
[1] In 1995, data on attainment rates at all education levels were not available for American Indians/Alaska Natives and persons of Two or more races.

Reference tables: *Digest of Education Statistics 2015*, tables 104.20 and 104.65
Related indicators: International Educational Attainment, Annual Earnings of Young Adults, Trends in Employment Rates by Educational Attainment [*The Condition of Education 2013 Spotlight*]

Glossary: Associate's degree, Bachelor's degree, Educational attainment (Current Population Survey), High school completer, High school diploma, Master's degree, Postsecondary education, Racial/ethnic group

International Educational Attainment

The OECD average percentage of the adult population with a postsecondary degree increased by 11 percentage points between 2001 and 2014, from 22 to 33 percent. During the same period, the percentage of U.S. adults with a postsecondary degree increased by 7 percentage points, from 37 to 44 percent.

The Organization for Economic Cooperation and Development (OECD) is an organization of 34 countries whose purpose is to promote trade and economic growth. In 2014, some 17 out of 33 countries[1] belonging to the OECD reported that more than 80 percent of their adult populations (ages 25 to 64) had completed high school.[2,3] Among OECD countries, the percentages of high school completers ranged from under 45 percent in Mexico, Turkey, and Portugal to over 90 percent in Poland, the Slovak Republic, Estonia, and the Czech Republic. Additionally, 20 out of 33 OECD countries reported that more than 30 percent of their adult populations had earned postsecondary degrees.[4] The percentages of adults earning a postsecondary degree ranged from under 20 percent in Turkey, Italy, and Mexico to 45 percent or more in Luxembourg, Israel, and Canada.

In most OECD countries, except for the United States and Estonia, higher percentages of the youngest adult age group surveyed (those ages 25 to 34) than of the oldest adult age group (ages 55 to 64) had completed high school in 2014. Across OECD countries, the average percentage of those completing high school was higher for 25- to 34-year-olds (83 percent) than for 55- to 64-year-olds (66 percent). The United States was the only country in which the high school completion percentages were not measurably different between the youngest and oldest age groups; the rates for both age groups were 90 percent. In Estonia, a lower percentage of 25- to 34-year-olds (89 percent) than of 55- to 64-year-olds (92 percent) had completed high school. Over 80 percent of 55- to 64-year-olds had completed high school in six other countries: Poland, Switzerland, the Slovak Republic, Canada, Germany, and the Czech Republic.

Figure 1. Percentage of the population that had completed high school in Organization for Economic Cooperation and Development (OECD) countries, by selected age groups: 2014

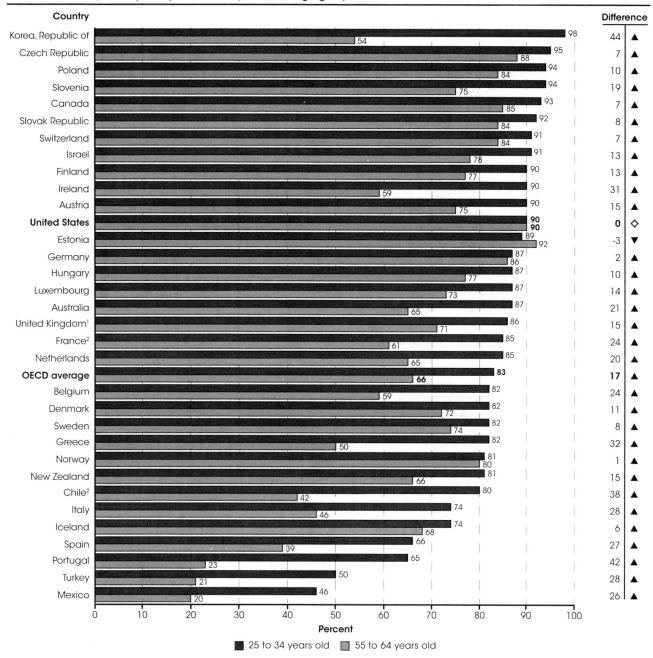

▲ 25 to 34 years old   ▨ 55 to 64 years old

▲ The percentage of 25- to 34-year-olds who had completed high school is higher than the percentage of 55- to 64-year-olds who had completed high school.
▼ The percentage of 25- to 34-year-olds who had completed high school is lower than the percentage of 55- to 64-year-olds who had completed high school.
◇ The percentages of 25- to 34-year-olds and 55- to 64-year-olds who had completed high school are not significantly different.
[1] Data include some persons (18 percent of the total) who have completed a sufficient volume and standard of programs, any one of which individually would be classified as a program that only partially completes the high school (or upper secondary) level of education.
[2] Data from 2013 reported for 2014.
NOTE: Data not available for Japan. The International Standard Classification of Education (ISCED) was most recently revised in 2011. Data in this figure refer to degrees classified as ISCED level 3, which corresponds to high school completion in the United States. The OECD average refers to the mean of the data values for all reporting OECD countries, to which each country reporting data contributes equally. Although rounded numbers are displayed, the figures are based on unrounded estimates.
SOURCE: Organization for Economic Cooperation and Development (OECD), *Education at a Glance, 2015.* See *Digest of Education Statistics 2015,* table 603.10.

Figure 2. Percentage of the population with a postsecondary degree in Organization for Economic Cooperation and Development (OECD) countries, by selected age groups: 2014

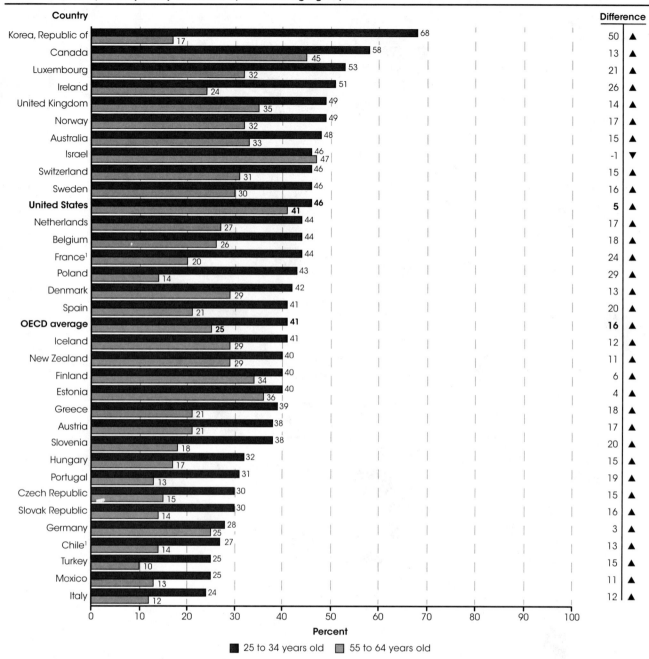

▀ 25 to 34 years old ▨ 55 to 64 years old

▲ The percentage of 25- to 34-year-olds with any postsecondary degree is higher than the percentage of 55- to 64-year-olds with any postsecondary degree.
▼ The percentage of 25- to 34-year-olds with any postsecondary degree is lower than the percentage of 55- to 64-year-olds with any postsecondary degree.
[1] Data from 2013 reported for 2014.
NOTE: Data in this figure include all postsecondary degrees, which correspond to degrees at the associate's level and above in the United States. The International Standard Classification of Education (ISCED) was most recently revised in 2011. Under ISCED 2011, postsecondary degrees are classified at the following levels: level 5 (corresponding to an associate's degree in the United States), level 6 (a bachelor's or equivalent degree), level 7 (a master's or equivalent degree), and level 8 (a doctoral or equivalent degree). 2014 estimates for Japan are excluded from the figure because data for postsecondary degree completion rates excluded short-cycle tertiary education, which corresponds to the associate's degree in the United States. Although rounded numbers are displayed, the figures are based on unrounded estimates.
SOURCE: Organization for Economic Cooperation and Development (OECD), *Education at a Glance, 2015.* See *Digest of Education Statistics 2015,* table 603.20.

The same general pattern of higher percentages of the youngest age groups attaining higher levels of education also applied to the attainment of postsecondary degrees in 2014. In all OECD countries except Israel, a higher percentage of 25- to 34-year-olds than of 55- to 64-year-olds had earned a postsecondary degree in 2014. Across OECD countries, 41 percent of 25- to 34-year-olds had earned a postsecondary degree in 2014, compared with 25 percent of 55- to 64-year-olds. In the United States, 46 percent of 25- to 34-year-olds and 41 percent of 55- to 64-year-olds had earned a postsecondary degree. Forty percent or more of 55- to 64-year-olds had earned a postsecondary degree in two other countries: Canada and Israel.

Figure 3. Percentage of the population 25 to 64 years old that had completed high school in Organization for Economic Cooperation and Development (OECD) countries: 2001 and 2014

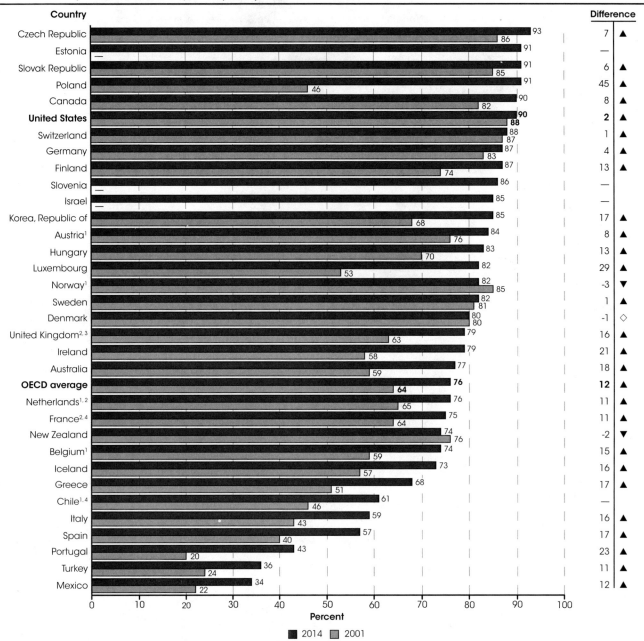

▲ The 2014 percentage is higher than the 2001 percentage.
▼ The 2014 percentage is lower than the 2001 percentage.
◇ The 2014 and 2001 percentages are not significantly different.
— Not available.
[1] Data from 2000 reported for 2001.
[2] Data in 2001 include some short secondary (ISCED 3C) programs.
[3] Data for 2014 include some persons (18 percent of the total) who have completed a sufficient volume and standard of programs, any one of which individually would be classified as a program that only partially completes the high school (or upper secondary) level of education.
[4] Data from 2013 reported for 2014.
NOTE: Data not available for Japan in 2014. The International Standard Classification of Education (ISCED) was most recently revised in 2011. The previous version, ISCED 1997, was used to calculate all data for 2012 and earlier years. For OECD countries, data for 2014 were calculated using ISCED 2011 and may not be comparable to data for earlier years. Data in this figure refer to degrees classified as ISCED level 3, which corresponds to high school completion in the United States, with the following exceptions: Programs classified under ISCED 1997 as level 3C short programs do not correspond to high school completion; these short programs are excluded from this table except where otherwise noted. Programs classified under ISCED 2011 as only partially completing level 3 are also excluded except where otherwise noted. Although rounded numbers are displayed, the figures are based on unrounded estimates.
SOURCE: Organization for Economic Cooperation and Development (OECD), *Education at a Glance, 2003 and 2015*. See *Digest of Education Statistics 2015*, table 603.10.

The percentage of 25- to 64-year-olds who had completed a high school education was higher in 2014 than in 2001 in each OECD country with reported data, with the exceptions of New Zealand and Norway, where high school completion rates in 2014 were between 2 and 3 percentage points lower than they were in 2001, and Denmark, where high school completion rates were not measurably different between the two years.[5] The OECD average percentage of the adult population completing a high school education increased by 12 percentage points, from 64 percent in 2001 to 76 percent in 2014. The percentage of adults in the United States who had completed high school increased from 88 to 90 percent during this period. For 25- to 34-year-olds, the OECD average percentage with a high school education was 9 percentage points higher in 2014 (83 percent) than in 2001 (74 percent), while the percentage of U.S. young adults with a high school education was 2 percentage points higher (90 vs. 88 percent).

Figure 4. Percentage of the population 25 to 64 years old with a postsecondary degree in Organization for Economic Cooperation and Development (OECD) countries: 2001 and 2014

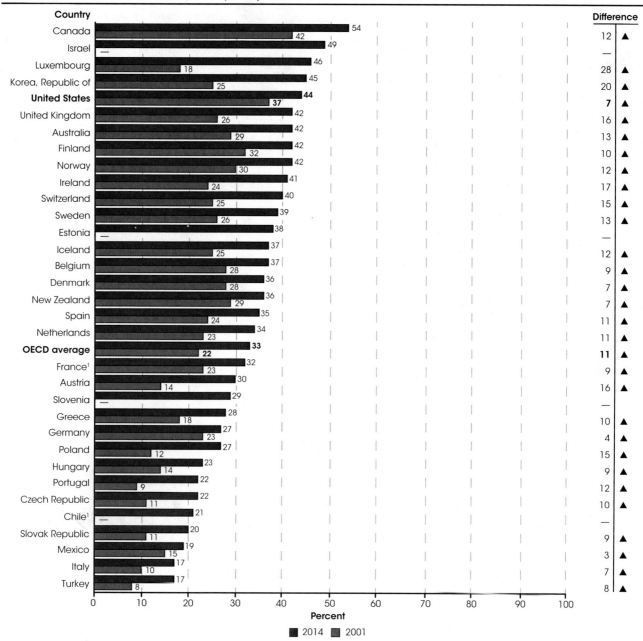

▲ The 2014 percentage is higher than the 2001 percentage.
— Not available.
[1] Data from 2013 reported for 2014.
NOTE: Data in this figure include all postsecondary degrees, which correspond to degrees at the associate's level and above in the United States. The International Standard Classification of Education (ISCED) was most recently revised in 2011. The previous version, ISCED 1997, was used to calculate all data for 2013 and earlier years. For OECD countries, data for 2014 were calculated using ISCED 2011 and may not be comparable to data for earlier years. Under ISCED 2011, postsecondary degrees are classified at the following levels: level 5 (corresponding to an associate's degree in the United States), level 6 (a bachelor's or equivalent degree), level 7 (a master's or equivalent degree), and level 8 (a doctoral or equivalent degree). 2014 estimates for Japan are excluded from the figure because data for postsecondary degree completion rates excluded short-cycle tertiary education, which corresponds to the associate's degree in the United States. Although rounded numbers are displayed, the figures are based on unrounded estimates.
SOURCE: Organization for Economic Cooperation and Development (OECD), *Education at a Glance, 2003 and 2015.* See *Digest of Education Statistics 2015,* table 603.20.

All countries with data reported that the percentages of 25- to 64-year-olds who had earned a postsecondary degree were higher in 2014 than in 2001. The OECD average percentage of the adult population with a postsecondary degree increased by 11 percentage points between 2001 and 2014, from 22 to 33 percent. During the same period, the percentage of U.S. adults with a postsecondary degree increased by 7 percentage points, from 37 to 44 percent.

For 25- to 34-year-olds, the OECD average percentage with a postsecondary degree rose from 28 percent in 2001 to 41 percent in 2014, an increase of 13 percentage points. The comparable percentage for young adults in the United States increased by 7 percentage points, from 39 to 46 percent. As a result of the relatively larger increases in postsecondary degree attainment among young adult populations in several other OECD countries, the gap in attainment at this level of education between the U.S. and the OECD average percentages decreased between 2001 and 2014. In 2001, the rate of attainment of a postsecondary degree among 25- to 34-year-olds in the United States was 11 percentage points higher than the OECD average; by 2014, this difference had decreased to 5 percentage points.

Endnotes:

[1] In 2014, Japan did not report data on high school completion rates. In addition, data for Japan's postsecondary degree completion rates excluded short-cycle tertiary education, which corresponds to the associate's degree in the United States. Due to these limitations, estimates for Japan are excluded from the indicator.

[2] Attainment data in this indicator refer to comparable levels of degrees, as classified by the International Standard Classification of Education (ISCED). ISCED was most recently revised in 2011. The previous version, ISCED 1997, was used to calculate all data for 2013 and earlier years. For OECD countries, data for 2014 were calculated using ISCED 2011 and may not be comparable to data for earlier years.

[3] Data in this section refer to degrees classified as ISCED level 3, which corresponds to high school completion in the United States, with the following exceptions: Programs classified under ISCED 1997 as level 3C short programs do not correspond to high school completion; these short programs are excluded from this section except for France and the United Kingdom. Programs classified under ISCED 2011 as only partially completing level 3 are also excluded except for the United Kingdom.

[4] Here, postsecondary degrees are those that correspond to the associate's or higher level in the United States. Under ISCED 2011, postsecondary degrees are classified at the following levels: level 5 (corresponding to an associate's degree in the United States), level 6 (a bachelor's or equivalent degree), level 7 (a master's or equivalent degree), and level 8 (a doctoral or equivalent degree).

[5] In 2001, Estonia, Slovenia, and Israel did not report data on high school completion rates.

Reference tables: *Digest of Education Statistics 2015*, tables 603.10 and 603.20

Related indicators: Educational Attainment of Young Adults, Education Expenditures by Country, International Assessments, Trends in Employment Rates by Educational Attainment [*The Condition of Education 2013 Spotlight*]

Glossary: Educational attainment, High school completer, International Standard Classification of Education (ISCED), Organization for Economic Cooperation and Development (OECD), Postsecondary education

Annual Earnings of Young Adults

In 2014, the median earnings of young adults with a bachelor's degree ($49,900) were 66 percent higher than the median earnings of young adult high school completers ($30,000). The median earnings of young adult high school completers were 20 percent higher than the median earnings of those without a high school credential ($25,000).

This indicator examines the annual earnings of young adults ages 25–34. Many people in this age group have recently completed their education and may be entering the workforce or transitioning from part-time to full-time work. In 2014, some 67 percent of young adults ages 25–34 who were in the labor force worked full time, year round (i.e., worked 35 or more hours per week for 50 or more weeks per year). The percentage of young adults working full time, year round was generally higher for those with higher levels of educational attainment. For example, 73 percent of young adults with a bachelor's degree worked full time, year round in 2014, compared with 65 percent of young adult high school completers (those with only a high school diploma or its equivalent).

Figure 1. Percentage of the labor force ages 25–34 who worked full time, year round, by educational attainment: 2000–2014

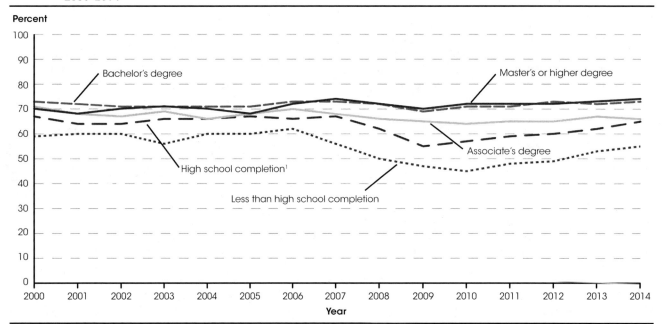

[1] Includes equivalency credentials, such as the GED credential.
NOTE: *Full-time, year-round workers* are those who worked 35 or more hours per week for 50 or more weeks per year.
SOURCE: U.S. Department of Commerce, Census Bureau, Current Population Survey (CPS), "Annual Social and Economic Supplement," 2001–2015; and previously unpublished tabulations. See *Digest of Education Statistics 2015*, table 502.30.

Changes over time in the percentage of young adults in the labor force who worked full time, year round varied by level of educational attainment. From 2000 to 2014, the percentage of young adults without a high school credential (i.e., without a high school diploma or its equivalent) who worked full time, year round decreased from 59 to 55 percent. The corresponding percentage for young adults with an associate's degree decreased from 71 to 66 percent. In contrast, the percentage of young adults with a master's or higher degree who worked full time, year round increased from 70 to 74 percent during the same period. However, from 2000 to 2014 the percentages of young adult high school completers and young adults with a bachelor's degree who worked full time, year round did not change measurably. Between 2013 and 2014, the percentages of young adults working full time, year round did not change measurably for most levels of educational attainment. The one exception was the percentage of young adult high school completers who worked full time, year round, which was higher in 2014 (65 percent) than in 2013 (62 percent).

Figure 2. Median annual earnings of full-time, year-round workers ages 25–34, by educational attainment: 2014

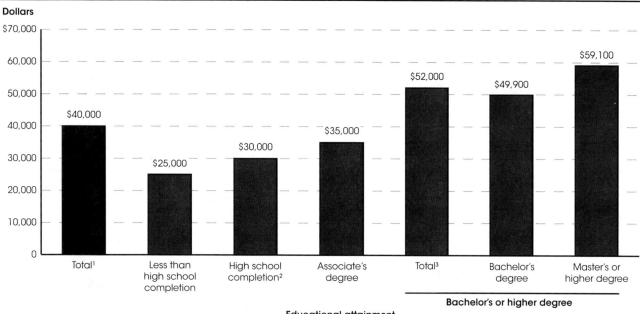

¹ Represents median annual earnings of all full-time, year-round workers ages 25–34.
² Includes equivalency credentials, such as the GED credential.
³ Represents median annual earnings of full-time, year-round workers ages 25–34 with a bachelor's or higher degree.
NOTE: *Full-time, year-round workers* are those who worked 35 or more hours per week for 50 or more weeks per year.
SOURCE: U.S. Department of Commerce, Census Bureau, Current Population Survey (CPS), "Annual Social and Economic Supplement," 2015. See *Digest of Education Statistics 2015*, table 502.30.

For young adults ages 25–34 who worked full time, year round, higher educational attainment was associated with higher median earnings¹; this pattern was consistent from 2000 through 2014. For example, in 2014 the median earnings of young adults with a bachelor's degree ($49,900) were 66 percent higher than the median earnings of young adult high school completers ($30,000). The median earnings of young adult high school completers were 20 percent higher than the median earnings of those without a high school credential ($25,000). In addition, median earnings of young adults with a master's or higher degree were $59,100 in 2014, some 18 percent higher than the median earnings of young adults with a bachelor's degree. This pattern of higher earnings associated with higher levels of educational attainment also held for both male and female young adults as well as for White, Black, Hispanic, and Asian young adults.

Figure 3. Median annual earnings of full-time, year-round workers ages 25–34, by educational attainment: 2000–2014

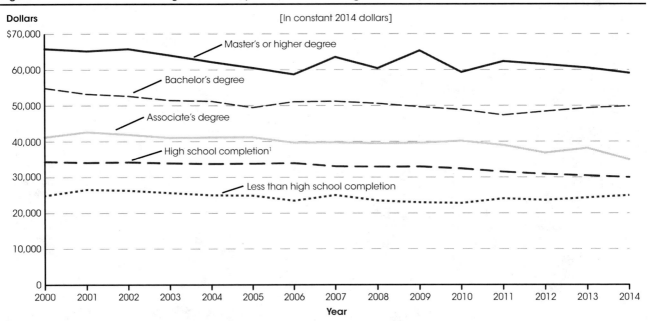

[1] Includes equivalency credentials, such as the GED credential.
NOTE: Earnings are presented in constant 2014 dollars, based on the Consumer Price Index (CPI), to eliminate inflationary factors and to allow for direct comparison across years. *Full-time, year-round workers* are those who worked 35 or more hours per week for 50 or more weeks per year.
SOURCE: U.S. Department of Commerce, Census Bureau, Current Population Survey (CPS), "Annual Social and Economic Supplement," 2001–2015; and previously unpublished tabulations. See *Digest of Education Statistics 2015*, table 502.30.

Median earnings (in constant 2014 dollars)[2] of young adults declined from 2000 to 2014 at most educational attainment levels, except for those who did not complete high school, for whom there was no measurable change in median earnings. During this period, the median earnings of young adult high school completers declined from $34,400 to $30,000 (a 13 percent decrease), and the median earnings of young adults with an associate's degree declined from $41,200 to $35,000 (a 15 percent decrease). In addition, the median earnings of young adults with a bachelor's degree declined from $54,900 to $49,900 (a 9 percent decrease), and the median earnings of young adults with a master's or higher degree declined from $65,900 to $59,100 (a 10 percent decrease). With the exception of high school completers, median annual earnings for young adults did not change measurably between 2013 and 2014; earnings declined for high school completers during this period.

Gaps in median earnings between young adults with varying levels of educational attainment exhibited different patterns between 2000 and 2014. The difference in median earnings between adult high school completers and those without a high school credential was smaller in 2014 than in 2000. In 2000, median earnings of young adult high school completers were $9,500 higher than median earnings of those without a high school credential; in 2014, this difference in median earnings was $5,000. Differences in median earnings between those with a bachelor's degree and high school completers and between those with a bachelor's degree and those with a master's or higher degree did not change measurably during the same period.

Figure 4.   Median annual earnings of full-time, year-round workers ages 25–34, by educational attainment and sex: 2014

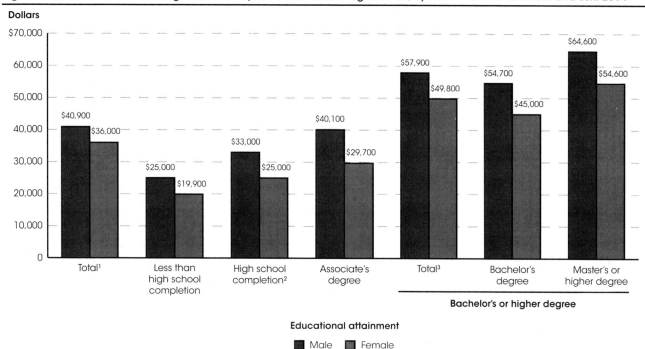

Educational attainment
■ Male   ■ Female

[1] Represents median annual earnings of all full-time, year-round workers ages 25–34.
[2] Includes equivalency credentials, such as the GED credential.
[3] Represents median annual earnings of full-time, year-round workers ages 25–34 with a bachelor's or higher degree.
NOTE: *Full-time, year-round workers* are those who worked 35 or more hours per week for 50 or more weeks per year.
SOURCE: U.S. Department of Commerce, Census Bureau, Current Population Survey (CPS), "Annual Social and Economic Supplement," 2015. See *Digest of Education Statistics 2015*, table 502.30.

In 2014, median earnings of young adult males were higher than median earnings of young adult females at every level of educational attainment. For example, median earnings of young adult males with an associate's degree were $40,100 in 2014, while median earnings of their female counterparts were $29,700. The median earning of young adult males with a high school credential were $33,000, compared with $25,000 for their female counterparts. In the same year, median earnings for White young adults exceeded the corresponding median earnings for Black and Hispanic young adults at all attainment levels except the master's or higher degree level, where there was no measurable difference in median earnings between White and Hispanic young adults. For instance, median earnings in 2014 for young adults with a bachelor's degree were $49,900 for White young adults, $44,800 for Black young adults, and $44,200 for Hispanic young adults. Among those with a bachelor's degree and those with a master's or higher degree, Asian young adults had higher median earnings than their Black, Hispanic, and White peers. For example, median earnings in 2014 for young adults with at least a master's degree were $73,100 for Asian young adults, $57,900 for White young adults, $57,100 for Hispanic young adults, and $49,200 for Black young adults.

Endnotes:
[1] Differences in earnings may also reflect other factors, such as differences in occupation. See the Employment Outcomes of Bachelor's Degree Recipients indicator.

[2] Constant dollars based on the Consumer Price Index, prepared by the Bureau of Labor Statistics, U.S. Department of Labor.

Reference tables: *Digest of Education Statistics 2015*, table 502.30
Related indicators: Employment and Unemployment Rates by Educational Attainment

Glossary: Associate's degree, Bachelor's degree, Constant dollars, Educational attainment (Current Population Survey), Employment status, High school completer, High school diploma, Master's degree, Median earnings, Racial/ethnic group

Employment and Unemployment Rates by Educational Attainment

The employment rate was higher for people with higher levels of educational attainment than for those with lower levels of educational attainment. For example, among 20- to 24-year-olds in 2015, the employment rate was 89 percent for those with a bachelor's or higher degree and 51 percent for those who did not complete high school.

This indicator examines recent trends in two distinct yet related measures of labor market conditions—the employment rate (also known as the employment to population ratio) and the unemployment rate—by age group and educational attainment level. For each age group, the *employment rate* is the number of persons in that age group who are employed as a percentage of the civilian population in that age group. The *unemployment rate* is the percentage of persons in the civilian labor force (i.e., all civilians who are employed or seeking employment) who are not working and who made specific efforts to find employment sometime during the prior 4 weeks. Trends in the unemployment rate reflect net changes in the relative number of people who are looking for work, while the employment rate reflects whether the economy is generating jobs relative to population growth in a specific age group.

Figure 1. Employment to population ratios of 20- to 24-year-olds, by sex and educational attainment: 2015

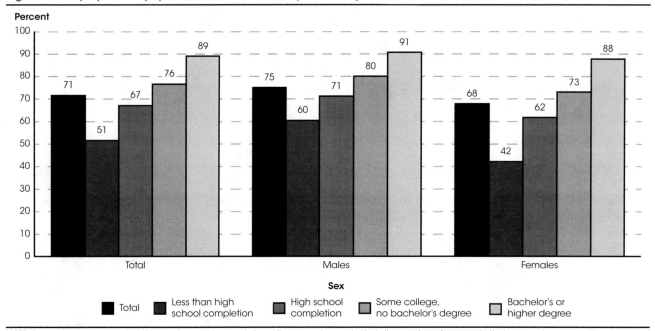

NOTE: For each group presented, the employment to population ratio, or employment rate, is the number of persons in that group who are employed as a percentage of the civilian population in that group. Data exclude persons enrolled in school. "Some college, no bachelor's degree" includes persons with an associate's degree. "High school completion" includes equivalency credentials, such as the GED credential.
SOURCE: U.S. Department of Labor, Bureau of Labor Statistics, Office of Employment and Unemployment Statistics, unpublished annual average data from the Current Population Survey (CPS), 2015. See *Digest of Education Statistics 2015*, tables 501.50, 501.60, and 501.70.

The employment rate was higher for those with higher levels of educational attainment. For example, in 2015, the employment rate for 20- to 24-year-olds (also referred to as "young adults" in this indicator) with a bachelor's degree or higher was higher than the rate for young adults with some college but no bachelor's degree (89 vs. 76 percent). The employment rate for young adults with some college was higher than the rate for those who had completed high school (67 percent), which was, in turn, higher than the employment rate for those who had not finished high school (51 percent). This pattern of a positive relationship between employment rates and educational attainment was also seen for 25- to 64-year-olds (also referred to as "older adults" in this indicator).

Employment rates were generally higher for young adult males than females at each level of educational attainment in 2015. The overall employment rate for young adult males was higher than the rate for young adult females (75 vs. 68 percent). The employment rate was also higher for male than for female young adults who had some college (80 vs. 73 percent). Similarly, the employment rate for young adults who had completed high school was higher for males than for females (71 vs. 62 percent), and the rate for young adults who had not completed high school was higher for males than for females (60 vs. 42 percent). However, there was no measurable difference between young adult males and females who had a bachelor's degree (91 and 88 percent, respectively). For older adults, employment rates were higher for males than for females at each level of educational attainment.

Figure 2. Employment to population ratios of 20- to 24-year-olds, by educational attainment: Selected years, 2000 through 2015

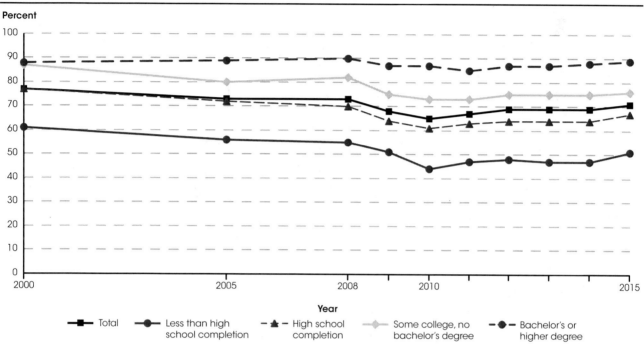

NOTE: For each group presented, the employment to population ratio, or employment rate, is the number of persons in that age group who are employed as a percentage of the civilian population in that age group. Data exclude persons enrolled in school. "Some college, no bachelor's degree" includes persons with an associate's degree. "High school completion" includes equivalency credentials, such as the GED credential.
SOURCE: U.S. Department of Labor, Bureau of Labor Statistics, Office of Employment and Unemployment Statistics, unpublished annual average data from the Current Population Survey (CPS), selected years, 2000 through 2015. See *Digest of Education Statistics 2015*, table 501.50.

During the period from 2008 to 2010, the U.S. economy experienced a recession.[1] For young adults, the employment rate was lower in 2008, when the recession began, than it was in 2000 (73 vs. 77 percent). The employment rate was even lower in 2010 (65 percent), after the end of the recession, than it was in 2008. While the employment rate for young adults was higher in 2015 (71 percent) than in 2010, the 2015 rate was still lower than the rates in 2008 and 2000. Similar patterns in the employment rate were found for young adults with some college and young adults who had completed high school, as well as for older adults. For young adults who had not completed high school, the employment rate was higher in 2015 (51 percent) than it had been in 2010 (44 percent), but was not measurably different than it had been in 2008 (55 percent).

Figure 3. Unemployment rates of 20- to 24-year-olds, by sex and educational attainment: 2015

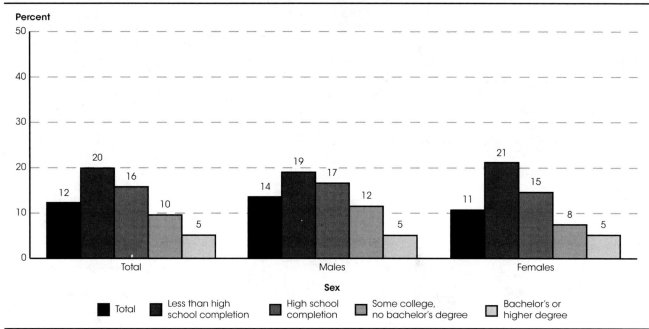

NOTE: The unemployment rate is the percentage of persons in the civilian labor force who are not working and who made specific efforts to find employment sometime during the prior 4 weeks. The civilian labor force consists of all civilians who are employed or seeking employment. Data exclude persons enrolled in school. "Some college, no bachelor's degree" includes persons with an associate's degree. "High school completion" includes equivalency credentials, such as the GED credential.
SOURCE: U.S. Department of Labor, Bureau of Labor Statistics, Office of Employment and Unemployment Statistics, unpublished annual average data from the Current Population Survey (CPS), 2015. See *Digest of Education Statistics 2015*, tables 501.80, 501.85, and 501.90.

Generally, the unemployment rate was lower for those with higher levels of educational attainment. For example, in 2015, the unemployment rate for young adults with at least a bachelor's degree was lower than the rate for young adults with some college (5 vs. 10 percent), and the unemployment rate for young adults with some college was lower than the rate for those who had completed high school (16 percent). This pattern of unemployment rates being lower for those with higher levels of educational attainment was generally also seen for males and females. Specifically, for both males and females, unemployment rates were generally lowest for those who had at least

a bachelor's degree (5 percent in each case), and were lower for those who had some college (12 and 8 percent, respectively) than for those who had not attended college (15 to 21 percent).

In 2015, the overall unemployment rate for 20- to 24-year-olds was higher for males than for females (14 vs. 11 percent); the rate for 20- to 24-year-olds who had some college was also higher for males than for females (12 vs. 8 percent). However, there were no measurable differences between unemployment rates of male and female 20- to 24-year-olds at other levels of educational attainment.

Figure 4. Unemployment rates of 20- to 24-year-olds, by educational attainment: Selected years, 2000 through 2015

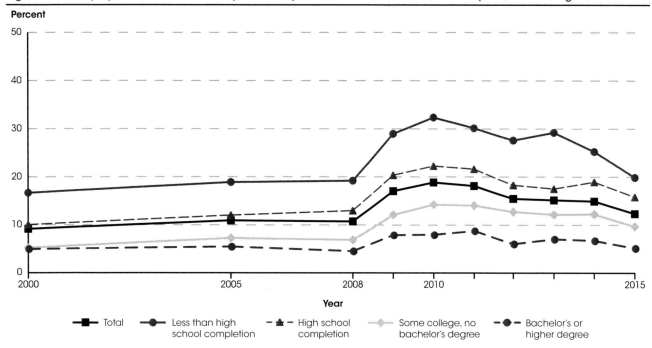

NOTE: The unemployment rate is the percentage of persons in the civilian labor force who are not working and who made specific efforts to find employment sometime during the prior 4 weeks. The civilian labor force consists of all civilians who are employed or seeking employment. Data exclude persons enrolled in school. "Some college, no bachelor's degree" includes persons with an associate's degree. "High school completion" includes equivalency credentials, such as the GED credential.
SOURCE: U.S. Department of Labor, Bureau of Labor Statistics, Office of Employment and Unemployment Statistics, unpublished annual average data from the Current Population Survey (CPS), selected years, 2000 through 2015. See *Digest of Education Statistics 2015*, table 501.80.

For young adults, the unemployment rate at the end of the recession in 2010 (19 percent) was higher than it was both at the beginning of the recession in 2008 and prior to the recession in 2000 (11 and 9 percent, respectively). In 2015, the unemployment rate for young adults (12 percent) was lower than it was in 2010, but higher than it was in both 2008 and 2000. Similar patterns were found for young adults with some college and young adults who had graduated from high school. For each of the four levels of educational attainment, the unemployment rate for young adults was lower in 2015 than it was in 2010. Also, the unemployment rate for young adults who either had some college or had completed high school was higher in 2015 than in 2008. There were no measurable differences between the unemployment rates in 2015 and 2008 for young adults who had not completed high school and for young adults who had earned a bachelor's degree.

Endnotes:
[1] The National Bureau of Economic Research determined that the recession began in December 2007 and continued through June 2009. See http://www.nber.org/cycles.html.

Reference tables: *Digest of Education Statistics 2015*, tables 501.50, 501.60, 501.70, 501.80, 501.85, and 501.90
Related indicators: Annual Earnings of Young Adults, Trends in Employment Rates by Educational Attainment [*The Condition of Education 2013 Spotlight*]

Glossary: Bachelor's degree, College, Educational attainment (Current Population Survey), Employment status, High school completer

Family Characteristics of School-Age Children

In 2014, approximately 20 percent of school-age children were in families living in poverty. The percentage of school-age children living in poverty ranged across the United States from 12 percent in Maryland to 29 percent in Mississippi.

Parents' educational attainment and household poverty status are associated with the quality of children's educational experiences and their academic achievement, whether they are in public school, in private school, or being homeschooled.[1] For example, research suggests that living in poverty during early childhood is related to lower levels of academic performance, beginning in kindergarten and extending through elementary and high school, and lower rates of high school completion.[2,3]

Figure 1. Percentage distribution of 5- to 17-year-olds, by parents' highest level of educational attainment: 2014

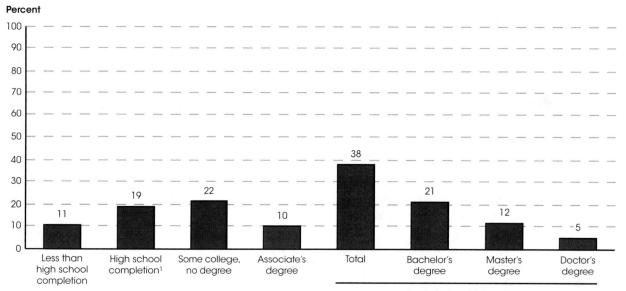

[1] Includes parents who completed high school through equivalency programs, such as a GED program.
NOTE: Parents' highest level of educational attainment is the highest level of education attained by any parent residing in the same household as the child. Parents include adoptive and stepparents but exclude parents not residing in the same household as their child. Detail may not sum to totals because of rounding.
SOURCE: U.S. Department of Commerce, Census Bureau, American Community Survey (ACS), 2014. See *Digest of Education Statistics 2015*, table 104.70.

In 2014, about 38 percent of school-age children (those ages 5 to 17) had parents whose highest level of educational attainment[4] was a bachelor's or higher degree: 21 percent had parents who had completed a bachelor's degree, 12 percent had parents who had completed a master's degree, and 5 percent had parents who had completed a doctor's degree. In addition, 11 percent of school-age children had parents who had not completed high school, 19 percent had parents who had only completed high school,[5] 22 percent had parents who attended some college but did not receive a degree, and 10 percent had parents who had completed an associate's degree.

Figure 2.   Percentage of 5- to 17-year-olds, by child's race/ethnicity and parents' highest level of educational attainment: 2014

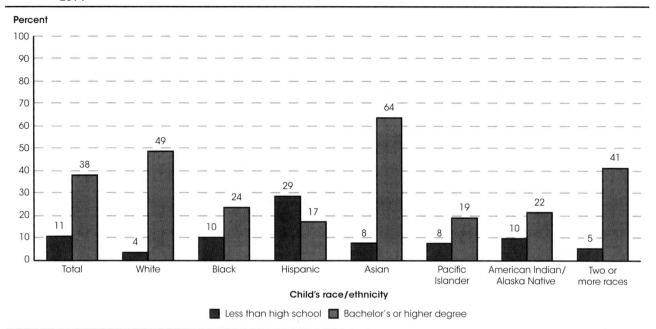

NOTE: Parents' highest level of educational attainment is the highest level of education attained by any parent residing in the same household as the child. Parents include adoptive and stepparents but exclude parents not residing in the same household as their child. Race categories exclude persons of Hispanic ethnicity.
SOURCE: U.S. Department of Commerce, Census Bureau, American Community Survey (ACS), 2014. See *Digest of Education Statistics 2015*, table 104.70.

In 2014, the percentage of school-age children (those ages 5 to 17) whose parents had completed a bachelor's or higher degree was higher than the percentage whose parents had not completed high school (38 vs. 11 percent). This pattern held for White, Black, Asian, and American Indian/Alaska Native children, as well as children of Two or more races, although the margins were wider for some groups than others. For example, among Asian school-age children, 64 percent had parents who had completed a bachelor's or higher degree versus 8 percent whose parents had not completed high school. Among American Indian/Alaska Native children, 22 percent had parents who had completed a bachelor's or higher degree, compared with 10 percent whose parents who had not completed high school. On the other hand, for Hispanic school-age children, the percentage whose parents had not

completed high school was higher than the percentage whose parents had completed a bachelor's or higher degree (29 vs. 17 percent). Despite the apparent difference, the percentage of Pacific Islander children whose parents had not completed high school was not measurably different from the percentage whose parents had completed a bachelor's or higher degree.

In 2014, approximately 10.7 million school-age children (those ages 5 to 17)[6] were in families living in poverty.[7] The percentage of school-age children living in poverty in 2014 (20 percent) was higher than it was over a decade earlier, in 2000 (15 percent). However, the poverty rate for school-age children in 2014 was lower than in 2013 (21 percent).

Figure 3.   Percentage of 5- to 17-year-olds in families living in poverty, by state: 2014

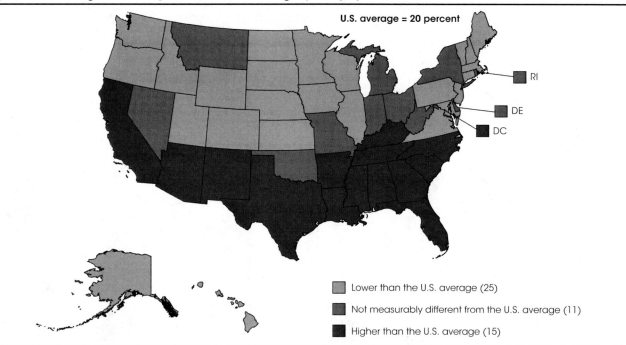

U.S. average = 20 percent

RI

DE

DC

Lower than the U.S. average (25)

Not measurably different from the U.S. average (11)

Higher than the U.S. average (15)

NOTE: The measure of child poverty includes all children who are related to the householder by birth, marriage, or adoption (except a child who is the spouse of the householder). The householder is the person (or one of the people) who owns or rents (maintains) the housing unit.
SOURCE: U.S. Department of Commerce, Census Bureau, American Community Survey (ACS), 2014. See *Digest of Education Statistics 2015*, table 102.40.

While the national average poverty rate for school-age children (those ages 5 to 17) was 20 percent in 2014, the poverty rates among the states ranged from 12 percent in Maryland to 29 percent in Mississippi. Twenty-five states had poverty rates for school-age children that were lower than the national average, 14 states and the District of Columbia had rates that were higher than the national average, and 11 states had rates that were not measurably different from the national average. Of the 15 jurisdictions (14 states and the District of Columbia) that had poverty rates higher than the national average, the majority (12) were located in the South. The poverty rate for school-age children was higher in 2014 than it was in 2000 in 41 states, while the rate did not change measurably during this period in the remaining 9 states and the District of Columbia.[6]

Figure 4. Percentage of children under age 18 in families living in poverty, by race/ethnicity: 2009 and 2014

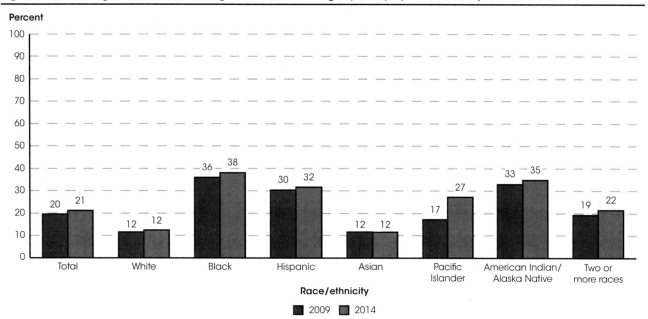

NOTE: The measure of child poverty includes all children who are related to the householder by birth, marriage, or adoption (except a child who is the spouse of the householder). The householder is the person (or one of the people) who owns or rents (maintains) the housing unit. Race categories exclude persons of Hispanic ethnicity. Although rounded numbers are displayed, the figures are based on unrounded estimates.
SOURCE: U.S. Department of Commerce, Census Bureau, American Community Survey (ACS), 2009 and 2014. See *Digest of Education Statistics 2015*, table 102.60.

In 2014, approximately 15.3 million, or 21 percent, of all children under the age of 18 were in families living in poverty; this population includes the 10.7 million school-age 5- to 17-year-olds previously discussed and 4.6 million children under age 5 living in poverty. The percentage of children under age 18 living in poverty varied across racial/ethnic groups. In 2014, the percentage living in poverty was highest for Black children (38 percent), followed by American Indian/Alaska Native children (35 percent), Hispanic children (32 percent), Pacific Islander children (27 percent), and children of Two or more races (22 percent). The poverty rates were lower for White and Asian children (12 percent

each) than for children from other racial/ethnic groups. The overall percentage of children under age 18 living in poverty in 2014 (21 percent) was higher than in 2009 (20 percent). This pattern was also observed for White, Black, Hispanic, and Pacific Islander children and for children of Two or more races (although the difference for White children was less than one percentage point). For example, 38 percent of Black children lived in poverty in 2014, compared with 36 percent in 2009. However, the percentages of Asian children and American Indian/Alaska Native children living in poverty were not measurably different in 2014 than in 2009.

Figure 5. Percentage of children under age 18 in families living in poverty, by selected Hispanic subgroups: 2014

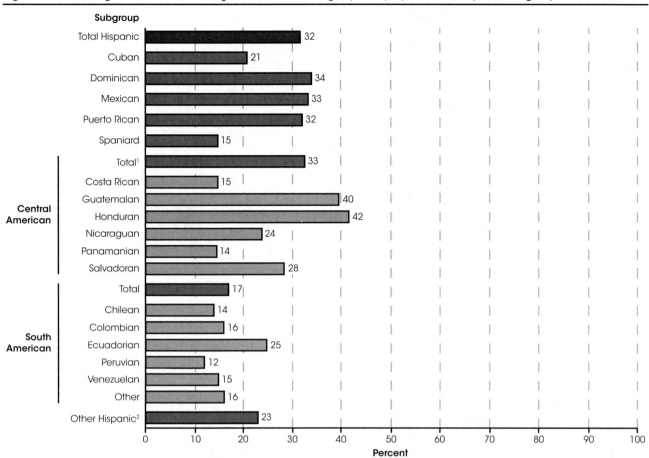

[1] Includes other Central American subgroups not shown separately.
[2] Includes children from Hispanic countries other than the ones shown.
NOTE: The measure of child poverty includes all children who are related to the householder by birth, marriage, or adoption (except a child who is the spouse of the householder). The householder is the person (or one of the people) who owns or rents (maintains) the housing unit.
SOURCE: U.S. Department of Commerce, Census Bureau, American Community Survey (ACS), 2014. See *Digest of Education Statistics 2015*, table 102.60.

In 2014, the overall rate of Hispanic children under age 18 living in poverty (32 percent) was higher than the national average of 21 percent. However, there was a range of rates among Hispanic subgroups, with some rates being lower than the national average. For example, the poverty rates for Peruvian children (12 percent) as well as Chilean and Panamanian children (14 percent each) were lower than the national average, while the rates for Guatemalan children (40 percent) and Honduran children (42 percent) were higher than the national average.

Figure 6.   Percentage of children under age 18 in families living in poverty, by selected Asian subgroups: 2014

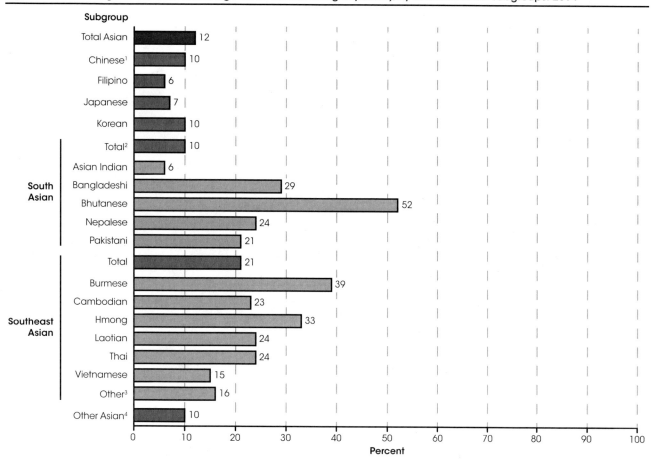

[1] Includes Taiwanese.
[2] In addition to the South Asian subgroups shown, also includes Sri Lankan.
[3] Other Southeast Asian consists of Indonesian and Malaysian.
[4] "Other Asian" refers to children from Asian countries other than the ones shown.
NOTE: The measure of child poverty includes all children who are related to the householder by birth, marriage, or adoption (except a child who is the spouse of the householder). The householder is the person (or one of the people) who owns or rents (maintains) the housing unit.
SOURCE: U.S. Department of Commerce, Census Bureau, American Community Survey (ACS), 2014. See *Digest of Education Statistics 2015*, table 102.60.

The overall rate of Asian children under age 18 living in poverty (12 percent) was lower than the national average, but there was a range of rates among Asian subgroups, with some rates being higher than the national average. For example, the poverty rates for Bhutanese children (52 percent) and Burmese children (39 percent) were higher than the national average, while the rates for Filipino and Asian Indian children (6 percent each) were lower than the national average.

Figure 7. Percentage of children under age 18 in families living in poverty, by race/ethnicity and family structure: 2014

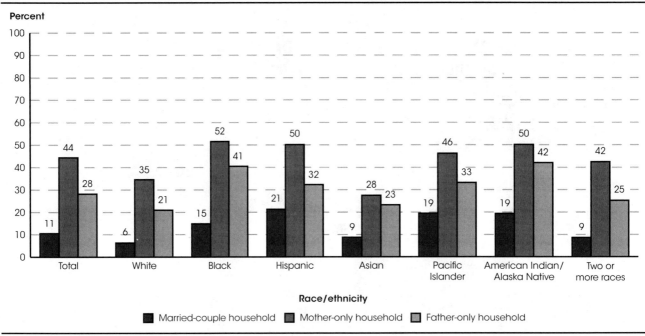

NOTE: The measure of child poverty includes all children who are related to the householder by birth, marriage, or adoption (except a child who is the spouse of the householder). The householder is the person (or one of the people) who owns or rents (maintains) the housing unit. To determine family structure, children are classified by their parents' marital status or, if no parents are present in the household, by the marital status of the householder who is related to the children. Mother-only households are those that have only a female householder, and father-only households are those that have only a male householder. Race categories exclude persons of Hispanic ethnicity.
SOURCE: U.S. Department of Commerce, Census Bureau, American Community Survey (ACS), 2014. See *Digest of Education Statistics 2015*, table 102.60.

For children under age 18 in 2014, those living in a mother-only household had the highest rate of poverty (44 percent) and those living in a father-only household had the next highest rate (28 percent). Children living in a married-couple household had the lowest rate of poverty, at 11 percent. This pattern of children living in married-couple households having the lowest rate of poverty was observed across most racial/ethnic groups—Pacific Islander children are an exception to this pattern. The apparent difference between the estimates for children in married-couple households and those in father-only households was not statistically significant. In 2014, for example, among Black children under age 18 the poverty rates were 52 percent for children living in a mother-only household, 41 percent for those living in a father-only household, and 15 percent for those living in a married-couple household.

The poverty rates for Black, Hispanic, and American Indian/Alaska Native children for each family type were higher than the corresponding national poverty rates in 2014. In contrast, the poverty rates for White and Asian children were lower than the national poverty rates. Among children living in mother-only households in 2014, the poverty rates for Black (52 percent), Hispanic (50 percent), and American Indian/Alaska Native children (50 percent) were higher than the national poverty rate (44 percent), while the rates for White (35 percent) and Asian children (28 percent) were lower than the national poverty rate. Among children living in married-couple households in 2014, the poverty rates for Black (15 percent), Hispanic (21 percent), Pacific Islander (19 percent), and American Indian/Alaska Native (19 percent) children were higher than the national poverty rate (11 percent), while the rates for White (6 percent) and Asian (9 percent) children as well as children of Two or more races (9 percent) were lower than the national rate.

Endnotes:

[1] Aud, S., Fox, M., and KewalRamani, A. (2010). *Status and Trends in the Education of Racial and Ethnic Groups 2010* (NCES 2010-015). U.S. Department of Education. Washington, DC: National Center for Education Statistics.

[2] Ross, T., Kena, G., Rathbun, A., KewalRamani, A., Zhang, J., Kristapovich, P., and Manning, E. (2012). *Higher Education: Gaps in Access and Persistence Study* (NCES 2012-046). U.S. Department of Education. Washington, DC: National Center for Education Statistics.

[3] Mulligan, G.M., Hastedt, S., and McCarroll, J.C. (2012). *First-Time Kindergartners in 2010–11: First Findings From the Kindergarten Rounds of the Early Childhood Longitudinal Study, Kindergarten Class of 2010–11 (ECLS-K:2011)* (NCES 2012-049). U.S. Department of Education. Washington, DC: National Center for Education Statistics.

[4] In this indicator, parents' highest level of educational attainment is the highest level of education attained by any parent residing in the same household as the child.

[5] Includes parents who completed high school through equivalency programs, such as a GED program.

[6] See *Digest of Education 2015*, table 102.40.

[7] In this indicator, data on household income and the number of people living in the household are combined with the poverty threshold, published by the Census Bureau, to determine the poverty status of children. A household includes all families in which children are related to the householder by birth or adoption, or through marriage. The householder is the person (or one of the people) who owns or rents (maintains) the housing unit. In 2014, the poverty threshold for a family of four with two related children under 18 years old was $24,008 (http://www.census.gov/hhes/www/poverty/data/threshld/thresh14.xls).

Reference tables: *Digest of Education Statistics 2015*, tables 102.40, 102.60, and 104.70

Related indicators: Concentration of Public School Students Eligible for Free or Reduced-Price Lunch, Disparities in Educational Outcomes Among Male Youth [*The Condition of Education 2015 Spotlight*]

Glossary: Bachelor's degree, College, Doctor's degree, Educational attainment, High school completer, Household, Master's degree, Poverty (official measure), Racial/ethnic group

The indicators in this chapter of *The Condition of Education* describe trends in enrollments across all levels of education. Enrollment is a key indicator of the scope of and access to educational opportunities, and functions as a basic descriptor of American education. Changes in enrollment may impact the demand for educational resources such as qualified teachers, physical facilities, and funding levels, all of which are required to provide high-quality education for our nation's students.

The indicators in this chapter include information on enrollment rates by age group as well as by level of the education system, namely, preprimary, elementary and secondary, undergraduate, graduate and professional, and adult education. Some of the indicators in this chapter provide information about the characteristics of the students who are enrolled in formal education and, in some cases, how enrollment rates of different types of students vary across schools.

This chapter's indicators, as well as additional indicators on participation in education, are available at *The Condition of Education* website: http://nces.ed.gov/programs/coe.

Chapter 2

Participation in Education

Enrollment Trends by Age

In 2014, some 93 percent of 5- to 6-year-olds and 98 percent of 7- to 13-year-olds were enrolled in elementary or secondary school. In that same year, 68 percent of 18- to 19-year-olds and 38 percent of 20- to 24-year-olds were enrolled in a secondary school or postsecondary institution. For all age groups from 3 to 34, total school enrollment rates were not measurably different in 2014 than they were in 2013.

From 1990 to 2014, school enrollment rates increased for those ages 3–4, 18–19, 20–24, and 25–29; however, enrollment rates decreased for those ages 5–6, 7–13, and 14–15, and enrollment rates for those ages 16–17 and 30–34 did not change measurably. In addition, for all age groups from 3 to 34, total school enrollment rates were not measurably different in 2014 than they were in 2013.

Changes in the number of students enrolled in school can stem from fluctuations in population size or shifts in enrollment rates. Enrollment rates may also vary in response to changes in state compulsory attendance requirements, changes in the prevalence of homeschooling, changes in perceptions regarding the cost or value of education (particularly at the preschool and college levels), and changes in the amount of time it takes to complete a degree. The enrollment rates presented in this indicator reflect enrollment in public, parochial, or other private schools, including nursery schools, kindergartens, elementary schools, high schools, colleges, universities, and professional schools.[1]

Figure 1. Percentage of the population ages 3–17 enrolled in school, by age group: October 1990–2014

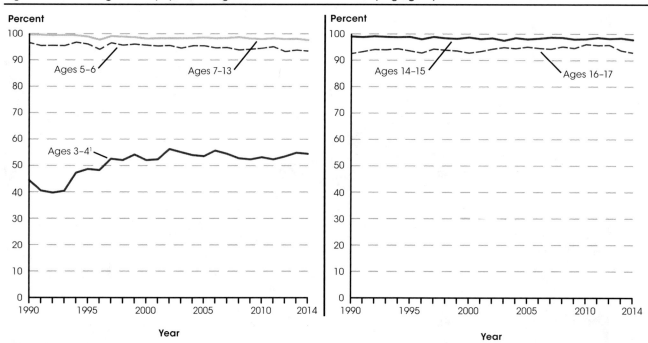

[1] Beginning in 1994, preprimary enrollment data were collected using new procedures. As a result, pre-1994 data may not be comparable to data from 1994 or later.
SOURCE: U.S. Department of Commerce, Census Bureau, Current Population Survey (CPS), October Supplement, 1990–2014. See *Digest of Education Statistics 2015*, table 103.20.

Between 1990 and 2014, the enrollment rate for children ages 3–4, who are typically enrolled in nursery school or preschool, increased from 44 to 54 percent, with most of the growth occurring between 1990 and 2000. Despite an overall decrease from 1990 to 2014, the enrollment rate for children ages 5–6, who are typically enrolled in kindergarten or first grade, fluctuated between 94 and 97 percent in the 1990s, and then declined

from 96 percent in 2000 to 93 percent in 2014. The enrollment rate for 7- to 13-year-olds decreased from nearly 100 percent in 1990 to 98 percent in 2014, while the enrollment rate for 14- to 15-year-olds decreased from 99 percent to 98 percent during the same period. Meanwhile, the enrollment rate for 16- to 17-year-olds in 2014 was not measurably different from the rate in 1990.

Figure 2.   Percentage of the population ages 18–19 enrolled in school, by education level: October 1990–2014

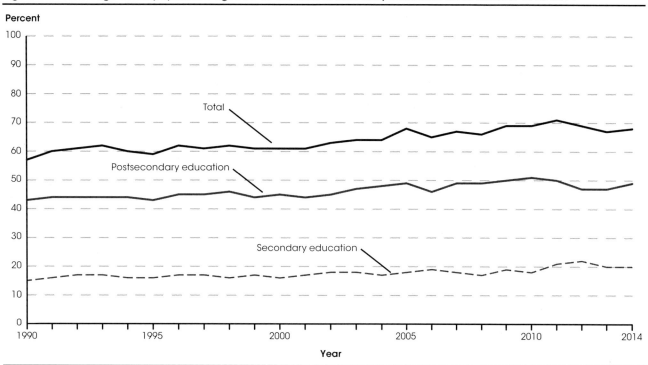

SOURCE: U.S. Department of Commerce, Census Bureau, Current Population Survey (CPS), October Supplement, 1990–2014. See *Digest of Education Statistics 2015*, table 103.20.

Young adults ages 18–19 are typically transitioning into postsecondary education or the workforce. Between 1990 and 2014, the overall enrollment rate (i.e., enrollment at both the secondary level and the postsecondary level) for young adults ages 18–19 increased from 57 to 68 percent. The enrollment rate during this period for these young adults increased from 15 to 20 percent at the secondary level and from 43 to 49 percent at the postsecondary

level. Most of the increase in the overall enrollment rate for this age group took place during the later part of this period. From 2000 to 2014, the overall enrollment rate for those in this age range increased from 61 to 68 percent; the enrollment rate increased from 16 to 20 percent at the secondary level and from 45 to 49 percent at the postsecondary level.

Figure 3. Percentage of the population ages 20–34 enrolled in school, by age group: October 1990–2014

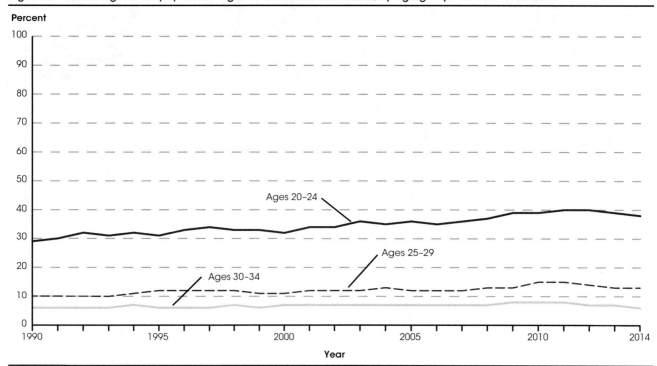

SOURCE: U.S. Department of Commerce, Census Bureau, Current Population Survey (CPS), October Supplement, 1990–2014. See *Digest of Education Statistics 2015*, table 103.20.

Most 20- to 34-year-old students are enrolled in college or graduate school. Between 1990 and 2014, the enrollment rate for 20- to 24-year-olds increased from 29 to 38 percent, while the enrollment rate increased from 10 to 13 percent for 25- to 29-year-olds. During this same period, the enrollment rate for 30- to 34-year-olds did not change measurably. Between 2000 and 2014,

the enrollment rate for 20- to 24-year-olds increased from 32 to 38 percent and the rate for 25- to 29-year-olds increased from 11 to 13 percent. Although the enrollment rate for 30- to 34-year-olds in 2014 (6 percent) was not measurably different from the rate in 2000, the enrollment rate for this age group fluctuated over this period.

Endnotes:
[1] Schooling other than in regular, graded schools is counted only if the credits obtained are regarded as transferable to a school in the regular school system.

Changes in enrollment rates over time may also reflect changes in participation in regular, graded schools.

Reference tables: *Digest of Education Statistics 2015*, table 103.20
Related indicators: Preschool Enrollment and Kindergarten Enrollment, Public School Enrollment, Charter School Enrollment, Private School Enrollment, Undergraduate Enrollment, Postbaccalaureate Enrollment

Glossary: College, Elementary school, Enrollment, Postsecondary education, Secondary school

This page intentionally left blank.

Preschool and Kindergarten Enrollment

In 2014, the overall percentage of 3- to 5-year-olds enrolled in preschool programs was higher for children whose parents had a graduate or professional degree (49 percent), as compared to those whose parents had a bachelor's degree (43 percent), an associate's degree (38 percent), some college (35 percent), a high school credential (32 percent), and less than a high school credential (28 percent).

Preprimary programs are groups or classes that are organized to provide educational experiences for children and include kindergarten and preschool programs.[1] Child care programs that are not primarily designed to provide educational experiences, such as daycare programs, are not included in preprimary programs. From 1990 to 2014, the percentage of 3- to 5-year-olds enrolled in preprimary programs increased from 59 to 65 percent, with all of the growth occurring during the earlier part of the period, between 1990 and 2000.

Figure 1.   Percentage of 3-, 4-, and 5-year-old children enrolled in preprimary programs: 1990 through 2014

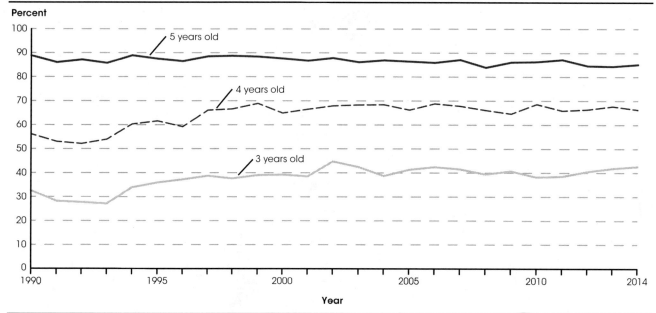

NOTE: "Preprimary programs" are groups or classes that are organized to provide educational experiences for children and include kindergarten, preschool, and nursery school programs. Enrollment data for 5-year-olds include only those students in preprimary programs and do not include those enrolled in primary programs. Beginning in 1994, new procedures were used in the Current Population Survey to collect preprimary enrollment data. As a result, pre-1994 data may not be comparable to data from 1994 or later. Data are based on sample surveys of the civilian noninstitutionalized population.
SOURCE: U.S. Department of Commerce, Census Bureau, Current Population Survey (CPS), October 1990 through 2014. See *Digest of Education Statistics 2015*, table 202.10.

The percentages of 3-year-olds and 4-year-olds enrolled in preprimary programs in 2014 (43 and 66 percent, respectively) were higher than the percentages enrolled in 1990 (33 and 56 percent, respectively), but were not measurably different from the percentages enrolled in 2000 and 2013. In contrast, the percentage of 5-year-olds enrolled in preprimary programs declined from 89 percent in 1990 to 85 percent in 2014. The percentage of 5-year-olds enrolled in preprimary programs in 2014 was not measurably different from the percentage enrolled in 2013.

Figure 2. Percentage of 3- to 5-year-old children in preprimary programs attending full-day programs, by program type: 1990 through 2014

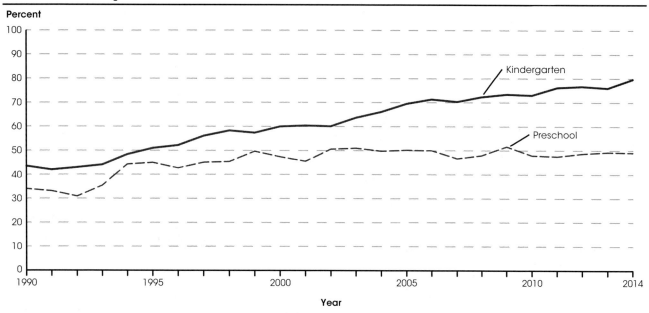

NOTE: "Preprimary programs" are groups or classes that are organized to provide educational experiences for children and include kindergarten, preschool, and nursery school programs. Enrollment data for 5-year-olds include only those students in preprimary programs and do not include those enrolled in primary programs. Beginning in 1994, new procedures were used in the Current Population Survey to collect preprimary enrollment data. As a result, pre-1994 data may not be comparable to data from 1994 or later. Data are based on sample surveys of the civilian noninstitutionalized population.
SOURCE: U.S. Department of Commerce, Census Bureau, Current Population Survey (CPS), October 1990 through 2014. See *Digest of Education Statistics 2015*, table 202.10.

The percentage of 3- to 5-year-olds in preschool programs who attended for the full day increased from 34 percent in 1990 to 49 percent in 2014, with all of the growth occurring during the earlier part of the period, between 1990 and 2000. The percentage of 3- to 5-year-old children in kindergarten programs who attended for the full day nearly doubled between 1990 and 2014, increasing from 44 percent to 80 percent. The percentage in 2014 was also higher than the percentage in 2013 (76 percent).

Figure 3. Percentage of 3- to 5-year-old children enrolled in preschool programs, by child age and attendance status: October 2014

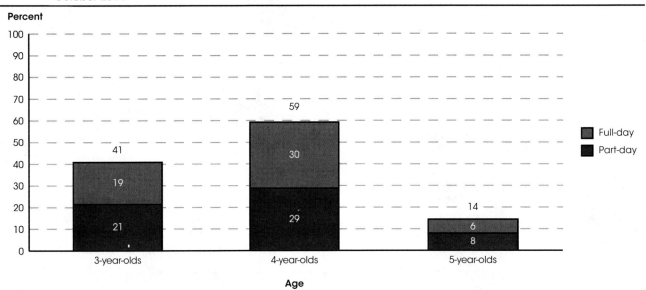

NOTE: Enrollment data include only those children in preschool programs and do not include those enrolled in kindergarten or primary programs. Data are based on sample surveys of the civilian noninstitutionalized population. Detail may not sum to totals because of rounding.
SOURCE: U.S. Department of Commerce, Census Bureau, Current Population Survey (CPS), October 2014. See *Digest of Education Statistics 2015*, table 202.20.

In 2014, most 3- to 4-year-old children who were enrolled in preprimary programs attended preschool programs, while most 5-year-old children who were enrolled in preprimary programs attended kindergarten. A higher percentage of 4-year-olds (59 percent) than of 3-year-olds (41 percent) attended preschool, and both percentages were higher than the percentage of 5-year-olds who attended preschool (14 percent)—a pattern which emerged across both part-day and full-day attendance status.

Figure 4.   Percentage of 3- to 5-year-old children enrolled in preschool programs, by race/ethnicity and attendance status: October 2014

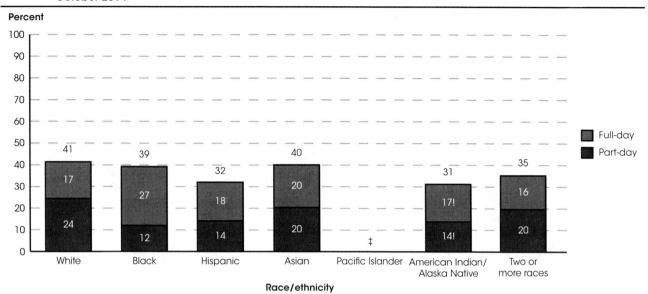

! Interpret data with caution. The coefficient of variation (CV) for this estimate is between 30 and 50 percent.
‡ Reporting standards not met. Either there are too few cases for a reliable estimate or the coefficient of variation (CV) is 50 percent or greater.
NOTE: Race categories exclude persons of Hispanic ethnicity. Enrollment data include only those children in preschool programs and do not include those enrolled in kindergarten or primary programs. Data are based on sample surveys of the civilian noninstitutionalized population. Detail may not sum to totals because of rounding.
SOURCE: U.S. Department of Commerce, Census Bureau, Current Population Survey (CPS), October 2014. See *Digest of Education Statistics 2015,* table 202.20.

In 2014, a lower percentage of Hispanic 3- to 5-year-olds (32 percent) were enrolled in preschool programs than of White (41 percent) and Black (39 percent) 3- to 5-year-olds. In terms of attendance status, a higher percentage of White (24 percent) and Asian (20 percent) children attended preschool part-day than of Hispanic (14 percent) and Black (12 percent) children in 2014.

Additionally, a higher percentage of children of Two or more races attended preschool part-day (20 percent) than of Black children. A higher percentage of Black children attended preschool for the full day (27 percent) than the percentages of children who were Asian (20 percent), Hispanic (18 percent), White (17 percent), and of Two or more races (16 percent).

Figure 5.   Percentage of 3- to 5-year-old children enrolled in preschool programs, by parents' highest level of education and attendance status: October 2014

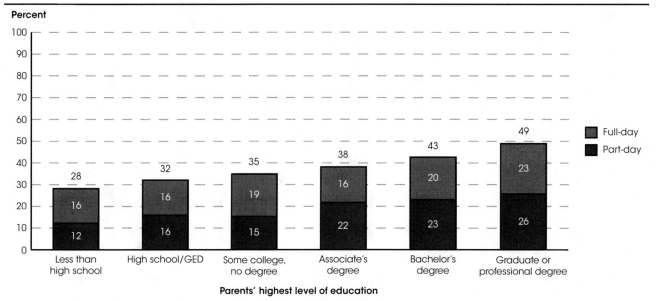

NOTE: Enrollment data include only those children in preschool programs and do not include those enrolled in kindergarten or primary programs. *Parents' highest level of education* is defined as the highest level of education attained by the most educated parent who lives in the household with the child. Data are based on sample surveys of the civilian noninstitutionalized population. Detail may not sum to totals because of rounding.
SOURCE: U.S. Department of Commerce, Census Bureau, Current Population Survey (CPS), October 2014. See *Digest of Education Statistics 2015*, table 202.20.

Enrollment in preschool programs varied by parents' highest level of education, defined as the highest level of education attained by the most educated parent in the child's household. In 2014, the overall percentage of 3- to 5-year-olds enrolled in preschool programs was higher for those children whose parents had a graduate or professional degree (49 percent), as compared to those whose parents had a bachelor's degree (43 percent), an associate's degree (38 percent), some college (35 percent), a high school credential (32 percent), and less than a high school credential (28 percent). The overall preschool enrollment percentage was also higher for those children whose parents had a bachelor's degree than for those whose parents had some college, a high school credential, and less than a high school credential.

The percentage of 3- to 5-year-olds enrolled in preschool programs who attended full-day or part-day programs

also varied by parents' highest level of education. In 2014, enrollment in part-day preschool programs was higher for those children whose parents had a graduate or professional degree (26 percent), a bachelor's degree (23 percent), and an associate's degree (22 percent), as compared to the part-day preschool enrollment rates for children whose parents' highest level of education was some college (15 percent), a high school credential (16 percent), and less than a high school credential (12 percent). For full-day preschool enrollment, the percentage was higher for those children whose parents had a graduate or professional degree (23 percent) than for those children whose parents had an associate's degree (16 percent), a high school credential (16 percent), and less than a high school credential (16 percent).

Figure 6.   Percentage of 3- to 4-year-old children enrolled in school, by OECD country: 2013

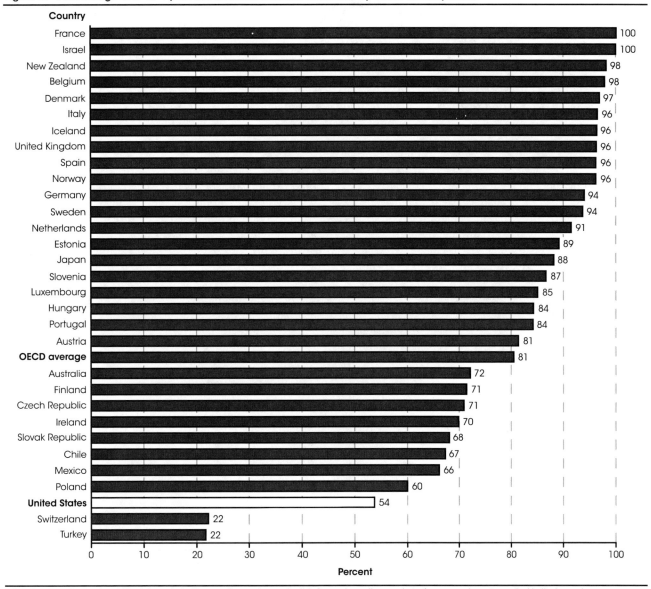

NOTE: Enrollment rates should be interpreted with care. For each country, this figure shows the number of persons who are enrolled in that country as a percentage of that country's total population in the 3- to 4-year-old age group. However, some of a country's population may be enrolled in a different country, and some persons enrolled in the country may be residents of a different country. Enrollment rates may be underestimated for countries such as Luxembourg that are net exporters of students and may be overestimated for countries that are net importers. "OECD average" refers to the mean of the data values for all reporting Organization for Economic Cooperation and Development (OECD) countries, to which each country reporting data contributes equally. SOURCE: Organization for Economic Cooperation and Development (OECD), *Education at a Glance 2015*. See *Digest of Education Statistics 2015*, table 601.35.

In 2013, some 54 percent of 3- to 4-year-olds in the United States were enrolled in school, compared to the average of 81 percent enrollment for the Organization for Economic Cooperation and Development (OECD) countries. Among the 31 OECD countries reporting data that year, the percentage of 3- to 4-year-olds enrolled in school ranged from 22 percent in Turkey and Switzerland to 100 percent in Israel and France.

Endnotes:
[1] Preschool programs are also known as nursery school programs.

Reference tables: *Digest of Education Statistics 2015,* tables 202.10, 202.20, and 601.35

Related indicators: Public School Enrollment; Private School Enrollment; Kindergarten Entry Status: On-Time, Delayed-Entry, Repeating Kindergartners [*The Condition of Education 2013 Spotlight*]

Glossary: Associate's degree, Bachelor's degree, Educational attainment (Current Population Survey), Enrollment, High school completer, Organization for Economic Cooperation and Development (OECD), Preschool, Racial/ethnic group

Public School Enrollment

Between school year 2013–14 and 2025–26, total public school enrollment in preK through grade 12 is projected to increase by 3 percent (from 50.0 million to 51.4 million students), with changes across states ranging from an increase of 39 percent in the District of Columbia to a decrease of 15 percent in New Hampshire.

Changes in public school enrollment are largely reflective of demographic changes in the population. This indicator discusses overall changes in public school enrollment (including both traditional public school and public charter school), as well as changes within grade levels and by state. In school year 2013–14, some

50.0 million students were enrolled in public elementary and secondary schools. Of these students, 70 percent were enrolled in prekindergarten (preK) through grade 8, and the remaining 30 percent were enrolled in grades 9 through 12.

Figure 1. Actual and projected public school enrollment in prekindergarten (preK) through grade 12, by grade level: Selected school years, 2003–04 through 2025–26

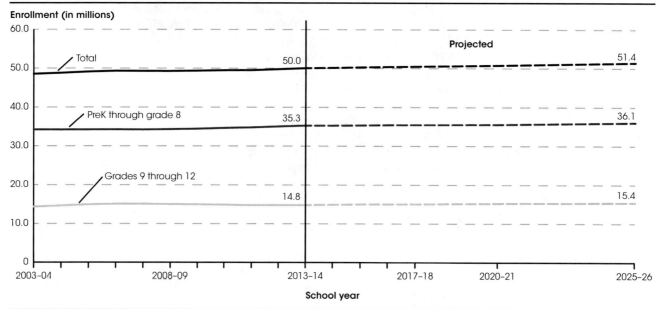

SOURCE: U.S. Department of Education, National Center for Education Statistics, Common Core of Data (CCD), "State Nonfiscal Survey of Public Elementary/Secondary Education," 2003–04 through 2013–14; and State Public Elementary and Secondary Enrollment Projection Model, 1980 through 2025. See *Digest of Education Statistics 2015*, tables 203.20, 203.25, and 203.30.

Total public school enrollment increased steadily throughout the 1990s and 2000s. Between 2003–04 and 2013–14, total public school enrollment increased by 3 percent, reaching 50.0 million students. From 2013–14 to 2025–26 (the last year for which projected data are available), total public school enrollment is projected to increase by 3 percent to 51.4 million students.

Reflecting the increase in total public school enrollment, enrollment in preK through grade 8 also rose throughout the 1990s and 2000s. Between 2003–04 and 2013–14, enrollment in preK through grade 8 increased by

3 percent, reaching 35.3 million students. Public school enrollment in preK through grade 8 is projected to increase by 2 percent to 36.1 million students in 2025–26. Public school enrollment in grades 9 through 12 increased in the 1990s and the early 2000s. In more recent years, enrollment in grades 9 through 12 increased between 2003–04 and 2007–08 to 15.1 million students, and then decreased by 2 percent to 14.8 million in 2013–14. Between 2013–14 and 2025–26, enrollment in grades 9 through 12 is projected to increase by 4 percent to 15.4 million students.

Total public school enrollment in preK through grade 12 increased in 30 states and the District of Columbia from 2003–04 to 2013–14, with increases of 15 percent or more occurring in five states (Utah, Texas, Idaho, Nevada, and Colorado). During this period, total enrollment declined in the other 20 states, with decreases of 10 percent or more occurring in four states (Michigan, Rhode Island, Vermont, and New Hampshire).

Figure 2. Projected percentage change in public school enrollment in prekindergarten through grade 12, by state: Between school years 2013–14 and 2025–26

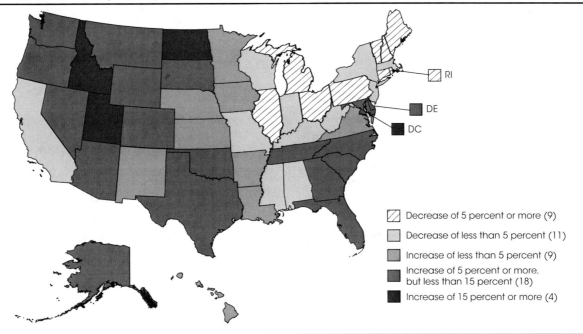

SOURCE: U.S. Department of Education, National Center for Education Statistics, Common Core of Data (CCD), "State Nonfiscal Survey of Public Elementary/Secondary Education," 2013–14; and State Public Elementary and Secondary Enrollment Projection Model, 1980 through 2025. See *Digest of Education Statistics 2015*, table 203.20.

Changes in total enrollment are also projected to vary across the nation from 2013–14 to 2025–26. The District of Columbia is projected to see the largest percentage increase (39 percent) in total enrollment, while the state with the largest projected percentage increase is North Dakota (30 percent). The states that are projected to have the largest percentage decreases are New Hampshire (15 percent) and Connecticut (14 percent).

Between 2013–14 and 2025–26, changes in public school enrollment are also projected to differ by state in preK through grade 8 as well as in grades 9 through 12. Reflecting the expected national enrollment increase during this period, 30 states and the District of Columbia

are expected to have enrollment increases in preK through grade 8, and 32 states and the District of Columbia are expected to have enrollment increases in grades 9 through 12. In preK through grade 8, enrollment is projected to increase by 15 percent or more in the District of Columbia, North Dakota, and Utah, but it is projected to decrease by 10 percent or more in Connecticut, New Hampshire, Maine, and Vermont. Enrollment in grades 9 through 12 is expected to increase by 15 percent or more in the District of Columbia and six states (North Dakota, Idaho, Utah, Texas, Wyoming, and Nevada), but it is projected to decrease by 10 percent or more in five states (New Hampshire, Connecticut, Maine, Michigan, and Vermont).

Reference tables: *Digest of Education Statistics 2015,* tables 203.20, 203.25, and 203.30; tables ESE 90 through ESE 03 at http://nces.ed.gov/surveys/AnnualReports/historicaltables.asp

Related indicators: Enrollment Trends by Age, Charter School Enrollment, Private School Enrollment, Characteristics of Traditional Public and Public Charter Schools, Teachers and Pupil/Teacher Ratios

Glossary: Elementary school, Enrollment, Prekindergarten, Public school or institution, Secondary school

Charter School Enrollment

Between school years 2003-04 and 2013-14, overall public charter school enrollment increased from 0.8 million to 2.5 million. During this period, the percentage of public school students who attended charter schools increased from 1.6 to 5.1 percent.

A *public charter school* is a publicly funded school that is typically governed by a group or organization under a legislative contract (or charter) with the state or jurisdiction. The charter exempts the school from certain state or local rules and regulations. In return for flexibility and autonomy, the charter school must meet the accountability standards outlined in its charter. A school's charter is reviewed periodically (typically every 3 to 5 years) by the group or jurisdiction that granted it and can be revoked if guidelines on curriculum and management are not followed or if the accountability standards are not met.[1]

The first law allowing the establishment of charter schools was passed in Minnesota in 1991.[2] As of school year 2013–14, charter school legislation had been passed in 42 states and the District of Columbia.[3] The states in which charter school legislation had not been passed by that year were Alabama, Kentucky, Montana, Nebraska, North Dakota, South Dakota, Vermont, and West Virginia. Despite legislative approval for charter schools in Mississippi and Washington, none were operating in these states in 2013–14.

Figure 1. Percentage distribution of public charter schools, by enrollment size: School years 2003-04 and 2013-14

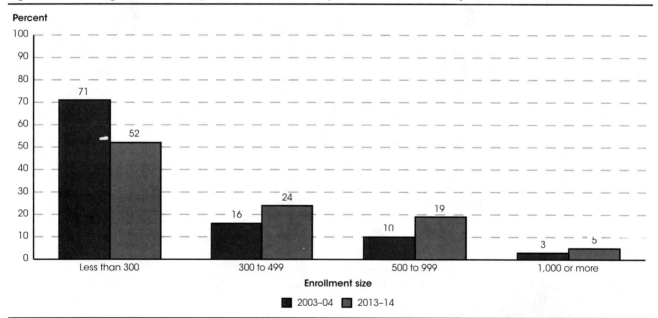

SOURCE: U.S. Department of Education, National Center for Education Statistics, Common Core of Data (CCD), "Public Elementary/Secondary School Universe Survey," 2003-04 and 2013-14. See *Digest of Education Statistics 2015*, table 216.30.

Between school years 2003–04 and 2013–14, the percentage of all public schools that were public charter schools increased from 3.1 to 6.6 percent, and the total number of public charter schools increased from 3,000 to 6,500. In addition to increasing in number, charter schools have generally increased in enrollment size over the last decade. From 2003–04 to 2013–14, the percentages of charter schools with 300–499, 500–999, and 1,000 or more students each increased, while the percentage of charter schools with fewer than 300 students decreased. Similar patterns were observed from 2012–13 to 2013–14.

Figure 2.   Charter school enrollment, by school level: Selected school years, 2003-04 through 2013-14

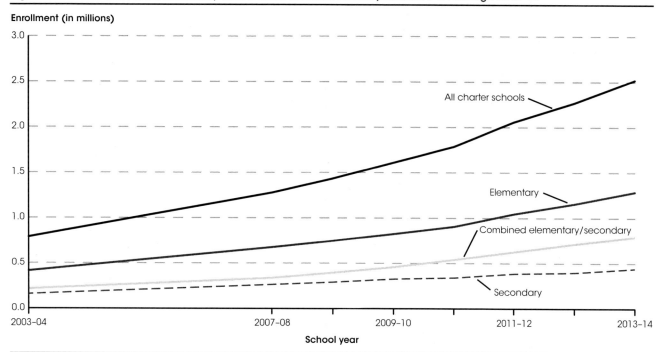

NOTE: "Elementary" includes schools beginning with grade 6 or below and with no grade higher than 8. "Secondary" includes schools with no grade lower than 7. "Combined elementary/secondary" includes schools beginning with grade 6 or below and ending with grade 9 or above. Other schools not classified by grade span are included in the "All charter schools" count but are not presented separately in the figure.
SOURCE: U.S. Department of Education, National Center for Education Statistics, Common Core of Data (CCD), "Public Elementary/Secondary School Universe Survey," selected school years, 2003-04 through 2013-14. See *Digest of Education Statistics 2015*, table 216.20.

The number of students enrolled in public charter schools between school years 2003–04 and 2013–14 increased from 0.8 million to 2.5 million. During that period, larger numbers of charter school students were enrolled in elementary schools than in any of the following types of charter schools: secondary, combined, and other types that were not classified by grade span. The percentage of public school students who attended charter schools increased from 1.6 to 5.1 percent during this period, following an increase of 1.7 million in the number of charter school students and a decrease of 0.4 million in the number of traditional public school students (see the Public School Enrollment indicator). Between 2012–13 and 2013–14, the number of students enrolled in public charter schools increased from 2.3 million to 2.5 million.

Figure 3. Percentage of all public school students enrolled in public charter schools, by state: School year 2013–14

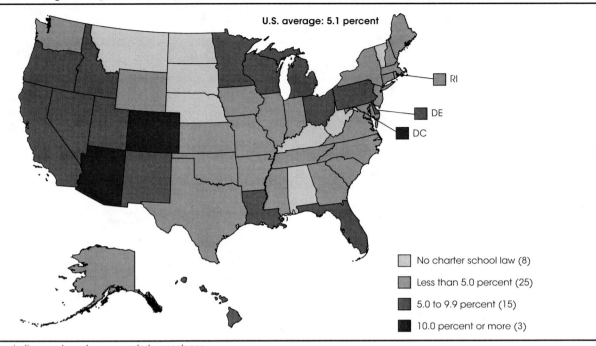

U.S. average: 5.1 percent

No charter school law (8)

Less than 5.0 percent (25)

5.0 to 9.9 percent (15)

10.0 percent or more (3)

NOTE: Categorizations are based on unrounded percentages.
SOURCE: U.S. Department of Education, National Center for Education Statistics, Common Core of Data (CCD), "Public Elementary/Secondary School Universe Survey," 2013–14. See *Digest of Education Statistics 2015*, table 216.90.

In school year 2013–14, California had the largest number of students enrolled in charter schools (513,400, representing 8 percent of total public school students in the state), and the District of Columbia had the highest percentage of public school students enrolled in charter schools (42 percent, representing 33,200 students). After the District of Columbia, Arizona had the next highest percentage (18 percent) of charter school enrollment as a percentage of total public school enrollment.

Between school years 2003–04 and 2013–14, charter schools experienced changes in their demographic composition similar to those seen at traditional public

schools. The percentage of charter school students who were Hispanic increased (from 21 to 30 percent), as did the percentage who were Asian/Pacific Islander (from 3 to 4 percent). In contrast, the percentage of charter school students who were White decreased from 42 to 35 percent. The percentages decreased for Black (from 32 to 27 percent) and American Indian/Alaska Native (from 2 to 1 percent) charter school students, as well. Data were collected for charter school students of Two or more races beginning in 2009–10. Students of Two or more races accounted for 3 percent of the charter school population in 2013–14.

Figure 4. Percentage distribution of public charter school students, by race/ethnicity: School years 2003–04 and 2013–14

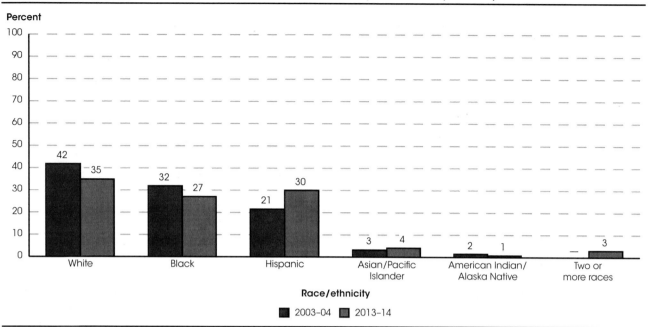

— Not available.
NOTE: Data for the "Two or more races" category were not available prior to 2009–10. Race categories exclude persons of Hispanic ethnicity.
SOURCE: U.S. Department of Education, National Center for Education Statistics, Common Core of Data (CCD), "Public Elementary/Secondary School Universe Survey," 2003–04 and 2013–14. See *Digest of Education Statistics 2015*, table 216.30.

In school year 2013–14, the percentage of students attending high-poverty schools—schools in which more than 75 percent of students qualify for free or reduced-price lunch (FRPL) under the National School Lunch Program—was higher for charter school students (37 percent) than for traditional public school students (24 percent). In the same year, 20 percent each of charter school students and of traditional public school students attended low-poverty schools, those in which 25 percent or less of students qualify for FRPL.

Endnotes:

[1] Nelson, B., Berman, P., Ericson, J., Kamprath, N., Perry, R., Silverman, D., and Solomon, D. (2000). *The State of Charter Schools 2000*. National Center for Education Statistics, Office of Educational Research and Improvement, U.S. Department of Education. Washington, DC. Retrieved September 30, 2015, from http://files.eric.ed.gov/fulltext/ED437724.pdf.
[2] Finnigan, K., Adelman, N., Anderson, L., Cotton, L., Donnelly, M., and Price, T. (2004). *Evaluation of the Public Charter Schools Program: Final Report*. U.S. Department of Education, Office of the Deputy Secretary. Washington, DC: Policy and Program Studies Service. Retrieved September 30, 2015, from https://www2.ed.gov/rschstat/eval/choice/pcsp-final/finalreport.pdf.
[3] The Center for Education Reform. (2015). Choice and Charter Schools: Charter School Law. Retrieved September 22, 2015, from www.edreform.com/issues/choice-charter-schools/laws-legislation.

Reference tables: *Digest of Education Statistics 2015*, tables 216.20, 216.30, and 216.90
Related indicators: Characteristics of Traditional Public and Public Charter Schools

Glossary: Charter school, Combined school, Elementary school, Enrollment, Free or reduced-price lunch, National School Lunch Program, Public school or institution, Racial/ethnic group, Secondary school, Student membership, Traditional public school

Private School Enrollment

Private school enrollment in prekindergarten (preK) through grade 12 increased from 5.9 million students in 1995–96 to 6.3 million in 2001–02, and then declined to 5.4 million in 2013–14.

In school year 2013–14, some 5.4 million students (or 10 percent of all elementary and secondary students) were enrolled in private elementary and secondary schools.[1] The percentage of all elementary and secondary students enrolled in private schools decreased from 12 percent in 1995–96 to 10 percent in 2013–14, and is projected to continue to decrease to 9 percent in 2025–26 (the last year for which projected data are available).

Figure 1. Actual and projected private school enrollment in prekindergarten (preK) through grade 12, by grade level: School years 2003–04 through 2025–26

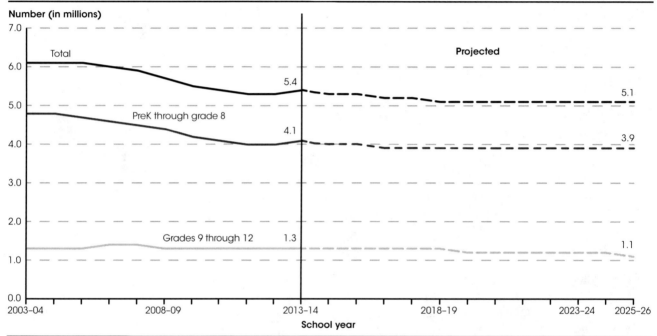

NOTE: Prekindergarten students who are enrolled in private schools that do not offer kindergarten or higher grades are not included in this analysis. Detail may not sum to totals because of rounding.
SOURCE: U.S. Department of Education, National Center for Education Statistics, Private School Universe Survey (PSS), 2003–04 through 2013–14; National Elementary and Secondary Enrollment Projection Model, 1972 through 2025. See *Digest of Education Statistics 2015*, table 105.30.

Private school enrollment in prekindergarten (preK) through grade 12 increased from 5.9 million in 1995–96 to 6.3 million in 2001–02, and then declined to 5.4 million in 2013–14. More recently, total private school enrollment decreased by 12 percent between 2003–04 and 2013–14; enrollment is projected to decrease by 6 percent to 5.1 million students in 2025–26.

Similar to overall private school enrollment, private school enrollment in preK through grade 8 increased from 4.8 million students in 1995–96 to 5.0 million in 2001–02 before decreasing to 4.1 million in 2013–14. Between 2003–04 and 2013–14, private school enrollment in preK through grade 8 decreased by 15 percent. Enrollment is expected to decrease by a further 3 percent to 3.9 million students in 2025–26. Private school enrollment in grades 9 through 12 increased from 1.2 million students in 1995–96 to a peak of 1.4 million in 2007–08; enrollment then fluctuated from 2007–08 to 2013–14. From 2013–14 to 2025–26, private school enrollment in grades 9 through 12 is expected to decrease by 13 percent, from 1.3 million to 1.1 million students.

Figure 2. Private elementary and secondary school enrollment, by school orientation: Selected school years, 2003–04 through 2013–14

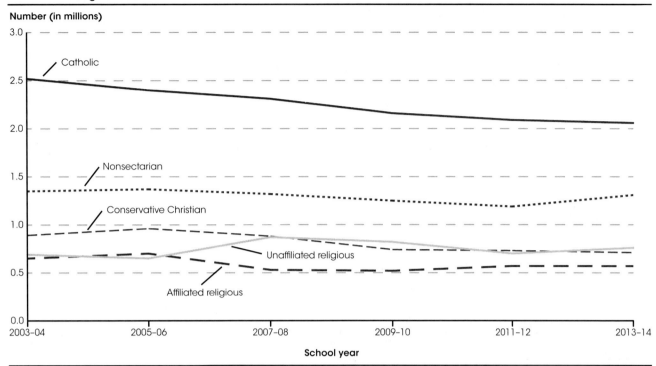

Number (in millions)

NOTE: Prekindergarten students who are enrolled in private schools that do not offer kindergarten or higher grades are not included in this analysis. Catholic schools include parochial, diocesan, and private Catholic schools. Conservative Christian schools have membership in at least one of four associations: Accelerated Christian Education, American Association of Christian Schools, Association of Christian Schools International, or Oral Roberts University Education Fellowship. Affiliated religious schools belong to associations of schools with a specific religious orientation other than Catholic or conservative Christian. Unaffiliated religious schools have a religious orientation or purpose but are not classified as Catholic, conservative Christian, or affiliated religious. Nonsectarian schools do not have a religious orientation or purpose.
SOURCE: U.S. Department of Education, National Center for Education Statistics, Private School Universe Survey (PSS), selected years, 2003–04 through 2013–14. See *Digest of Education Statistics 2015*, table 205.20.

In 2013–14, some 38 percent of all private school students were enrolled in Catholic schools. The number of private school students enrolled in Catholic schools decreased from 2.5 million in 2003–04 to 2.1 million in 2013–14. The decrease in the number of students enrolled in Catholic schools was primarily due to a decline in the number of students enrolled in Catholic parochial schools (1.2 million in 2003–04 compared to 740,000 in 2013–14). The numbers of students enrolled

in conservative Christian (707,000) and affiliated religious (565,000) schools in 2013–14 were also lower than in 2003–04, while the number of students enrolled in unaffiliated religious schools (758,000) in 2013–14 was higher than in 2003–04. The number of students enrolled in nonsectarian schools (1.3 million) in 2013–14 was not measurably different from the number enrolled in 2003–04.

Figure 3. Percentage distribution of private elementary and secondary school enrollment, by school level and orientation: School year 2013–14

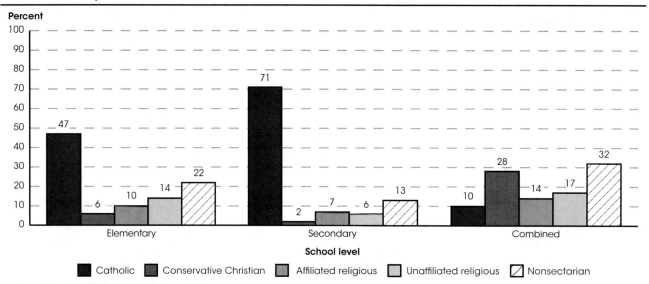

NOTE: Prekindergarten students who are enrolled in private schools that do not offer kindergarten or higher grades are not included in this analysis. Elementary schools have grade 6 or lower and no grade higher than 8. Secondary schools have no grade lower than 7. Combined schools include those that have grades lower than 7 and higher than 8, as well as those that do not classify students by grade level. Catholic schools include parochial, diocesan, and private Catholic schools. Conservative Christian schools have membership in at least one of four associations: Accelerated Christian Education, American Association of Christian Schools, Association of Christian Schools International, or Oral Roberts University Education Fellowship. Affiliated religious schools belong to associations of schools with a specific religious orientation other than Catholic or conservative Christian. Unaffiliated religious schools have a religious orientation or purpose but are not classified as Catholic, conservative Christian, or affiliated religious. Nonsectarian schools do not have a religious orientation or purpose. Detail may not sum to totals because of rounding.
SOURCE: U.S. Department of Education, National Center for Education Statistics, Private School Universe Survey (PSS), 2013–14. See *Digest of Education Statistics 2015*, table 205.30.

In 2013–14, the percentage of private elementary[2] students enrolled in Catholic schools was 47 percent, which was higher than the percentage of students enrolled in nonsectarian (22 percent), unaffiliated religious (14 percent), affiliated religious (10 percent), and conservative Christian (6 percent) schools. Similarly, a higher percentage of private secondary[3] students were

enrolled in Catholic schools (71 percent) than in any other school orientation. In contrast to the large percentages of private school students enrolled in Catholic elementary and secondary schools, Catholic students made up a smaller percentage (10 percent) of private school students enrolled in combined[4] elementary/secondary schools.

Figure 4.   Percentage distribution of private elementary and secondary school enrollment, by school locale and orientation: School year 2013–14

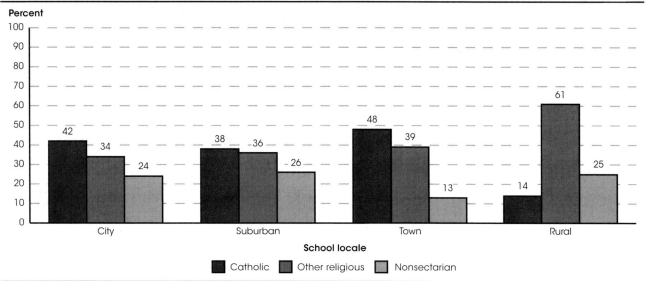

NOTE: Prekindergarten students who are enrolled in private schools that do not offer kindergarten or higher grades are not included in this analysis. Catholic schools include parochial, diocesan, and private Catholic schools. Other religious schools include conservative Christian, affiliated religious, and unaffiliated religious schools. Conservative Christian schools have membership in at least one of four associations: Accelerated Christian Education, American Association of Christian Schools, Association of Christian Schools International, or Oral Roberts University Education Fellowship. Affiliated religious schools belong to associations of schools with a specific religious orientation other than Catholic or conservative Christian. Unaffiliated religious schools have a religious orientation or purpose but are not classified as Catholic, conservative Christian, or affiliated religious. Nonsectarian schools do not have a religious orientation or purpose. Detail may not sum to totals because of rounding.
SOURCE: U.S. Department of Education, National Center for Education Statistics, Private School Universe Survey (PSS), 2013–14. See *Digest of Education Statistics 2015,* table 205.30.

In 2013–14, higher percentages of private school students in cities and towns were enrolled in Catholic schools than in other religious[5] or nonsectarian schools. For example, in towns, 48 percent of private school students were enrolled in Catholic schools, while 39 percent were enrolled in other religious schools and 13 percent were enrolled in nonsectarian schools. In contrast, a lower percentage of private school students in rural areas were enrolled in Catholic schools (14 percent) than nonsectarian (25 percent) or other religious (61 percent) schools. Additionally, while the percentage of private school students in suburbs enrolled in Catholic schools (38 percent) was higher than the percentage enrolled in nonsectarian schools (26 percent), it was not measurably different from the percentage enrolled in other religious schools.

Figure 5. Percentage distribution of private elementary and secondary school enrollment, by race/ethnicity and school orientation: School year 2013-14

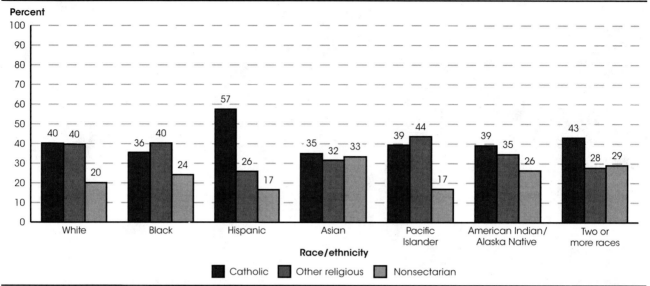

NOTE: Prekindergarten students who are enrolled in private schools that do not offer kindergarten or higher grades are not included in this analysis. Catholic schools include parochial, diocesan, and private Catholic schools. Other religious schools include conservative Christian, affiliated religious, and unaffiliated religious schools. Conservative Christian schools have membership in at least one of four associations: Accelerated Christian Education, American Association of Christian Schools, Association of Christian Schools International, or Oral Roberts University Education Fellowship. Affiliated religious schools belong to associations of schools with a specific religious orientation other than Catholic or conservative Christian. Unaffiliated religious schools have a religious orientation or purpose but are not classified as Catholic, conservative Christian, or affiliated religious. Nonsectarian schools do not have a religious orientation or purpose. Race categories exclude persons of Hispanic ethnicity. Percentage distribution is based on the students for whom race/ethnicity was reported. Detail may not sum to totals because of rounding. Although rounded numbers are displayed, the figures are based on unrounded estimates. SOURCE: U.S. Department of Education, National Center for Education Statistics, Private School Universe Survey (PSS), 2013-14. See *Digest of Education Statistics 2015*, table 205.30.

There were also differences in private school enrollment by school orientation within racial/ethnic groups. Among Hispanic, Asian, and American Indian/Alaska Native students as well as students of Two or more races, higher percentages of private school students were enrolled in Catholic schools than other religious schools in 2013–14. For example, 57 percent of Hispanic private school students were enrolled in Catholic schools, while 26 percent were enrolled in other religious schools. In contrast, lower percentages of Black (36 percent) and Pacific Islander (39 percent) private school students were enrolled in Catholic schools in 2013–14 than in other religious schools (40 and 44 percent, respectively). In addition, for all racial/ethnic groups other than Asian, higher percentages of private school students were enrolled in Catholic schools than nonsectarian schools. For example, 40 percent of White private school students were enrolled in Catholic schools compared to 20 percent enrolled in nonsectarian schools. The percentage of Asian students enrolled in Catholic schools (35 percent) was not measurably different from the percentage enrolled in nonsectarian schools (33 percent).

Endnotes:

[1] Prekindergarten students who are enrolled in private schools that do not offer kindergarten or higher grades are not included in this analysis.
[2] Elementary schools have grade 6 or lower and no grade higher than 8. This category is not comparable to the preK through grade 8 category used elsewhere in this indicator.
[3] Secondary schools have one or more of grades 7 through 12 and have no grade lower than grade 7. This category is not comparable to the grades 9 through 12 category used elsewhere in this indicator.
[4] Combined schools include grades lower than 7 and higher than 8, as well as those that do not classify students by grade level.
[5] Other religious schools include conservative Christian, affiliated religious, and unaffiliated religious schools.

Reference tables: *Digest of Education Statistics 2015*, tables 105.30, 205.20, and 205.30
Related indicators: Public School Enrollment, Teachers and Pupil/Teacher Ratios

Glossary: Catholic school, Combined school, Elementary school, Enrollment, Locale codes, Nonsectarian school, Other religious school, Prekindergarten, Private school, Racial/ethnic group, Secondary school

This page intentionally left blank.

Racial/Ethnic Enrollment in Public Schools

Between fall 2003 and fall 2013, the number of White students enrolled in public elementary and secondary schools decreased from 28.4 million to 25.2 million, and the percentage who were White decreased from 59 to 50 percent. In contrast, the number of Hispanic students enrolled increased from 9.0 million to 12.5 million, and the percentage who were Hispanic increased from 19 to 25 percent.

Overall enrollment in public elementary and secondary schools increased from 48.5 million to 50.0 million between fall 2003 and fall 2013, and is projected to continue increasing to 51.4 million in fall 2025 (the most recent year for which projected data are available).

In addition, racial/ethnic distributions of public school students across the country and within its regions have shifted. These changing distributions may reflect demographic shifts in the population.

Figure 1. Percentage distribution of students enrolled in public elementary and secondary schools, by race/ethnicity: Fall 2003, fall 2013, and fall 2025

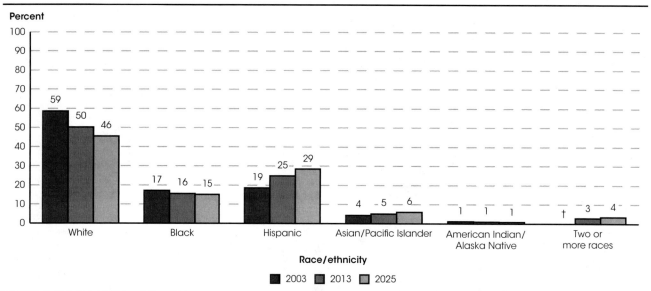

† Not applicable.
NOTE: Race categories exclude persons of Hispanic ethnicity. Prior to 2008, separate data on students of Two or more races were not collected. Although rounded numbers are displayed, the figures are based on unrounded estimates. Detail may not sum to totals because of rounding. Data for 2025 are projected.
SOURCE: U.S. Department of Education, National Center for Education Statistics, Common Core of Data (CCD), "State Nonfiscal Survey of Public Elementary and Secondary Education," 2003–04 and 2013–14; and National Elementary and Secondary Enrollment by Race/Ethnicity Projection Model, 1972 through 2025. See *Digest of Education Statistics 2015*, table 203.50.

From fall 2003 through fall 2013, the number of White students enrolled in public elementary and secondary schools decreased from 28.4 million to 25.2 million, and the percentage of students who were White decreased from 59 to 50 percent. In contrast, the number of Hispanic students enrolled during this period increased from 9.0 million to 12.5 million, and the percentage who were Hispanic increased from 19 to 25 percent. The number of Black students enrolled decreased from 8.3 million to 7.8 million, and the percentage who were Black decreased from 17 to 16 percent. Since fall 2002, the percentage of students enrolled in public schools who were Hispanic has exceeded the percentage who were Black. Additionally, the number of American Indian/Alaska Native students enrolled from fall 2003 to fall

2013 decreased from 0.6 million to 0.5 million, and the percentage who were American Indian/Alaska Native remained around 1 percent.

The number of White students enrolled in public schools is projected to continue decreasing between fall 2014 and fall 2025 (from 25.0 million to 23.5 million) and to account for 46 percent of total enrollment in 2025. The percentage of students enrolled who are White is projected to be less than 50 percent beginning in 2014 and is projected to continue to decline as the enrollments of Hispanic students and Asian/Pacific Islander students increase. The number of Hispanic students is projected to increase from 12.7 million in 2014 to 14.7 million in 2025 and to account for 29 percent of total enrollment in 2025. The number of Asian/Pacific Islander students is projected to increase from 2.6 million to 3.1 million between 2014 and 2025 and to account for 6 percent of total enrollment in 2025. The number of Black students is projected to fluctuate around 7.8 million during this period, and the percentage of students who are Black is projected to decrease by less than 1 percent to 15 percent in 2025. Additionally, the number of American Indian/Alaska Native students is projected to continue decreasing during this period (from 0.5 million to 0.4 million) and to account for 1 percent of total enrollment in 2025.

Figure 2. Number of students enrolled in public elementary and secondary schools, by region and race/ethnicity: Fall 2003 through fall 2013

Number (in millions)

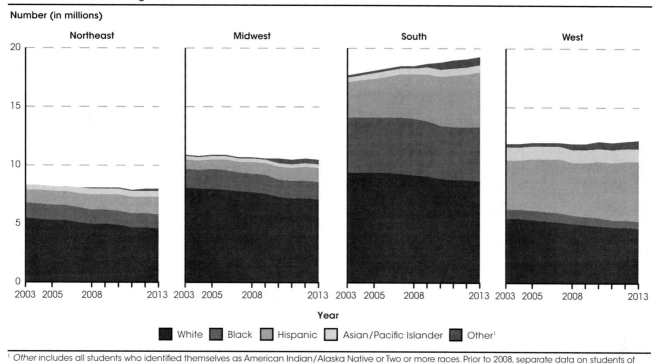

White   Black   Hispanic   Asian/Pacific Islander   Other[1]

[1] *Other* includes all students who identified themselves as American Indian/Alaska Native or Two or more races. Prior to 2008, separate data on students of Two or more races were not collected. In 2008 and 2009, data on students of Two or more races were reported by only a small number of states.
NOTE: Race categories exclude persons of Hispanic ethnicity.
SOURCE: U.S. Department of Education, National Center for Education Statistics, Common Core of Data (CCD), "State Nonfiscal Survey of Public Elementary and Secondary Education," 2003–04 through 2013–14. See *Digest of Education Statistics 2015*, table 203.50.

Changes between fall 2003 and fall 2013 in the racial/ethnic distribution of public school enrollment differed by region. During this time, both the number and the percentage of public school students who were White decreased in all regions. The percentage of students who were White decreased by 7 percentage points in the Midwest and 8 percentage points each in the Northeast, South, and West. Both the number and the percentage of students who were Hispanic increased in all four regions. The percentage of students who were Hispanic increased by 5 percentage points in both the Midwest and Northeast, 6 percentage points in the West, and 7 percentage points in the South. From 2003 through 2013, both the number and the percentage of students who were Black decreased in all regions. The percentage of students who were Black decreased by 1 percentage point each in the Northeast, Midwest, and West and 3 percentage points in the South. The number of Asian/Pacific Islander students fluctuated in the West and increased in the other three regions. Similarly, the percentage of public school students who were Asian/Pacific Islander remained about the same in the West but increased by 1 percentage point in both the Midwest and South and 2 percentage points in the Northeast.

Changes in the racial/ethnic distribution of public school enrollment between 2003 and 2013 also differed by state. In all 50 states, the percentage of students enrolled who were White was lower in 2013 than in 2003, with the decrease ranging from 15 percentage points in Nevada to 2 percentage points in Louisiana, Mississippi, and South Carolina. However, in the District of Columbia the percentage of public school students who were White increased by 5 percentage points over the same period. In all states and the District of Columbia, the percentage of students enrolled who were Hispanic was higher in 2013 than in 2003; the increase was largest in Nevada (10 percentage points) and smallest in Vermont and West Virginia (less than 1 percentage point each). The percentage of public school students who were Black was higher in 2013 than in 2003 in 13 states where the increases were 2 percentage points or less. In the remaining states and the District of Columbia, the percentage of public school students who were Black was lower in 2013 than in 2003 (the largest decrease, 11 percentage points, occurred in the District of Columbia).

Figure 3. Percentage distribution of students enrolled in public elementary and secondary schools, by region and race/ethnicity: Fall 2013

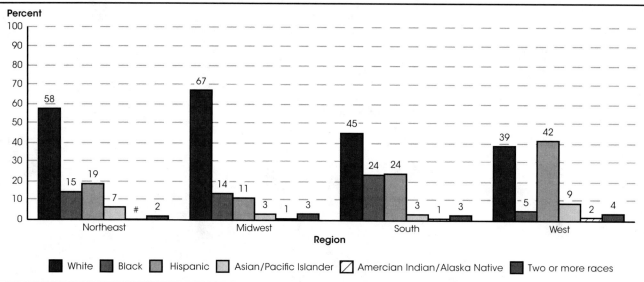

Rounds to zero.
NOTE: Race categories exclude persons of Hispanic ethnicity. Although rounded numbers are displayed, the figures are based on unrounded estimates. Detail may not sum to totals because of rounding.
SOURCE: U.S. Department of Education, National Center for Education Statistics, Common Core of Data (CCD), "State Nonfiscal Survey of Public Elementary and Secondary Education," 2013–14. See *Digest of Education Statistics 2015*, table 203.50.

In fall 2013, the racial/ethnic distribution of public school enrollment differed by region. In most regions, the percentage of public school students who were White was at least 21 percentage points greater than the percentage who were Hispanic. However, in the West, the percentage of public school students who were White (39 percent) was 3 percentage points lower than the percentage who were Hispanic (42 percent). The percentage of public school students who were Black ranged from 5 percent in the West to 24 percent in the South. Fourteen percent of public school students in the Midwest and 15 percent of public school students in the Northeast were Black; both percentages are within 2 percentage points of the overall percentage of public school students who were Black (16 percent). The percentage of public school students who were Asian/Pacific Islander ranged from 3 percent in both the Midwest and South to 9 percent in the West. American Indian/Alaska Native students accounted for 2 percent or less of student enrollment in every region of the United States. Students of Two or more races made up 2 percent of enrollment in the Northeast, 3 percent of enrollment in both the South and Midwest, and 4 percent of enrollment in the West.

Reference tables: *Digest of Education Statistics 2015,* tables 203.50 and 203.70
Related indicators: Public School Enrollment

Glossary: Elementary school, Enrollment, Geographic region, Public school or institution, Racial/ethnic group, Secondary school

This page intentionally left blank.

English Language Learners in Public Schools

The percentage of public school students in the United States who were English language learners (ELL) was higher in school year 2013-14 (9.3 percent) than in 2003-04 (8.8 percent) and 2012–13 (9.2 percent). In 2013-14, five of the six states with the highest percentages of ELL students in their public schools were located in the West.

Students who are English language learners (ELL) participate in appropriate programs of language assistance, such as English as a Second Language, High Intensity Language Training, and bilingual education, to help ensure that they attain English proficiency, develop high levels of academic attainment in English, and meet the same academic content and academic achievement standards that all students are expected to meet. Participation in these types of programs can improve students' English language proficiency which, in turn, has been associated with improved educational outcomes.[1] The percentage of public school students in the United States who were English language learners was higher in school year 2013–14 (9.3 percent, or an estimated 4.5 million students) than in 2003–04 (8.8 percent, or an estimated 4.2 million students) and 2012–13 (9.2 percent, or an estimated 4.4 million students).

Figure 1.   Percentage of public school students who were English language learners, by state: School year 2013–14

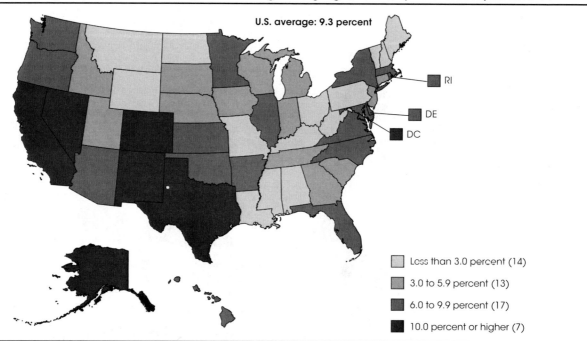

U.S. average: 9.3 percent

RI
DE
DC

Less than 3.0 percent (14)
3.0 to 5.9 percent (13)
6.0 to 9.9 percent (17)
10.0 percent or higher (7)

NOTE: Categorization based on unrounded percentages.
SOURCE: U.S. Department of Education, National Center for Education Statistics, Common Core of Data (CCD), "Local Education Agency Universe Survey," 2013–14. See *Digest of Education Statistics 2015*, table 204.20.

In 2013–14, five of the six states with the highest percentages of ELL students in their public schools were in the West. In the District of Columbia and six states— Alaska, California, Colorado, Nevada, New Mexico, and Texas—10.0 percent or more of public school students were English language learners, with California having the highest percentage, at 22.7 percent. Seventeen states had percentages of ELL public school enrollment between 6.0 and 9.9 percent. These states were Arizona, Arkansas,

Delaware, Florida, Hawaii, Illinois, Kansas, Maryland, Massachusetts, Minnesota, New York, North Carolina, Oklahoma, Oregon, Rhode Island, Virginia, and Washington. In 13 states, the percentage of ELL students in public schools was between 3.0 and 5.9 percent; this percentage was less than 3.0 percent in 14 states, with West Virginia having the lowest percentage, at 0.7 percent.

The percentage of ELL students in public schools increased between 2003–04 and 2013–14 in all but 14 states, with the largest percentage-point increase occurring in Kansas (4.6 percentage points) and the largest percentage-point decrease occurring in Arizona (9.8 percentage points). Between 2012–13 and 2013–14, the percentage of ELL students in public schools decreased in 20 states, with the largest decrease occurring in Idaho (1.4 percentage points). In contrast, 30 states and the District of Columbia experienced an increase in the percentage of ELL students, with the largest increase occurring in Kansas (0.6 percentage points).

Figure 2. Percentage of public school students who were English language learners, by locale: School year 2013–14

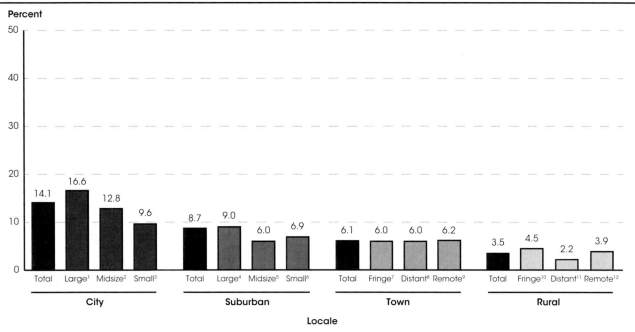

1 Located inside an urbanized area and inside a principal city with a population of at least 250,000.
2 Located inside an urbanized area and inside a principal city with a population of at least 100,000 but less than 250,000.
3 Located inside an urbanized area and inside a principal city with a population less than 100,000.
4 Located inside an urbanized area and outside a principal city with a population of 250,000 or more.
5 Located inside an urbanized area and outside a principal city with a population of at least 100,000 but less than 250,000.
6 Located inside an urbanized area and outside a principal city with a population less than 100,000.
7 Located inside an urban cluster that is 10 miles or less from an urbanized area.
8 Located inside an urban cluster that is more than 10 but less than or equal to 35 miles from an urbanized area.
9 Located inside an urban cluster that is more than 35 miles from an urbanized area.
10 Located outside any urbanized area or urban cluster but 5 miles or less from an urbanized area or 2.5 miles or less from an urban cluster.
11 Located outside any urbanized area or urban cluster and more than 5 but less than or equal to 25 miles from an urbanized area, or more than 2.5 miles but less than or equal to 10 miles from an urban cluster.
12 Located outside any urbanized area or urban cluster, more than 25 miles from an urbanized area, and more than 10 miles from an urban cluster.
NOTE: Locales are based on an address's proximity to an urbanized area. Data in this figure are based on the locales of school districts rather than the locales of the schools themselves.
SOURCE: U.S. Department of Education, National Center for Education Statistics, Common Core of Data (CCD), "Local Education Agency Universe Survey," 2013–14. See *Digest of Education Statistics 2015*, table 214.40.

In 2013–14, the percentage of students in ELL programs was generally higher for school districts in more urbanized areas than for those in less urbanized areas. For example, ELL students in cities made up an average of 14.1 percent of total public school enrollment, ranging from 9.6 percent in small cities to 16.6 percent in large cities. In suburban areas, ELL students constituted an average of 8.7 percent of public school enrollment, ranging from 6.0 percent in midsize suburban areas to 9.0 percent in large suburban areas. Towns and rural areas are subdivided into fringe, distant, and remote areas according to their proximity to urban centers, with fringe being the closest to an urban center and remote being the farthest from one. In towns, ELL students made up an average of 6.1 percent of public school enrollment, ranging from 6.0 percent in fringe and distant areas to 6.2 percent in remote areas. In rural areas, ELL students made up an average of 3.5 percent of public student enrollment, ranging from 2.2 percent in distant areas to 4.5 percent in fringe areas.

Table 1.   Ten most commonly reported home languages of English language learner (ELL) students: School year 2013–14

Home language	Number of ELL students	Percentage distribution of ELL students[1]	Number of ELL students as a percentage of total enrollment
Spanish, Castilian	3,770,816	76.5	7.7
Arabic	109,170	2.2	0.2
Chinese	107,825	2.2	0.2
English[2]	91,669	1.9	0.2
Vietnamese	89,705	1.8	0.2
Hmong	39,860	0.8	0.1
Haitian, Haitian Creole	37,371	0.8	0.1
Somali	34,472	0.7	0.1
Russian	33,821	0.7	0.1
Korean	32,445	0.7	0.1

[1] Details do not sum to 100 because not all categories are reported.
[2] Examples of situations in which English might be reported as an English learner's home language include students who live in multilingual households and students adopted from other countries who speak English at home but also have been raised speaking another language.
SOURCE: U.S. Department of Education, National Center for Education Statistics, ED*Facts* file 141, Data Group 678, extracted November 3, 2015; Common Core of Data (CCD), "State Nonfiscal Survey of Public Elementary and Secondary Education," 2013–14. See *Digest of Education Statistics 2015*, table 204.27.

Spanish was the home language of nearly 3.8 million ELL students in 2013–14, representing 76.5 percent of all ELL students and 7.7 percent of all public K–12 students. Arabic and Chinese were the next most common home languages, reported for approximately 109,000 and 108,000 students, respectively. English (91,700 students) was the fourth most commonly reported home language, which may reflect students who live in multilingual households or students adopted from other countries who had been raised speaking another language but currently live in households where English is spoken. Vietnamese (89,700), Hmong (39,900), Haitian (37,400), Somali (34,500), Russian (33,800), and Korean (32,400) round out the top ten most commonly reported home languages for ELL students in 2013–14.

Figure 3. Percentage of public K–12 students identified as English language learners, by grade level: School year 2013–14

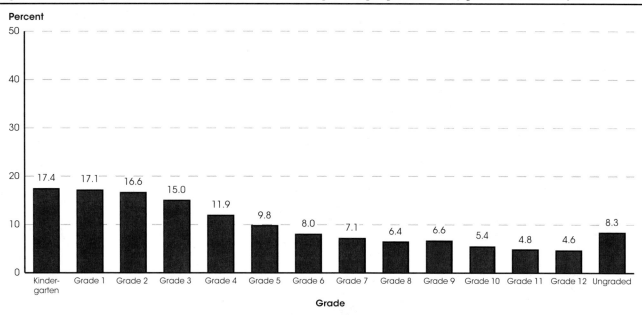

SOURCE: U.S. Department of Education, National Center for Education Statistics, ED*Facts* file 141, Data Group 678, extracted November 3, 2015; Common Core of Data (CCD), "State Nonfiscal Survey of Public Elementary and Secondary Education," 2013–14. See *Digest of Education Statistics 2015*, table 204.27.

In 2013–14, a greater percentage of public school students in lower grades than in upper grades were identified as ELL students. For example, 17.4 percent of kindergarteners were identified as ELL students, compared to 8.0 percent of 6th-graders and 6.4 percent of 8th-graders. Among 12th-graders, only 4.6 percent of students were identified as ELL students.

Endnotes:
[1] Ross, T., Kena, G., Rathbun, A., KewalRamani, A., Zhang, J., Kristapovich, P., and Manning, E. (2012). *Higher Education: Gaps in Access and Persistence Study* (NCES 2012-046). U.S. Department of Education. Washington, DC: National Center for Education Statistics.

Reference tables: *Digest of Education Statistics 2015,* tables 204.20, 204.27, and 214.40
Related indicators: Reading Performance, Mathematics Performance

Glossary: English language learner (ELL), Enrollment, Geographic region, Household, Locale codes, Public school or institution, School district

Children and Youth with Disabilities

In 2013-14, the number of children and youth ages 3-21 receiving special education services was 6.5 million, or about 13 percent of all public school students. Among students receiving special education services, 35 percent had specific learning disabilities.

Enacted in 1975, the Individuals with Disabilities Education Act (IDEA), formerly known as the Education for All Handicapped Children Act (EAHCA), mandates the provision of a free and appropriate public school education for eligible students ages 3–21. Eligible students are those identified by a team of professionals as having a disability that adversely affects academic performance and as being in need of special education and related services. Data collection activities to monitor compliance with IDEA began in 1976.

From school years 1990–91 through 2004–05, the number of children and youth ages 3–21 who received special education services increased from 4.7 million, or 11 percent of total public school enrollment, to 6.7 million, or 14 percent of total public school enrollment. Both the number and percentage of students served under IDEA declined from 2004–05 through 2011–12. There was evidence that the number and percentage of students served leveled off in 2012–13 and 2013–14. By 2013–14, the number of students served under IDEA was 6.5 million, or 13 percent of total public school enrollment.

Figure 1. Percentage distribution of children ages 3–21 served under the Individuals with Disabilities Education Act (IDEA), Part B, by disability type: School year 2013-14

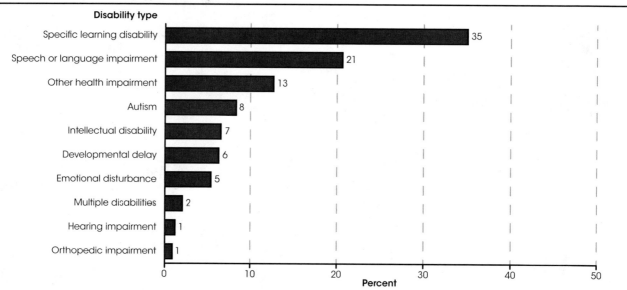

NOTE: Deaf-blindness, traumatic brain injury, and visual impairment are not shown because they each account for less than 0.5 percent of children served under IDEA. Due to categories not shown, detail does not sum to total. Although rounded numbers are displayed, the figures are based on unrounded estimates.
SOURCE: U.S. Department of Education, Office of Special Education Programs, Individuals with Disabilities Education Act (IDEA) database, retrieved September 25, 2015, from http://www2.ed.gov/programs/osepidea/618-data/state-level-data-files/index.html#bcc. See *Digest of Education Statistics 2015*, table 204.30.

In school year 2013–14, a higher percentage of children and youth ages 3–21 received special education services under IDEA for specific learning disabilities than for any other type of disability. A specific learning disability is a disorder in one or more of the basic psychological processes involved in understanding or using language, spoken or written, that may manifest itself in an imperfect ability to listen, think, speak, read, write, spell, or do mathematical calculations. In 2013–14, some 35 percent of all students receiving special education services had specific learning disabilities, 21 percent had speech or language impairments, and 13 percent had other health impairments (including having limited strength, vitality, or alertness due to chronic or acute health problems such as a heart condition, tuberculosis, rheumatic fever, nephritis, asthma, sickle cell anemia, hemophilia, epilepsy, lead poisoning, leukemia, or diabetes). Students with autism, intellectual disabilities, developmental delays, or emotional disturbances each accounted for between 5 and

8 percent of students served under IDEA. Students with multiple disabilities, hearing impairments, orthopedic impairments, visual impairments, traumatic brain injuries, or deaf-blindness each accounted for 2 percent or less of those served under IDEA.

Figure 2. Percentage, of total enrollment, of children ages 3–21 served under the Individuals with Disabilities Education Act (IDEA), Part B, by race/ethnicity: School year 2013–14

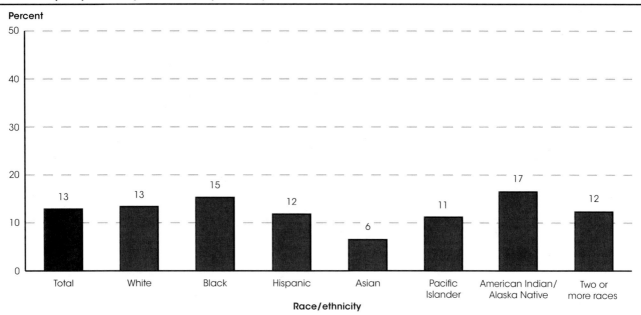

NOTE: Race categories exclude persons of Hispanic ethnicity. Although rounded numbers are displayed, the figures are based on unrounded estimates.
SOURCE: U.S. Department of Education, Office of Special Education Programs, Individuals with Disabilities Education Act (IDEA) database, retrieved September 25, 2015, from http://www2.ed.gov/programs/osepidea/618-data/state-level-data-files/index.html#bcc; and National Center for Education Statistics, Common Core of Data (CCD), "State Nonfiscal Survey of Public Elementary/Secondary Education," 2013–14. See *Digest of Education Statistics 2015*, tables 204.30 and 204.50.

In school year 2013–14, children and youth ages 3–21 served under IDEA as a percentage of total enrollment in public schools differed by race/ethnicity. The percentage of students served under IDEA was highest for American Indian/Alaska Native students (17 percent), followed by Black students (15 percent), White students (13 percent), students of Two or more races (12 percent), Hispanic students (12 percent), Pacific Islander students (11 percent), and Asian students (6 percent). In most racial/ethnic groups, the percentage of children and youth receiving services for specific learning disabilities combined with the percentage receiving services for speech or language impairments accounted for over 50 percent of children and youth served under IDEA. The percentage distribution of various types of special education services received by students ages 3–21 in 2013–14 differed by race/ethnicity. For example, the percentage of students with disabilities receiving services

under IDEA for specific learning disabilities was lower among Asian students (22 percent) than among students overall (35 percent). However, the percentage of students with disabilities receiving services under IDEA for autism was higher among Asian students (19 percent) than among students overall (8 percent). Additionally, of students who were served under IDEA, 8 percent of Black students and 7 percent of students of Two or more races, compared to 5 percent of students served under IDEA overall, received services for emotional disturbances. Among children and youth who received services under IDEA, the percentages of American Indian/Alaska Native students (10 percent), Pacific Islander students (8 percent), and students of Two or more races (8 percent) who received services for developmental delays were higher than the percentage of students overall receiving services for developmental delays (6 percent).

Separate data on special education services for males and females are available only for students ages 6–21. Among those 6- to 21-year-olds enrolled in public schools in 2013–14, a higher percentage of males (16 percent) than females (9 percent) received special education services under IDEA. The percentage distribution of students ages 6–21 who received various types of special education services in 2013–14 differed by sex. For example, the percentage of students served under IDEA who received services for specific learning disabilities was higher among female students (44 percent) than among male students (37 percent), while the percentage served under IDEA who received services for autism was higher among male students (11 percent) than among female students (4 percent).

Figure 3. Percentage of students ages 6–21 served under the Individuals with Disabilities Education Act (IDEA), Part B, placed in a regular public school environment, by amount of time spent inside general classes: Selected school years, 1990–91 through 2013–14

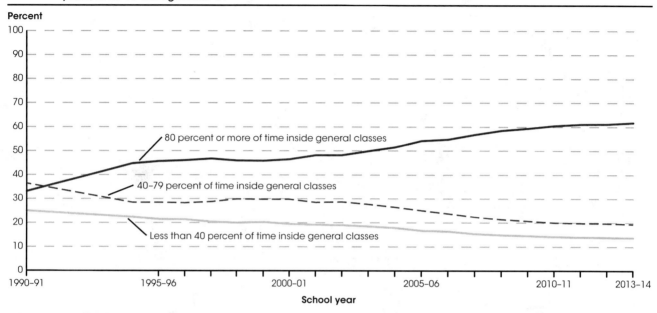

SOURCE: U.S. Department of Education, Office of Special Education Programs, Individuals with Disabilities Education Act (IDEA) database, retrieved October 29, 2015, from http://www2.ed.gov/programs/osepidea/618-data/state-level-data-files/index.html#bcc. See *Digest of Education Statistics 2015*, table 204.60.

Educational environment data are available for students ages 6–21 served under IDEA. About 95 percent of children and youth ages 6–21 who were served under IDEA in 2013–14 were enrolled in regular schools. Some 3 percent of students ages 6–21 who were served under IDEA were enrolled in separate schools (public or private) for students with disabilities; 1 percent were placed by their parents in regular private schools; and less than 1 percent each were in separate residential facilities (public or private), homebound or in hospitals, or in correctional facilities. Among all students ages 6–21 who were served under IDEA, the percentage who spent most of the school day (i.e., 80 percent or more of time) in general classes in regular schools increased from 33 percent in 1990–91 to 62 percent in 2013–14. In contrast, during the same period, the percentage of those who spent 40 to 79 percent of the school day in general classes declined from 36 to 19 percent, and the percentage of those who spent less than 40 percent of time inside general classes also declined, from 25 to 14 percent. In 2013–14, the percentage of students served under IDEA who spent most of the school day in general classes was highest for students with speech or language impairments (87 percent). Approximately two-thirds of students with specific learning disabilities (68 percent), visual impairments (65 percent), other health impairments (64 percent), and developmental delays (63 percent) spent most of the school day in general classes. In contrast, 16 percent of students with intellectual disabilities and 13 percent of students with multiple disabilities spent most of the school day in general classes.

Data are also available for students ages 14–21 served under IDEA who exited school during school year 2012–13, including exit reason. In 2012–13, approximately 396,000 students ages 14–21 who received special education services under IDEA exited school: almost two-thirds (65 percent) graduated with a regular high school diploma, 14 percent received an alternative certificate,[1] 19 percent dropped out, 1 percent reached maximum age, and less than one-half of 1 percent died.

Figure 4.   Percentage of students ages 14–21 served under the Individuals with Disabilities Education Act (IDEA), Part B, who exited school, by exit reason and race/ethnicity: School year 2012–13

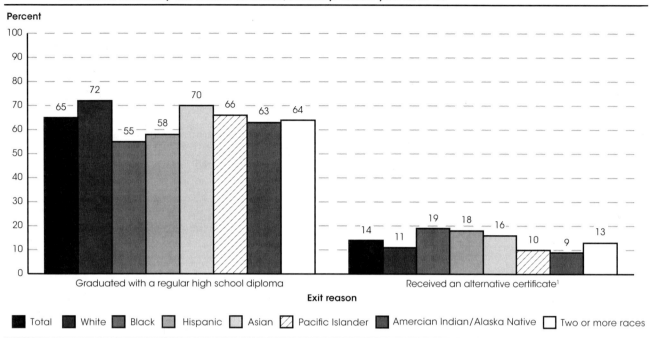

[1] Received a certificate of completion, modified diploma, or some similar document, but did not meet the same standards for graduation as those for students without disabilities.
NOTE: Race categories exclude persons of Hispanic ethnicity.
SOURCE: U.S. Department of Education, Office of Special Education Programs, Individuals with Disabilities Education Act (IDEA) Section 618 Data Products: State Level Data Files, retrieved November 30, 2015, from http://www2.ed.gov/programs/osepidea/618-data/state-level-data-files/index.html. See *Digest of Education Statistics 2015,* table 219.90.

Of the students ages 14–21 served under IDEA who exited school, the percentage who graduated with a regular high school diploma was highest among White students (72 percent) and lowest among Black students (55 percent). The percentage of students served under IDEA who received an alternative certificate was highest among Black students (19 percent) and lowest among American Indian/Alaska Native students (9 percent). The percentage of students served under IDEA who exited special education due to dropping out in 2012–13 was highest among American Indian/Alaska Native students (27 percent) and lowest among Asian students (9 percent).

The percentage of students ages 14–21 served under IDEA who graduated with a regular high school diploma

in 2012–13 differed by type of disability. The percentage of students ages 14–21 served under IDEA who graduated with a regular high school diploma was highest among students with visual impairments (77 percent) and lowest among those with intellectual disabilities (43 percent). The percentage of students served under IDEA who received an alternative certificate was highest among students with intellectual disabilities (33 percent) and lowest among students with speech or language impairments (9 percent). The percentage of students served under IDEA who dropped out in 2012–13 was highest among students with emotional disturbance (35 percent) and lowest among students with autism (7 percent).

Endnotes:

[1] Received a certificate of completion, modified diploma, or some similar document, but did not meet the same standards for graduation as those for students without disabilities.

Reference tables: *Digest of Education Statistics 2015,* tables 204.30, 204.50, 204.60, and 219.90

Related indicators: N/A

Glossary: Disabilities, children with; Enrollment; High school completer; High school diploma; Individuals with Disabilities Education Act (IDEA); Private school; Public school or institution; Racial/ethnic group; Regular school

Undergraduate Enrollment

Total undergraduate enrollment in degree-granting postsecondary institutions increased 31 percent from 13.2 million in 2000 to 17.3 million in 2014. By 2025, total undergraduate enrollment is projected to increase to 19.8 million students.

In fall 2014, total undergraduate enrollment in degree-granting postsecondary institutions was 17.3 million students, an increase of 31 percent from 2000, when enrollment was 13.2 million students. While total undergraduate enrollment increased by 37 percent between 2000 and 2010, enrollment decreased by 4 percent between 2010 and 2014. Undergraduate enrollment is projected to increase 14 percent from 17.3 million to 19.8 million students between 2014 and 2025.

Figure 1. Actual and projected undergraduate enrollment in degree-granting postsecondary institutions, by sex: Fall 2000–2025

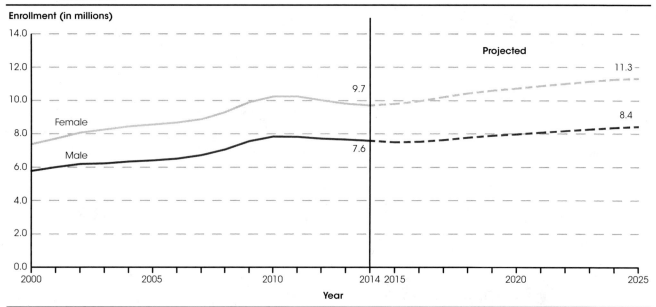

NOTE: Data include unclassified undergraduate students. Degree-granting institutions grant associate's or higher degrees and participate in Title IV federal financial aid programs. Projections are based on data through 2014. Some data have been revised from previously published figures.
SOURCE: U.S. Department of Education, National Center for Education Statistics, Integrated Postsecondary Education Data System (IPEDS), Spring 2001 through Spring 2015, Fall Enrollment component; and Enrollment in Degree-Granting Institutions Projection Model, 1980 through 2025. See *Digest of Education Statistics 2015*, table 303.70.

In fall 2014, female students made up 56 percent of total undergraduate enrollment at 9.7 million, and male students made up 44 percent at 7.6 million. Between 2000 and 2014, enrollment for both groups showed similar patterns of change. During this period, female enrollment increased by 32 percent and male enrollment increased by 31 percent. Most of the increases occurred between 2005 and 2010, when female enrollment increased by 20 percent and male enrollment increased by 22 percent. However, between 2010 and 2014 both female and male enrollments decreased (by 5 percent and 3 percent, respectively). Between 2014 and 2025, female enrollment is projected to increase by 17 percent (from 9.7 million to 11.3 million students), and male enrollment is projected to increase by 11 percent (from 7.6 million to 8.4 million students).

Figure 2. Undergraduate enrollment in degree-granting postsecondary institutions, by race/ethnicity: Fall 2000–2014

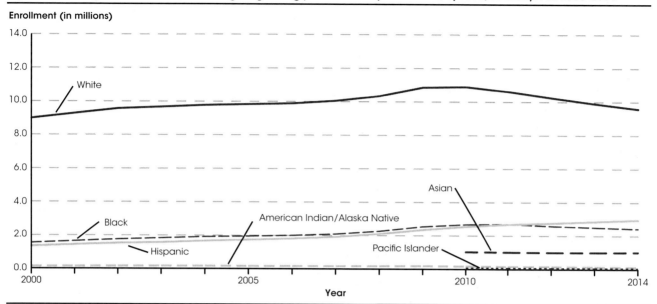

NOTE: Race categories exclude persons of Hispanic ethnicity. Prior to 2010, separate data on Asian and Pacific Islander students were not available. Data include unclassified undergraduate students. Degree-granting institutions grant associate's or higher degrees and participate in Title IV federal financial aid programs. Some data have been revised from previously published figures.
SOURCE: U.S. Department of Education, National Center for Education Statistics, Integrated Postsecondary Education Data System (IPEDS), Spring 2001 through Spring 2015, Fall Enrollment component. See *Digest of Education Statistics 2015*, table 306.10.

Of the 17.3 million undergraduate students in fall 2014, some 9.6 million were White, 3.0 million were Hispanic, 2.4 million were Black, 1.0 million were Asian, 0.1 million were American Indian/Alaska Native, and 0.1 million were Pacific Islander. Between 2000 and 2014, Hispanic enrollment more than doubled (a 119 percent increase from 1.4 million to 3.0 million students), Black enrollment increased by 57 percent (from 1.5 million

to 2.4 million students), and White enrollment increased by 7 percent (from 9.0 million to 9.6 million students). Despite the general increases, the number of undergraduate students was lower in 2014 than in 2010 for most groups; the exception was Hispanic students, whose enrollment increased by 16 percent during this period.

Figure 3. Actual and projected undergraduate enrollment in degree-granting postsecondary institutions, by attendance status: Fall 2000–2025

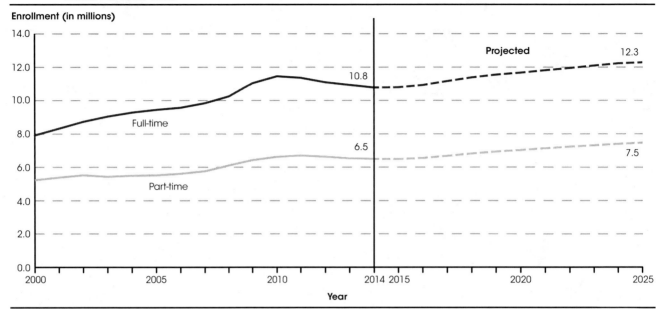

NOTE: Data include unclassified undergraduate students. Degree-granting institutions grant associate's or higher degrees and participate in Title IV federal financial aid programs. Projections are based on data through 2014. Some data have been revised from previously published figures.
SOURCE: U.S. Department of Education, National Center for Education Statistics, Integrated Postsecondary Education Data System (IPEDS), Spring 2001 through Spring 2015, Fall Enrollment component; and Enrollment in Degree-Granting Institutions Projection Model, 1980 through 2025. See *Digest of Education Statistics 2015*, table 303.70.

In fall 2014, there were 10.8 million full-time and 6.5 million part-time undergraduate students. Enrollment for both full- and part-time students has generally increased since 2000, particularly between 2000 and 2010, when full-time enrollment increased by 45 percent and part-time enrollment increased by 27 percent. However, full-time enrollment was 6 percent lower in 2014 than in 2010, and part-time enrollment was 2 percent lower in 2014 than in 2010. Between 2014 and 2025, full-time enrollment is projected to increase by 14 percent (from 10.8 million to 12.3 million students) and part-time enrollment is projected to increase by 15 percent (from 6.5 million to 7.5 million students).

Figure 4.   Undergraduate enrollment in degree-granting postsecondary institutions, by control of institution: Fall 2000–2014

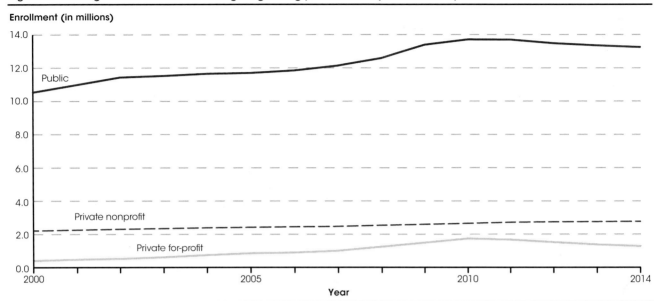

NOTE: Data include unclassified undergraduate students. Degree-granting institutions grant associate's or higher degrees and participate in Title IV federal financial aid programs. Some data have been revised from previously published figures.
SOURCE: U.S. Department of Education, National Center for Education Statistics, Integrated Postsecondary Education Data System (IPEDS), IPEDS Spring 2001 through Spring 2015, Fall Enrollment component. See *Digest of Education Statistics 2015*, table 303.70.

The increase in undergraduate enrollment from fall 2000 to fall 2014 occurred at a faster rate at private for-profit institutions (217 percent) than at public institutions (26 percent) and private nonprofit institutions (25 percent), although in 2000 undergraduate enrollment at private for-profit institutions was relatively small, at 0.4 million students. Enrollment at private for-profit institutions quadrupled from 0.4 million to 1.7 million students from 2000 to 2010. In comparison, enrollment increased by 30 percent at public institutions (from 10.5 million to 13.7 million students) and by 20 percent

at private nonprofit institutions (from 2.2 million to 2.7 million students) during this period. More recently, the pattern of enrollment at private for-profit institutions has changed. After reaching a peak in 2010, enrollment at private for-profit institutions decreased by 26 percent (from 1.7 million to 1.3 million students) between 2010 and 2014. In contrast, enrollment at public institutions decreased by 3 percent (from 13.7 million to 13.2 million students) during this period, while enrollment at private nonprofit institutions increased by 4 percent (from 2.7 million to 2.8 million students).

Figure 5. Actual and projected undergraduate enrollment in degree-granting postsecondary institutions, by level of institution: Fall 2000–2025

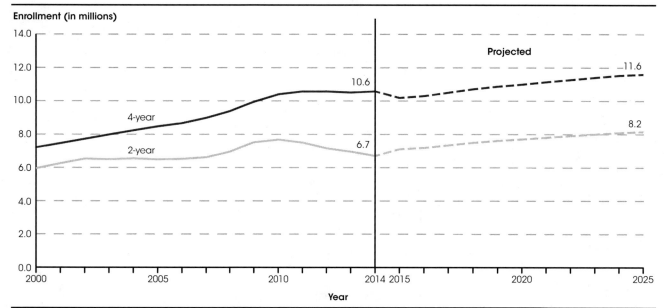

NOTE: Data include unclassified undergraduate students. Degree-granting institutions grant associate's or higher degrees and participate in Title IV federal financial aid programs. Projections are based on data through 2014. Some data have been revised from previously published figures.
SOURCE: U.S. Department of Education, National Center for Education Statistics, Integrated Postsecondary Education Data System (IPEDS), IPEDS Spring 2001 through Spring 2015, Fall Enrollment component; and Enrollment in Degree-Granting Institutions Projection Model, 1980 through 2025. See *Digest of Education Statistics 2015*, table 303.70.

In fall 2014, the 10.6 million students at 4-year institutions made up 61 percent of undergraduate enrollment; the remaining 39 percent (6.7 million students) were enrolled at 2-year institutions. Between 2000 and 2010, enrollment increased by 44 percent at 4-year institutions and by 29 percent at 2-year institutions. More recently, enrollment patterns have changed. Enrollment was 2 percent higher at 4-year institutions and 13 percent lower at 2-year institutions in 2014 than in 2010. Between 2010 and 2014, public

4-year institutions had the highest percentage increase in undergraduate enrollment (6 percent) among all types of institutions by control and level, and private for-profit 2-year institutions had the highest percentage decrease (34 percent). Between 2014 and 2025, enrollment at 2-year institutions is projected to increase by 21 percent to 8.2 million students, while enrollment at 4-year institutions is projected to increase by 10 percent to 11.6 million students.

Figure 6. Percentage of undergraduate students at degree-granting postsecondary institutions who enrolled exclusively in distance education courses, by control and level of institution: Fall 2014

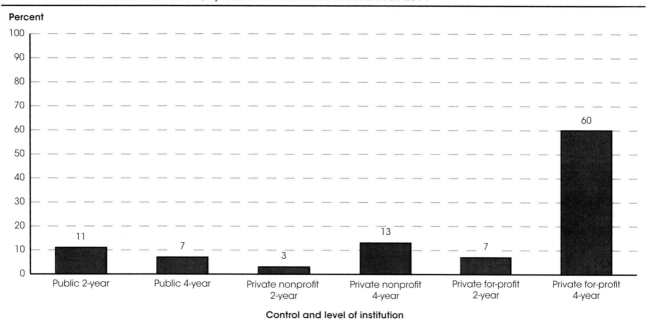

NOTE: Degree-granting institutions grant associate's or higher degrees and participate in Title IV federal financial aid programs. Distance education uses one or more technologies to deliver instruction to students who are separated from their instructor as well as to support regular and substantive interaction between students and instructors synchronously or asynchronously. Technologies used for instruction may include the following: Internet; one-way and two-way transmissions through open broadcasts, closed circuit, cable, microwave, broadband lines, fiber optics, satellite, or wireless communication devices; audio conferencing; and videocassettes, DVDs, and CD-ROMs, only if the videocassettes, DVDs, and CD-ROMs are used in a course in conjunction with the technologies listed above.
SOURCE: U.S. Department of Education, National Center for Education Statistics, Integrated Postsecondary Education Data System (IPEDS), Spring 2015, Fall Enrollment component. See *Digest of Education Statistics 2015*, table 311.15.

Distance education[1] courses and programs provide students with flexible learning opportunities. In fall 2014, nearly a quarter of undergraduate students (4.8 million) participated in distance education, with 2.1 million students, or 12 percent of total undergraduate enrollment, exclusively taking distance education courses. Of the 2.1 million undergraduate students who exclusively took distance education courses, 1.2 million students were enrolled at institutions located in the same state in which they resided, and 0.8 million were enrolled at institutions in a different state.

The percentage of undergraduate students enrolled exclusively in distance education courses differed by institutional control. In fall 2014, a higher percentage of students at private for-profit institutions (48 percent) exclusively took distance education courses than did students at private nonprofit institutions (13 percent) and public institutions (9 percent). In particular, a higher percentage of students at private for-profit 4-year institutions exclusively took distance education courses (60 percent) than did students at any other control and level of institution. (Percentages at these institutions ranged from 3 percent at private nonprofit 2-year institutions to 13 percent at private nonprofit 4-year institutions.)

Endnotes:

[1] Distance education uses one or more technologies to deliver instruction to students who are separated from their instructor as well as to support regular and substantive interaction between students and instructors synchronously or asynchronously. Technologies used for instruction may include the following: Internet; one-way and two-way transmissions through open broadcasts,

closed circuit, cable, microwave, broadband lines, fiber optics, satellite, or wireless communication devices; audio conferencing; and videocassettes, DVDs, and CD-ROMs, only if the videocassettes, DVDs, and CD-ROMs are used in a course in conjunction with the technologies listed above.

Reference tables: *Digest of Education Statistics 2015,* tables 303.70, 306.10, and 311.15

Related indicators: Enrollment Trends by Age, Postbaccalaureate Enrollment, Characteristics of Degree-Granting Postsecondary Institutions

Glossary: For-profit institution, Full-time enrollment, Higher education institutions, Nonprofit institution, Part-time enrollment, Private institution, Public school or institution, Undergraduate students

Postbaccalaureate Enrollment

Total enrollment in postbaccalaureate degree programs was 2.9 million students in fall 2014. Between 2014 and 2025, postbaccalaureate enrollment is projected to increase by 21 percent, to 3.5 million students.

In fall 2014, some 2.9 million students were enrolled in postbaccalaureate degree programs. Postbaccalaureate degree programs include master's and doctoral programs, as well as programs such as law, medicine, and dentistry. Postbaccalaureate enrollment increased by 36 percent between 2000 and 2010. More recently, the pattern of enrollment in postbaccalaureate degree programs has changed; postbaccalaureate enrollment was 1 percent lower in 2014 than in 2010. Between 2014 and 2025, postbaccalaureate enrollment is projected to increase by 21 percent, to 3.5 million students.

Figure 1. Actual and projected postbaccalaureate enrollment in degree-granting postsecondary institutions, by sex: Fall 2000–2025

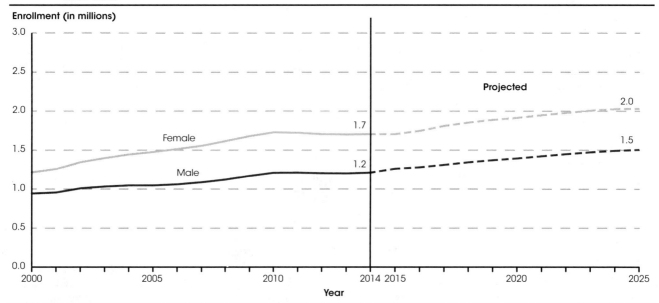

NOTE: Postbaccalaureate degree programs include master's and doctoral programs, as well as programs such as law, medicine, and dentistry. Degree-granting institutions grant associate's or higher degrees and participate in Title IV federal financial aid programs. Projections are based on data through 2014. Some data have been revised from previously published figures.
SOURCE: U.S. Department of Education, National Center for Education Statistics, Integrated Postsecondary Education Data System (IPEDS), Spring 2001 through Spring 2015, Fall Enrollment component; and Enrollment in Degree-Granting Institutions Projection Model, 1980 through 2025. See *Digest of Education Statistics 2015*, table 303.80.

In fall 2014, female students made up 58 percent of total postbaccalaureate enrollment, at 1.7 million, and male students made up 42 percent, at 1.2 million. Female enrollment has generally increased at a faster rate than male enrollment since 2000. For example, between 2000 and 2010, female enrollment increased by 42 percent, while male enrollment increased by 28 percent. However, female enrollment was 1 percent lower in 2014 than in 2010, while male enrollment was less than 1 percent higher in 2014 than in 2010. Between 2014 and 2025, male enrollment is projected to increase by 24 percent, from 1.2 million to 1.5 million students, while female enrollment is projected to increase by 19 percent, from 1.7 million to 2.0 million students.

Figure 2. Postbaccalaureate enrollment in degree-granting postsecondary institutions, by race/ethnicity: Fall 2000–2014

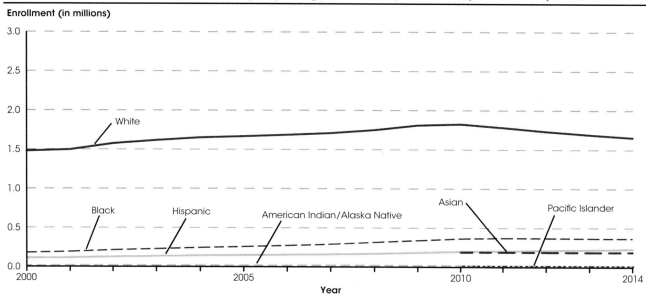

NOTE: Postbaccalaureate degree programs include master's and doctoral programs, as well as programs such as law, medicine, and dentistry. Race categories exclude persons of Hispanic ethnicity. Prior to 2010, separate data on Asian and Pacific Islander students were not available. Data include unclassified graduate students. Degree-granting institutions grant associate's or higher degrees and participate in Title IV federal financial aid programs. Some data have been revised from previously published figures.
SOURCE: U.S. Department of Education, National Center for Education Statistics, Integrated Postsecondary Education Data System (IPEDS), IPEDS Spring 2001 through Spring 2015, Fall Enrollment component. See *Digest of Education Statistics 2015*, table 306.10.

Of the 2.9 million postbaccalaureate students enrolled in fall 2014, some 1,656,000 were White, 366,000 were Black, 230,000 were Hispanic, 191,000 were Asian, 14,000 were American Indian/Alaska Native, and 7,000 were Pacific Islander. Between 2000 and 2014, both Black and Hispanic enrollment more than doubled, with Black enrollment increasing from 181,000 to 366,000 students and Hispanic enrollment increasing from 111,000 to 230,000 students. White enrollment was 12 percent

higher in 2014 than in 2000 (1.7 million vs. 1.5 million students) and American Indian/Alaska Native enrollment was 13 percent higher (14,000 vs. 13,000 students). More recently, the number of postbaccalaureate students was higher in 2014 than in 2010 for most groups; the exceptions were White and American Indian/Alaska Native students, whose enrollment decreased during this period.

Figure 3. Actual and projected postbaccalaureate enrollment in degree-granting postsecondary institutions, by attendance status: Fall 2000–2025

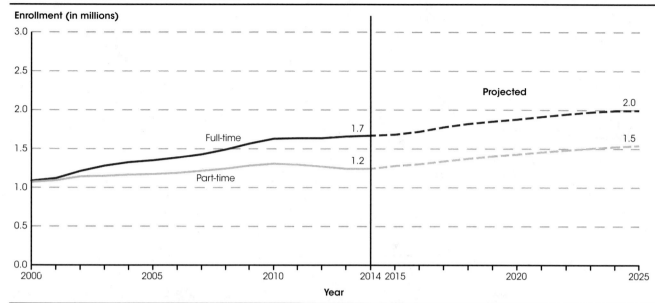

NOTE: Postbaccalaureate degree programs include master's and doctoral programs, as well as programs such as law, medicine, and dentistry. Degree-granting institutions grant associate's or higher degrees and participate in Title IV federal financial aid programs. Projections are based on data through 2014. Some data have been revised from previously published figures.
SOURCE: U.S. Department of Education, National Center for Education Statistics, Integrated Postsecondary Education Data System (IPEDS), IPEDS Spring 2001 through Spring 2015, Fall Enrollment component; and Enrollment in Degree-Granting Institutions Projection Model, 1980 through 2025. See *Digest of Education Statistics 2015*, table 303.80.

In fall 2014, there were 1.7 million full-time postbaccalaureate students and 1.2 million part-time students. Since 2000, full-time enrollment has increased at a faster rate (54 percent) than part-time enrollment (16 percent). Between 2000 and 2010, full-time enrollment increased by 50 percent, while part-time enrollment increased by 22 percent. More recently, between 2010 and 2014, full-time enrollment increased by 2 percent but part-time enrollment decreased by 5 percent. Between 2014 and 2025, however, part-time enrollment is projected to increase at a faster rate (24 percent) than full-time enrollment (19 percent).

Figure 4. Postbaccalaureate enrollment in degree-granting postsecondary institutions, by control of institution: Fall 2000–2014

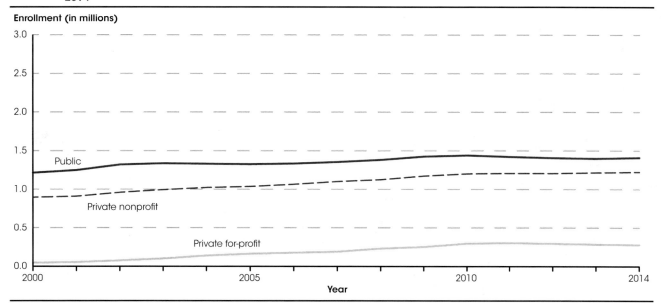

Enrollment (in millions)

NOTE: Postbaccalaureate degree programs include master's and doctoral programs, as well as programs such as law, medicine, and dentistry. Degree-granting institutions grant associate's or higher degrees and participate in Title IV federal financial aid programs. Some data have been revised from previously published figures.
SOURCE: U.S. Department of Education, National Center for Education Statistics, Integrated Postsecondary Education Data System (IPEDS), Spring 2001 through Spring 2015, Fall Enrollment component. See *Digest of Education Statistics 2015*, table 303.80.

From fall 2000 to fall 2014, postbaccalaureate enrollment grew at a faster rate at private for-profit institutions (an increase of 493 percent) than at private nonprofit institutions (an increase of 37 percent) and public institutions (an increase of 16 percent), although in 2000 enrollment at private for-profit institutions was relatively small, at 47,000 students. Between 2000 and 2010, postbaccalaureate enrollment increased by 528 percent at private for-profit institutions, while enrollment increased by 34 percent at private nonprofit institutions and by 19 percent at public institutions.

Figure 5. Percentage of postbaccalaureate students enrolled in degree-granting postsecondary institutions, by participation in distance education and control of institution: Fall 2014

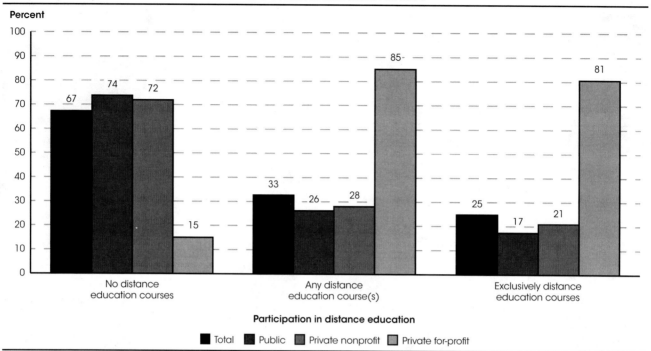

NOTE: Postbaccalaureate degree programs include master's and doctoral programs, as well as programs such as law, medicine, and dentistry. Distance education uses one or more technologies to deliver instruction to students who are separated from their instructor as well as to support regular and substantive interaction between students and the instructors synchronously or asynchronously. Technologies used for instruction may include the following: Internet; one-way and two-way transmissions through open broadcasts, closed circuit, cable, microwave, broadband lines, fiber optics, satellite, or wireless communication devices; audio conferencing; and videocassettes, DVDs, and CD-ROMs, only if the videocassettes, DVDs, and CD-ROMs are used in a course in conjunction with the technologies listed above. Degree-granting institutions grant associate's or higher degrees and participate in Title IV federal financial aid programs.
SOURCE: U.S. Department of Education, National Center for Education Statistics, Integrated Postsecondary Education Data System (IPEDS), Spring 2015, Fall Enrollment component. See *Digest of Education Statistics 2015*, table 311.15.

Distance education[1] courses and programs provide flexible learning opportunities to postbaccalaureate students. In fall 2014, one third (33 percent) of total postbaccalaureate students (953,000) participated in distance education, with one quarter (25 percent) of total postbaccalaureate students (726,000) exclusively taking distance education courses.[2] Of the 726,000 students who exclusively took distance education courses, 298,000 were enrolled at institutions located in the same state in which they resided, and 383,000 were enrolled at institutions in a different state.

The percentage of postbaccalaureate students enrolled exclusively in distance education courses differed by institutional control. In fall 2014, the percentage of students who exclusively took distance education courses was higher for those enrolled at private for-profit institutions (81 percent) than for those at private nonprofit (21 percent) and public (17 percent) institutions. The percentage of students who did not take any distance education courses was higher for those enrolled at public (74 percent) and private nonprofit (72 percent) institutions than for those at private for-profit institutions (15 percent).

Endnotes:
[1] Distance education uses one or more technologies to deliver instruction to students who are separated from their instructors as well as to support regular and substantive interaction between students and instructors synchronously or asynchronously. Technologies used for instruction may include the following: Internet; one-way and two-way transmissions through open broadcasts, closed circuit, cable, microwave, broadband lines, fiber optics, satellite,

or wireless communication devices; audio conferencing; and videocassettes, DVDs, and CD-ROMs, only if the videocassettes, DVDs, and CD-ROMs are used in a course in conjunction with the technologies listed above.
[2] In comparison, 12 percent of undergraduate students exclusively took distance education courses (see the Undergraduate Enrollment indicator).

Reference tables: *Digest of Education Statistics 2015*, tables 303.80, 306.10, and 311.15

Related indicators: Enrollment Trends by Age, Undergraduate Enrollment, College Participation Rates, Characteristics of Degree-Granting Postsecondary Institutions

Glossary: Control of institutions, Distance education, Enrollment, For-profit institution, Full-time enrollment, Nonprofit institution, Part-time enrollment, Postbaccalaureate enrollment, Private institution, Public school or institution, Racial/ethnic group

This page intentionally left blank.

The indicators in this chapter of *The Condition of Education* measure aspects of elementary and secondary education in the United States. The indicators examine school characteristics and climate; principals, teachers and staff; elementary and secondary financial resources; student assessments; and other measures of the progress students make as they move through the education system, such as graduation rates.

In this chapter, particular attention is given to how various subgroups in the population proceed through school and attain different levels of education, as well as the factors that are associated with their progress along the way. The indicators on student achievement illustrate how students are performing on assessments in reading, mathematics, science, and other academic subject areas. Other indicators describe aspects of the context of learning in elementary and secondary schools.

This chapter's indicators, as well as additional indicators on elementary and secondary education, are available at *The Condition of Education* website: http://nces.ed.gov/programs/coe.

Chapter 3

Elementary and Secondary Education

Characteristics of Traditional Public and Public Charter Schools

High-poverty schools, in which more than 75 percent of the students qualify for free or reduced-price lunch under the National School Lunch Program, accounted for 25 percent of all public schools in 2013–14. In that year, 24 percent of traditional public schools were high-poverty, compared with 39 percent of charter schools.

In school year 2013–14, there were 98,270 public schools in the United States, including 91,810 traditional public schools and 6,470 charter schools. The total number of schools was higher in 2013–14 than in 2003–04, when there was a total of 95,730 public schools, including 92,750 traditional public schools and 2,980 charter schools. Between school years 2003–04 and 2013–14, the percentage of all public schools that were charter schools increased from 3 to 7 percent, while the percentage that were traditional public schools decreased from 97 to 93 percent. Between 2012–13 and 2013–14, the number of charter schools increased by 390 while the number of traditional public schools decreased by 570. See the Charter School Enrollment indicator for a description of charter schools and charter school legislation.

Figure 1. Percentage distribution of traditional public schools and charter schools, by school level: School year 2013–14

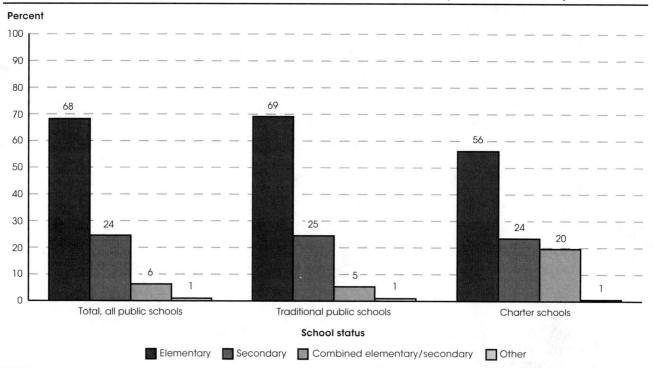

NOTE: "Elementary" includes schools beginning with grade 6 or below and with no grade higher than 8. "Secondary" includes schools with no grade lower than 7. "Combined elementary/secondary" includes schools beginning with grade 6 or below and ending with grade 9 or above. "Other" includes schools not classified by grade span. Detail may not sum to 100 percent because of rounding.
SOURCE: U.S. Department of Education, National Center for Education Statistics, Common Core of Data (CCD), "Public Elementary/Secondary School Universe Survey," 2013-14. See *Digest of Education Statistics 2015*, table 216.30.

Over two-thirds of traditional public schools (69 percent) were elementary schools in 2013–14, versus 56 percent of charter schools. By contrast, 20 percent of charter schools in 2013–14 were combined elementary/secondary schools (schools beginning with grade 6 or below and ending with grade 9 or above), compared with 5 percent of traditional public schools.

Figure 2. Percentage of traditional public schools and charter schools, by racial/ethnic concentration: School years 2003–04 and 2013–14

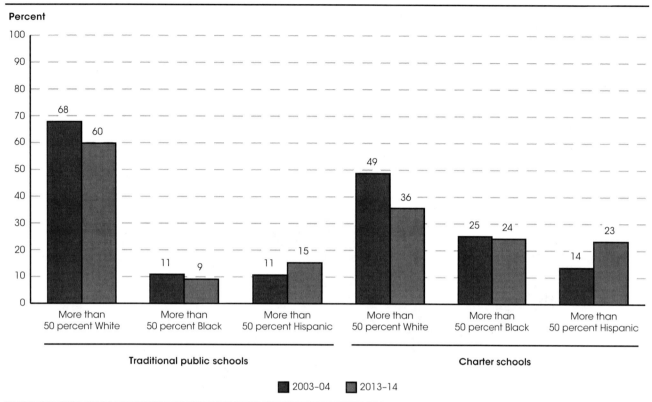

NOTE: Race categories exclude persons of Hispanic ethnicity.
SOURCE: U.S. Department of Education, National Center for Education Statistics, Common Core of Data (CCD), "Public Elementary/Secondary School Universe Survey," 2003–04 and 2013–14. See *Digest of Education Statistics 2015*, table 216.30.

In 2013–14, in a majority (60 percent) of traditional public schools more than half of the students were White, while in 9 percent more than half of the students were Black and in 15 percent more than half of the students were Hispanic. In comparison, 36 percent of charter schools had more than 50 percent White enrollment, 24 percent had more than 50 percent Black enrollment, and 23 percent had more than 50 percent Hispanic enrollment. For both traditional public and public charter schools, the percentages of schools that had more than

50 percent White enrollment or more than 50 percent Black enrollment were lower in 2013–14 than in 2003–04, while the percentage of schools that had more than 50 percent Hispanic enrollment was higher in 2013–14 than in 2003–04. These shifts reflect, in part, changes in student demographics overall. Between 2004 and 2014, the percentage of children ages 5 to 17 who were White decreased from 59 to 53 percent, the percentage who were Black decreased from 15 to 14 percent, and the percentage who were Hispanic increased from 18 to 24 percent.

Figure 3. Percentage of traditional public schools and charter schools, by percentage of students eligible for free or reduced-price lunch: School year 2013–14

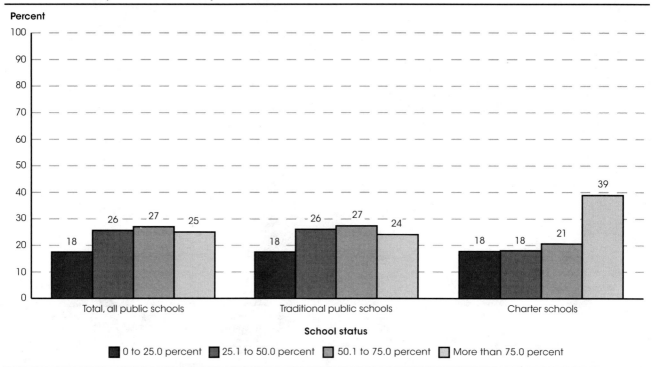

NOTE: The category "missing/school does not participate" is not included in this figure; thus, the sum of the free or reduced-price lunch eligible categories does not equal 100 percent. The National School Lunch Program is a federally assisted meal program. To be eligible for free lunch under the program, a student must be from a household with an income at or below 130 percent of the poverty threshold; to be eligible for reduced-price lunch, a student must be from a household with an income between 130 percent and 185 percent of the poverty threshold.
SOURCE: U.S. Department of Education, National Center for Education Statistics, Common Core of Data (CCD), "Public Elementary/Secondary School Universe Survey," 2013–14. See *Digest of Education Statistics 2015*, table 216.30.

High-poverty schools, in which more than 75 percent of the students qualify for free or reduced-price lunch under the National School Lunch Program, accounted for 25 percent of all public schools in 2013–14. In that year, 24 percent of traditional public schools were high-poverty, compared with 39 percent of charter schools.

Figure 4. Percentage distribution of traditional public schools and charter schools, by school locale and region: School year 2013–14

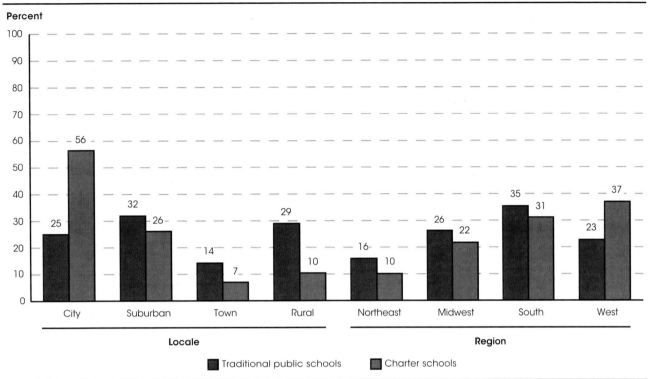

NOTE: Detail may not sum to totals due to rounding.
SOURCE: U.S. Department of Education, National Center for Education Statistics, Common Core of Data (CCD), "Public Elementary/Secondary School Universe Survey," 2013–14. See *Digest of Education Statistics 2015*, table 216.30.

In school year 2013–14, the majority of charter schools (56 percent) were in cities, compared with 25 percent of traditional public schools. In contrast, 10 percent of charter schools were in rural areas, compared with 29 percent of traditional public schools.

Regionally, the highest percentage of traditional public schools in 2013–14 was in the South (35 percent),

followed by the Midwest (26 percent), the West (23 percent), and the Northeast (16 percent). Charter schools followed a different pattern. In 2013–14, some 31 percent of charter schools were in the South, 22 percent were in the Midwest, 37 percent were in the West, and 10 percent were in the Northeast.

Reference tables: *Digest of Education Statistics 2015*, tables 101.20, 216.20, and 216.30
Related indicators: Public School Enrollment, Charter School Enrollment, Racial/Ethnic Enrollment in Public Schools, Concentration of Public School Students Eligible for Free or Reduced-Price Lunch

Glossary: Charter school, Combined school, Elementary school, Enrollment, Free or reduced-price lunch, Geographic region, Locale codes, National School Lunch Program, Private school, Public school or institution, Racial/ethnic group, Secondary school, Traditional public school

Concentration of Public School Students Eligible for Free or Reduced-Price Lunch

In school year 2012–13, higher percentages of Black, Hispanic, and American Indian/Alaska Native students attended high-poverty public schools than did Pacific Islander students, students of Two or more races, Asian students, and White students (ordered by descending percentages).

The percentage of students eligible for free or reduced-price lunch (FRPL) under the National School Lunch Program provides a proxy measure for the concentration of low-income students within a school. Children from families with incomes at or below 130 percent of the poverty level are eligible for free meals. Those from families with incomes that are between 130 percent and 185 percent of the poverty level are eligible for reduced-price meals. In this indicator, public schools (including both traditional and charter) are divided into categories by FRPL eligibility. High-poverty schools are defined

as public schools where more than 75.0 percent of the students are eligible for FRPL, and mid-high poverty schools are those schools where 50.1 to 75.0 percent of the students are eligible for FRPL. Low-poverty schools are defined as public schools where 25.0 percent or less of the students are eligible for FRPL, and mid-low poverty schools are those schools where 25.1 to 50.0 percent of the students are eligible for FRPL. In school year 2012–13, some 21 percent of public school students attended low-poverty schools, and 24 percent of public school students attended high-poverty schools.

Figure 1.   Percentage of public school students in low-poverty and high-poverty schools, by race/ethnicity: School year 2012–13

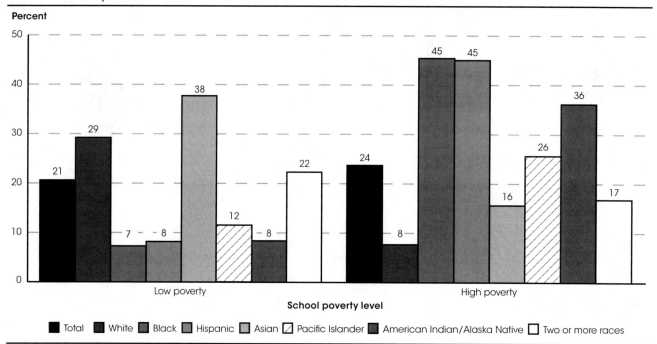

NOTE: High-poverty schools are defined as public schools where more than 75.0 percent of the students are eligible for free or reduced-price lunch (FRPL), and low-poverty schools are defined as public schools where 25.0 percent or less of the students are eligible for FRPL. Race categories exclude persons of Hispanic ethnicity.
SOURCE: U.S. Department of Education, National Center for Education Statistics, Common Core of Data (CCD), "Public Elementary/Secondary School Universe Survey," 2012–13. See *Digest of Education Statistics 2014*, table 216.60.

The percentages of students in low-poverty and high-poverty schools varied by race/ethnicity. In school year 2012–13, higher percentages of Asian students (38 percent), White students (29 percent), and students of Two or more races (22 percent) attended low-poverty public schools than did Pacific Islander (12 percent), American Indian/Alaska Native (8 percent), Hispanic

(8 percent), and Black (7 percent) students. In contrast, higher percentages of Black (45 percent), Hispanic (45 percent), and American Indian/Alaska Native (36 percent) students attended high-poverty public schools than did Pacific Islander students (26 percent), students of Two or more races (17 percent), Asian students (16 percent), and White students (8 percent).

Figure 2. Percentage of public school students, by school poverty level and school locale: School year 2012–13

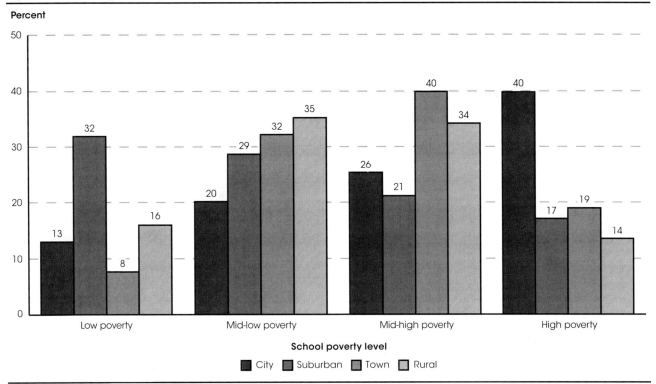

Percent

School poverty level

■ City ■ Suburban ■ Town ■ Rural

NOTE: This figure does not include schools for which information on free or reduced-price lunch (FRPL) is missing or schools that did not participate in the National School Lunch Program (NSLP). The NSLP is a federally assisted meal program. To be eligible for free lunch under the program, a student must be from a household with an income at or below 130 percent of the poverty threshold; to be eligible for reduced-price lunch, a student must be from a household with an income between 130 percent and 185 percent of the poverty threshold. High-poverty schools are defined as public schools where more than 75.0 percent of the students are eligible for FRPL, and mid-high poverty schools are those schools where 50.1 to 75.0 percent of the students are eligible for FRPL. Low-poverty schools are defined as public schools where 25.0 percent or less of the students are eligible for FRPL, and mid-low poverty schools are those schools where 25.1 to 50.0 percent of the students are eligible for FRPL. Detail may not sum to totals because of rounding.
SOURCE: U.S. Department of Education, National Center for Education Statistics, Common Core of Data (CCD), "Public Elementary/Secondary School Universe Survey," 2012–13. See *Digest of Education Statistics 2014*, table 216.60.

The distribution of schools at different poverty concentrations varied by school locale (i.e., city, suburb, town, or rural). In school year 2012–13, some 40 percent of students attending city schools were in a high-poverty school, compared with 14 percent of students attending rural schools, 17 percent of students attending suburban schools, and 19 percent of students attending town schools. In contrast, the percentage of students attending suburban schools who were in a low-poverty school (32 percent) was about four times as large as the corresponding percentage of students attending town schools (8 percent). The percentage of students attending suburban schools who were in a low-poverty school was also higher than the percentages of students attending city and rural schools who were in a low-poverty school (13 and 16 percent, respectively). In addition, a majority (65 percent) of students attending city schools were in a high-poverty or mid-high poverty school while a majority (61 percent) of students attending suburban schools were in a low-poverty or mid-low poverty school.

Reference tables: *Digest of Education Statistics 2014*, tables 216.30 and 216.60; *Digest of Education Statistics 2013*, table 216.30

Related indicators: Family Characteristics of School-Age Children

Glossary: Free or reduced-price lunch, Locale codes, National School Lunch Program, Poverty (official measure), Public school or institution, Racial/ethnic group

School Crime and Safety

Through nearly two decades of decline, the rate of nonfatal victimization of 12- to 18-year-old students at school fell from 181 victimizations per 1,000 students in 1992 to 33 per 1,000 students in 2014. The rate of nonfatal victimization of these students occurring away from school also declined from 173 to 24 victimizations per 1,000 students during the same period.

Between 1992 and 2014, the rates of total nonfatal victimization of 12- to 18-year-old students declined both at school[1] and away from school. During these years, the rates of theft, violent crime, and serious violent crime—subsets of total nonfatal victimization—against 12- to 18-year-old students also generally declined. Nonfatal victimizations include theft and all violent crime. Violent crime includes serious violent crime (rape, sexual assault, robbery, and aggravated assault) and simple assault.

Figure 1. Rate of nonfatal victimization per 1,000 students ages 12–18, by type of victimization and location: 1992 through 2014

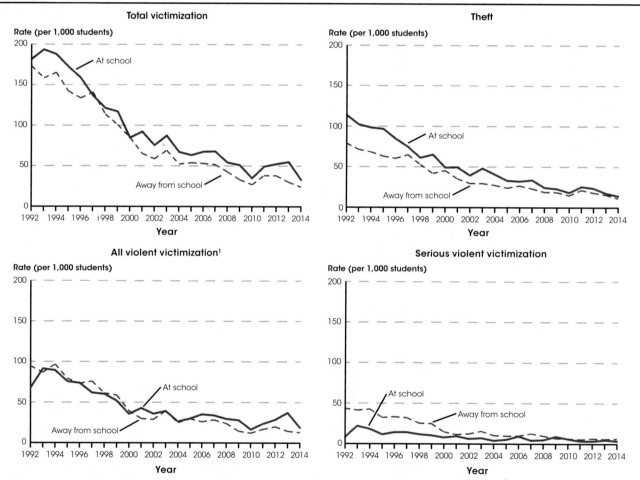

[1] Violent victimization includes serious violent victimization.
NOTE: "Total victimization" includes theft and violent crimes. "Theft" includes attempted and completed purse-snatching, completed pickpocketing, and all attempted and completed thefts, with the exception of motor vehicle thefts. "Theft" does not include robbery, which involves the threat or use of force and is classified as a serious violent crime. "All violent victimization" includes serious violent crimes as well as simple assault. "Serious violent victimization" includes the crimes of rape, sexual assault, robbery, and aggravated assault. "At school" includes inside the school building, on school property, or on the way to or from school. Due to methodological differences, use caution when comparing 2006 estimates to other years.
SOURCE: U.S. Department of Justice, Bureau of Justice Statistics, National Crime Victimization Survey (NCVS), 1992–2014. See *Digest of Education Statistics 2015*, table 228.20.

In 2014, students ages 12–18 reported 850,000 victimizations (theft and violent crime) at school and 621,000 victimizations away from school. These figures translate to total nonfatal victimization rates of 33 victimizations per 1,000 students at school and 24 per 1,000 students away from school; these rates were not measurably different. From 1992 to 2014, the rate of nonfatal victimization of students at school declined from 181 to 33 victimizations per 1,000 students. The rate of nonfatal victimization of students away from school also declined, from 173 to 24 victimizations per 1,000 students.

Between 1992 and 2014, the rate of theft against students ages 12–18 at school declined (from 114 to 14 thefts per 1,000 students), as did the rate away from school (from 79 to 11 thefts per 1,000 students). Thus, the difference between the theft rates was 35 thefts per 1,000 students in 1992. In 2014, there was no measurable difference between these rates.

Rates of nonfatal violent victimization of 12- to 18-year-old students also decreased both at and away from school between 1992 and 2014. During this period, there was a decline in the rate of violent victimization at school (from 68 to 19 violent victimizations per 1,000 students) as well as away from school (from 94 to 13 violent victimizations per 1,000). In 1992, more violent victimizations occurred away from school (94 per 1,000 students) than at school (68 per 1,000 students); in 2014 the rate of occurrence at school did not differ measurably from the rate of occurrence away from school.

The rate of nonfatal serious violent victimization of students ages 12–18 at school in 2014 was lower than the rate in 1992 (4 serious violent victimizations at school per 1,000 students in 2014, compared with 8 per 1,000 students in 1992). The rate of serious violent victimization away from school decreased from 43 to 6 victimizations per 1,000 students between 1992 and 2014. The difference between rates of serious violent victimization at school and away from school also narrowed over the past two decades. There were 35 more serious violent victimizations per 1,000 students away from school than at school in 1992; there was no measurable difference between the rates of these victimizations at school and away from school in 2014.

Figure 2. Rate of nonfatal victimization per 1,000 students ages 12–18 at and away from school, by type of victimization and age: 2014

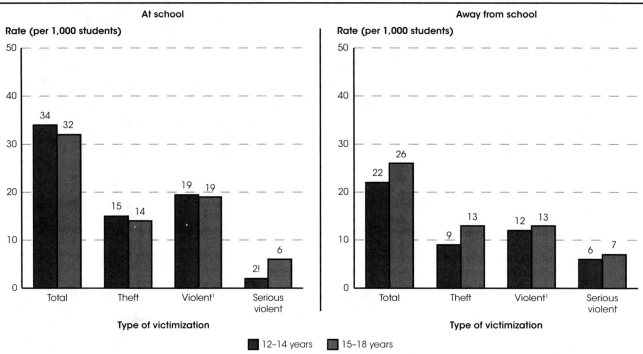

! Interpret with caution. The coefficient of variation (CV) for this estimate is between 30 and 50 percent.
[1] Violent victimization includes serious violent victimization.
NOTE: "Total victimization" includes theft and violent crimes. "Theft" includes attempted and completed purse-snatching, completed pickpocketing, and all attempted and completed thefts, with the exception of motor vehicle thefts. "Theft" does not include robbery, which involves the threat or use of force and is classified as a serious violent crime. "Violent victimization" includes serious violent crimes as well as simple assault. "Serious violent victimization" includes the crimes of rape, sexual assault, robbery, and aggravated assault. "At school" includes inside the school building, on school property, or on the way to or from school. Detail may not sum to totals because of rounding.
SOURCE: U.S. Department of Justice, Bureau of Justice Statistics, National Crime Victimization Survey (NCVS), 2014. See *Digest of Education Statistics 2015*, table 228.25.

For the most part, the rates of nonfatal victimization for 12- to 18-year-old students in 2014 did not measurably differ by sex or age group. Both at school and away from school, the rates of total nonfatal victimization, theft, violent victimization, and serious violent victimization did not measurably differ between males and females in 2014. However, the rate of serious violent victimization at school was lower for students ages 12–14 (2 per 1,000 students) than for students ages 15–18 (6 per 1,000 students). The rates of violent victimization and theft occurring at school did not differ measurably by age group, nor did the rates of theft, violent victimization, and serious violent victimization occurring away from school.

Figure 3. Percentage of public schools that used selected safety and security measures: 1999–2000, 2009–10, and 2013–14

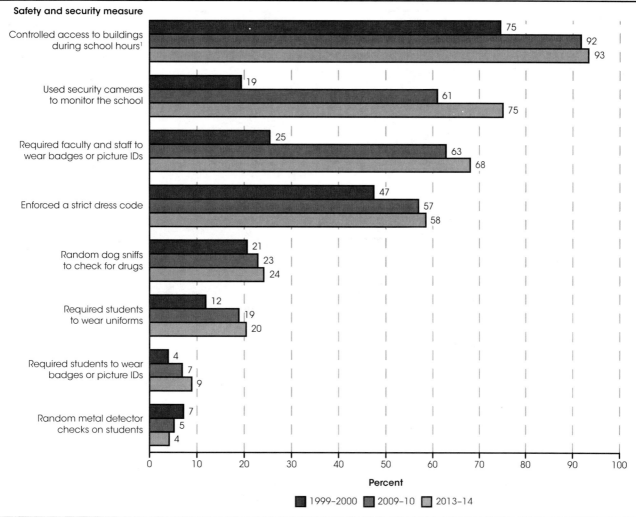

Safety and security measure

Controlled access to buildings during school hours[1]: 75, 92, 93

Used security cameras to monitor the school: 19, 61, 75

Required faculty and staff to wear badges or picture IDs: 25, 63, 68

Enforced a strict dress code: 47, 57, 58

Random dog sniffs to check for drugs: 21, 23, 24

Required students to wear uniforms: 12, 19, 20

Required students to wear badges or picture IDs: 4, 7, 9

Random metal detector checks on students: 7, 5, 4

Percent

■ 1999–2000   ▨ 2009–10   ▢ 2013–14

[1] For example, locked or monitored doors.
NOTE: Data for 2013–14 were collected using the Fast Response Survey System, while data for earlier years were collected using the School Survey on Crime and Safety (SSOCS). The 2013–14 survey was designed to allow comparisons with SSOCS data. However, respondents to the 2013–14 survey could choose either to complete the survey on paper (and mail it back) or to complete the survey online, whereas respondents to SSOCS did not have the option of completing the survey online. The 2013–14 survey also relied on a smaller sample. The smaller sample size and change in survey administration may have impacted 2013–14 results.
SOURCE: U.S. Department of Education, National Center for Education Statistics, 1999–2000 and 2009–10 School Survey on Crime and Safety (SSOCS), 2000 and 2010; Fast Response Survey System (FRSS), "School Safety and Discipline: 2013–14," FRSS 106, 2014. See *Digest of Education Statistics 2015*, table 233.50.

Schools use a variety of practices and procedures to promote the safety of students, faculty, and staff. Certain practices, such as locking or monitoring doors and gates, are intended to limit or control access to school campuses, while others, such as the use of metal detectors and security cameras, are intended to monitor or restrict students' and visitors' behavior on campus. The percentages of public schools reporting the use of various safety and security measures tended to be higher in 2013–14 than in prior years. For example, the percentage of public schools reporting the use of security cameras increased from 19 percent in 1999–2000 to 75 percent

in 2013–14. Similarly, the percentage of public schools reporting that they controlled access to school buildings increased from 75 percent to 93 percent during this time. From 1999–2000 to 2013–14, use of the following safety and security measures also increased: requiring faculty and staff to wear badges or picture IDs, enforcing a strict dress code, using random dog sniffs, requiring school uniforms, and requiring students to wear badges or picture IDs. Conversely, the percentage of schools that reported using random metal detector checks decreased from 7 percent in 1999–2000 to 4 percent in 2013–14.

Figure 4. Percentage of public schools with one or more full-time or part-time security staff present at least once a week, by employment status: Selected years 2005–06 through 2013–14

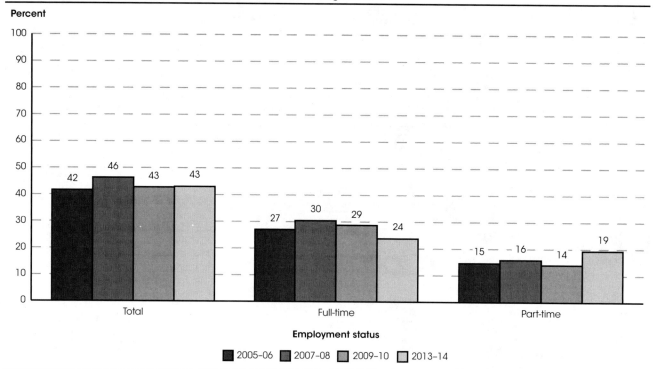

NOTE: Data for 2013–14 were collected using the Fast Response Survey System, while data for earlier years were collected using the School Survey on Crime and Safety (SSOCS). The 2013–14 survey was designed to allow comparisons with SSOCS data. However, respondents to the 2013–14 survey could choose either to complete the survey on paper (and mail it back) or to complete the survey online, whereas respondents to SSOCS did not have the option of completing the survey online. The 2013–14 survey also relied on a smaller sample. The smaller sample size and change in survey administration may have impacted 2013–14 results. Detail may not sum to totals because of rounding.
SOURCE: U.S. Department of Education, National Center for Education Statistics, 2005–06, 2007–08, and 2009–10 School Survey on Crime and Safety (SSOCS), 2006, 2008, and 2010; Fast Response Survey System (FRSS), "School Safety and Discipline: 2013–14," FRSS 106, 2014. See *Digest of Education Statistics 2015*, table 233.70.

In the 2013–14 school year, 43 percent of public schools reported the presence of one or more security guards, security personnel, School Resource Officers (SROs), or sworn law enforcement officers who were not SROs at their school at least once a week during the school year.[2] The percentage of public schools reporting the presence of any security staff in 2013–14 was not measurably different than in 2005–06, 2007–08, and 2009–10. However, the percentage of public schools reporting the presence of full-time security staff was lower in 2013–14 (24 percent) than in prior years, while the percentage of public schools reporting part-time only security staff in 2013–14 (19 percent) was higher than it was in prior years.

Endnotes:

[1] At school includes inside the school building, on school property, or on the way to or from school.
[2] Security guards or security personnel do not include law enforcement. School Resource Officers include all career law enforcement officers with arrest authority who have specialized training and are assigned to work in collaboration with school organizations.

Reference tables: *Digest of Education Statistics 2015*, tables 228.20, 228.25, 233.50, and 233.70

Glossary: Public school or institution

This page intentionally left blank.

Teachers and Pupil/Teacher Ratios

Of the 6.2 million staff members in public elementary and secondary schools in fall 2013, half (3.1 million) were teachers. The pupil/teacher ratio in public schools declined from 15.9 in 2003 to 15.3 in 2008. In the years after 2008, the pupil/teacher ratio rose, reaching 16.1 in 2013.

Of the 6.2 million staff members in public elementary and secondary schools in fall 2013, half (3.1 million) were teachers. There were 738,000 instructional aides, such as teachers' assistants, who made up another 12 percent of total staff. The percentages of public school staff have changed little in recent years. For example, between fall 2003 and fall 2013 the percentage of staff members who were teachers decreased 1 percentage point (from 51 to 50 percent), and the percentage of staff members who were instructional aides over this period increased less than 1 percentage point to 12 percent in 2013. By comparison, in fall 1969 teachers represented 60 percent of public school staff, and instructional aides represented 2 percent of public school staff.

Figure 1.   Teachers as a percentage of staff in public elementary and secondary school systems, by state: Fall 2013

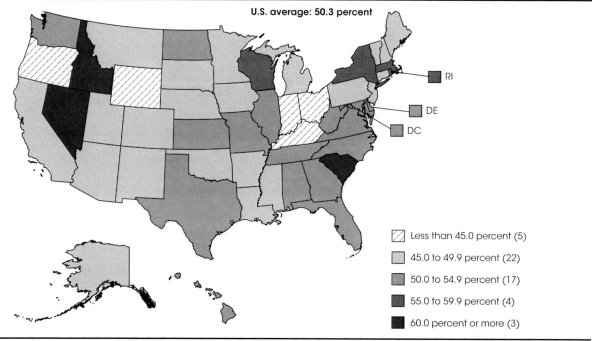

U.S. average: 50.3 percent

RI
DE
DC

Less than 45.0 percent (5)
45.0 to 49.9 percent (22)
50.0 to 54.9 percent (17)
55.0 to 59.9 percent (4)
60.0 percent or more (3)

NOTE: The U.S. average includes imputations for underreporting and nonreporting states. The calculations of teachers as a percentage of staff for Alaska, California, Idaho, Illinois, Montana, Nevada, New Jersey, Pennsylvania, and West Virginia include imputations to correct for underreporting.
SOURCE: U.S. Department of Education, National Center for Education Statistics, Common Core of Data (CCD), "State Nonfiscal Survey of Public Elementary/ Secondary Education," 2013–14. See *Digest of Education Statistics 2015*, table 213.40.

Teachers constituted between 45 and 55 percent of public school staff in 38 states and the District of Columbia in 2013. There were, however, five states where teachers made up less than 45 percent of public school staff (Indiana, Ohio, Kentucky, Wyoming, and Oregon) and seven states where teachers made up more than 55 percent of public school staff (Massachusetts, Wisconsin, Rhode Island, New York, Idaho, Nevada, and South Carolina).

Figure 2. Public and private elementary and secondary school pupil/teacher ratios: Fall 2003 through fall 2013

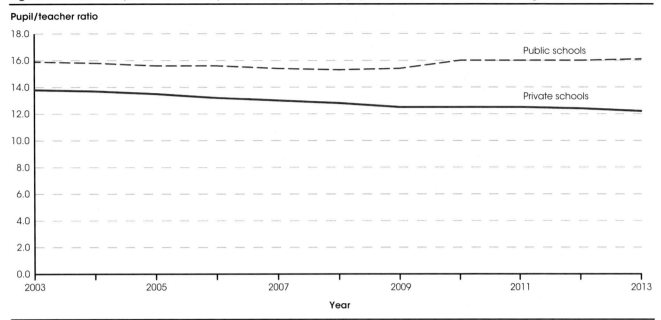

NOTE: Data for teachers are expressed in full-time equivalents (FTEs). Data for public schools include prekindergarten through grade 12. Data for private schools include prekindergarten through grade 12 in schools offering kindergarten or higher grades. The pupil/teacher ratio includes teachers for students with disabilities and other special teachers. Ratios for public schools reflect totals reported by states and differ from totals reported by schools or school districts. Some data have been revised from previously published figures.
SOURCE: U.S. Department of Education, National Center for Education Statistics, Common Core of Data (CCD), "State Nonfiscal Survey of Public Elementary/Secondary Education," 2003–04 through 2013–14; and Private School Universe Survey (PSS), 2003–04 through 2013–14. See *Digest of Education Statistics 2015*, table 208.20.

The number of students per teacher, or the pupil/teacher ratio,[1] has generally been decreasing over more than 50 years at both public and private schools. In fall 1955, there were 1.1 million public and 145,000 private elementary and secondary school teachers in the United States. By fall 2013, these numbers had nearly tripled to 3.1 million for public school teachers and to 441,000 for private school teachers. However, increases in student enrollment were proportionally smaller over this period: from 30.7 million to 50.0 million public school students (a 63 percent increase) and from 4.6 million to 5.4 million private school students (a 17 percent increase). For public schools, the pupil/teacher ratio fell from 26.9 in 1955 to 15.9 in 2003. The ratio continued this decline until 2008, when it dropped to 15.3. In the years after 2008, the pupil/teacher ratio rose, reaching 16.1 in 2013. The private school pupil/teacher ratio decreased more steeply (from 31.7 to 12.2 students per teacher) between 1955 and 2013 than did the public school ratio. The pupil/teacher ratio has been lower for private schools than for public schools since 1972.

Figure 3. Percentage of public elementary and secondary school teachers who had less than 2 years of teaching experience, by state: 2011–12

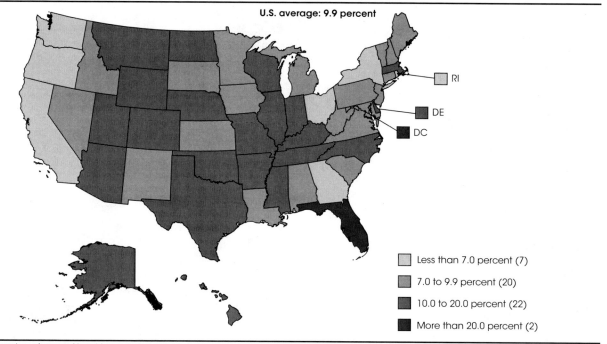

U.S. average: 9.9 percent

Less than 7.0 percent (7)

7.0 to 9.9 percent (20)

10.0 to 20.0 percent (22)

More than 20.0 percent (2)

NOTE: The number of years of teaching experience includes the current year and any prior years teaching in any school, subject, or grade. Does not include any student teaching or other similar preparation experiences.
SOURCE: U.S. Department of Education, Office for Civil Rights, Civil Rights Data Collection, "2011–12 Classroom Teachers Estimations." See *Digest of Education Statistics 2015*, table 209.25.

The Civil Rights Data Collection reports information on years of teaching experience for all public elementary and secondary school teachers. Of the 3.1 million public school teachers in 2011–12, some 310,300 teachers, or 10 percent, had less than 2 years of teaching experience. In 42 states, between 7 and 20 percent of public school teachers had less than 2 years of teaching experience. However, in seven states (Rhode Island, Washington, Oregon, New York, Ohio, California, and Georgia), less than 7 percent of public school teachers had less than 2 years of teaching experience, and in Florida and the District of Columbia, more than 20 percent of public school teachers had less than 2 years of teaching experience. While 6 percent of public school teachers overall were in their first year of teaching in 2011–12,

the percentages of first-year teachers that year ranged from 2 percent in Pennsylvania to 19 percent in Florida.

Data on public school teachers' licensing and certification are also available from the Civil Rights Data Collection. Overall, 97 percent of public elementary and secondary school teachers in 2011–12 met all licensing certification requirements of the state in which they taught. In 20 states, more than 99 percent of public school teachers in 2011–12 met all state licensing certification requirements. In another 18 states, between 97 and 99 percent of public school teachers met all state licensing certification requirements. However, in Florida and the District of Columbia, less than 90 percent of teachers met all state licensing certification requirements.

Endnotes:
[1] The pupil/teacher ratio measures the number of students per teacher. It reflects teacher workload and the availability of teachers' services to their students. The lower the pupil/teacher ratio, the higher the availability of teacher services to students. The pupil/teacher ratio is not the same as class size, however. Class size can be described as the

number of students a teacher faces during a given period of instruction. The relationship between these two measures of teacher workload is affected by a variety of factors, including the number of classes a teacher is responsible for and the number of classes taken by students.

Reference tables: *Digest of Education Statistics 2015*, tables 208.20, 209.25, 213.10, 213.40

Related indicators: Public School Enrollment, Private School Enrollment

Glossary: Elementary school, Private school, Public school or institution, Pupil/teacher ratio, Secondary school

This page intentionally left blank.

Public School Revenue Sources

From school years 2002-03 through 2012-13, total elementary and secondary public school revenues increased from $572 billion to $618 billion (in constant dollars). From 2011-12 through 2012-13, total revenues for public elementary and secondary schools decreased by $4 billion, or 1 percent.

From school years 2002–03 through 2012–13, total elementary and secondary public school revenues increased from $572 billion to $618 billion (in constant 2014–15 dollars), an 8 percent increase, adjusting for inflation using the Consumer Price Index (CPI).[1] This

increase was accompanied by a 3 percent increase in total elementary and secondary public school enrollment, from 48 million students in 2002–03 to 50 million students in 2012–13 (see the Public School Enrollment indicator).

Figure 1.   Revenues for public elementary and secondary schools, by revenue source: School years 2002-03 through 2012-13

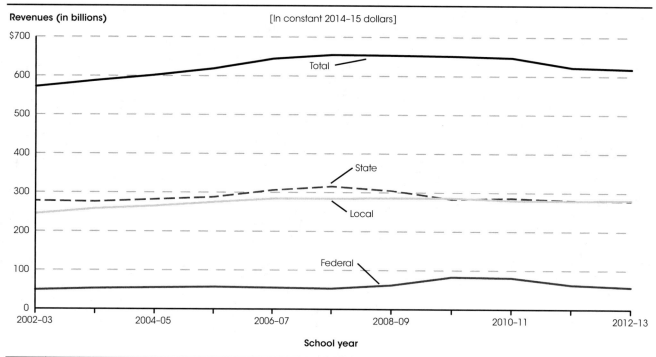

NOTE: Revenues are in constant 2014-15 dollars, adjusted using the Consumer Price Index (CPI).
SOURCE: U.S. Department of Education, National Center for Education Statistics, Common Core of Data (CCD), "National Public Education Financial Survey," 2002-03 through 2012-13. See *Digest of Education Statistics 2015*, table 235.10.

Federal revenues increased by 70 percent from 2002–03 to 2009–10 (from $49 billion to $83 billion), but then decreased each year from 2009–10 to 2012–13, falling by 31 percent to $57 billion over the period. From 2002–03 through 2012–13, local revenues increased by 15 percent to $281 billion in 2012–13. State revenues fluctuated between $276 billion and $316 billion during this period, and they were about the same in 2012–13 as in 2002–03 ($279 billion and $278 billion, respectively). During this period, federal revenues peaked in 2009–10 at $83 billion, while local revenues peaked in 2008–09 at $286 billion and state revenues peaked in 2007–08 at $316 billion.

Between school years 2002–03 and 2012–13, the percentage of total revenues coming from federal sources fluctuated between 8 and 13 percent, accounting for 9 percent of total revenues in both 2002–03 and 2012–13. Local sources accounted for 46 percent of total revenues in 2012–13, their highest percentage in the 2002–03 to 2012–13 period. The percentage of total revenues from state sources decreased from 49 percent in school year 2002–03 to 45 percent in school year 2012–13. From school year 2002–03 through school year 2012–13, the percentage of revenues from state sources was highest in 2002–03 (49 percent) and lowest in 2009–10 (43 percent).

More recently, from school year 2011–12 through school year 2012–13, total revenues for public elementary and secondary schools decreased by $4 billion in constant 2014–15 dollars (1 percent), from $622 billion to $618 billion. Between these years, federal revenues declined by $6 billion (10 percent) and state revenues declined by $0.4 billion (0.2 percent). Local revenues increased by $2.4 billion (1 percent), reflecting a $2.6 billion (1 percent) increase in revenues from local property taxes, a $0.2 billion increase in other local public revenues, and a $0.4 billion decrease in private revenues (consisting of revenues from gifts, and tuition and fees from patrons).

In school year 2012–13, there were significant variations across the states in the percentages of public school revenues coming from state, local, and federal sources of revenue. In 22 states, at least half of education revenues came from state governments, while in 14 states and the District of Columbia at least half came from local revenues. In the remaining 14 states, Arizona, Colorado, Florida, Georgia, Louisiana, Maryland, Montana, Ohio, Oklahoma, Oregon, South Carolina, Tennessee, Texas, and Wisconsin, no single revenue source made up more than half of education revenues.

Figure 2. State revenues for public elementary and secondary schools as a percentage of total public school revenues, by state: School year 2012–13

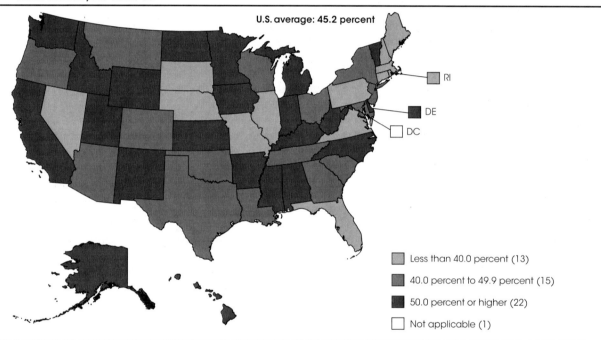

NOTE: All 50 states and the District of Columbia are included in the U.S. average, even though the District of Columbia does not receive any state revenue. The District of Columbia and Hawaii have only one school district each; therefore, neither is comparable to the other states. Categorizations are based on unrounded percentages. Excludes revenues for state education agencies.
SOURCE: U.S. Department of Education, National Center for Education Statistics, Common Core of Data (CCD), "National Public Education Financial Survey," 2012–13. See *Digest of Education Statistics 2015*, table 235.20.

In school year 2012–13, the percentages of public school revenues coming from state sources were highest in Vermont and Hawaii (89 and 84 percent, respectively), and lowest in South Dakota and Illinois (31 and 26 percent, respectively). The percentage of revenues coming from federal sources was highest in Mississippi (16 percent), followed by New Mexico, Louisiana, and South Dakota (15 percent each); the percentages were lowest in New York, Connecticut, and New Jersey

(5, 4, and 4 percent, respectively). Among all states, the percentage of revenues coming from local sources was highest in Illinois (65 percent), followed by New Hampshire and Nebraska (59 percent each), and lowest in Vermont and Hawaii (4 and 2 percent, respectively). Ninety percent of the revenues for the District of Columbia were from local sources; the remaining 10 percent of these revenues were from federal sources.

Figure 3. Property tax revenues for public elementary and secondary schools as a percentage of total public school revenues, by state: School year 2012–13

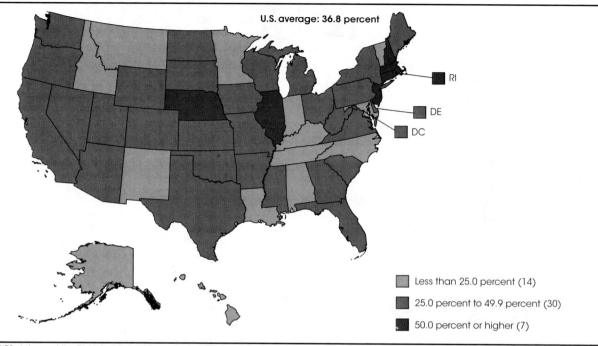

U.S. average: 36.8 percent

Less than 25.0 percent (14)

25.0 percent to 49.9 percent (30)

50.0 percent or higher (7)

NOTE: All 50 states and the District of Columbia are included in the U.S. average. The District of Columbia and Hawaii have only one school district each; therefore, neither is comparable to the other states. Categorizations are based on unrounded percentages.
SOURCE: U.S. Department of Education, National Center for Education Statistics, Common Core of Data (CCD), "National Public Education Financial Survey," 2012–13. See *Digest of Education Statistics 2015*, table 235.20.

On a national basis in 2012–13, $222 billion, or 81 percent, of total local revenues for public and elementary secondary school districts were derived from local property taxes. The percentages of total revenues from local property taxes differed by state. In 2012–13, Illinois had the highest percentage of revenues from property taxes, at 57 percent. Six other states had percentages of revenues from property taxes of 50 percent or more (in descending order): New Hampshire, Connecticut,

Nebraska, New Jersey, Massachusetts, and Rhode Island. Vermont and Hawaii[2] had the lowest percentages of revenues from property taxes (0.1 percent and 0 percent, respectively). In 12 other states, property taxes made up less than 25 percent of education revenues (in descending order): Montana, Maryland, Kentucky, Indiana, North Carolina, Idaho, Tennessee, Minnesota, Louisiana, Alabama, New Mexico, and Alaska.

Endnotes:

[1] Constant dollars based on the Consumer Price Index (CPI), prepared by the Bureau of Labor Statistics, U.S. Department of Labor, adjusted to a school-year basis.

[2] Hawaii has only one school district, which receives no funding from property taxes.

Reference tables: *Digest of Education Statistics 2015*, tables 235.10 and 235.20; *Digest of Education Statistics 2014*, table 203.20

Related indicators: Public School Expenditures

Glossary: Constant dollars, Consumer Price Index (CPI), Elementary school, Property tax, Public school or institution, Revenue, School district, Secondary school

This page intentionally left blank.

Public School Expenditures

Current expenditures per student in public elementary and secondary schools increased by 5 percent overall between 2002-03 and 2012-13; however, expenditures per student peaked in 2008-09 at $11,621 and decreased each year since then, after adjusting for inflation. The amount for 2012-13 ($11,011) was less than 1 percent lower than the amount for 2011-12 ($11,074).

Total expenditures for public elementary and secondary schools in the United States amounted to $620 billion in 2012–13, or $12,296 per public school student enrolled in the fall (in constant 2014–15 dollars, based on the Consumer Price Index). These expenditures include $11,011 per student in current expenditures for the operation of schools; $931 for capital outlay (i.e., expenditures for property and for buildings and alterations completed by school district staff or contractors); and $355 for interest on school debt.

Figure 1. Total expenditures per student in fall enrollment in public elementary and secondary schools, by type of expenditure: School years 2002-03 through 2012-13

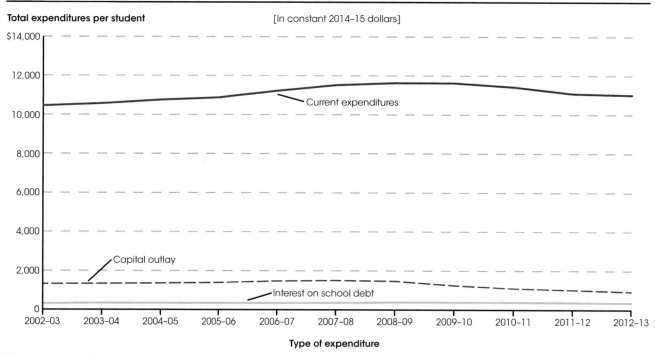

Total expenditures per student   [In constant 2014-15 dollars]

Type of expenditure

NOTE: Current expenditures, Capital outlay, and Interest on school debt are subcategories of Total expenditures. Current expenditures include instruction, support services, food services, and enterprise operations. Capital outlay includes expenditures for property and for buildings and alterations completed by school district staff or contractors. Expenditures are reported in constant 2014-15 dollars, based on the Consumer Price Index (CPI).
SOURCE: U.S. Department of Education, National Center for Education Statistics, Common Core of Data (CCD), "National Public Education Financial Survey," 2002-03 through 2012-13. See *Digest of Education Statistics 2015*, tables 236.10, 236.55, and 236.60.

From 2002–03 to 2012–13, current expenditures per student enrolled in the fall in public elementary and secondary schools increased by 5 percent (from $10,455 to $11,011 in constant 2014–15 dollars). Current expenditures per student peaked in 2008–09 at $11,621 and have decreased each year since then. While current expenditures per pupil declined $64 from 2011–12 to 2012–13, this decline was smaller than the declines from 2009–10 to 2010–11 and from 2010–11 to 2011–12 ($200 and $340, respectively.)

Interest payments on school debt per student in fall enrollment increased by 14 percent (from $310 to $355 in constant 2014–15 dollars) during the period from 2002–03 to 2012–13. Capital outlay expenditures per student in 2012–13 ($931) were 29 percent lower than the 2002–03 amount ($1,317) and 9 percent lower than the 2011–12 amount ($1,023); however, there were some fluctuations during this period.

Figure 2. Current expenditures per student in fall enrollment in public elementary and secondary schools, by function of expenditure: School years 2002-03, 2007-08, and 2012-13

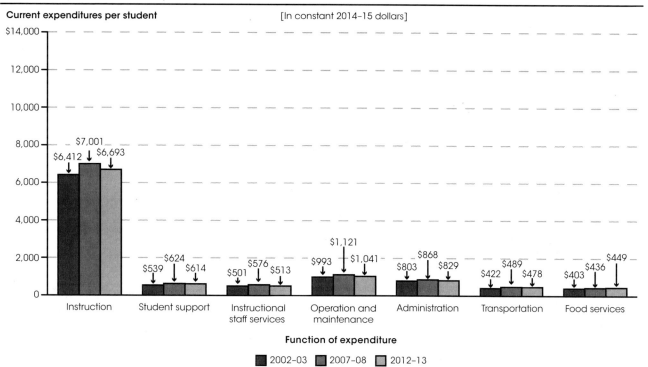

NOTE: Instruction, Student support, Instructional staff services, Operation and maintenance, Administration, Transportation, and Food services are subcategories of Current expenditures. Student support includes expenditures for guidance, health, attendance, and speech pathology services. Instructional staff services include expenditures for curriculum development, staff training, libraries, and media and computer centers. Administration includes both general administration and school administration. Transportation refers to student transportation. Expenditures are reported in constant 2014-15 dollars, based on the Consumer Price Index (CPI).
SOURCE: U.S. Department of Education, National Center for Education Statistics, Common Core of Data (CCD), "National Public Education Financial Survey," 2002-03, 2007-08, and 2012-13. See *Digest of Education Statistics 2015*, table 236.60.

In addition to being reported by type, expenditures are also reported by function, which describes the activity for which a service or material object is acquired. Current expenditures per student (in constant 2014–15 dollars) increased for most functions between 2002–03 and 2012–13, though expenditures for each function in 2012–13 were within a percentage point of their value in 2011–12. In 2012–13, instruction—the single largest component of current expenditures—was $6,693 per student, or 61 percent of current expenditures. Instruction expenditures include salaries and benefits of teachers and teaching assistants as well as costs for instructional materials and instructional services provided under contract. Between 2002–03 and 2012–13, expenditures per student for instruction increased by 4 percent (from

$6,412 to $6,693), though they peaked in 2009–10 at $7,110. Expenditures between 2002–03 and 2012–13 for most other major school functions increased more rapidly, although, with the exception of food services, all function categories peaked within a year of 2008–09. For example, expenditures per student for student support services, such as guidance and health personnel, increased by 14 percent from 2002–03 to 2012–13 (from $539 to $614), but peaked in 2009–10 at $645. Expenditures per student for instructional staff services, including curriculum development, staff training, libraries, and media and computer centers, were 2 percent higher in 2012–13 than in 2002–03 ($513 versus $501) and peaked in 2007–08 at $576. Expenditures per student for food services, however, were highest in 2012–13 ($449).

Figure 3. Percentage of current expenditures per student in fall enrollment in public elementary and secondary schools, by type of expenditure: School years 2002-03, 2007-08, and 2012-13

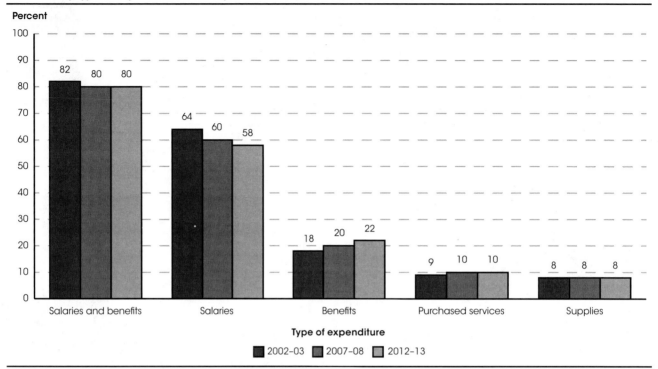

NOTE: Salaries and benefits, Salaries, Benefits, Purchased services, and Supplies are subcategories of Current expenditures. Purchased services include expenditures for contracts for food, transportation, or janitorial services, or professional development for teachers. Supplies include expenditures for items ranging from books to heating oil. Detail may not sum to totals because of rounding.
SOURCE: U.S. Department of Education, National Center for Education Statistics, Common Core of Data (CCD), "National Public Education Financial Survey," 2002-03, 2007-08, and 2012-13. See *Digest of Education Statistics 2015*, table 236.60.

Current expenditures for education can also be expressed in terms of the percentage of funds going toward salaries, benefits, purchased services, or supplies. On a national basis in 2012–13, approximately 80 percent of current expenditures were for salaries and benefits for staff. Approximately 10 percent of current expenditures were for purchased services, which include a wide variety of items, such as contracts for food, transportation, and janitorial services, and for professional development for teachers. This expenditure distribution shifted only slightly from 2002–03 to 2012–13, when expenditures for purchased services increased from 9 to 10 percent. Eight percent of school expenditures in 2012–13 were for supplies, ranging from books to heating oil. The percentages of expenditures for supplies changed less than one percentage point over the period from 2002–03 to 2012–13. There were, however, shifts within the distribution of salaries and benefits for staff, as the proportion of school budgets for staff salaries decreased from 64 percent in 2002–03 to 58 percent in 2012–13, and the proportion of staff benefits increased from 18 to 22 percent during this period.

Reference tables: *Digest of Education Statistics 2015,* tables 236.10, 236.55, and 236.60
Related indicators: Public School Revenue Sources

Glossary: Capital outlay; Constant dollars; Consumer Price Index (CPI); Current expenditures (elementary/secondary); Elementary school; Expenditures per pupil; Expenditures, total; Interest on debt; Public school or institution; Salary; Secondary school

This page intentionally left blank.

Education Expenditures by Country

In 2012, the United States spent $11,700 per full-time-equivalent (FTE) student on elementary/secondary education, which was 31 percent higher than the OECD average of $9,000. At the postsecondary level, the United States spent $26,600 per FTE student, which was 79 percent higher than the OECD average of $14,800.

This indicator uses material from the Organization for Economic Cooperation and Development (OECD) report *Education at a Glance 2015* to compare countries' expenditures on education using two measures: *expenditures per full-time-equivalent (FTE) student from both public and private sources* and *total education expenditures as a percentage of gross domestic product (GDP)*. The OECD is an organization of 34 countries whose purpose is to promote trade and economic growth. Education expenditures are from public revenue sources (governments) and private revenue sources, and include current and capital expenditures. Private sources include payments from households for school-based expenses such as tuition, transportation fees, book rentals, and food services, as well as public funding via subsidies to households, private fees for education services, and other private spending that goes through the educational institution. *The total education expenditures as a percentage of GDP* measure allows for a comparison of countries' expenditures relative to their ability to finance education. Purchasing power parity (PPP) indexes are used to convert other currencies to U.S. dollars (i.e., absolute terms).

A country's wealth (defined as GDP per capita) is positively associated with expenditures per FTE student on education at the elementary/secondary level as well as at the postsecondary level. In terms of OECD countries that reported expenditures per FTE student in 2012 at both of these education levels, 13 of the 15 countries with the highest GDP per capita (Switzerland, Norway, the United States, the Netherlands, Ireland, Austria, Sweden, Germany, Belgium, Finland, France, the United Kingdom, and Japan) had education expenditures per FTE student that were higher than the OECD average at both the elementary/secondary level and the postsecondary level. The two exceptions were Australia, with lower elementary/secondary level expenditures per FTE student ($8,800, in current dollars) than the OECD average ($9,000), and Iceland, with lower postsecondary level expenditures per FTE student ($9,400) than the OECD average ($14,800). Each of the 15 countries with the lowest GDP per capita (Mexico, Turkey, Chile, Hungary, Poland, Estonia, the Slovak Republic, Portugal, Slovenia, the Czech Republic, Israel, the Republic of Korea, New Zealand, Spain, and Italy) had education expenditures per FTE student that were lower than the OECD average at both the elementary/secondary level and the postsecondary level.

Figure 1. Annual expenditures per full-time-equivalent (FTE) student for elementary and secondary education in selected Organization for Economic Cooperation and Development (OECD) countries, by gross domestic product (GDP) per capita: 2012

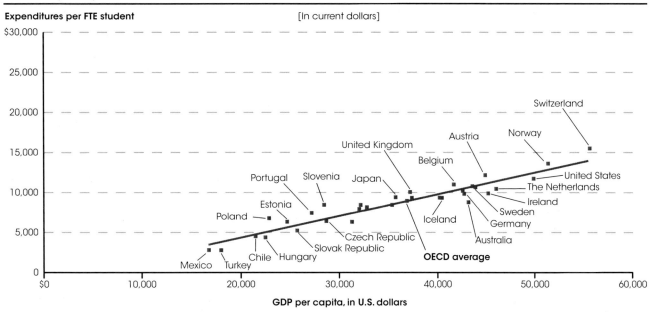

— Linear relationship between spending and country wealth for 32 OECD countries reporting data (elementary/secondary): r^2 = .90; slope = 0.27; intercept = -1022.

NOTE: Not all countries are labeled in the figure. The countries that are not labeled include Canada, Denmark, Finland, France, Israel, Italy, New Zealand, Spain, and The Republic of Korea. Data for those countries may be found in *Digest of Education Statistics 2015*, table 605.10. Data for Luxembourg are excluded from the figure because of anomalies in that country's GDP per capita data (large revenues from international finance institutions in Luxembourg distort the wealth of that country's population). Data for Greece are excluded because expenditure data are not available for 2011 and 2012. Expenditure and GDP data for Canada are for 2011. Expenditures for International Standard Classification of Education (ISCED) level 4 (postsecondary non-higher education) are included in elementary and secondary education unless otherwise noted. Expenditure data for Canada, France, Italy, and the United States do not include postsecondary non-higher education. Expenditure data for Ireland, Italy, Poland, Portugal, and Switzerland include public institutions only.
SOURCE: Organization for Economic Cooperation and Development (OECD), *Education at a Glance, 2015*. See *Digest of Education Statistics 2015*, table 605.10.

Expenditures per FTE student varied widely across OECD countries. At the elementary/secondary level, expenditures per FTE student in 2012 included low values such as $2,800 each for Turkey and Mexico. Switzerland had the highest value of $15,500. The United States spent $11,700 per FTE student at the elementary/secondary level, which was 31 percent higher than the average of $9,000 for OECD member countries reporting data.

Figure 2. Annual expenditures per full-time-equivalent (FTE) student for postsecondary education in selected Organization for Economic Cooperation and Development (OECD) countries, by gross domestic product (GDP) per capita: 2012

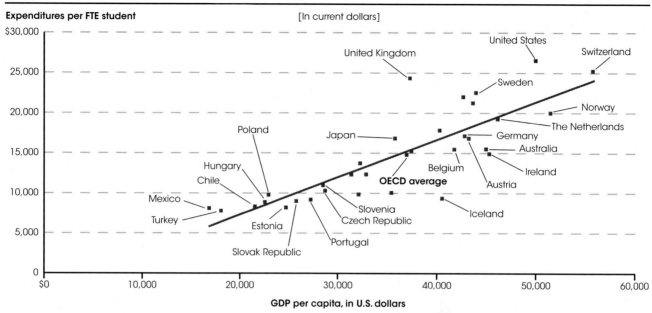

— Linear relationship between spending and country wealth for 32 OECD countries reporting data (postsecondary): r^2 = .70; slope = 0.47; intercept = -2042.
NOTE: Not all countries are labeled in the figure. The countries that are not labeled include Canada, Denmark, Finland, France, Israel, Italy, New Zealand, Spain, and The Republic of Korea. Data for those countries may be found in *Digest of Education Statistics 2015*, table 605.10. Data for Luxembourg are excluded from the figure because of anomalies in that country's GDP per capita data (large revenues from international finance institutions in Luxembourg distort the wealth of that country's population). Data for Greece are excluded because expenditure data are not available for 2011 and 2012. Expenditure and GDP data for Canada and Denmark are for 2011. Expenditure data for Denmark, Japan, Portugal, and the United States include postsecondary non-higher education. Expenditure data for Canada, Ireland, Portugal, and Switzerland include public institutions only.
SOURCE: Organization for Economic Cooperation and Development (OECD), *Education at a Glance, 2015*. See *Digest of Education Statistics 2015*, table 605.10.

At the postsecondary level, expenditures per FTE student in 2012 included low values such as $7,800 for Turkey and $8,100 for Mexico. The United States had the highest postsecondary expenditures per FTE student at $26,600, which were 79 percent higher than the OECD average of $14,800.

Figure 3. Direct expenditures on education as a percentage of gross domestic product (GDP) for Organization for Economic Cooperation and Development (OECD) countries with the highest percentages, by level of education: 2012

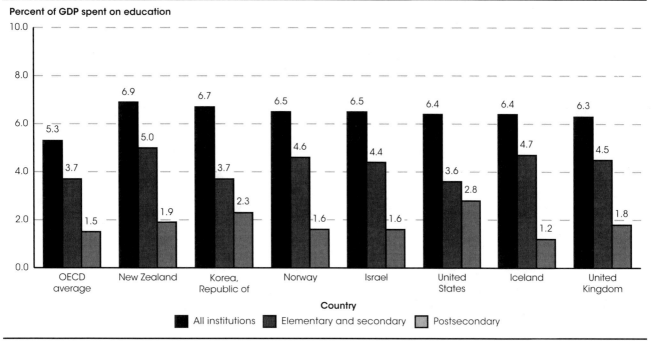

NOTE: Data for Chile are excluded because data are for 2013 instead of 2012. Expenditures for International Standard Classification of Education (ISCED) level 4 (postsecondary non-higher education) are included in elementary and secondary education, except for in the United States, where they are included in postsecondary education. "All institutions" total includes expenditures that could not be reported by level of education.
SOURCE: Organization for Economic Cooperation and Development (OECD), *Education at a Glance, 2015.* See *Digest of Education Statistics 2015,* table 605.20.

Among the 30 OECD countries reporting data in 2012, seven countries, including the United States, spent over 6.0 percent of their GDP on total education expenditures: New Zealand (6.9 percent), the Republic of Korea (6.7 percent), Norway (6.5 percent), Israel (6.5 percent), the United States (6.4 percent), Iceland (6.4 percent), and the United Kingdom (6.3 percent).

In terms of countries' education expenditures by education level in 2012, the percentage of GDP the United States spent on elementary/secondary education (3.6 percent) was slightly lower than the OECD average (3.7 percent).

Fifteen OECD countries spent less than 3.7 percent of their GDP on elementary/secondary education, seven countries spent between 3.7 and 4.0 percent, and nine countries spent more than 4.0 percent. New Zealand (5.0 percent) spent the highest percentage of GDP on elementary/secondary education. At the postsecondary level, spending as a percentage of GDP by the United States (2.8 percent) was higher than the OECD average (1.5 percent) and higher than that of any other OECD country reporting data. Only one other country spent more than 2.0 percent of its GDP on postsecondary education: the Republic of Korea (2.3 percent).

Reference tables: *Digest of Education Statistics 2015*, tables 605.10 and 605.20
Related indicators: International Educational Attainment

Glossary: Elementary school, Expenditures per pupil, Full-time-equivalent (FTE) enrollment, Gross domestic product (GDP), International Standard Classification of Education (ISCED), Organization for Economic Cooperation and Development (OECD), Postsecondary education, Purchasing Power Parity (PPP) indexes

Reading Performance

While the 2015 average 4th-grade reading score was not measurably different from the 2013 score, the average 8th-grade score was lower in 2015 than in 2013, according to data from the National Assessment of Educational Progress. At grade 12, the average reading score in 2015 was not measurably different from that in 2013.

The National Assessment of Educational Progress (NAEP) assesses student performance in reading at grades 4, 8, and 12 in both public and private schools across the nation. NAEP reading scores range from 0 to 500 for all grade levels. NAEP achievement levels define what students should know and be able to do:

Basic indicates partial mastery of fundamental skills, and *Proficient* indicates demonstrated competency over challenging subject matter. NAEP reading assessments have been administered periodically since 1992. The most recent reading assessments were conducted in 2015 for grades 4, 8, and 12.

Figure 1. Average National Assessment of Educational Progress (NAEP) reading scale scores of 4th-, 8th-, and 12th-grade students: Selected years, 1992–2015

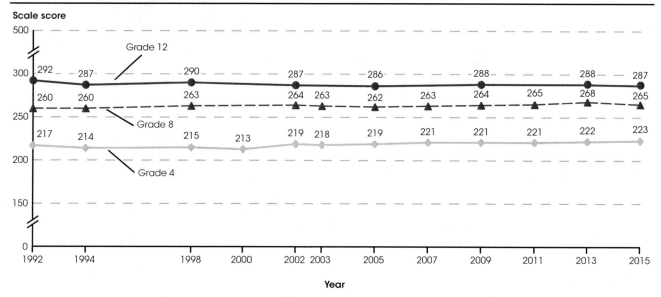

NOTE: Includes public and private schools. The reading scale scores range from 0 to 500. Assessment was not conducted for grade 8 in 2000 or for grade 12 in 2000, 2003, 2007, and 2011. Testing accommodations (e.g., extended time, small group testing) for children with disabilities and English language learners were not permitted in 1992 and 1994.
SOURCE: U.S. Department of Education, National Center for Education Statistics, National Assessment of Educational Progress (NAEP), selected years, 1992–2015 Reading Assessments, NAEP Data Explorer. See *Digest of Education Statistics 2015*, table 221.10.

In 2015, the average reading score for 4th-grade students (223) was not measurably different from the 2013 score, but it was higher than the score in 1992 (217). For 8th-grade students, the average reading score in 2015 (265) was lower than in 2013 (268), but it was higher than

in 1992 (260). In 2015, the average reading score for 12th-grade students (287) was not measurably different from the score in 2013, but it was 5 points lower than in 1992 (292).

Figure 2.   Percentage of 4th-, 8th-, and 12th-grade students across National Assessment of Educational Progress (NAEP) reading achievement levels: Selected years, 1992–2015

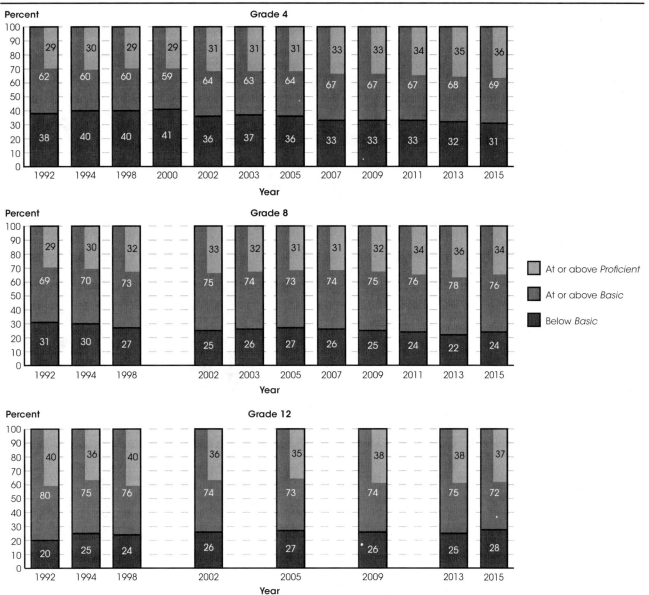

NOTE: Includes public and private schools. Achievement levels define what students should know and be able to do: *Basic* indicates partial mastery of fundamental skills, and *Proficient* indicates demonstrated competency over challenging subject matter. Assessment was not conducted for grade 8 in 2000 or for grade 12 in 2000, 2003, 2007, and 2011. Testing accommodations (e.g., extended time, small group testing) for children with disabilities and English language learners were not permitted in 1992 and 1994. Although rounded numbers are displayed, the figures are based on unrounded estimates. Detail may not sum to totals because of rounding.
SOURCE: U.S. Department of Education, National Center for Education Statistics, National Assessment of Educational Progress (NAEP), selected years, 1992–2015 Reading Assessments, NAEP Data Explorer. See *Digest of Education Statistics 2015,* table 221.12.

In 2015, the percentage of 4th-grade students performing at or above the *Basic* achievement level (69 percent) was not measurably different from the percentage in 2013, but it was higher than the percentage in 1992 (62 percent). In addition, the percentage of 4th-grade students performing at or above the *Proficient* achievement level in 2015 (36 percent) was not measurably different from the percentage in 2013, but it was higher than the percentage in 1992 (29 percent). Among 8th-grade students, the percentage performing at or above *Basic* in 2015 (76 percent) was lower than in 2013 (78 percent). However, the percentage was higher in 2015 than in

1992 (69 percent). Similarly, a lower percentage of 8th-grade students performed at or above *Proficient* in 2015 (34 percent) than in 2013 (36 percent), but the percentage in 2015 was higher than in 1992 (29 percent). Among 12th-grade students, the percentage performing at or above *Basic* in 2015 (72 percent) was lower than the percentage in 2013 (75 percent) and 1992 (80 percent). The percentage of 12th-graders performing at or above *Proficient* in 2015 (37 percent) was not measurably different from the percentage in 2013, but it was lower than the percentage in 1992 (40 percent).

Figure 3.   Average National Assessment of Educational Progress (NAEP) reading scale scores of 4th- and 8th-grade students, by race/ethnicity: 1992, 2013, and 2015

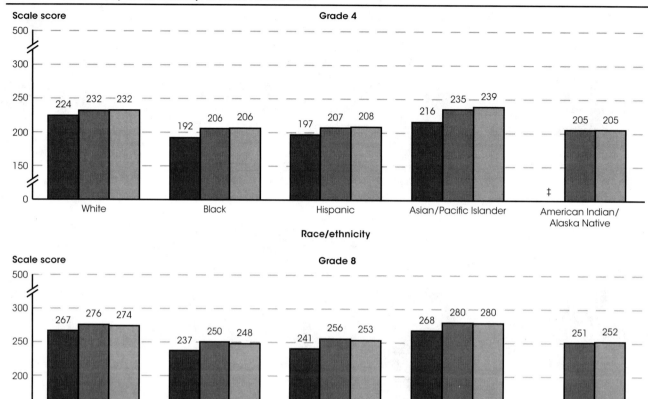

‡ Reporting standards not met (too few cases for a reliable estimate).
NOTE: Includes public and private schools. The reading scale scores range from 0 to 500. Testing accommodations (e.g., extended time, small group testing) for children with disabilities and English language learners were not permitted in 1992. Race categories exclude persons of Hispanic ethnicity. Although rounded numbers are displayed, the figures are based on unrounded estimates.
SOURCE: U.S. Department of Education, National Center for Education Statistics, National Assessment of Educational Progress (NAEP), 1992, 2013, and 2015 Reading Assessments, NAEP Data Explorer. See *Digest of Education Statistics 2015*, table 221.10.

At grade 4, the average 2015 reading scores for White (232), Black (206), Hispanic (208), and Asian/Pacific Islander students (239) were not measurably different from the corresponding scores in 2013, but their average scores were all higher in 2015 than in 1992. At grade 8, average 2015 reading scores for White (274), Black (248), and Hispanic (253) students were lower than the scores in 2013 (276, 250, and 256, respectively), while the average 2015 reading score for Asian/Pacific Islander (280) students was not measurably different from the score in 2013. Consistent with the findings at grade 4, the average reading scores for White, Black, Hispanic, and Asian/Pacific Islander 8th-grade students were higher in 2015 than in 1992. In 2015, the average scores for American Indian/Alaska Native 4th-graders (205) and 8th-graders (252) were not measurably different from the scores in 2013 and 1994, the first year that data were available for American Indian/Alaska Native students at both

grades. Starting in 2011, separate data for Asian students, Pacific Islander students, and students of Two or more races were collected. At both grades 4 and 8, the 2015 average reading scores for Asian students, Pacific Islander students, and students of Two or more races were not measurably different from the scores in 2013 and 2011.

Closing achievement gaps is a goal of both national and state education policies. From 1992 through 2015, the average reading scores for White 4th- and 8th-graders were higher than those of their Black and Hispanic peers. Although the White-Black and White-Hispanic achievement gaps did not change measurably from 2013 to 2015 at either grade 4 or 8, some of the racial/ethnic achievement gaps have narrowed since 1992. At grade 4, the White-Black gap narrowed from 32 points in 1992 to 26 points in 2015; at grade 8, the White-Hispanic gap narrowed from 26 points in 1992 to 21 points in 2015.

Figure 4. Average National Assessment of Educational Progress (NAEP) reading scale scores of 4th- and 8th-grade students, by sex: 1992, 2013, and 2015

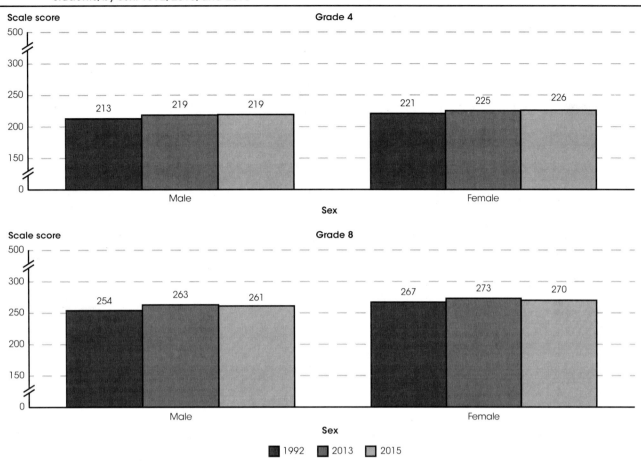

NOTE: Includes public and private schools. The reading scale scores range from 0 to 500. Testing accommodations (e.g., extended time, small group testing) for children with disabilities and English language learners were not permitted in 1992. Although rounded numbers are displayed, the figures are based on unrounded estimates.
SOURCE: U.S. Department of Education, National Center for Education Statistics, National Assessment of Educational Progress (NAEP), 1992, 2013, and 2015 Reading Assessments, NAEP Data Explorer. See *Digest of Education Statistics 2015*, table 221.10.

At grade 4, the average reading scores for male (219) and female (226) students in 2015 were not measurably different from those in 2013 but were higher than those in 1992 (213 and 221, respectively). At grade 8, the average reading score for male students in 2015 (261) was lower than in 2013 (263) but higher than the score in 1992 (254). Similarly, the average score for female 8th-grade students was lower in 2015 (270) than in 2013 (273) but higher than in 1992 (267). Since 1992, female students have scored higher than male students at both grades 4 and 8. The 2015 gender gap for 4th-grade students was not measurably different from the corresponding gaps in 2013 and 1992. The 2015 gender gap for 8th-grade students was not measurably different from the corresponding gap in 2013, but the 2015 gap (10 points) was smaller than the gap in 1992 (13 points).

Since 1998, NAEP has collected data regarding student English language learner (ELL) status.[1] For all available assessment years, the NAEP average reading scores for non-ELL 4th- and 8th-grade students were higher than the scores for their ELL peers. In 2015, the achievement gap between non-ELL and ELL students was 37 points at the 4th-grade level and 45 points at the 8th-grade level; these gaps were not measurably different from the achievement gaps observed in 2013 and 1998.

In 2015, the average reading score for 4th-grade students in high-poverty[2] public schools (205) was lower than the average scores for 4th-grade students in mid-high poverty schools (219), mid-low poverty schools (228), and low-poverty schools (241). At grade 8, the average 2015 reading score for students in high-poverty public schools (248) was lower than the average scores for students in mid-high poverty schools (261), mid-low poverty schools (269), and low-poverty schools (281). In 2015, the achievement gap between the students at high-poverty public schools and low-poverty schools was 36 points at grade 4 and 33 points at grade 8. These 2015 achievement gaps were not measurably different from the corresponding achievement gaps between students at high-poverty and low-poverty schools at grades 4 and 8 in 2005, 2007, 2009, 2011, and 2013.

Figure 5. Average National Assessment of Educational Progress (NAEP) reading scale scores of 12th-grade students, by race/ethnicity and sex: 1992, 2013, and 2015

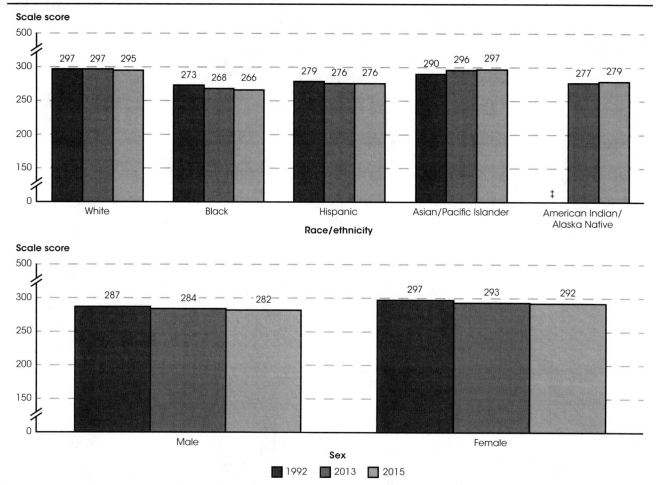

‡ Reporting standards not met (too few cases for a reliable estimate).
NOTE: Includes public and private schools. The reading scale scores range from 0 to 500. Testing accommodations (e.g., extended time, small group testing) for children with disabilities and English language learners were not permitted in 1992. Race categories exclude persons of Hispanic ethnicity. Although rounded numbers are displayed, the figures are based on unrounded estimates.
SOURCE: U.S. Department of Education, National Center for Education Statistics, National Assessment of Educational Progress (NAEP), 1992, 2013, and 2015 Reading Assessments, NAEP Data Explorer. See *Digest of Education Statistics 2015*, table 221.10.

At grade 12, the average 2015 reading scores for White (295), Hispanic (276), and Asian/Pacific Islander students (297) were not measurably different from the scores in 2013 and 1992. For Black students, the 2015 average score (266) was lower than the 1992 score (273) but was not measurably different from the 2013 score. The average score for American Indian/Alaska Native students in 2015 (279) was not measurably different from the 2013 score. Starting in 2011, separate data for Asian students, Pacific Islander students, and students of Two or more races were collected. The 2015 average scores for Asian students and students of Two or more races were not measurably different from the scores in 2013.[3] Achievement gaps in reading were also evident for 12th-grade students. The White-Black gap was wider in 2015 (30 points) than in 1992 (24 points), while the White-Hispanic gap in 2015 (20 points) was not measurably different from the gap in any previous assessment year.

The 2015 average reading scores for male (282) and female (292) 12th-grade students were not measurably different from the scores in 2013 but were lower than the scores in 1992 (287 and 297, respectively). The achievement gap between male and female students at grade 12 in 2015 (10 points) was not measurably different from the corresponding gaps in 2013 and 1992. In 2015, non-ELL 12th-grade students scored higher than their ELL peers by 49 points. The achievement gap between non-ELL and ELL students in 2015 was not measurably different from the gaps in both 2013 and 1998.[1]

In 2015, the average reading score for 12th-grade students in high-poverty public schools (266) was lower than the average scores for 12th-grade students in mid-high poverty schools (282), mid-low poverty schools (289), and low-poverty schools (298). The achievement gap between the students at high-poverty schools and low-poverty schools was 32 points in 2015, which was not measurably different from the gap in previous assessment years.

NAEP results also permit state-level comparisons of the reading abilities of 4th- and 8th-grade students in public schools. In 2015, the average reading scores across the states varied for public school students in both grades. At grade 4, the national public school average score was 221 and scores across states ranged from 207 to 235. In 21 states, average scores for public school students were higher than the national public school average score.

Average scores for public school students in 16 states were not measurably different from the national public school average. However, average scores in the District of Columbia and the remaining 13 states were lower than the national public school average. At grade 8, the national public school average score was 264 and scores across states ranged from 248 to 275. In 2015, 8th-grade average scores for public school students in 27 states were

Figure 6. Change in average National Assessment of Educational Progress (NAEP) reading scale scores of 4th- and 8th-grade public school students, by state: 2013 and 2015

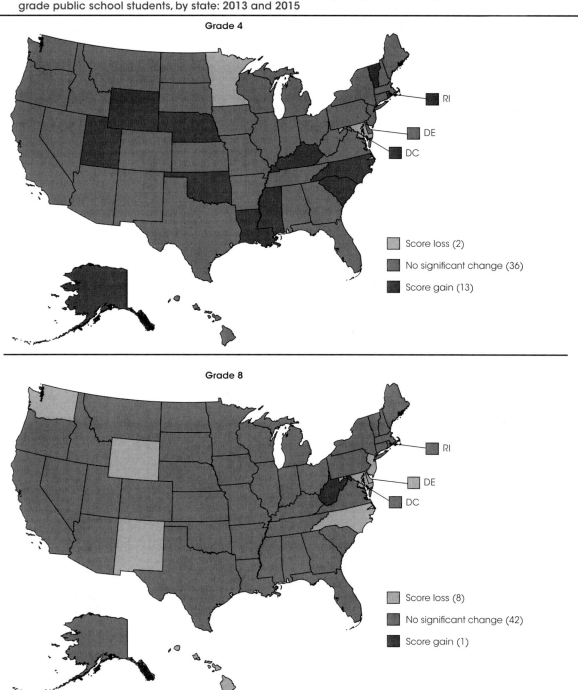

NOTE: The reading scale scores range from 0 to 500. "Gain" is defined as a significant increase from 2013 to 2015, "no change" is defined as no significant change from 2013 to 2015, and "loss" is defined as a significant decrease from 2013 to 2015.
SOURCE: U.S. Department of Education, National Center for Education Statistics, National Assessment of Educational Progress (NAEP), 2013 and 2015 Reading Assessments, NAEP Data Explorer. See *Digest of Education Statistics 2015*, tables 221.40 and 221.60.

higher than the national public school average, and public school students in 10 states had average scores that were not measurably different from the national public school average. However, 8th-grade public school students in the District of Columbia and 13 states had average scores that were lower than the national public school average.

While there was no measurable change from 2013 to 2015 in the average reading score for 4th-grade public school students nationally, average scores were higher in 2015 than in 2013 in the District of Columbia and 12 states. Average 4th-grade scores were lower in 2015 than in 2013 in Maryland and Minnesota, while scores in all remaining states did not change measurably from 2013 to 2015. The

average reading score for 8th-grade public school students was lower in 2015 than in 2013 nationally and in 8 states. However, 8th-grade students in West Virginia scored higher in 2015 than in 2013. In the remaining states, scores did not change measurably from 2013 to 2015.

NAEP also collects public school data from urban districts at grades 4 and 8 based on the same reading assessment used to report national and state results. Twenty-one urban districts participated in 2015. The Trial Urban District Assessment (TUDA) is intended to focus attention on urban education and to measure the educational progress of participating large urban districts.

Figure 7. Average National Assessment of Educational Progress (NAEP) reading scale scores of 4th- and 8th-grade public school students, by jurisdiction: 2015

Jurisdiction	Grade 4	Grade 8
Nation (public)	221	264
Large city	⬇ 214	⬇ 257
Albuquerque (NM)	⬇ 207	⬇ 251
Atlanta (GA)	⬇ 212	⬇ 252
Austin (TX)	◆ 220	◆ 261
Baltimore City (MD)	⬇ 199	⬇ 243
Boston (MA)	◆ 219	⬇ 258
Charlotte (NC)	⬆ 226	◆ 263
Chicago (IL)	⬇ 213	⬇ 257
Cleveland (OH)	⬇ 197	⬇ 240
Dallas (TX)	⬇ 204	⬇ 250
Detroit (MI)	⬇ 186	⬇ 237
District of Columbia (DC)	⬇ 214	⬇ 245
Duval County (FL)	⬆ 225	◆ 264
Fresno (CA)	⬇ 199	⬇ 242
Hillsborough County (FL)	⬆ 230	◆ 261
Houston (TX)	⬇ 210	⬇ 252
Jefferson County (KY)	◆ 222	◆ 261
Los Angeles (CA)	⬇ 204	⬇ 251
Miami-Dade (FL)	⬆ 226	◆ 265
New York City (NY)	⬇ 214	⬇ 258
Philadelphia (PA)	⬇ 201	⬇ 248
San Diego (CA)	⬇ 216	◆ 262

⬆ Higher average score than national average score　⬇ Lower average score than national average score　◆ No significant difference between urban district and national average score

NOTE: The reading scale scores range from 0 to 500. "Large city" includes students from all cities in the nation with populations of 250,000 or more, including the participating districts.
SOURCE: U.S. Department of Education, National Center for Education Statistics, National Assessment of Educational Progress (NAEP), 2015 Reading Assessments, NAEP Data Explorer. See *Digest of Education Statistics 2015*, table 221.80.

In 2015, the average reading score for 4th-grade public school students in large cities[4] (214) was lower than the national public school average reading score (221). Additionally, at grade 4, average scores for public school students in urban districts participating in TUDA ranged from 186 to 230. Public school 4th-grade students in 4 urban districts (Charlotte, Duval County, Hillsborough County, and Miami-Dade) had average scores higher than the national public school average, while students in 3 urban districts (Austin, Boston, and Jefferson County) had scores that were not measurably different from the national public school average. However, public school 4th-grade students in 14 urban districts had scores lower than the national public school average. Similarly, the average reading score for 8th-grade public school students in large cities (257) was lower than the national public school average score (264). At grade 8, average scores for public school students in urban districts participating in TUDA in 2015 ranged from 237 to 265. None of the urban districts had average 8th-grade scores higher than the national public school average. Eighth-grade public school students in 7 urban districts had average scores that

were not measurably different from the national public school average. Eighth-grade public school students in the remaining 14 districts had average scores lower than the national public school average.

Of the 20 urban districts that participated in the Trial Urban District Assessment in both 2013 and 2015, average 4th- and 8th-grade reading scores in some districts changed over time. Fourth-grade public school students in 4 urban districts (Boston, Chicago, Cleveland, and the District of Columbia) performed better in reading in 2015 than in 2013. While there was a decline in 4th-grade public school students' average scores in Baltimore City, the average scores for students in the remaining 15 urban districts showed no measurable change between 2013 and 2015. Eighth-grade public school students in Miami-Dade scored higher in 2015 than in 2013 while 8th-grade students in 3 urban districts (Albuquerque, Baltimore City, and Hillsborough County) had lower average scores in 2015 than in 2013. Average scores for 8th-grade students in all other participating urban districts did not change measurably.

Endnotes:

[1] In the mid- to late-1990s, NAEP began a transition to include accommodations for ELL students and other students with special needs. Thus, 2015 data for ELL students are compared with data for 1998 instead of 1992 as in the remainder of the indicator.

[2] High-poverty schools are defined as public schools where 76 to 100 percent of the students are eligible for free or reduced-price lunch (FRPL). Mid-high poverty schools are those schools where 51 to 75 percent of the students are eligible for FRPL, and mid-low poverty schools are those

schools where 26 to 50 percent of the students are eligible for FRPL. Low-poverty schools are defined as public schools where 25 percent or less of the students are eligible for FRPL.

[3] A comparison between the two most recent assessment periods is not possible for Pacific Islander students because reporting standards were not met for these students in 2015.

[4] Large cities include students from all cities in the nation with populations of 250,000 or more, including the participating urban districts.

Reference tables: *Digest of Education Statistics 2015*, tables 221.10, 221.12, 221.40, 221.60, and 221.80
Related indicators: English Language Learners in Public Schools, Mathematics Performance, International Assessments, Reading and Mathematics Score Trends [*web-only*]

Glossary: Achievement gap; Achievement levels, NAEP; English language learner (ELL); Public school or institution; Racial/ethnic group

Mathematics Performance

The average 4th- and 8th-grade mathematics scores in 2015 were lower than the scores in 2013 but were higher than the scores in 1990, according to data from the National Assessment of Educational Progress. At grade 12, the average mathematics score in 2015 was lower than the score in 2013, but not measurably different from the score in 2005.

The National Assessment of Educational Progress (NAEP) assesses student performance in mathematics at grades 4, 8, and 12 in both public and private schools across the nation. NAEP mathematics scores range from 0 to 500 for grades 4 and 8 and from 0 to 300 for grade 12. NAEP achievement levels define what students should know and be able to do: *Basic* indicates partial mastery of

fundamental skills, and *Proficient* indicates demonstrated competency over challenging subject matter. NAEP mathematics assessments have been administered periodically since 1990. The most recent mathematics assessments were conducted in 2015 for grades 4, 8, and 12.

Figure 1. Average National Assessment of Educational Progress (NAEP) mathematics scale scores of 4th- and 8th-grade students: Selected years, 1990–2015

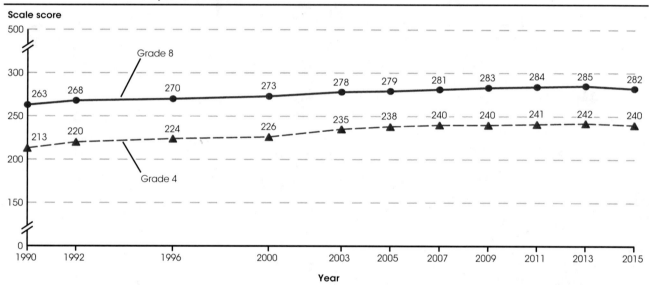

NOTE: Includes public and private schools. At grades 4 and 8, the mathematics scale scores range from 0 to 500. Testing accommodations (e.g., extended time, small group testing) for children with disabilities and English language learners were not permitted in 1990 and 1992.
SOURCE: U.S. Department of Education, National Center for Education Statistics, National Assessment of Educational Progress (NAEP), selected years, 1990–2015 Mathematics Assessments, NAEP Data Explorer. See *Digest of Education Statistics 2015*, table 222.10.

In 2015, for the first time, the average mathematics scores for 4th- and 8th-grade students were lower than the average scores in the previous assessment year. The average 4th-grade mathematics score in 2015 (240) was lower than the score in 2013 (242), although it was higher than the score in 1990 (213). The average 8th-grade mathematics score in 2015 (282) was lower than the score in 2013

(285). However, the average 8th-grade score in 2015 was higher than the score in 1990 (263). The average 12th-grade mathematics score in 2015 (152) was lower than the score in 2013 (153), but not measurably different from the score in 2005, the first year the revised assessment was administered.[1]

Figure 2. Percentage of 4th-, 8th-, and 12th-grade students across National Assessment of Educational Progress (NAEP) mathematics achievement levels: Selected years, 1990–2015

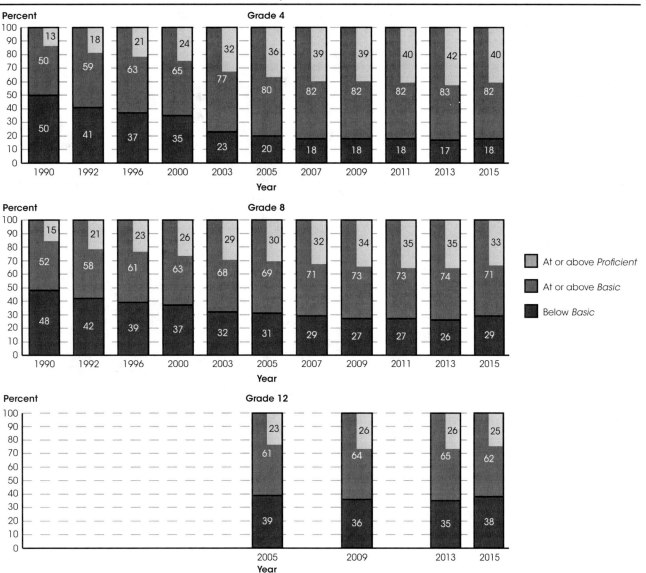

NOTE: Includes public and private schools. Achievement levels define what students should know and be able to do: *Basic* indicates partial mastery of fundamental skills, and *Proficient* indicates demonstrated competency over challenging subject matter. In 2005, there were major changes to the framework and content of the grade 12 assessment, and, as a result, scores from 2005 and later assessment years cannot be compared with scores and results from earlier assessment years. Assessment was not conducted for grade 12 in 2000, 2003, 2007, and 2011. Testing accommodations (e.g., extended time, small group testing) for children with disabilities and English language learners were not permitted in 1990 and 1992. Although rounded numbers are displayed, the figures are based on unrounded estimates. Detail may not sum to totals because of rounding.
SOURCE: U.S. Department of Education, National Center for Education Statistics, National Assessment of Educational Progress (NAEP), selected years, 1990–2015 Mathematics Assessments, NAEP Data Explorer. See *Digest of Education Statistics 2015*, table 222.12.

In 2015, some 82 percent of 4th-grade students performed at or above the *Basic* achievement level in mathematics, and 40 percent performed at or above the *Proficient* level. While the percentage of 4th-grade students performing at or above *Basic* in 2015 was lower than in 2013 (83 percent), it was higher than the percentage in 1990 (50 percent). The percentage of 4th-grade students performing at or above *Proficient* in 2015 (40 percent) was lower than in 2013 (42 percent). However, the percentage of 4th-grade students performing at or above *Proficient* in 2015 was higher than in 1990 (13 percent). In 2015, some 71 percent of 8th-grade students performed at or above *Basic* in mathematics, and 33 percent performed at or above *Proficient*. The percentage of 8th-grade students

performing at or above *Basic* was lower in 2015 than in 2013 (74 percent), but was higher than the percentage in 1990 (52 percent). The percentage of 8th-grade students who scored at or above *Proficient* in 2015 (33 percent) was also lower than the percentage in 2013 (35 percent), but was higher than the percentage in 1990 (15 percent). The percentage of 12th-grade students performing at or above *Basic* in 2015 (62 percent) was lower than the percentage in 2013 (65 percent), but not measurably different from the percentage in 2005. The percentage performing at or above *Proficient* (25 percent) was not measurably different from the percentages in 2013 and in 2005.

Figure 3.   Average National Assessment of Educational Progress (NAEP) mathematics scale scores of 4th- and 8th-grade students, by race/ethnicity: 1990, 2013, and 2015

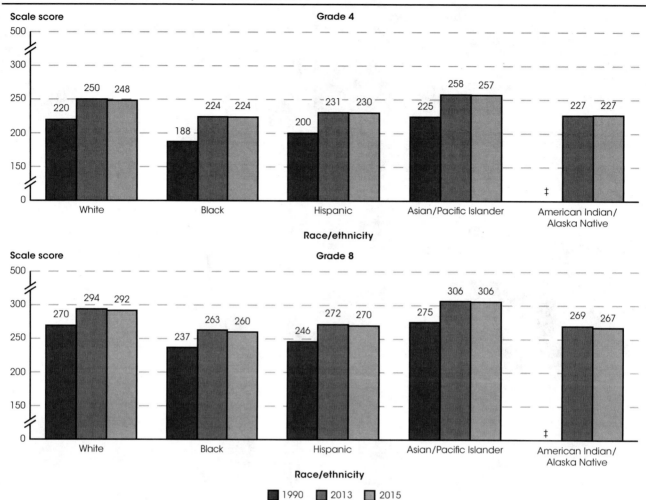

‡ Reporting standards not met (too few cases for a reliable estimate).
NOTE: Includes public and private schools. At grades 4 and 8, the mathematics scale scores range from 0 to 500. Testing accommodations (e.g., extended time, small group testing) for children with disabilities and English language learners were not permitted in 1990. Race categories exclude persons of Hispanic ethnicity. Although rounded numbers are displayed, the figures are based on unrounded estimates.
SOURCE: U.S. Department of Education, National Center for Education Statistics, National Assessment of Educational Progress (NAEP), 1990, 2013, and 2015 Mathematics Assessments, NAEP Data Explorer. See *Digest of Education Statistics 2015*, table 222.10.

At grade 4, the average mathematics score in 2015 for White students (248) was lower than the score in 2013 (250), while the average scores in 2015 for Black (224), Hispanic (230), and Asian/Pacific Islander (257) students were not measurably different from the 2013 scores. However, the 4th-grade average scores for White, Black, Hispanic, and Asian/Pacific Islander students were all higher in 2015 than in 1990. The 2015 average score for 4th-grade American Indian/Alaska Native students (227) was not measurably different from the scores in 2013 and in 1996, the first year that data were available for these students. At grade 8, the average scores for White (292), Black (260), and Hispanic students (270) were lower in 2015 than in 2013 (294, 263, and 272, respectively). The 2015 average score for Asian/Pacific Islander students (306) was not measurably different from the score in 2013. However, the average scores for 8th-grade White, Black, Hispanic, and Asian/Pacific Islander students were all higher in 2015 than in 1990. The 2015 average score

for 8th-grade American Indian/Alaska Native students (267) was not measurably different from the scores in 2013 and in 2000, the first year data were available for these students. Starting in 2011, separate data for Asian students, Pacific Islander students, and students of Two or more races were collected. At grades 4 and 8, the 2015 average mathematics scores for Asian students, Pacific Islander students, and students of Two or more races were not measurably different from the scores in 2013 and 2011.

Closing achievement gaps is a goal of both national and state education policies. In 2015, and in all previous assessment years since 1990, the average mathematics scores for White students in grades 4 and 8 have been higher than the scores of their Black and Hispanic peers. For both grades, there was some narrowing of racial/ethnic achievement gaps since the early 1990s. For example, the White-Black achievement gap at grade 4 narrowed from 32 points in 1990 to 24 points in 2015. Additionally, this 4th-grade White-Black achievement gap narrowed from 26 points in 2013 to 24 points in 2015, due to a decrease in White students' scores from 2013 to 2015. The 4th-grade White-Hispanic achievement gap in 2015 (18 points) was not measurably different from

the gap in 2013. In 2015, the 8th-grade achievement gaps between White and Black students' average scores (32 points) and between White and Hispanic students' scores (22 points) were not measurably different from 2013.

Figure 4. Average National Assessment of Educational Progress (NAEP) mathematics scale scores of 4th- and 8th-grade students, by sex: 1990, 2013, and 2015

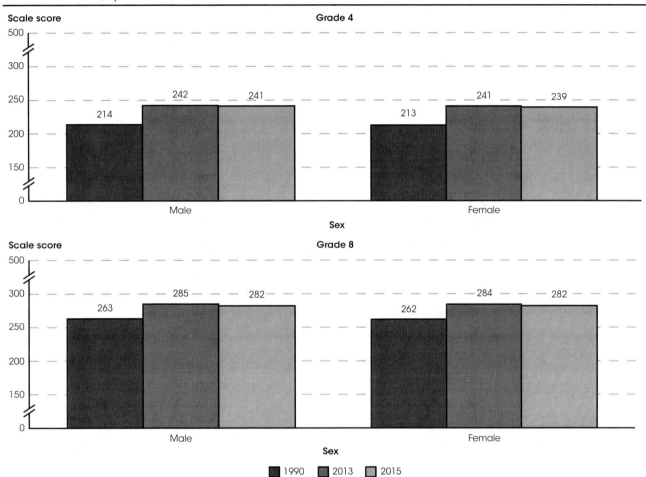

NOTE: Includes public and private schools. At grades 4 and 8, the mathematics scale scores range from 0 to 500. Testing accommodations (e.g., extended time, small group testing) for children with disabilities and English language learners were not permitted in 1990. Although rounded numbers are displayed, the figures are based on unrounded estimates.
SOURCE: U.S. Department of Education, National Center for Education Statistics, National Assessment of Educational Progress (NAEP), 1990, 2013, and 2015 Mathematics Assessments, NAEP Data Explorer. See *Digest of Education Statistics 2015*, table 222.10.

The average mathematics score in 2015 for male 4th-grade students (241) was not measurably different from the score in 2013, but was higher than the score in 1990 (214). For female 4th-grade students, the 2015 average score (239) was lower than the score in 2013 (241), but was higher than the score in 1990 (213). The average mathematics score in 2015 for male 8th-grade students (282) was lower than the score in 2013 (285), but was higher than the score in 1990 (263). Similarly, for female 8th-grade students, the average score in 2015 (282) was lower than in 2013 (284), but was higher than the score

in 1990 (262). In 2015, there was a 2 point gap between the mathematics scores for male and female students at grade 4, which was not measurably different from the gaps in 2013 and 1990. At grade 8, no measurable gender achievement gap was observed in 1990, 2013, and 2015.

Since 1996, NAEP has collected data on student English language learner (ELL) status for grades 4 and 8.[2] For all available years of data, the average mathematics scores for non-ELL 4th- and 8th-grade students were higher than their ELL peers' scores. In 2015, the achievement gap between non-ELL and ELL students was 25 points at grade 4 and 38 points at grade 8. At grade 4, this achievement gap was not measurably different from the gap observed in any assessment year since 1996. At grade 8, the achievement gap between non-ELL and ELL students narrowed from 46 points in 1996 and 41 points in 2013 to 38 points in 2015.

In 2015, the average mathematics score for 4th-grade students in high-poverty[3] public schools (226) was lower than the average scores for 4th-grade students in mid-high poverty schools (237), mid-low poverty schools (245),

and low-poverty schools (257). At grade 8, the average 2015 mathematics score for students in high-poverty public schools (264) was lower than the average scores for students in mid-high poverty schools (276), mid-low poverty schools (287), and low-poverty schools (301). In 2015, the achievement gap between the students at high-poverty public schools and low-poverty schools was 30 points at grade 4 and 38 points at grade 8. At both grades 4 and 8, this achievement gap was not measurably different from the gap observed in any assessment year since 2005.

Figure 5. Average National Assessment of Educational Progress (NAEP) mathematics scale scores of 12th-grade students, by sex and race/ethnicity: 2005, 2013, and 2015

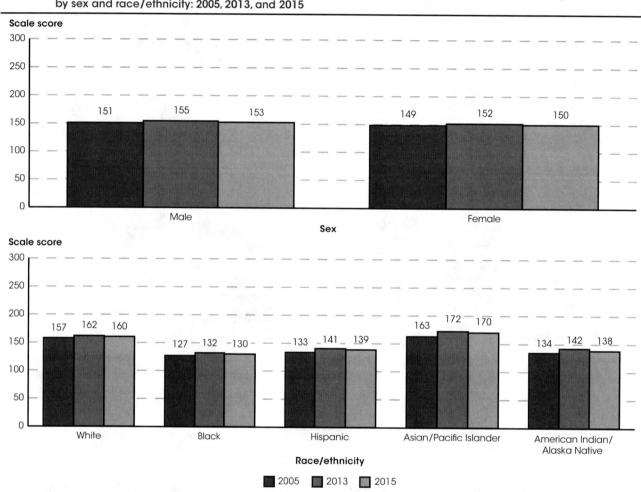

NOTE: Includes public and private schools. At grade 12, the mathematics scale scores range from 0 to 300. Race categories exclude persons of Hispanic ethnicity. Although rounded numbers are displayed, the figures are based on unrounded estimates.
SOURCE: U.S. Department of Education, National Center for Education Statistics, National Assessment of Educational Progress (NAEP), 2005, 2013, and 2015 Mathematics Assessments, NAEP Data Explorer. See *Digest of Education Statistics 2015*, table 222.10.

At grade 12, the average 2015 scores for White (160), Black (130), Hispanic (139), Asian/Pacific Islander (170), and American Indian/Alaska Native students (138) were not measurably different from the scores in 2013. However, the average scores for all racial/ethnic groups were higher in 2015 than in 2005, except the score for

American Indian/Alaska Native students, which was not measurably different. Starting in 2011, separate data for Asian students, Pacific Islander students, and students of Two or more races were collected. The 2015 average scores for Asian students and students of Two or more races were not measurably different from the scores in 2013.[4] The average mathematics scores for White 12th-grade students were higher than the scores for their Black, Hispanic, and American Indian/Alaska Native peers in 2005, 2009, 2013, and 2015. There were no measurable changes in racial/ethnic achievement gaps during this period.

Average mathematics scores in 2015 for 12th-grade male (153) and female (150) students were lower than the scores in 2013 (155 and 152, respectively) and were not measurably different from the scores in 2005. In 2005, 2009, 2013, and 2015, the gender gap for 12th-grade students remained at 3 points. The average scores for non-ELL 12th-grade students in 2005 (151), 2009 (154), 2013 (155), and 2015 (153) were higher than their ELL peers' scores in these years (120, 117, 109, and 115, respectively). The achievement gap between non-ELL and ELL students narrowed from 46 points in 2013 to 37 points in 2015.

In 2015, the average mathematics score for 12th-grade students in high-poverty public schools (129) was lower than the average scores for 12th-grade students in mid-high poverty schools (145), mid-low poverty schools (154), and low-poverty schools (164). The achievement gap between the students at high-poverty schools and low-poverty schools was 36 points in 2015, which was not measurably different from the gap in previous assessment years.

NAEP results also permit state-level comparisons of the mathematics achievement of 4th- and 8th-grade students in public schools. In 2015, the average mathematics scores varied across the states for public school students in both grades. At grade 4, the national public school average score was 240, and scores across states ranged from 231 to 251. In 20 states, the average score for public school 4th-grade students was higher than the national public school average score. In 14 states, the average mathematics score for 4th-grade public school students was not measurably different from the national public school average. However, average scores in the District of Columbia and the remaining 16 states were lower than the national public school average. At grade 8, the 2015 national public school average score was 281, and scores among public school students across states ranged from 263 to 297. In 2015, 8th-grade average scores for public school students in 22 states were higher than the national public school average, and in 14 states, the average scores for public school 8th-grade students were not measurably different from the national public school average. However, public school 8th-grade students in the District of Columbia and 14 states had average scores that were lower than the national public school average.

Figure 6. Change in average National Assessment of Educational Progress (NAEP) mathematics scale scores of 4th- and 8th-grade public school students, by state: 2013 and 2015

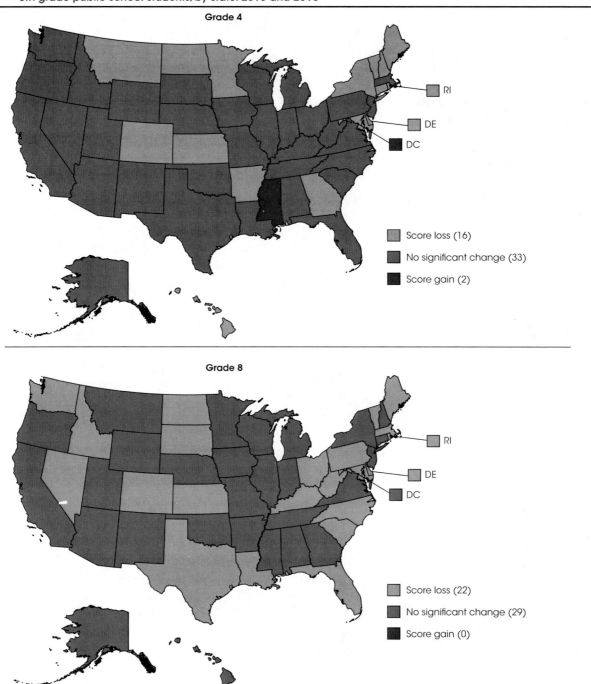

Grade 4

Score loss (16)

No significant change (33)

Score gain (2)

Grade 8

Score loss (22)

No significant change (29)

Score gain (0)

NOTE: At grades 4 and 8, the National Assessment of Educational Progress (NAEP) mathematics scale ranges from 0 to 500. "Gain" is defined as a significant increase from 2013 to 2015, "no change" is defined as no significant change from 2013 to 2015, and "loss" is defined as a significant decrease from 2013 to 2015.
SOURCE: U.S. Department of Education, National Center for Education Statistics, National Assessment of Educational Progress (NAEP), 2013 and 2015 Mathematics Assessments, NAEP Data Explorer. See *Digest of Education Statistics 2015*, tables 222.50 and 222.60.

The average mathematics score for 4th-grade public school students across the nation was lower in 2015 (240) than in 2013 (241). Average 4th-grade mathematics scores for public school students were also lower in 2015 than in 2013 in 16 states. However, the mathematics average score for 4th-grade students in Mississippi and the District of Columbia were higher in 2015 than in 2013. Scores were not measurably different in the other states during this

period. The national public school average mathematics score for 8th-grade students was lower in 2015 (281) than in 2013 (284). Similarly, 22 states had lower 8th-grade average scores in 2015 than in 2013, while scores for the remaining 28 states and the District of Columbia were not measurably different between 2013 and 2015. During this time, no state experienced a score increase at the 8th-grade level.

Figure 7. Average National Assessment of Educational Progress (NAEP) mathematics scale scores of 4th- and 8th-grade public school students, by jurisdiction: 2015

Jurisdiction	Grade 4	Grade 8
Nation (public)	240	281
Large city	⬇ 234	⬇ 274
Albuquerque (NM)	⬇ 231	⬇ 271
Atlanta (GA)	⬇ 228	⬇ 266
Austin (TX)	⬆ 246	⬆ 284
Baltimore City (MD)	⬇ 215	⬇ 255
Boston (MA)	⬇ 236	◆ 281
Charlotte (NC)	⬆ 248	⬆ 286
Chicago (IL)	⬇ 232	⬇ 275
Cleveland (OH)	⬇ 219	⬇ 254
Dallas (TX)	◆ 238	⬇ 271
Detroit (MI)	⬇ 205	⬇ 244
District of Columbia (DC)	⬇ 232	⬇ 258
Duval County (FL)	⬆ 243	⬇ 275
Fresno (CA)	⬇ 218	⬇ 257
Hillsborough County (FL)	⬆ 244	⬇ 276
Houston (TX)	◆ 239	⬇ 276
Jefferson County (KY)	⬇ 236	⬇ 272
Los Angeles (CA)	⬇ 224	⬇ 263
Miami-Dade (FL)	◆ 242	⬇ 274
New York City (NY)	⬇ 231	⬇ 275
Philadelphia (PA)	⬇ 217	⬇ 267
San Diego (CA)	⬇ 233	◆ 280

⬆ Higher average score than national average score   ⬇ Lower average score than national average score   ◆ No significant difference between urban district and national average score

NOTE: At grades 4 and 8, the mathematics scale scores range from 0 to 500. "Large city" includes students from all cities in the nation with populations of 250,000 or more, including the participating districts.
SOURCE: U.S. Department of Education, National Center for Education Statistics, National Assessment of Educational Progress (NAEP), 2015 Mathematics Assessments, NAEP Data Explorer. See *Digest of Education Statistics 2015*, table 222.80.

NAEP also collects public school data from urban districts at grades 4 and 8, based on the same mathematics assessment used to report national and state results. In 2015, 21 urban districts participated. The Trial Urban District Assessment (TUDA) is intended to focus attention on urban education and to measure the educational progress of participating large urban districts.

In 2015, average mathematics scores across participating urban districts varied for both grades. The average mathematics scores of 4th-grade public school students in large cities[5] (234) was lower than the national public school average score (240). At grade 4, average urban district scores for public school students in participating districts ranged from 205 to 248. Students in four urban districts (Austin, Charlotte, Duval County, and Hillsborough County) had average scores higher than the national public school average, while students in three urban districts had scores that were not measurably different from the national public school average. However, students in the remaining 14 urban districts had average scores lower than the national public school average. At grade 8, average urban district scores for public school students in participating districts in 2015 ranged from 244 to 286. The average mathematics score of 8th-grade public school students in large cities (274) was lower than the national public school average score (281). Eighth-grade students in Austin and Charlotte had average scores that were higher than the national public school average, and 8th-grade students in Boston and San Diego had average scores that were not measurably

different from the national public school average. However, students in the remaining 17 urban districts had scores lower than the national public school average.

Of the 20 urban districts that participated in the Trial Urban District Assessment in both 2013 and 2015, average mathematics scores at 4th and 8th grade in some urban districts changed over time. The average scores for 4th-grade students in Dallas, the District of Columbia, and Miami-Dade were higher in 2015 than in 2013. The averages scores for 4th-grade students in 10 participating urban districts were not measurably different between 2013 and 2015. However, the average scores for 4th-grade students in the remaining seven urban districts were lower in 2015 than in 2013. At grade 8, students in Chicago had higher average scores in 2015 than did their peers in 2013. Average mathematics scores for 8th-grade students in 16 participating urban districts were not measurably different during this same period. However, 8th-grade students in the remaining three districts (Dallas, Hillsborough County, and Houston) scored lower in 2015 on average than in 2013.

Endnotes:

[1] The 2005 mathematics framework for grade 12 introduced changes from the previous framework in order to reflect adjustments in curricular emphases and to ensure an appropriate balance of content. Consequently, the 12th-grade mathematics results in 2005 and subsequent years could not be compared to previous assessments, and a new trend line was established beginning in 2005.
[2] In the mid- to late-1990s, NAEP began a transition to include accommodations for ELL students and other students with special needs. Thus, 2015 data for ELL students are compared with data for 1996 instead of 1990 as in the remainder of the indicator.
[3] High-poverty schools are defined as public schools where more than 76 percent of the students are eligible for free or

reduced-price lunch (FRPL). Mid-high poverty schools are those schools where 51 to 75 percent of the students are eligible for FRPL, and mid-low poverty schools are those schools where 26 to 50 percent of the students are eligible for FRPL. Low-poverty schools are defined as public schools where 25 percent or less of the students are eligible for FRPL.
[4] A comparison between the two most recent assessment periods is not possible for Pacific Islander students because reporting standards were not met for these students in 2015.
[5] Large cities include students from all cities in the nation with populations of 250,000 or more, including the participating districts.

Reference tables: *Digest of Education Statistics 2015*, tables 222.10, 222.12, 222.50, 222.60, and 222.80
Related indicators: English Language Learners in Public Schools, Reading Performance, International Assessments, Reading and Mathematics Score Trends [*web-only*]

Glossary: Achievement gap; Achievement levels, NAEP; English language learner (ELL); Public school or institution; Racial/ethnic group

This page intentionally left blank.

International Assessments

Among 15-year-old students, 29 education systems had higher average scores than the United States in mathematics literacy, 22 had higher average scores in science literacy, and 19 had higher average scores in reading literacy, according to the 2012 Program for International Student Assessment (PISA).

The Program for International Student Assessment (PISA), coordinated by the Organization for Economic Cooperation and Development (OECD), has measured the performance of 15-year-old students in mathematics, science, and reading literacy every 3 years since 2000. In 2012, PISA was administered in 65 countries and education systems, including all 34 member countries of the OECD. In addition to participating in the U.S. national sample, three states—Connecticut, Florida, and Massachusetts—opted to participate as individual education systems and had separate samples of public schools and public-school students included in PISA to obtain state-level results. PISA 2012 results are reported by average scale score (from 0 to 1,000) as well as by the percentage of students reaching particular proficiency levels. Proficiency results are presented in terms of the percentages of students reaching proficiency level 5 or above (i.e., percentages of top performers) and the percentages of students performing below proficiency level 2 (i.e., percentages of low performers).

Table 1. Average scores of 15-year-old students on the Program for International Student Assessment (PISA) mathematics literacy scale, by education system: 2012

Education system	Average score		Education system	Average score	
OECD average	494	⬤	OECD average	494	⬤
Shanghai-CHN	613	⬤	Lithuania	479	
Singapore	573	⬤	Sweden	478	
Hong Kong-CHN	561	⬤	Hungary	477	
Chinese Taipei-CHN	560	⬤	Croatia	471	▼
Korea, Republic of	554	⬤	Israel	466	▼
Macao-CHN	538	⬤	Greece	453	▼
Japan	536	⬤	Serbia, Republic of	449	▼
Liechtenstein	535	⬤	Turkey	448	▼
Switzerland	531	⬤	Romania	445	▼
Netherlands	523	⬤	Cyprus	440	▼
Estonia	521	⬤	Bulgaria	439	▼
Finland	519	⬤	United Arab Emirates	434	▼
Canada	518	⬤	Kazakhstan	432	▼
Poland	518	⬤	Thailand	427	▼
Belgium	515	⬤	Chile	423	▼
Germany	514	⬤	Malaysia	421	▼
Vietnam	511	⬤	Mexico	413	▼
Austria	506	⬤	Montenegro, Republic of	410	▼
Australia	504	⬤	Uruguay	409	▼
Ireland	501	⬤	Costa Rica	407	▼
Slovenia	501	⬤	Albania	394	▼
Denmark	500	⬤	Brazil	391	▼
New Zealand	500	⬤	Argentina	388	▼
Czech Republic	499	⬤	Tunisia	388	▼
France	495	⬤	Jordan	386	▼
United Kingdom	494	⬤	Colombia	376	▼
Iceland	493	⬤	Qatar	376	▼
Latvia	491	⬤	Indonesia	375	▼
Luxembourg	490	⬤	Peru	368	▼
Norway	489				
Portugal	487				
Italy	485				
Spain	484		**U.S. state education systems**		
Russian Federation	482		Massachusetts	514	⬤
Slovak Republic	482		Connecticut	506	⬤
United States	**481**		Florida	467	▼

⬤ Average score is higher than U.S. average score.
▼ Average score is lower than U.S. average score.
NOTE: Education systems are ordered by 2012 average score. The Organization for Economic Cooperation and Development (OECD) average is the average of the national averages of the OECD member countries, with each country weighted equally. Scores are reported on a scale from 0 to 1,000. All average scores reported as higher or lower than the U.S. average score are different at the .05 level of statistical significance. Italics indicate non-OECD education systems. Results for Connecticut, Florida, and Massachusetts are for public school students only.
SOURCE: Organization for Economic Cooperation and Development (OECD), Program for International Student Assessment (PISA), 2012. See *Digest of Education Statistics 2013*, table 602.60.

In 2012, average scores in mathematics literacy ranged from 368 in Peru to 613 in Shanghai-CHN. The U.S. average mathematics score (481) was lower than the average for all OECD countries (494). Twenty-nine education systems and two U.S. states had higher average mathematics scores than the U.S. average score and nine had scores not measurably different from the U.S. score. The 29 education systems with scores higher than the U.S. average score were Shanghai-CHN, Singapore, Hong Kong-CHN, Chinese Taipei-CHN, the Republic of Korea, Macao-CHN, Japan, Liechtenstein, Switzerland, the Netherlands, Estonia, Finland, Canada, Poland, Belgium, Germany, Vietnam, Austria, Australia, Ireland,

Slovenia, Denmark, New Zealand, the Czech Republic, France, the United Kingdom, Iceland, Latvia, and Luxembourg. Within the United States, Massachusetts (514) and Connecticut (506) had scores higher than the U.S. average.

In addition to scoring above the U.S. average, Massachusetts scored above the OECD average. Connecticut scored above the U.S. national average, but its score was not measurably different from the OECD average. Florida's average score (467) was below the U.S. national average.

Figure 1. Percentage of 15-year-old students performing on the Program for International Student Assessment (PISA) mathematics literacy scale, by selected proficiency level and education system: 2012

Education system	Below level 2	Levels 5 and above
OECD average	23*	13*
Shanghai-CHN	4*	55*
Singapore	8*	40*
Chinese Taipei-CHN	13*	37*
Hong Kong-CHN	9*	34*
Korea, Republic of	9*	31*
Liechtenstein	14*	25*
Macao-CHN	11*	24*
Japan	11*	24*
Switzerland	12*	21*
Belgium	19*	20*
Netherlands	15*	19*
Germany	18*	17*
Poland	14*	17*
Canada	14*	16*
Finland	12*	15*
New Zealand	23*	15*
Australia	20*	15*
Estonia	11*	15*
Austria	19*	14*
Slovenia	20*	14*
Vietnam	14*	13*
France	22*	13*
Czech Republic	21*	13*
United Kingdom	22	12*
Luxembourg	24	11*
Iceland	21*	11*
Slovak Republic	27	11
Ireland	17*	11*
Portugal	25	11
Denmark	17*	10
Italy	25	10
Norway	22*	9
Israel	34*	9
Hungary	28	9
United States	26	9
Lithuania	26	8

Education system	Below level 2	Levels 5 and above
OECD average	23*	13*
Sweden	27	8
Spain	24	8
Latvia	20*	8
Russian Federation	24	8
Croatia	30*	7
Turkey	42*	6*
Serbia, Republic of	39*	5*
Bulgaria	44*	4*
Greece	36*	4*
Cyprus	42*	4*
United Arab Emirates	46*	3†
Romania	41*	3†
Thailand	50*	3†
Qatar	70*	2*†
Chile	52*	2*†
Uruguay	56*	1*
Malaysia	52*	1*
Montenegro, Republic of	57*	1*
Kazakhstan	45*	1!*
Albania	61*	1*
Tunisia	68*	1!*
Brazil	67*	1*
Mexico	55*	1*
Peru	75*	1!*
Costa Rica	60*	1!*†
Jordan	69*	‡
Columbia	74*	#!*
Indonesia	76*	‡
Argentina	66*	#!*

U.S. state education systems

Education system	Below level 2	Levels 5 and above
Massachusetts	18*	19*
Connecticut	21*	16*
Florida	30*	6*

■ Below level 2
▓ Levels 5 and above
\# Rounds to zero.
! Interpret data with caution. The coefficient of variation (CV) for this estimate is between 30 and 50 percent.
‡ Reporting standards not met. Either there are too few cases for a reliable estimate or the coefficient of variation (CV) is 50 percent or greater.
* $p < .05$. Significantly different from the U.S. percentage at the .05 level of statistical significance.
NOTE: Education systems are ordered by 2012 percentages of 15-year-olds at levels 5 and above. To reach a particular proficiency level, a student must correctly answer a majority of items at that level. Students were classified into mathematics proficiency levels according to their scores. Exact cut scores are as follows: below level 1 (a score less than or equal to 357.77); level 1 (a score greater than 357.77 and less than or equal to 420.07); level 2 (a score greater than 420.07 and less than or equal to 482.38); level 3 (a score greater than 482.38 and less than or equal to 544.68); level 4 (a score greater than 544.68 and less than or equal to 606.99); level 5 (a score greater than 606.99 and less than or equal to 669.30); and level 6 (a score greater than 669.30). Scores are reported on a scale from 0 to 1,000. The Organization for Economic Cooperation and Development (OECD) average is the average of the national percentages of the OECD member countries, with each country weighted equally. Italics indicate non-OECD education systems. Results for Connecticut, Florida, and Massachusetts are for public school students only.
SOURCE: Organization for Economic Cooperation and Development (OECD), Program for International Student Assessment (PISA), 2012. See *Digest of Education Statistics 2013*, table 602.60.

PISA reports mathematics literacy in terms of six proficiency levels, with level 1 being the lowest and level 6 being the highest. Students scoring at proficiency levels 5 and above are considered to be top performers since they have demonstrated advanced mathematical thinking and reasoning skills required to solve problems of greater complexity. The percentage of top performers in the United States was lower than the average of the OECD countries' percentages of top performers (9 vs.

13 percent). Percentages of top performers ranged from near 0 percent in Colombia and Argentina to 55 percent in Shanghai-CHN. Twenty-seven education systems and two U.S. states had higher percentages of top performers in mathematics literacy than the United States. Massachusetts and Connecticut both had higher percentages of top performers (19 and 16 percent, respectively) than the United States (9 percent), while Florida had a lower percentage (6 percent).

A higher percentage (26 percent) of 15-year-olds in the United States scored below proficiency level 2 in mathematics literacy than the average of the OECD countries' percentages (23 percent). Percentages of low performers ranged from 4 percent in Shanghai-CHN to 76 percent in Indonesia. Twenty-nine education systems and two U.S. states had lower percentages of low performers than the United States in mathematics literacy. The U.S. percentage of low performers was higher than the percentages for both Massachusetts (18 percent) and Connecticut (21 percent). The percentage of low performers in Florida (30 percent) was not measurably different from the U.S. percentage.

Table 2. Average scores of 15-year-old students on the Program for International Student Assessment (PISA) science literacy scale, by education system: 2012

Education system	Average score	Education system	Average score
OECD average	501	OECD average	501
Shanghai-CHN	580 ⬦	Russian Federation	486 ▼
Hong Kong-CHN	555 ⬦	Sweden	485 ▼
Singapore	551 ⬦	Iceland	478 ▼
Japan	547 ⬦	Slovak Republic	471 ▼
Finland	545 ⬦	Israel	470 ▼
Estonia	541 ⬦	Greece	467 ▼
Korea, Republic of	538 ⬦	Turkey	463 ▼
Vietnam	528 ⬦	*United Arab Emirates*	448 ▼
Poland	526 ⬦	*Bulgaria*	446 ▼
Canada	525 ⬦	Chile	445 ▼
Liechtenstein	525 ⬦	*Serbia, Republic of*	445 ▼
Germany	524 ⬦	*Thailand*	444 ▼
Chinese Taipei-CHN	523 ⬦	Romania	439 ▼
Netherlands	522 ⬦	*Cyprus*	438 ▼
Ireland	522 ⬦	*Costa Rica*	429 ▼
Australia	521 ⬦	*Kazakhstan*	425 ▼
Macao-CHN	521 ⬦	*Malaysia*	420 ▼
New Zealand	516 ⬦	*Uruguay*	416 ▼
Switzerland	515 ⬦	Mexico	415 ▼
Slovenia	514 ⬦	*Montenegro, Republic of*	410 ▼
United Kingdom	514 ⬦	*Jordan*	409 ▼
Czech Republic	508 ⬦	*Argentina*	406 ▼
Austria	506	*Brazil*	405 ▼
Belgium	505	*Colombia*	399 ▼
Latvia	502	*Tunisia*	398 ▼
France	499	*Albania*	397 ▼
Denmark	498	*Qatar*	384 ▼
United States	**497**	*Indonesia*	382 ▼
Spain	496	*Peru*	373 ▼
Lithuania	496		
Norway	495		
Hungary	494		
Italy	494	**U.S. state education systems**	
Croatia	491	*Massachusetts*	527 ⬦
Luxembourg	491	*Connecticut*	521 ⬦
Portugal	489	*Florida*	485

⬦ Average score is higher than U.S. average score.
▼ Average score is lower than U.S. average score.
NOTE: Education systems are ordered by 2012 average score. The Organization for Economic Cooperation and Development (OECD) average is the average of the national averages of the OECD member countries, with each country weighted equally. Scores are reported on a scale from 0 to 1,000. All average scores reported as higher or lower than the U.S. average score are different at the .05 level of statistical significance. Italics indicate non-OECD education systems. Results for Connecticut, Florida, and Massachusetts are for public school students only.
SOURCE: Organization for Economic Cooperation and Development (OECD), Program for International Student Assessment (PISA), 2012. See *Digest of Education Statistics 2013*, table 602.70.

In science literacy, average scores ranged from 373 in Peru to 580 in Shanghai-CHN. The U.S. average science score (497) was not measurably different from the OECD average (501). Twenty-two education systems and 2 U.S. states had higher average science scores than the United States, and 13 systems and 1 U.S. state had scores that were not measurably different. The 22 education systems with higher scores than the U.S. average score were Shanghai-CHN, Hong Kong-CHN, Singapore, Japan, Finland, Estonia, the Republic of Korea, Vietnam, Poland, Canada, Liechtenstein, Germany, Chinese Taipei-CHN, the Netherlands, Ireland, Australia, Macao-CHN, New Zealand, Switzerland, Slovenia, the United Kingdom, and the Czech Republic. Within the United States, Massachusetts and Connecticut scored above the U.S. average.

In addition to scoring above the U.S. national average, Massachusetts (527) and Connecticut (521) also scored above the OECD average. Florida (485) had an average score not measurably different from the U.S. average and lower than the OECD average.

Figure 2. Percentage of 15-year-old students performing on the Program for International Student Assessment (PISA) science literacy scale, by selected proficiency level and education system: 2012

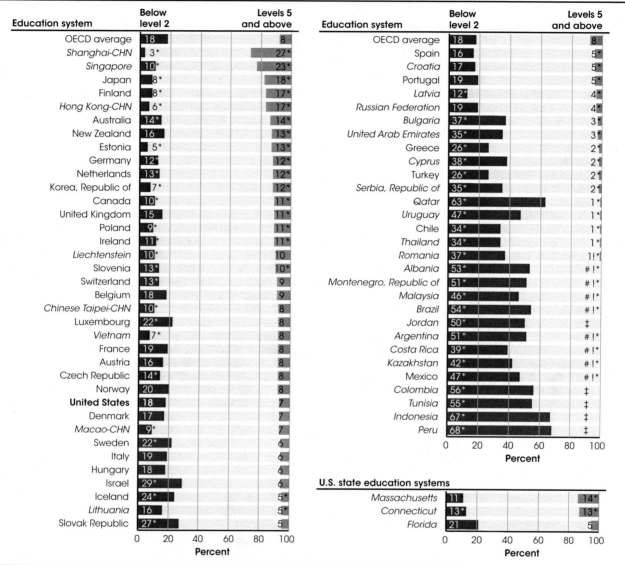

■ Below level 2
▨ Levels 5 and above
Rounds to zero.
! Interpret data with caution. The coefficient of variation (CV) for this estimate is between 30 and 50 percent.
‡ Reporting standards not met. Either there are too few cases for a reliable estimate or the coefficient of variation (CV) is 50 percent or greater.
* p < .05. Significantly different from the U.S. percentage at the .05 level of statistical significance.
NOTE: Education systems are ordered by 2012 percentages of 15-year-olds at levels 5 and above. To reach a particular proficiency level, a student must correctly answer a majority of items at that level. Students were classified into science proficiency levels according to their scores. Exact cut scores are as follows: below level 1 (a score less than or equal to 334.94); level 1 (a score greater than 334.94 and less than or equal to 409.54); level 2 (a score greater than 409.54 and less than or equal to 484.14); level 3 (a score greater than 484.14 and less than or equal to 558.73); level 4 (a score greater than 558.73 and less than or equal to 633.33); level 5 (a score greater than 633.33 and less than or equal to 707.93); and level 6 (a score greater than 707.93). Scores are reported on a scale from 0 to 1,000. The Organization for Economic Cooperation and Development (OECD) average is the average of the national percentages of the OECD member countries, with each country weighted equally. Italics indicate non-OECD education systems. Results for Connecticut, Florida, and Massachusetts are for public school students only.
SOURCE: Organization for Economic Cooperation and Development (OECD), Program for International Student Assessment (PISA), 2012. See *Digest of Education Statistics 2013*, table 602.70.

Similar to PISA's reporting of mathematics literacy, PISA also reports science literacy by six proficiency levels, with level 1 being the lowest and level 6 being the highest. Students performing at levels 5 and 6 can apply scientific knowledge in a variety of complex life situations. The percentage of U.S. top performers on the science literacy scale (7 percent) was not measurably different from the average of the OECD countries' percentages of top performers (8 percent). Percentages of top performers ranged from near 0 percent in eight education systems to 27 percent in Shanghai-CHN. Sixteen education systems and two U.S. states had percentages of top performers higher than the United States in science literacy. Massachusetts and Connecticut both had higher percentages of top performers (14 and 13 percent,

respectively) than the United States, while Florida had a percentage that was not measurably different (5 percent).

The percentage of U.S. students who scored below proficiency level 2 in science literacy was not measurably different from the average of the OECD countries' percentages (both 18 percent). Percentages of low performers ranged from 3 percent in Shanghai-CHN to 68 percent in Peru. Twenty-one education systems and two U.S. states, Massachusetts and Connecticut (11 and 13 percent, respectively), had lower percentages of low performers than the United States in science literacy. The percentage of low performers for Florida (21 percent) was not measurably different from the percentage for the United States.

Table 3. Average scores of 15-year-old students on the Program for International Student Assessment (PISA) reading literacy scale, by education system: 2012

Education system	Average score		Education system	Average score	
OECD average	496		OECD average	496	
Shanghai-CHN	570	⬆	Iceland	483	⬇
Hong Kong-CHN	545	⬆	Slovenia	481	⬇
Singapore	542	⬆	Lithuania	477	⬇
Japan	538	⬆	Greece	477	⬇
Korea, Republic of	536	⬆	Turkey	475	⬇
Finland	524	⬆	Russian Federation	475	⬇
Ireland	523	⬆	Slovak Republic	463	⬇
Chinese Taipei-CHN	523	⬆	Cyprus	449	⬇
Canada	523	⬆	Serbia, Republic of	446	⬇
Poland	518	⬆	United Arab Emirates	442	⬇
Estonia	516	⬆	Chile	441	⬇
Liechtenstein	516	⬆	Thailand	441	⬇
New Zealand	512	⬆	Costa Rica	441	⬇
Australia	512	⬆	Romania	438	⬇
Netherlands	511	⬆	Bulgaria	436	⬇
Switzerland	509	⬆	Mexico	424	⬇
Macao-CHN	509	⬆	Montenegro, Republic of	422	⬇
Belgium	509	⬆	Uruguay	411	⬇
Vietnam	508		Brazil	410	⬇
Germany	508	⬆	Tunisia	404	⬇
France	505		Colombia	403	⬇
Norway	504		Jordan	399	⬇
United Kingdom	499		Malaysia	398	⬇
United States	**498**		Indonesia	396	⬇
Denmark	496		Argentina	396	⬇
Czech Republic	493		Albania	394	⬇
Italy	490		Kazakhstan	393	⬇
Austria	490		Qatar	388	⬇
Latvia	489	⬇	Peru	384	⬇
Hungary	488				
Spain	488	⬇			
Luxembourg	488	⬇			
Portugal	488		**U.S. state education systems**		
Israel	486		Massachusetts	527	⬆
Croatia	485	⬇	Connecticut	521	⬆
Sweden	483	⬇	Florida	492	

⬆ Average score is higher than U.S. average score.
⬇ Average score is lower than U.S. average score.
NOTE: Education systems are ordered by 2012 average score. The Organization for Economic Cooperation and Development (OECD) average is the average of the national averages of the OECD member countries, with each country weighted equally. Scores are reported on a scale from 0 to 1,000. All average scores reported as higher or lower than the U.S. average score are different at the .05 level of statistical significance. Italics indicate non-OECD education systems. Results for Connecticut, Florida, and Massachusetts are for public school students only.
SOURCE: Organization for Economic Cooperation and Development (OECD), Program for International Student Assessment (PISA), 2012. See *Digest of Education Statistics 2013*, table 602.50.

In reading literacy, average scores ranged from 384 in Peru to 570 in Shanghai-CHN. The U.S. average score (498) was not measurably different from the OECD average (496). Nineteen education systems and 2 U.S. states had higher average reading scores and 11 education systems and 1 U.S. state had scores that were not measurably different. The 19 education systems with higher average scores than the United States in reading literacy were

Shanghai-CHN, Hong Kong-CHN, Singapore, Japan, the Republic of Korea, Finland, Ireland, Chinese Taipei-CHN, Canada, Poland, Estonia, Liechtenstein, New Zealand, Australia, the Netherlands, Switzerland, Macao-CHN, Belgium, and Germany. Within the United States, Massachusetts and Connecticut, scored above the US. average.

Figure 3. Percentage of 15-year-old students performing on the Program for International Student Assessment (PISA) reading literacy scale, by selected proficiency level and education system: 2012

Education system	Below level 2	Levels 5 and above
OECD average	18	8
Shanghai-CHN	3*	25*
Singapore	10*	21*
Japan	10*	18*
Hong Kong-CHN	7*	17*
Korea, Republic of	8*	14*
New Zealand	16	14*
Finland	11	13*
France	19	13*
Canada	11	13*
Chinese Taipei-CHN	11*	12*
Belgium	16	12*
Australia	14	12*
Ireland	10*	11*
Liechtenstein	12	11
Norway	16	10*
Poland	11	10
Netherlands	14	10
Israel	24*	10
Switzerland	14*	9
Germany	14	9
Luxembourg	22*	9
United Kingdom	17	9
Estonia	9*	8
United States	17	8
Sweden	23*	8
Macao-CHN	11	7
Italy	20*	7
Czech Republic	17	6*
Iceland	21*	6*
Portugal	19	6*
Hungary	20	6*
Spain	18	6*
Austria	19	6*
Denmark	15	5*
Greece	23*	5*
Slovenia	21*	5*

Education system	Below level 2	Levels 5 and above
OECD average	18	8
Russian Federation	22*	5*
Vietnam	9*	5*
Croatia	19	4*
Slovak Republic	28*	4*
Turkey	22*	4*
Bulgaria	39*	4*
Latvia	17	4*
Cyprus	33*	4*
Lithuania	21*	3*
Serbia, Republic of	33*	2*
United Arab Emirates	36*	2*
Qatar	57*	2*
Romania	37*	2*
Albania	52*	1*
Montenegro, Republic of	43*	1*
Uruguay	47*	1*
Thailand	33*	1*
Chile	33*	1*
Costa Rica	32*	1!*
Argentina	54*	1*
Brazil	49*	1*
Peru	60*	#!*
Mexico	41*	#*
Colombia	51*	#!*
Tunisia	49*	‡
Jordan	51*	‡
Malaysia	53*	‡
Indonesia	55*	‡
Kazakhstan	57*	‡

U.S. state education systems

	Below level 2	Levels 5 and above
Massachusetts	11*	16*
Connecticut	13	15*
Florida	17	6*

■ Below level 2
■ Levels 5 and above
Rounds to zero.
! Interpret data with caution. The coefficient of variation (CV) for this estimate is between 30 and 50 percent.
‡ Reporting standards not met. Either there are too few cases for a reliable estimate or the coefficient of variation (CV) is 50 percent or greater.
* $p < .05$. Significantly different from the U.S. percentage at the .05 level of statistical significance.
NOTE: Education systems are ordered by 2012 percentages of 15-year-olds at levels 5 and above. To reach a particular proficiency level, a student must correctly answer a majority of items at that level. Students were classified into reading proficiency levels according to their scores. Exact cut scores are as follows: below level 1b (a score less than or equal to 262.04); level 1b (a score greater than 262.04 and less than or equal to 334.75); level 1a (a score greater than 334.75 and less than or equal to 407.47); level 2 (a score greater than 407.47 and less than or equal to 480.18); level 3 (a score greater than 480.18 and less than or equal to 552.98); level 4 (a score greater than 552.98 and less than or equal to 625.61); level 5 (a score greater than 625.61 and less than or equal to 698.32); and level 6 (a score greater than 698.32). Scores are reported on a scale from 0 to 1,000. The Organization for Economic Cooperation and Development (OECD) average is the average of the national percentages of the OECD member countries, with each country weighted equally. Italics indicate non-OECD education systems. Results for Connecticut, Florida, and Massachusetts are for public school students only.
SOURCE: Organization for Economic Cooperation and Development (OECD), Program for International Student Assessment (PISA), 2012. See *Digest of Education Statistics 2013*, table 602.50.

In reading, Massachusetts (527) and Connecticut (521) scored above both the U.S. national average and the OECD average. Florida had an average reading score (492) that was not measurably different from either the U.S. average or the OECD average.

PISA reports reading literacy by seven proficiency levels, with level 1b being the lowest and level 6 being the highest. At levels 5 and 6, students have mastered sophisticated reading skills required to interpret and evaluate deeply embedded or abstract text. The percentage of U.S. top performers on the reading literacy scale was not measurably different from the average of the OECD countries' percentages of top performers (both 8 percent). Percentages of top performers ranged from near 0 percent in three education systems to 25 percent in Shanghai-CHN. Fourteen education systems and two U.S. states had percentages of top performers higher than the United States in reading literacy. Massachusetts and Connecticut both had higher percentages of top performers (16 and 15 percent, respectively) than the United States, while Florida had a lower percentage (6 percent).

The percentage of U.S. students who were low performers in reading literacy was not measurably different from the average of the OECD countries' percentages of low performers (17 and 18 percent, respectively). Percentages of low performers ranged from 3 percent in Shanghai-CHN to 60 percent in Peru. Fourteen education systems and one U.S. state had lower percentages of low performers than the United States in reading literacy. Massachusetts had a lower percentage (11 percent) than the United States, while Connecticut and Florida both

had percentages that were not measurably different (13 and 17 percent, respectively).

The United States also participates in the Trends in International Mathematics and Science Study (TIMSS) and the Progress in International Reading Literacy Study (PIRLS). Both assessments are coordinated by the TIMSS & PIRLS International Study Center at Boston College, under the auspices of the International Association for the Evaluation of Educational Achievement (IEA), an international organization of national research institutions and governmental research agencies. TIMSS assesses mathematics and science knowledge and skills at grades 4 and 8, and PIRLS assesses reading literacy at grade 4.

In 2011, there were 57 education systems that had TIMSS mathematics and science data at grade 4 and 56 education systems that had these data at grade 8. Education systems include countries (complete, independent, and political entities) and other benchmarking education systems (portions of a country, nation, kingdom, or emirate, or other non-national entities). These benchmarking systems are able to participate in TIMSS even though they may not be members of the IEA. Participating allows them the opportunity to assess their students' achievement and to view their curricula in an international context. In addition to participating in the U.S. national sample, several U.S. states participated individually and are included as education systems. At the 4th-grade level, two U.S. states (Florida and North Carolina) participated; at the 8th-grade level, nine U.S. states (Alabama, California, Colorado, Connecticut, Florida, Indiana, Massachusetts, Minnesota, and North Carolina) participated.

Table 4.   Average TIMSS mathematics assessment scale scores of 4th-grade students, by education system: 2011

Grade 4			Grade 4	
Education system	Average score		Education system	Average score
TIMSS scale average	500		TIMSS scale average	500
Singapore[1]	606 ⬤		New Zealand	486 ▼
Korea, Republic of	605 ⬤		Spain	482 ▼
Hong Kong-CHN[1]	602 ⬤		Romania	482 ▼
Chinese Taipei-CHN	591 ⬤		Poland	481 ▼
Japan	585 ⬤		Turkey	469 ▼
Northern Ireland-GBR[2]	562 ⬤		Azerbaijan[1,5]	463 ▼
Belgium (Flemish)-BEL	549 ⬤		Chile	462 ▼
Finland	545		Thailand	458 ▼
England-GBR	542		Armenia	452 ▼
Russian Federation	542		Georgia[3,5]	450 ▼
United States[1]	**541**		Bahrain	436 ▼
Netherlands[2]	540		United Arab Emirates	434 ▼
Denmark[1]	537		Iran, Islamic Republic of	431 ▼
Lithuania[1,3]	534 ▼		Qatar[1]	413 ▼
Portugal	532 ▼		Saudi Arabia	410 ▼
Germany	528 ▼		Oman[6]	385 ▼
Ireland	527 ▼		Tunisia[6]	359 ▼
Serbia, Republic of[1]	516 ▼		Kuwait[3,7]	342 ▼
Australia	516 ▼		Morocco[7]	335 ▼
Hungary	515 ▼		Yemen[7]	248 ▼
Slovenia	513 ▼			
Czech Republic	511 ▼			
Austria	508 ▼		**Benchmarking education systems**	
Italy	508 ▼		*North Carolina-USA*[1,3]	554 ▲
Slovak Republic	507 ▼		*Florida-USA*[3,8]	545
Sweden	504 ▼		*Quebec-CAN*	533 ▼
Kazakhstan[1]	501 ▼		*Ontario-CAN*	518 ▼
Malta	496 ▼		*Alberta-CAN*[1]	507 ▼
Norway[4]	495 ▼		*Dubai-UAE*	468 ▼
Croatia[1]	490 ▼		*Abu Dhabi-UAE*	417 ▼

⬤ Average score is higher than U.S. average score.
▼ Average score is lower than U.S. average score.
[1] National Defined Population covers 90 to 95 percent of National Target Population defined by TIMSS.
[2] Met guidelines for sample participation rates only after replacement schools were included.
[3] National Target Population does not include all of the International Target Population defined by TIMSS.
[4] Nearly satisfied guidelines for sample participation rates after replacement schools were included.
[5] Exclusion rates for Azerbaijan and Georgia are slightly underestimated as some conflict zones were not covered and no official statistics were available.
[6] The TIMSS International Study Center has reservations about the reliability of the average achievement score because the percentage of students with achievement too low for estimation exceeds 15 percent, though it is less than 25 percent.
[7] The TIMSS International Study Center has reservations about the reliability of the average achievement score because the percentage of students with achievement too low for estimation exceeds 25 percent.
[8] National Defined Population covers less than 90 percent, but at least 77 percent, of National Target Population defined by TIMSS.
NOTE: Education systems are ordered by 2011 average score. Italics indicate participants identified and counted in this report as an education system and not as a separate country. Trends in International Mathematics and Science Study (TIMSS) scores are reported on a scale from 0 to 1,000, with the scale average set at 500 and the standard deviation set at 100. The TIMSS average includes only education systems that are members of the International Association for the Evaluation of Educational Achievement (IEA), which develops and implements TIMSS at the international level. "Benchmarking" education systems are not members of the IEA and are therefore not included in the average. All U.S. state data are based on public school students only.
SOURCE: Provasnik, S., Kastberg, D., Ferraro, D., Lemanski, N., Roey, S., and Jenkins, F. (2012). *Highlights From TIMSS 2011: Mathematics and Science Achievement of U.S. Fourth- and Eighth-Grade Students in an International Context* (NCES 2013-009), table 3, data from the International Association for the Evaluation of Educational Achievement (IEA), Trends in International Mathematics and Science Study (TIMSS), 2011. See *Digest of Education Statistics 2013*, table 602.20.

At grade 4, the U.S. average mathematics score (541) in 2011 was higher than the TIMSS scale average (500). The United States was among the top 15 education systems in mathematics (8 education systems had higher average scores, and 6 had scores that were not measurably different), and the United States scored higher, on average, than 42 education systems. Seven education systems with average mathematics scores above the U.S. score were Belgium (Flemish)-BEL, Chinese Taipei-CHN,

Hong Kong-CHN, Japan, Northern Ireland-GBR, the Republic of Korea, and Singapore. Among the U.S. states that participated at grade 4, both North Carolina and Florida had average mathematics scores above the TIMSS scale average. North Carolina's score was higher than the U.S. national average; however, Florida's score was not measurably different from the U.S. national average in mathematics.

Table 5. Average TIMSS science assessment scale scores of 4th-grade students, by education system: 2011

Grade 4		Grade 4	
Education system	Average score	Education system	Average score
TIMSS scale average	500	TIMSS scale average	500
Korea, Republic of	587 ⬦	New Zealand	497 ▼
Singapore[1]	583 ⬦	Kazakhstan[1]	495 ▼
Finland	570 ⬦	Norway[4]	494 ▼
Japan	559 ⬦	Chile	480 ▼
Russian Federation	552 ⬦	Thailand	472 ▼
Chinese Taipei-CHN	552 ⬦	Turkey	463 ▼
United States[1]	**544**	Georgia[3,5]	455 ▼
Czech Republic	536 ▼	Iran, Islamic Republic of	453 ▼
Hong Kong-CHN[1]	535 ▼	Bahrain	449 ▼
Hungary	534 ▼	Malta	446 ▼
Sweden	533 ▼	Azerbaijan[1,5]	438 ▼
Slovak Republic	532 ▼	Saudi Arabia	429 ▼
Austria	532 ▼	United Arab Emirates	428 ▼
Netherlands[2]	531 ▼	Armenia	416 ▼
England-GBR	529 ▼	Qatar[1]	394 ▼
Denmark[1]	528 ▼	Oman	377 ▼
Germany	528 ▼	Kuwait[3,6]	347 ▼
Italy	524 ▼	Tunisia[6]	346 ▼
Portugal	522 ▼	Morocco[7]	264 ▼
Slovenia	520 ▼	Yemen[7]	209 ▼
Northern Ireland-GBR[2]	517 ▼		
Ireland	516 ▼		
Croatia[1]	516 ▼	**Benchmarking education systems**	
Australia	516 ▼	Florida-USA[3,8]	545
Serbia, Republic of[1]	516 ▼	Alberta-CAN[1]	541
Lithuania[1,3]	515 ▼	North Carolina-USA[1,3]	538
Belgium (Flemish)-BEL	509 ▼	Ontario-CAN	528 ▼
Romania	505 ▼	Quebec-CAN	516 ▼
Spain	505 ▼	Dubai-UAE	461 ▼
Poland	505 ▼	Abu Dhabi-UAE	411 ▼

⬦ Average score is higher than U.S. average score.
▼ Average score is lower than U.S. average score.
[1] National Defined Population covers 90 to 95 percent of National Target Population defined by TIMSS.
[2] Met guidelines for sample participation rates only after replacement schools were included.
[3] National Target Population does not include all of the International Target Population defined by TIMSS.
[4] Nearly satisfied guidelines for sample participation rates after replacement schools were included.
[5] Exclusion rates for Azerbaijan and Georgia are slightly underestimated as some conflict zones were not covered and no official statistics were available.
[6] The TIMSS International Study Center has reservations about the reliability of the average achievement score because the percentage of students with achievement too low for estimation exceeds 15 percent, though it is less than 25 percent.
[7] The TIMSS International Study Center has reservations about the reliability of the average achievement score because the percentage of students with achievement too low for estimation exceeds 25 percent.
[8] National Defined Population covers less than 90 percent, but at least 77 percent, of National Target Population defined by TIMSS.
NOTE: Education systems are ordered by 2011 average score. Italics indicate participants identified and counted in this report as an education system and not as a separate country. Trends in International Mathematics and Science Study (TIMSS) scores are reported on a scale from 0 to 1,000, with the scale average set at 500 and the standard deviation set at 100. The TIMSS average includes only education systems that are members of the International Association for the Evaluation of Educational Achievement (IEA), which develops and implements TIMSS at the international level. "Benchmarking" education systems are not members of the IEA and are therefore not included in the average. All U.S. state data are based on public school students only.
SOURCE: Provasnik, S., Kastberg, D., Ferraro, D., Lemanski, N., Roey, S., and Jenkins, F. (2012). Highlights From *TIMSS 2011: Mathematics and Science Achievement of U.S. Fourth- and Eighth-Grade Students in an International Context* (NCES 2013-009), table 26, data from the International Association for the Evaluation of Educational Achievement (IEA), Trends in International Mathematics and Science Study (TIMSS), 2011. See *Digest of Education Statistics 2013*, table 602.20.

At grade 4, the U.S. average science score (544) was higher than the TIMSS scale average of 500. The United States was among the top 10 education systems in science (6 education systems had higher average science scores, and 3 had scores that were not measurably different). The United States also scored higher, on average, than 47 education systems in 2011. The six education systems with average science scores above the U.S. score were Chinese Taipei-CHN, Finland, Japan, the Republic of Korea, the Russian Federation, and Singapore. Of the participating education systems within the United States, both Florida and North Carolina scored above the TIMSS scale average, but their science scores were not measurably different from the U.S. national average.

Table 6.   Average TIMSS mathematics assessment scale scores of 8th-grade students, by education system: 2011

Grade 8		Grade 8	
Education system	Average score	Education system	Average score
TIMSS scale average	500	TIMSS scale average	500
Korea, Republic of	613 ⬥	Chile	416 ▼
Singapore[1]	611 ⬥	Iran, Islamic Republic of[6]	415 ▼
Chinese Taipei-CHN	609 ⬥	Qatar[6]	410 ▼
Hong Kong-CHN	586 ⬥	Bahrain[6]	409 ▼
Japan	570 ⬥	Jordan[6]	406 ▼
Russian Federation[1]	539 ⬥	*Palestinian National Authority*[6]	404 ▼
Israel[2]	516	Saudi Arabia[6]	394 ▼
Finland	514	Indonesia[6]	386 ▼
United States[1]	**509**	Syrian Arab Republic[6]	380 ▼
England-GBR[3]	507	Morocco[7]	371 ▼
Hungary	505	Oman[6]	366 ▼
Australia	505	Ghana[7]	331 ▼
Slovenia	505		
Lithuania[4]	502		
Italy	498 ▼		
New Zealand	488 ▼	**Benchmarking education systems**	
Kazakhstan	487 ▼	*Massachusetts-USA*[1,4]	561 ⬥
Sweden	484 ▼	*Minnesota-USA*[4]	545 ⬥
Ukraine	479 ▼	*North Carolina-USA*[2,4]	537 ⬥
Norway	475 ▼	*Quebec-CAN*	532 ⬥
Armenia	467 ▼	*Indiana-USA*[1,4]	522 ⬥
Romania	458 ▼	*Colorado-USA*[4]	518
United Arab Emirates	456 ▼	*Connecticut-USA*[1,4]	518
Turkey	452 ▼	*Florida-USA*[1,4]	513
Lebanon	449 ▼	*Ontario-CAN*[1]	512
Malaysia	440 ▼	*Alberta-CAN*[1]	505
Georgia[4,5]	431 ▼	*California-USA*[1,4]	493 ▼
Thailand	427 ▼	*Dubai-UAE*	478 ▼
Macedonia, Republic of[6]	426 ▼	*Alabama-USA*[4]	466 ▼
Tunisia	425 ▼	*Abu Dhabi-UAE*	449 ▼

⬥ Average score is higher than U.S. average score.
▼ Average score is lower than U.S. average score.
[1] National Defined Population covers 90 to 95 percent of National Target Population defined by TIMSS.
[2] National Defined Population covers less than 90 percent, but at least 77 percent, of National Target Population defined by TIMSS.
[3] Nearly satisfied guidelines for sample participation rates after replacement schools were included.
[4] National Target Population does not include all of the International Target Population defined by TIMSS.
[5] Exclusion rates for Georgia are slightly underestimated as some conflict zones were not covered and no official statistics were available.
[6] The TIMSS International Study Center has reservations about the reliability of the average achievement score because the percentage of students with achievement too low for estimation exceeds 15 percent, though it is less than 25 percent.
[7] The TIMSS International Study Center has reservations about the reliability of the average achievement score because the percentage of students with achievement too low for estimation exceeds 25 percent.
NOTE: Education systems are ordered by 2011 average score. Italics indicate participants identified and counted in this report as an education system and not as a separate country. Trends in International Mathematics and Science Study (TIMSS) scores are reported on a scale from 0 to 1,000, with the scale average set at 500 and the standard deviation set at 100. The TIMSS average includes only education systems that are members of the International Association for the Evaluation of Educational Achievement (IEA), which develops and implements TIMSS at the international level. "Benchmarking" education systems are not members of the IEA and are therefore not included in the average. All U.S. state data are based on public school students only.
SOURCE: Provasnik, S., Kastberg, D., Ferraro, D., Lemanski, N., Roey, S., and Jenkins, F. (2012). *Highlights From TIMSS 2011: Mathematics and Science Achievement of U.S. Fourth- and Eighth-Grade Students in an International Context* (NCES 2013-009), table 4, data from the International Association for the Evaluation of Educational Achievement (IEA), Trends in International Mathematics and Science Study (TIMSS), 2011. See *Digest of Education Statistics 2013*, table 602.30.

At grade 8, the U.S. average mathematics score (509) was higher than the TIMSS scale average of 500. The United States was among the top 24 education systems in mathematics in 2011 (11 education systems had higher average scores, and 12 had scores that were not measurably different). In addition, the United States scored higher, on average, than 32 education systems. The 11 education systems with average mathematics scores above the U.S. score were Chinese Taipei-CHN, Hong Kong-CHN, Japan, Quebec-CAN, the Republic of Korea, the Russian Federation, Singapore, and, within the United States, Indiana, Massachusetts, Minnesota, and North Carolina.

In addition to scoring above the U.S. average in 8th-grade mathematics, Indiana, Massachusetts, Minnesota, and North Carolina also scored above the TIMSS scale average. Colorado, Connecticut, and Florida scored above the TIMSS scale average, but their scores were not measurably different from the U.S. national average. California's score was not measurably different from the TIMSS scale average, but it was below the U.S. national average; Alabama scored below both the TIMSS scale average and the U.S. national average in mathematics.

Table 7.   Average TIMSS science assessment scale scores of 8th-grade students, by education system: 2011

Grade 8			Grade 8		
Education system	Average score		Education system	Average score	
TIMSS scale average	500		TIMSS scale average	500	
Singapore[1]	590	⬥	Saudi Arabia	436	▼
Chinese Taipei-CHN	564	⬥	Malaysia	426	▼
Korea, Republic of	560	⬥	Syrian Arab Republic	426	▼
Japan	558	⬥	*Palestinian National Authority*	420	▼
Finland	552	⬥	Georgia[4,5]	420	▼
Slovenia	543	⬥	Oman	420	▼
Russian Federation[1]	542	⬥	Qatar	419	▼
Hong Kong-CHN	535	⬥	Macedonia, Republic of	407	▼
England-GBR[2]	533		Lebanon	406	▼
United States[1]	**525**		Indonesia	406	▼
Hungary	522		Morocco	376	▼
Australia	519		Ghana[6]	306	▼
Israel[3]	516				
Lithuania[4]	514	▼			
New Zealand	512	▼			
Sweden	509	▼	**Benchmarking education systems**		
Italy	501	▼	*Massachusetts-USA[1,4]*	567	⬥
Ukraine	501	▼	*Minnesota-USA[4]*	553	⬥
Norway	494	▼	*Alberta-CAN[1]*	546	⬥
Kazakhstan	490	▼	*Colorado-USA[4]*	542	⬥
Turkey	483	▼	*Indiana-USA[1,4]*	533	
Iran, Islamic Republic of	474	▼	*Connecticut-USA[1,4]*	532	
Romania	465	▼	*North Carolina-USA[3,4]*	532	
United Arab Emirates	465	▼	*Florida-USA[1,4]*	530	
Chile	461	▼	*Ontario-CAN[1]*	521	
Bahrain	452	▼	*Quebec-CAN*	520	
Thailand	451	▼	*California-USA[1,4]*	499	▼
Jordan	449	▼	*Alabama-USA[4]*	485	▼
Tunisia	439	▼	*Dubai-UAE*	485	▼
Armenia	437	▼	*Abu Dhabi-UAE*	461	▼

⬥ Average score is higher than U.S. average score.
▼ Average score is lower than U.S. average score.
[1] National Defined Population covers 90 to 95 percent of National Target Population defined by TIMSS.
[2] Nearly satisfied guidelines for sample participation rates after replacement schools were included.
[3] National Defined Population covers less than 90 percent, but at least 77 percent, of National Target Population defined by TIMSS.
[4] National Target Population does not include all of the International Target Population defined by TIMSS.
[5] Exclusion rates for Georgia are slightly underestimated as some conflict zones were not covered and no official statistics were available.
[6] The TIMSS International Study Center has reservations about the reliability of the average achievement score because the percentage of students with achievement too low for estimation exceeds 15 percent, though it is less than 25 percent.
NOTE: Education systems are ordered by 2011 average score. Italics indicate participants identified and counted in this report as an education system and not as a separate country. Trends in International Mathematics and Science Study (TIMSS) scores are reported on a scale from 0 to 1,000, with the scale average set at 500 and the standard deviation set at 100. The TIMSS average includes only education systems that are members of the International Association for the Evaluation of Educational Achievement (IEA), which develops and implements TIMSS at the international level. "Benchmarking" education systems are not members of the IEA and are therefore not included in the average. All U.S. state data are based on public school students only.
SOURCE: Provasnik, S., Kastberg, D., Ferraro, D., Lemanski, N., Roey, S., and Jenkins, F. (2012). *Highlights From TIMSS 2011: Mathematics and Science Achievement of U.S. Fourth- and Eighth-Grade Students in an International Context* (NCES 2013-009), table 27, data from the International Association for the Evaluation of Educational Achievement (IEA), Trends in International Mathematics and Science Study (TIMSS), 2011. See *Digest of Education Statistics 2013*, table 602.30.

At grade 8, the U.S. average science score (525) was higher than the TIMSS scale average of 500. The United States was among the top 23 education systems in science in 2011 (12 education systems had higher average scores, and 10 had scores that were not measurably different). The United States scored higher, on average, than 33 education systems. The 12 education systems with average science scores above the U.S. score were Alberta-CAN, Chinese Taipei-CHN, Finland, Hong Kong-CHN, Japan, the Republic of Korea, the Russian Federation, Singapore, Slovenia, and, within the United States, Colorado, Massachusetts, and Minnesota.

Aside from scoring above the U.S. average in 8th-grade science, Colorado, Massachusetts, and Minnesota also scored above the TIMSS scale average of 500. Connecticut, Florida, Indiana, and North Carolina scored above the TIMSS scale average, but their scores were not measurably different from the U.S. national average. California's score was not measurably different from the TIMSS scale average, but it was below the U.S. national average; Alabama scored below both the TIMSS scale average and the U.S. national average in science.

Figure 4. Number of instructional hours per year for 4th-grade students, by country or education system and subject: 2011

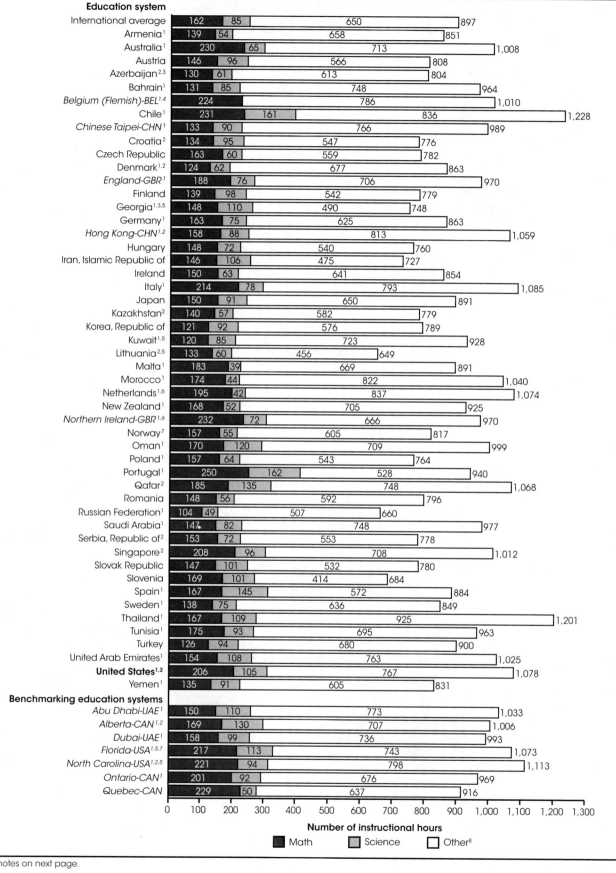

See notes on next page.

[1] Data for number of math, science, and/or total instructional hours are available for at least 50 percent but less than 85 percent of students.
[2] National Defined Population covers 90 to 95 percent of National Target Population defined by TIMSS.
[3] Exclusion rates for Azerbaijan and Georgia are slightly underestimated as some conflict zones were not covered and no official statistics were available.
[4] Data for instructional hours in science are not available. Other instructional hours calculated by subtracting instruction hours in mathematics from total instructional hours.
[5] National Target Population does not include all of the International Target Population defined by TIMSS.
[6] Met guidelines for sample participation rates only after replacement schools were included.
[7] National Defined Population covers less than 90 percent, but at least 77 percent, of National Target Population defined by TIMSS.
[8] Other instructional hours calculated by adding instructional hours in mathematics to instructional hours in science and then subtracting from total instructional hours.
NOTE: Italics indicate participants identified and counted in this report as an education system and not as a separate country. Instructional times shown in this table are actual or implemented times (as opposed to intended times prescribed by the curriculum). Principals reported total instructional hours per day and school days per year. Total instructional hours per year were calculated by multiplying the number of school days per year by the number of instructional hours per day. Teachers reported instructional hours per week in mathematics and science. Instructional hours per year in mathematics and science were calculated by dividing weekly instructional hours by the number of school days per week and then multiplying by the number of school days per year. International average instructional hours includes only education systems that are members of the International Association for the Evaluation of Educational Achievement (IAE), which develops and implements TIMSS at the international level. "Benchmarking" education systems are not members of the IEA and are therefore not included in the average. All U.S. state data are based on public school students only.
SOURCE: Mullis, I.V.S., Martin, M.O., Foy, P., and Arora, A. (2012). *TIMSS 2011 International Results in Mathematics*, exhibit 8.6, and Martin, M.O., Mullis, I.V.S., Foy, P., and Stanco, G.M. (2012). *TIMSS 2011 International Results in Science*, exhibit 8.6. See *Digest of Education Statistics 2013*, table 602.20.

In addition to assessing achievement in mathematics and science, TIMSS collects information from principals on the total number of annual instructional hours in school. TIMSS also collects information from teachers on the number of annual instructional hours spent on mathematics and science instruction at grades 4 and 8. In 2011, education systems (excluding the benchmarking participants) participating in TIMSS at grade 4 spent an average of 897 total hours on instructional time, of which an average of 162 hours (18 percent) were spent on mathematics instruction and 85 hours (9 percent) were spent on science instruction. In 2011, the average number of total instructional hours (1,078 hours) spent in the United States at grade 4 was higher than the international average (897 hours). The average numbers of instructional hours spent on grade 4 mathematics instruction (206 hours) and science instruction (105 hours) in the United States were also higher than the international averages (162 and 85 hours, respectively).

Figure 5. Number of instructional hours per year for 8th-grade students, by country or education system and subject: 2011

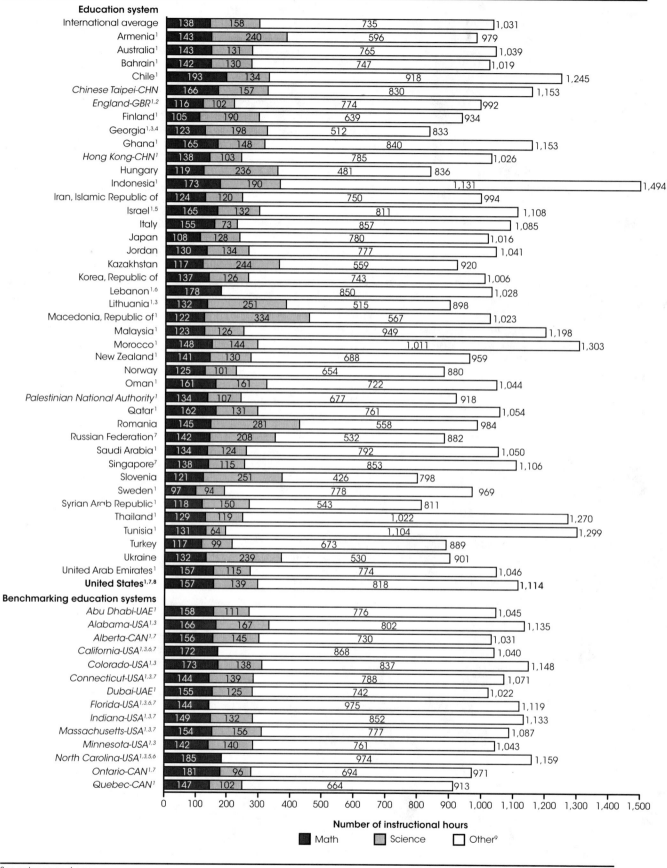

Number of instructional hours

■ Math ▨ Science □ Other[9]

[1] Data for number of math and/or science instructional hours are available for at least 50 percent but less than 85 percent of students.
[2] Nearly satisfied guidelines for sample participation rate after replacement schools were included.
[3] Target Population does not include all of the International Target Population defined by TIMSS.
[4] Exclusion rates for Georgia are slightly underestimated as some conflict zones were not covered and no official statistics were available.
[5] National Defined Population covers less than 90 percent, but at least 77 percent, of National Target Population defined by TIMSS.
[6] Data for instructional hours in science were not available. Other instructional hours calculated by subtracting instruction hours in mathematics from total instructional hours.
[7] National Defined Population covers 90 to 95 percent of National Target Population defined by TIMSS.
[8] Data for science are for 2007 and are from TIMSS 2007 International Results in Science. Met guidelines for sample participation rates only after substitute schools were included. Data for number of math instructional hours are available for at least 50 percent but less than 70 percent of students.
[9] Other instructional hours calculated by adding instructional hours in mathematics to instructional hours in science and then subtracting from total instructional hours.
NOTE: Instructional times shown in this table are actual or implemented times (as opposed to intended times prescribed by the curriculum). Principals reported total instructional hours per day and school days per year. Total instructional hours per year were calculated by multiplying the number of school days per year by the number of instructional hours per day. Teachers reported instructional hours per week in mathematics and science. Instructional hours per year in mathematics and science were calculated by dividing weekly instructional hours by the number of school days per week and then multiplying by the number of school days per year. International average instructional hours includes only education systems that are members of the International Association for the Evaluation of Educational Achievement (IAE), which develops and implements TIMSS at the international level. "Benchmarking" education systems are not members of the IEA and are therefore not included in the average. All U.S. state data are based on public school students only.
SOURCE: Mullis, I.V.S., Martin, M.O., Foy, P., and Arora, A. (2012). *TIMSS 2011 International Results in Mathematics*, exhibit 8.7, and Martin, M.O., Mullis, I.V.S., Foy, P., and Stanco, G.M. (2012). *TIMSS 2011 International Results in Science*, exhibit 8.7. See *Digest of Education Statistics 2013*, table 602.30.

At grade 8, education systems (excluding the benchmarking participants) participating in TIMSS spent an average of 1,031 total annual hours on instructional time in 2011, of which 138 hours (13 percent) were spent on mathematics instruction and 158 hours (15 percent) were spent on science instruction. Similar to the findings at grade 4, the United States' average number of total instructional hours at grade 8 (1,114 hours) was higher than the international average (1,031 hours). The average hours spent on grade 8 mathematics instruction (157 hours) in the United States was also higher than the international average (138 hours).

Table 8. Average PIRLS reading literacy assessment scale scores of 4th-grade students, by education system: 2011

Education system	Overall reading average scale score	Education system	Overall reading average scale score
PIRLS scale average	500	PIRLS scale average	500
Hong Kong-CHN[1]	571 ⬥	France	520 ▼
Russian Federation	568 ⬥	Spain	513 ▼
Finland	568 ⬥	Norway[5]	507 ▼
Singapore[2]	567 ⬥	Belgium (French)-BEL[2,3]	506 ▼
Northern Ireland-GBR[3]	558	Romania	502 ▼
United States[2]	**556**	Georgia[4,6]	488 ▼
Denmark[2]	554	Malta	477 ▼
Croatia[2]	553	Trinidad and Tobago	471 ▼
Chinese Taipei-CHN	553	Azerbaijan[2,6]	462 ▼
Ireland	552	Iran, Islamic Republic of	457 ▼
England-GBR[3]	552	Colombia	448 ▼
Canada[2]	548 ▼	United Arab Emirates	439 ▼
Netherlands[3]	546 ▼	Saudi Arabia	430 ▼
Czech Republic	545 ▼	Indonesia	428 ▼
Sweden	542 ▼	Qatar[2]	425 ▼
Italy	541 ▼	Oman[7]	391 ▼
Germany	541 ▼	Morocco[8]	310 ▼
Israel[1]	541 ▼		
Portugal	541 ▼		
Hungary	539 ▼	**Benchmarking education systems**	
Slovak Republic	535 ▼	Florida-USA[1,4]	569 ⬥
Bulgaria	532 ▼	Ontario-CAN[2]	552
New Zealand	531 ▼	Alberta-CAN[2]	548 ▼
Slovenia	530 ▼	Quebec-CAN	538 ▼
Austria	529 ▼	Andalusia-ESP	515 ▼
Lithuania[2,4]	528 ▼	Dubai-UAE	476 ▼
Australia	527 ▼	Maltese-MLT	457 ▼
Poland	526 ▼	Abu Dhabi-UAE	424 ▼

⬥ Average score is higher than U.S. average score.
▼ Average score is lower than U.S. average score.
[1] National Defined Population covers less than 90 percent of National Target Population defined by PIRLS.
[2] National Defined Population covers 90 percent to 95 percent of National Target Population defined by PIRLS.
[3] Met guidelines for sample participation rates only after replacement schools were included.
[4] National Target Population does not include all of the International Target Population defined by PIRLS.
[5] Nearly satisfied guidelines for sample participation rates after replacement schools were included.
[6] Exclusion rates for Azerbaijan and Georgia are slightly underestimated as some conflict zones were not covered and no official statistics were available.
[7] The PIRLS International Study Center has reservations about the reliability of the average achievement score because the percentage of students with achievement too low for estimation exceeds 15 percent, though it is less than 25 percent.
[8] The PIRLS International Study Center has reservations about the reliability of the average achievement score because the percentage of students with achievement too low for estimation exceeds 25 percent.
NOTE: Education systems are ordered by 2011 average score. Italics indicate participants identified and counted in this report as an education system and not as a separate country. The Progress in International Reading Literacy Study (PIRLS) scores are reported on a scale from 0 to 1,000, with the scale average set at 500 and the standard deviation set at 100. The PIRLS average includes only education systems that are members of the International Association for the Evaluation of Educational Achievement (IEA), which develops and implements PIRLS at the international level. "Benchmarking" education systems are not members of the IEA and are therefore not included in the average. All U.S. state data are based on public school students only.
SOURCE: Thompson, S., Provasnik, S., Kastberg, D., Ferraro, D., Lemanski, N., Roey, S., and Jenkins, F. (2012). *Highlights From PIRLS 2011: Reading Achievement of U.S. Fourth-Grade Students in an International Context* (NCES 2013-010), table 3, data from the International Association for the Evaluation of Educational Achievement (IEA), Progress in International Reading Literacy Study (PIRLS), 2011. See *Digest of Education Statistics 2013*, table 602.10.

In 2011, there were 53 education systems that had PIRLS reading literacy data at grade 4. These 53 education systems included both countries and other benchmarking education systems. In addition to participating in the U.S. national sample, Florida participated individually and was included as an education system. In 2011, the U.S. average 4th-grade reading literacy score (556) was higher than the PIRLS scale average (500). The United States was among the top 13 education systems in reading literacy (5 education systems had higher average scores, and 7 had scores that were not measurably different).

The United States scored higher, on average, than 40 education systems.

The five education systems with average reading scores above the U.S. score were Finland, Hong Kong-CHN, the Russian Federation, Singapore, and, within the United States, Florida. Additionally, Florida's average score (569) was higher than the PIRLS scale average. No education system scored higher than Florida, although four had scores that were not measurably different. Forty-eight education systems scored lower than Florida.

Reference tables: *Digest of Education Statistics 2013,* tables 602.10, 602.20, 602.30, 602.50, 602.60, and 602.70

Related indicators: Educational Attainment of Young Adults, International Educational Attainment, U.S. Student and Adult Performance on International Assessments of Educational Achievement [*The Condition of Education 2006 Special Analysis*], U.S. Performance Across International Assessments of Student Achievement [*The Condition of Education 2009 Special Analysis*]

Glossary: Organization for Economic Cooperation and Development (OECD)

High School Coursetaking

The percentages of high school graduates who had taken mathematics courses in algebra I, geometry, algebra II/trigonometry, analysis/precalculus, statistics/ probability, and calculus increased from 1990 to 2009. The percentages of high school graduates who had taken science courses in chemistry and physics also increased between 1990 and 2009.

In addition to administering student assessments, the National Assessment of Educational Progress (NAEP) periodically collects data on the transcripts of high school graduates. The transcript survey gathers information about the types of courses that graduates from regular and honors programs take, how many credits they earn, their grade point averages, and the relationship between coursetaking patterns and achievement. The transcript data include information only about the coursework that graduates completed while they were enrolled in grades 9 through 12.

Figure 1. Percentage of high school graduates who completed selected mathematics and science courses in high school: 1990 and 2009

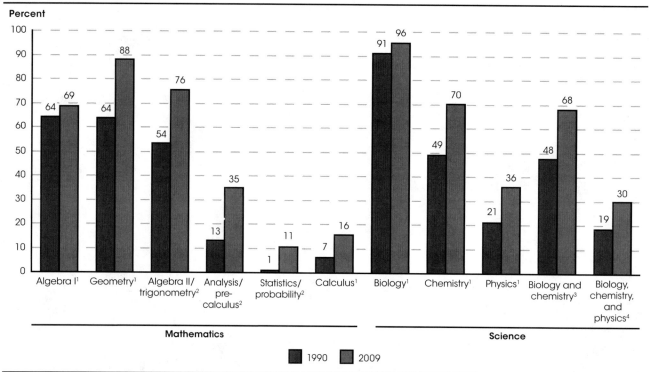

[1] Percentages are for students who earned at least one Carnegie credit.
[2] Percentages are for students who earned at least one-half of a Carnegie credit.
[3] Percentages are for students who earned at least one Carnegie credit each in biology and chemistry.
[4] Percentages are for students who earned at least one Carnegie credit each in biology, chemistry, and physics.
NOTE: For a transcript to be included in the analyses, the graduate had to receive either a standard or honors diploma.
SOURCE: U.S. Department of Education, National Center for Education Statistics, High School Transcript Study (HSTS), 1990 and 2009. See *Digest of Education Statistics 2013*, table 225.40.

The percentages of high school graduates who had completed mathematics courses in algebra I, geometry, algebra II/trigonometry, analysis/precalculus, statistics/ probability, and calculus increased between 1990 and 2009. For example, the percentage of graduates who had completed calculus increased from 7 percent to 16 percent between 1990 and 2009. Similarly, the percentage of graduates who had completed algebra II/trigonometry increased from 54 percent to 76 percent.

Between 1990 and 2009, the percentages of high school graduates who had taken various mathematics courses generally increased across subgroups. For example, the percentage of Hispanic graduates completing calculus increased from 4 percent in 1990 to 9 percent in 2009. Also, the percentage of Hispanic graduates completing algebra II/trigonometry increased from 40 percent to 71 percent. Similarly, the percentage of Black graduates completing calculus during this period increased from 3 to 6 percent, and the percentage completing algebra II/trigonometry increased from 44 to 71 percent. Although there were increases in mathematics coursetaking across racial/ethnic groups during this period, gaps between groups remained in terms of the percentages of graduates completing courses. For example, in 2009 higher percentages of Asian/Pacific Islander (42 percent) and White graduates (18 percent) had taken calculus than had their Black (6 percent) and Hispanic peers (9 percent). In 2009, there was no measurable difference between the percentages of males and females who had taken calculus (16 percent each). However, the percentage of females who had taken algebra II/trigonometry (78 percent) was higher than that of male graduates (74 percent).

The percentages of high school graduates who had taken science courses in chemistry and physics also increased between 1990 and 2009. The percentage of graduates who had taken chemistry increased from 49 to 70 percent, and the percentage of graduates who had completed physics courses increased from 21 to 36 percent. The percentage of graduates who earned at least one credit in biology, chemistry, and physics increased from 19 percent in 1990 to 30 percent in 2009.

The general increases in science coursetaking in biology, chemistry, and physics between 1990 and 2009 were reflected by increases for students of most racial/ethnic groups. For instance, the percentage of Hispanic graduates who had completed a chemistry course increased from 38 to 66 percent, and the percentage of Hispanic graduates who had completed at least one credit in biology, chemistry, and physics increased from 10 to 23 percent. Similarly, the percentage of Black graduates who had completed a chemistry course increased from 40 to 65 percent, and the percentage of Black graduates who had completed at least one credit in biology, chemistry, and physics increased from 12 to 22 percent. Although there were increases in coursetaking among student groups from 1990 to 2009, gaps between different subgroups in coursetaking remained. In 2009, a higher percentage of Asian (54 percent) and White (31 percent) graduates had completed the combination of biology, chemistry, and physics courses than had their Black and Hispanic peers (22 percent and 23 percent, respectively). A higher percentage of males (39 percent) than of females (33 percent) had completed a physics class in 2009; however, a higher percentage of females (73 percent) than of males (67 percent) had taken chemistry.

Figure 2. Average National Assessment of Educational Progress (NAEP) 12th-grade mathematics scale scores of high school graduates, by highest mathematics course taken and race/ethnicity: 2009

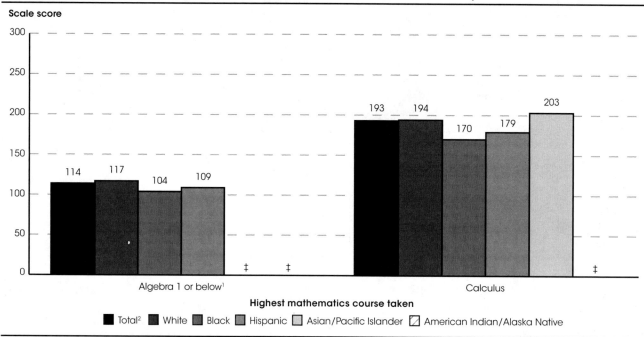

‡ Reporting standards not met (too few cases for a reliable estimate).
[1] Includes basic math, general math, applied math, pre-algebra, and algebra I.
[2] Includes other racial/ethnic groups not shown separately and cases that were missing information on race/ethnicity and/or sex of student.
NOTE: The scale of the NAEP mathematics assessment for grade 12 ranges from 0 to 300. For a transcript to be included in the analyses, the graduate had to receive either a standard or honors diploma. Race categories exclude persons of Hispanic ethnicity. Reporting standards were not met for American Indian/Alaska Native estimates; therefore, data for this racial group are not shown in the figure.
SOURCE: U.S. Department of Education, National Center for Education Statistics, National Assessment of Educational Progress (NAEP), 2009 Mathematics Assessment; and High School Transcript Study (HSTS), 2009. See *Digest of Education Statistics 2013*, table 222.40.

A higher percentage of 2009 graduates from private schools (85 percent) had taken courses in algebra II/trigonometry than had graduates from traditional public schools (75 percent), and a higher percentage of graduates from private schools (23 percent) had taken courses in calculus than had graduates from public schools (15 percent). Also, a higher percentage of private high school graduates (44 percent) had taken at least one credit in biology, chemistry, and physics than had graduates from traditional public schools (29 percent). A higher percentage of graduates from city (32 percent) and suburban (39 percent) schools had taken courses in biology, chemistry, and physics than had graduates from schools in towns (19 percent) or rural areas (20 percent).

In 2009, higher average scale scores on the National Assessment of Educational Progress (NAEP) 12th-grade mathematics assessment were associated with higher levels of high school mathematics coursetaking. For example,

graduates who had taken only algebra I or below had an average scale score of 114 (on a scale of 0–300), whereas graduates who had taken calculus had an average scale score of 193. In addition, among those students who had completed specific mathematics courses, there were differences across demographic subgroups. For graduates who had taken calculus, the average scale score was higher for males than for females (197 vs. 190). Average scale scores were also higher for students who had taken calculus who were Asian/Pacific Islander (203) and White (194) than for their Hispanic (179) and Black (170) peers. Among students who had taken calculus, the average scale score for those who had attended low-poverty schools (schools in which 0 to 25 percent of students receive, or are eligible to receive, free or reduced-price lunch under the National School Lunch Program) was 199, compared with a score of 163 for their peers at high-poverty schools (schools in which 75 to 100 percent of students receive, or are eligible to receive, free or reduced-price lunch).

Reference tables: *Digest of Education Statistics 2013,* tables 222.40 and 225.40

Related indicators: A Closer Look at High School Students in the United States Over the Last 20 Years [*The Condition of Education 2012 Special Analysis*]

Glossary: Free or reduced-price lunch, Locale codes, National School Lunch Program, Private school, Public school or institution, Racial/ethnic group

This page intentionally left blank.

Public High School Graduation Rates

In school year 2013-14, the adjusted cohort graduation rate (ACGR) for public high schools rose to an all-time high of 82 percent. This indicates that approximately 4 out of 5 students graduated with a regular high school diploma within 4 years of the first time they started 9th grade. Asian/Pacific Islander students had the highest ACGR (89 percent), followed by White (87 percent), Hispanic (76 percent), Black (73 percent), and American Indian/Alaska Native (70 percent) students.

This indicator examines two widely used measures of high school completion: the averaged freshman graduation rate (AFGR) and the adjusted cohort graduation rate (ACGR). Both rates measure the percentage of public school students who attain a regular high school diploma within 4 years of starting 9th grade for the first time. However, they differ in important ways. The AFGR is an estimate of the on-time 4-year graduation rate derived from aggregate student enrollment data and graduate counts. The ACGR, on the other hand, uses detailed student-level data to determine the percentage of students who graduate within 4 years of starting 9th grade for the first time. In many states, the data required to produce the ACGR have become available only in recent years. The AFGR estimate is less precise than the ACGR, but it can be estimated as far back as the 1960s.

Figure 1. Averaged freshman graduation rate (AFGR) for public high school students: School years 1990–91 through 2012–13

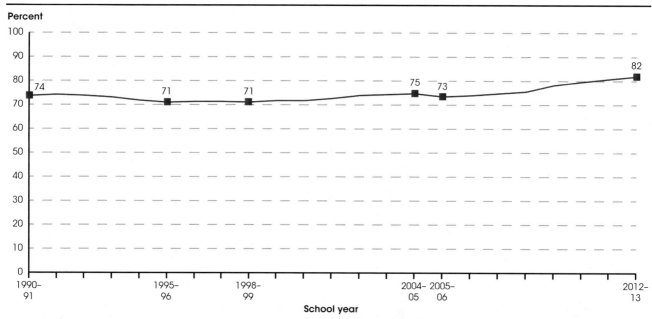

NOTE: The AFGR provides an estimate of the percentage of high school students who graduate within 4 years of first starting 9th grade. The rate uses aggregate student enrollment data to estimate the size of an incoming freshman class and aggregate counts of diplomas awarded 4 years later.
SOURCE: U.S. Department of Education, National Center for Education Statistics, Common Core of Data (CCD), "State Nonfiscal Survey of Public Elementary/Secondary Education," 1986–1987 through 2009–10; "State Dropout and Completion Data File," 2005–06 through 2012–13; *Public School Graduates and Dropouts From the Common Core of Data,* 2007–08 and 2008–09. See *Digest of Education Statistics 2015,* table 219.10.

In school year 2012–13, the national AFGR was 82 percent,[1] and some 3.2 million public high school students graduated with a regular diploma. The overall AFGR was higher for the graduating class of 2012–13 than for the class of 1990–91 (74 percent). However, from 1990–91 to 1995–96 the rate decreased from 74 to 71 percent. During the period from 1998–99 to 2004–05, the rate steadily increased from 71 to 75 percent. After dropping to 73 percent in 2005–06, the rate increased to 82 percent in 2012–13.

Figure 2. Adjusted cohort graduation rate (ACGR) for public high school students, by state: School year 2013–14

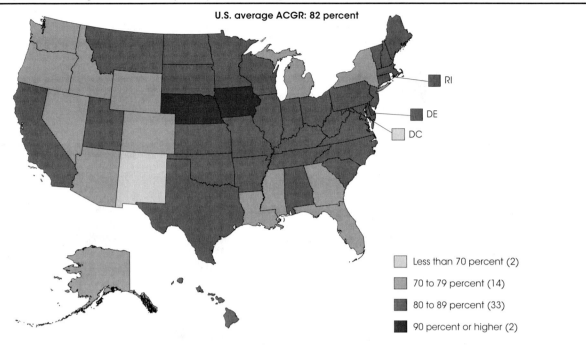

U.S. average ACGR: 82 percent

Less than 70 percent (2)

70 to 79 percent (14)

80 to 89 percent (33)

90 percent or higher (2)

NOTE: The adjusted cohort graduation rate (ACGR) is the percentage of public high school freshmen who graduate with a regular diploma within 4 years of starting 9th grade. The Bureau of Indian Education and Puerto Rico were not included in the United States 4-year ACGR estimate. The graduation rates displayed above have been rounded to whole numbers. The categorizations shown may vary slightly from how the unrounded rates would be categorized. SOURCE: U.S. Department of Education, Office of Elementary and Secondary Education, Consolidated State Performance Report, 2013–14. See *Digest of Education Statistics 2015*, table 219.46.

At the national level, the ACGR closely tracks the AFGR. The ACGR increased over the first 4 years in which it was collected by the U.S. Department of Education, from 79 percent in 2010–11 to 82 percent in 2013–14. These rates indicate that approximately 4 out of 5 students received a regular high school diploma within 4 years of first starting 9th grade.

In 2013–14, the state-level ACGRs ranged from 61 percent in the District of Columbia to 90 percent in Nebraska and 91 percent in Iowa. In addition to the District of Columbia, six states reported graduation rates at or below 75 percent: Louisiana (75 percent), Georgia (73 percent), Oregon (72 percent), Alaska (71 percent), Nevada (70 percent), and New Mexico (69 percent).

Figure 3. Adjusted cohort graduation rate (ACGR) for public high school students, by race/ethnicity: School year 2013–14

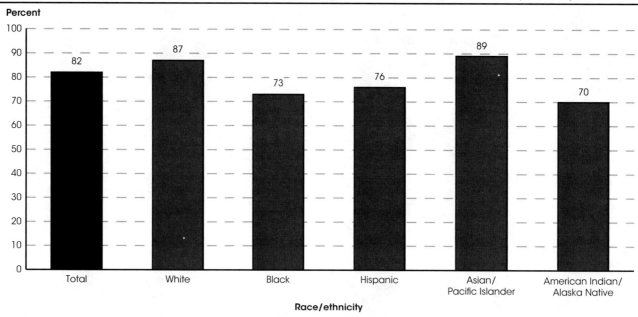

NOTE: The adjusted cohort graduation rate (ACGR) is the percentage of public high school freshmen who graduate with a regular diploma within 4 years of starting 9th grade. The Bureau of Indian Education and Puerto Rico were not included in United States 4-year ACGR estimates. Race categories exclude persons of Hispanic ethnicity.
SOURCE: U.S. Department of Education, Office of Elementary and Secondary Education, Consolidated State Performance Report, 2013–14. See *Digest of Education Statistics 2015*, table 219.46.

In 2013–14, the ACGRs for American Indian/Alaska Native (70 percent), Black (73 percent), and Hispanic (76 percent) students were below the national average of 82 percent. The ACGRs for White (87 percent) and Asian/Pacific Islander (89 percent) students were above the national average. Across states, ACGRs for White students ranged from 74 percent in Oregon to 94 percent in New Jersey, and were higher than the overall national ACGR of 82 percent in 38 states and the District of Columbia. The rates for Black students ranged from 54 percent in Nevada to 89 percent in Montana and were higher than the total national ACGR in five states (Alabama, Delaware, Montana, New Hampshire, and Texas). The ACGRs for Hispanic students ranged from 63 percent in

Minnesota to 89 percent in West Virginia and were higher than the overall national ACGR in eight states (Alabama, Arkansas, Delaware, Indiana, Kentucky, Nebraska, Texas, and West Virginia). For Asian/Pacific Islander students, ACGRs ranged from 74 percent in Alaska to 96 percent in New Jersey and were higher than the overall national ACGR in 45 states.[2] The ACGRs for American Indian/Alaska Native students ranged from 47 percent in South Dakota and Wyoming to 89 percent in Delaware and were higher than the total national ACGR in 11 states (Alabama, Arkansas, Connecticut, Delaware, Indiana, Kentucky, Maryland, Missouri, New Hampshire, New Jersey, and Texas).[3]

Figure 4.   Adjusted cohort graduation rate (ACGR) of White and Black public high school students, by state: 2013–14

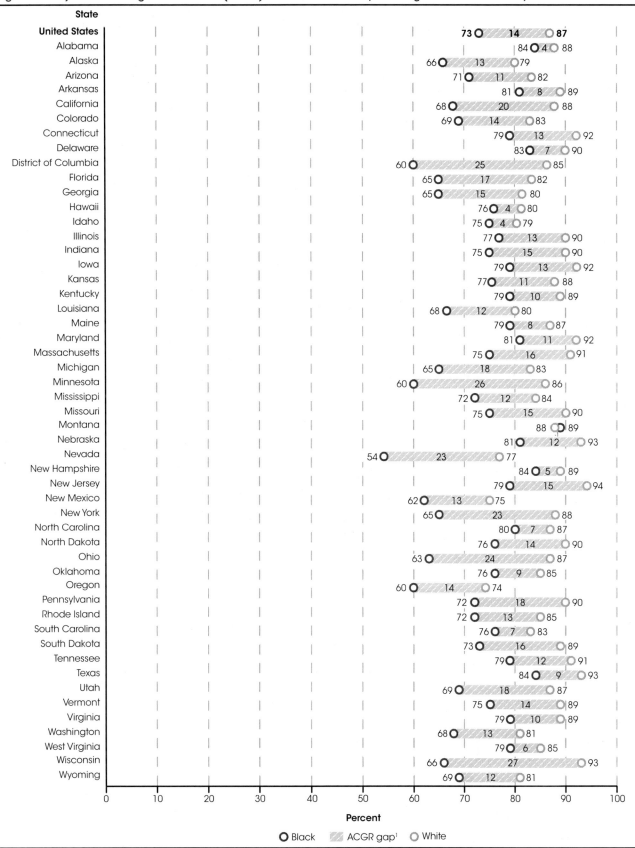

O Black   ▨ ACGR gap¹   O White

¹ The graduation rate gaps were calculated using graduation rates that were rounded to whole numbers. These gaps may vary slightly from those that would be calculated using unrounded rates.
NOTE: The adjusted cohort graduation rate (ACGR) is the percentage of public high school freshmen who graduate with a regular diploma within 4 years of starting 9th grade. The Bureau of Indian Education and Puerto Rico were not included in the United States 4-year ACGR estimate. Race categories exclude persons of Hispanic ethnicity.
SOURCE: U.S. Department of Education, Office of Elementary and Secondary Education, Consolidated State Performance Report, 2013–14. See *Digest of Education Statistics 2015*, table 219.46.

The national ACGR for White students (87 percent) was 14 percentage points[4] higher than the national ACGR for Black students (73 percent) in 2013–14. White public high school students had higher ACGRs than Black public high school students in all states except Montana, where the ACGRs for White and Black students were 88 and 89 percent, respectively. Wisconsin, Minnesota, the District of Columbia, Ohio, New York, and Nevada reported the largest gaps between White and Black students. In each of these states and the District of Columbia, the ACGR for White students was over 20 percentage points higher than the ACGR for Black students.

Figure 5. Adjusted cohort graduation rate (ACGR) of White and Hispanic public high school students, by state: 2013–14

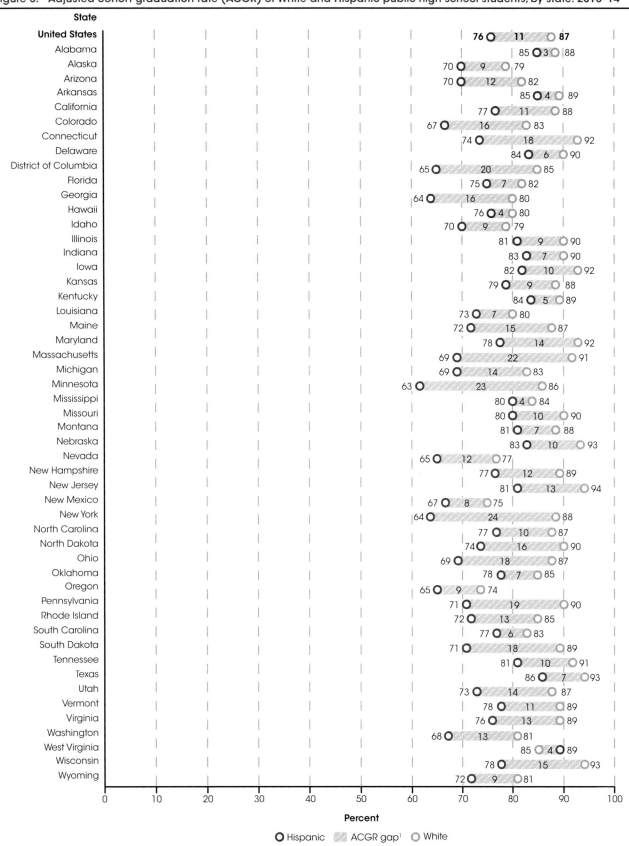

O Hispanic   ▨ ACGR gap[1]   O White

[1] The graduation rate gaps were calculated using graduation rates that were rounded to whole numbers. These gaps may vary slightly from those that would be calculated using unrounded rates.
NOTE: The adjusted cohort graduation rate (ACGR) is the percentage of public high school freshmen who graduate with a regular diploma within 4 years of starting 9th grade. The Bureau of Indian Education and Puerto Rico were not included in the United States 4-year ACGR estimate. Race categories exclude persons of Hispanic ethnicity.
SOURCE: U.S. Department of Education, Office of Elementary and Secondary Education, Consolidated State Performance Report, 2013–14. See *Digest of Education Statistics 2015*, table 219.46.

States reported similar gaps in ACGRs between White and Hispanic public high school students. The national ACGR for White students (87 percent) was 11 percentage points higher than the national ACGR for Hispanic students (76 percent) in 2013–14. The ACGRs for White students were higher than the ACGRs for Hispanic students in every state except West Virginia. In West Virginia the ACGR for Hispanic students (89 percent) was 4 percentage points higher than the ACGR for White students (85 percent). New York, Minnesota, and Massachusetts reported the largest gaps between White and Hispanic students. In each of these three states, the ACGR for White students was more than 20 percentage points higher than the ACGR for Hispanic students.

Endnotes:

[1] This indicator uses graduation rates that have been rounded to whole numbers. As such, comparisons among states and between racial and ethnic groups may differ slightly from comparisons based on unrounded rates.

[2] Discussion of ACGRs for Asian/Pacific Islander students excludes data for the District of Columbia. Data for the District of Columbia were suppressed due to small cell sizes.

[3] Discussion of ACGRs for American Indian/Alaska Native students excludes data for three jurisdictions: the District of Columbia, Vermont, and Virginia. Data for the District of Columbia and Vermont were suppressed due to small cell sizes, and data for Virginia were unavailable.

[4] Percentage point gaps were calculated using graduation rates that have been rounded to whole numbers.

Reference tables: *Digest of Education Statistics 2015*, tables 219.10 and 219.46

Related indicators: Educational Attainment of Young Adults, Status Dropout Rates

Glossary: Averaged freshman graduation rate (AFGR), High school completer, High school diploma, Public school or institution, Racial/ethnic group

This page intentionally left blank.

Status Dropout Rates

The status dropout rate decreased from 12.1 percent in 1990 to 6.5 percent in 2014, with most of the decline occurring since 2000. From 1990 to 2014, the Hispanic status dropout rate decreased by 21.8 percentage points, while the Black and White status dropout rates decreased by 5.8 and 3.7 percentage points, respectively. Nevertheless, in 2014 the Hispanic status dropout rate (10.6 percent) remained higher than the White (5.2 percent) and Black (7.4 percent) status dropout rates.

The *status dropout rate* represents the percentage of 16- to 24-year-olds (referred to as youth in this indicator) who are not enrolled in school and have not earned a high school credential (either a diploma or an equivalency credential such as a GED certificate).[1] Graduation rates reflect the percentage of students earning a regular diploma within 4 years of entering high school. Based on data from the Current Population Survey, the status dropout rate decreased from 12.1 percent in 1990 to 6.5 percent in 2014, with most of the decline occurring after 2000 (when it was 10.9 percent). However, there was no measurable difference between the 2013 rate and the 2014 rate.

Figure 1.   Status dropout rates of 16- to 24-year-olds, by sex: 1990 through 2014

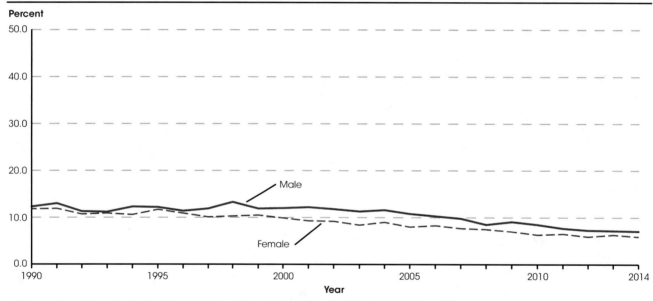

NOTE: The "status dropout rate" is the percentage of 16- to 24-year-olds who are not enrolled in school and have not earned a high school credential (either a diploma or an equivalency credential such as a GED certificate). Data are based on sample surveys of the civilian noninstitutionalized population, which excludes persons in prisons, persons in the military, and other persons not living in households.
SOURCE: U.S. Department of Commerce, Census Bureau, Current Population Survey (CPS), October 1990 through 2014. See *Digest of Education Statistics 2015*, table 219.70.

Between 1990 and 2014, the male status dropout rate declined from 12.3 to 7.1 percent, with nearly the entire decline occurring after 2000 (when it was 12.0 percent). For females, the rate declined from 11.8 percent in 1990 to 9.9 percent in 2000, and then decreased further to 5.9 percent in 2014. In 2014, the status dropout rate was higher for males than for females.

Figure 2.   Status dropout rates of 16- to 24-year-olds, by race/ethnicity: 1990 through 2014

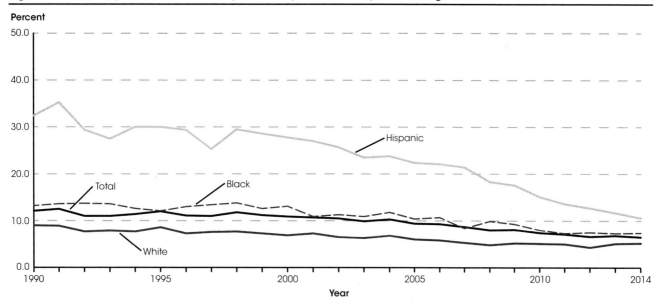

NOTE: The "status dropout rate" is the percentage of 16- to 24-year-olds who are not enrolled in school and have not earned a high school credential (either a diploma or an equivalency credential such as a GED certificate). Data are based on sample surveys of the civilian noninstitutionalized population, which excludes persons in prisons, persons in the military, and other persons not living in households. Data for all races include other racial/ethnic categories not separately shown. Race categories exclude persons of Hispanic ethnicity.
SOURCE: U.S. Department of Commerce, Census Bureau, Current Population Survey (CPS), October 1990 through 2014. See *Digest of Education Statistics 2015*, table 219.70.

In each year from 1990 to 2014, the status dropout rate was lower for White youth than for Black youth, and the rates for both White and Black youth were lower than the rate for Hispanic youth. During this period, the status dropout rate declined from 9.0 to 5.2 percent for White youth; from 13.2 to 7.4 percent for Black youth; and from 32.4 to 10.6 percent for Hispanic youth. As a result, the gap between White and Hispanic youth narrowed from 23.4 percentage points in 1990 to 5.3 percentage points in 2014. Most of this gap was narrowed between 2000 and 2014, when the gap between White and Hispanic youth declined from 20.9 to 5.3 percentage points. Although the rates for both White and Black youth declined from 1990 to 2014, the gap between the rates in 2014 did not measurably differ from the gap between the rates in 1990. However, the White-Black gap narrowed from 6.2 percentage points in 2000 to 2.2 percentage points in 2014.

Figure 3. Status dropout rates of 16- to 24-year-olds, by income level: 1990 through 2014

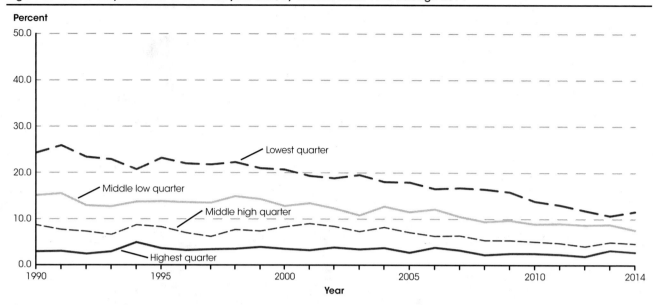

NOTE: The "status dropout rate" is the percentage of 16- to 24-year-olds who are not enrolled in school and have not earned a high school credential (either a diploma or an equivalency credential such as a GED certificate). The "lowest" quarter represents the bottom 25 percent of family incomes. The "middle low" quarter represents families between the 25th percentile and the median (50th percentile). The "middle high" quarter represents families with incomes between the median (50th percentile) and the 75th percentile. The "highest" quarter represents the top 25 percent of all family incomes. Data are based on sample surveys of the civilian noninstitutionalized population, which excludes persons in prisons, persons in the military, and other persons not living in households.
SOURCE: U.S. Department of Commerce, Census Bureau, Current Population Survey (CPS), October 1990 through 2014. See *Digest of Education Statistics 2015*, table 219.75.

The status dropout rate also declined for youth in low- and middle-income families between 1990 and 2014. Status dropout rates declined from 24.3 to 11.6 percent for those in families with the lowest incomes (the bottom 25 percent of all family incomes), from 15.1 to 7.6 percent for those in "middle low" income families (families with incomes between the 25th percentile and the median), and from 8.7 to 4.7 percent for those in "middle high" income families (families with incomes between the median and the 75th percentile). For those in the highest income families (the top 25 percent of all family incomes), the status dropout rate in 2014 (2.8 percent) was not measurably different from the status dropout rate in 1990 (2.9 percent). During this period, the status dropout rate for those in the highest income families was consistently lower than the rates for those in all other income groups. Conversely, the rates for those in the lowest income families were consistently higher than the rates for those in the "middle high" and "middle low" income families, with the exception of 2013, when the rates between those in the lowest income families and those in the "middle low" income families were not measurably different. While differences between those in the lowest income families and highest income families remained, the gap in the status dropout rate between these two groups narrowed from 21.4 percentage points in 1990 to 8.8 percentage points in 2014.

Figure 4. Percentage distribution of status dropouts, by years of school completed: 1990 through 2014

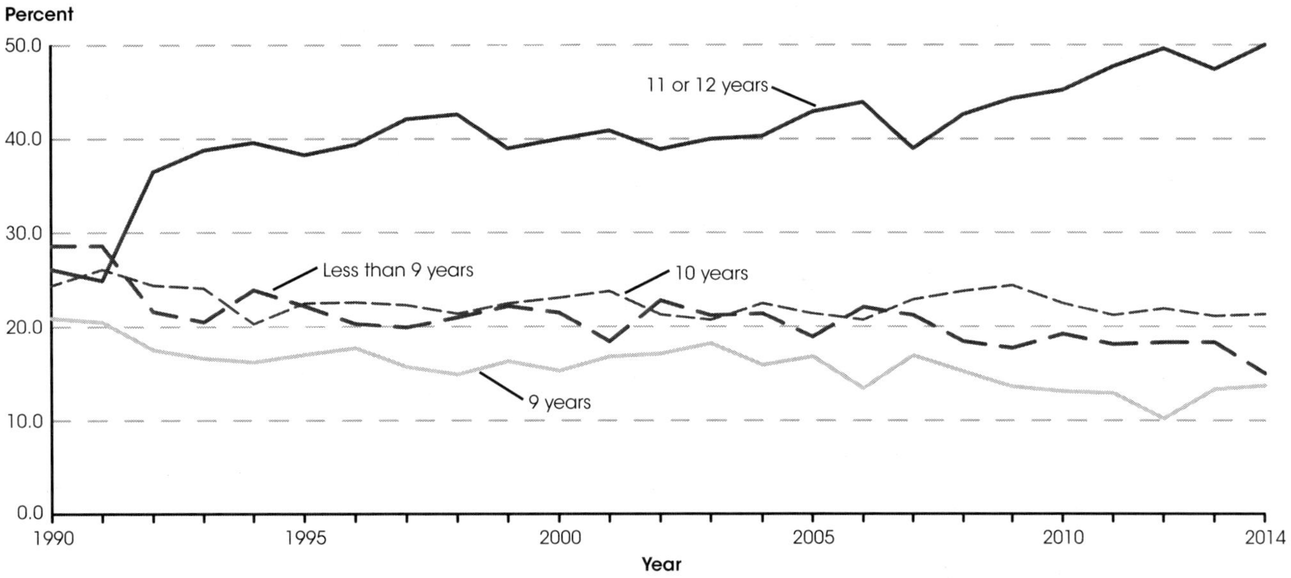

NOTE: "Status dropouts" are 16- to 24-year-olds who are not enrolled in school and have not earned a high school credential (either a diploma or an equivalency credential such as a GED certificate). Data are based on sample surveys of the civilian noninstitutionalized population, which excludes persons in prisons, persons in the military, and other persons not living in households.
SOURCE: U.S. Department of Commerce, Census Bureau, Current Population Survey (CPS), October 1990 through 2014. See *Digest of Education Statistics 2015*, table 219.75.

The decline in the overall status dropout rate from 12.1 percent in 1990 to 6.5 percent in 2014 coincided with a shift in the distribution of years of school completed by status dropouts, as fewer status dropouts completed less than 9 years of schooling while more completed 11 or 12 years of schooling. The percentage of status dropouts with less than 9 years of schooling decreased from 28.6 percent in 1990 to 15.0 percent in 2014. Conversely, the percentage of status dropouts who had completed 11 or 12 years of schooling but did not receive a diploma or GED certificate increased from 26.1 percent in 1990 to 50.0 percent in 2014.

Status dropout rates can also be calculated using data from the American Community Survey (ACS), which includes individuals living in households as well as institutional and noninstitutional group quarters. Institutional group quarters include adult and juvenile correctional facilities, nursing facilities, and other health care facilities. Noninstitutional group quarters include college and university housing, military quarters, facilities for workers and religious groups, and temporary shelters for the homeless. In 2014, the overall status dropout rate was 6.3 percent; in addition, this rate was lower for those living in households and noninstitutionalized group quarters (6.0 percent) than for those living in institutionalized group quarters (33.1 percent).

The total status dropout rate across individuals in households, institutional group quarters, and noninstitutional group quarters varied by race/ethnicity. The status dropout rate in 2014 was lower for Asian (2.5 percent) and White (4.4 percent) youth than for youth of Two or more races (5.0 percent) and Black (7.9 percent), Pacific Islander (10.6 percent), Hispanic (10.7 percent), and American Indian/Alaska Native (11.5 percent) youth. The Asian status dropout rate was also lower than the rate for White youth.

Figure 5.   Status dropout rates of 16- to 24-year-olds, by selected Hispanic subgroups: 2014

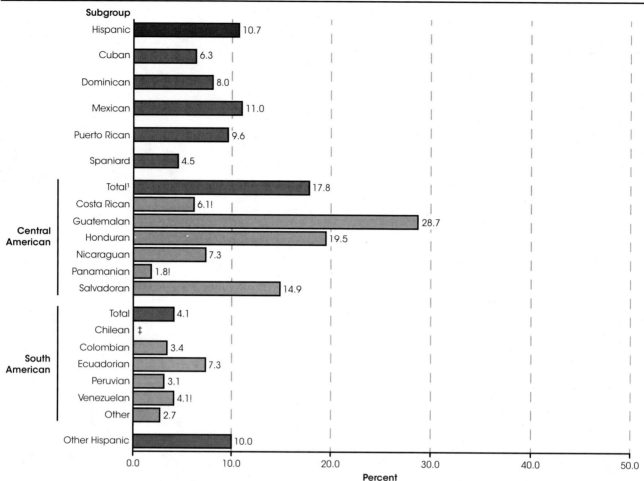

! Interpret data with caution. The coefficient of variation (CV) for this estimate is between 30 and 50 percent.
‡ Reporting standards not met. Either there are too few cases for a reliable estimate or the coefficient of variation (CV) is 50 percent or greater.
[1] Includes other Central American subgroups not shown separately.
NOTE: This figure uses a different data source than figure 2; therefore, estimates are not directly comparable to the estimates in figure 2. The status dropout rate is the percentage of 16- to 24-year-olds who are not enrolled in school and have not earned a high school credential (either a diploma or an equivalency credential such as a GED certificate). Data are based on sample surveys of persons living in households, noninstitutionalized group quarters (such as college or military housing), and institutionalized group quarters (such as correctional or nursing facilities).
SOURCE: U.S. Department of Commerce, Census Bureau, American Community Survey (ACS), 2014. See *Digest of Education Statistics 2015*, table 219.80.

Data from the ACS can also be used to estimate the status dropout rate for many specific Asian and Hispanic subgroups, including, for example, Mexican, Puerto Rican, Chinese, and Vietnamese youth. In 2014, the total high school status dropout rate for Hispanic youth was 10.7 percent. Status dropout rates for youth of Guatemalan (28.7 percent), Honduran (19.5 percent), and Salvadoran (14.9 percent) descent were higher than the total rate for all Hispanic youth. In addition, the

overall status dropout rate for Central American[2] youth (17.8 percent) was higher than the total Hispanic rate. The status dropout rates for the Mexican, Costa Rican, and Other Hispanic groups were not measurably different from the total Hispanic rate. The rates for the remaining Hispanic subgroups were lower than the total Hispanic rate. For example, the status dropout rate was 9.6 percent for Puerto Rican youth, 8.0 percent for Dominican youth, and 6.3 percent for Cuban youth.

Figure 6. Status dropout rates of 16- to 24-year-olds, by selected Asian subgroups: 2014

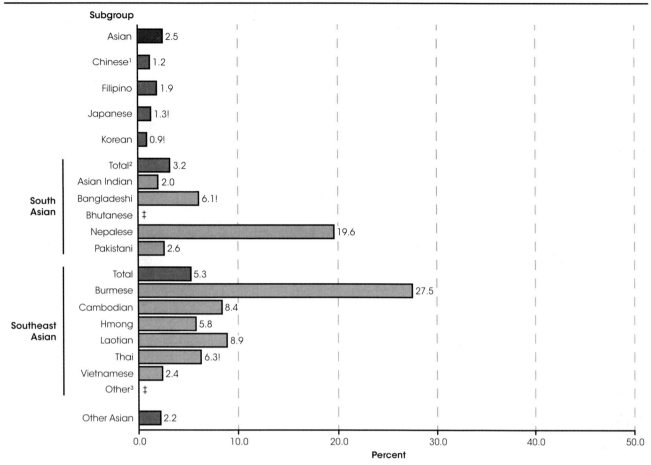

! Interpret data with caution. The coefficient of variation (CV) for this estimate is between 30 and 50 percent.
‡ Reporting standards not met. Either there are too few cases for a reliable estimate or the coefficient of variation (CV) is 50 percent or greater.
[1] Includes Taiwanese.
[2] In addition to the subgroups shown, also includes Sri Lankan.
[3] Consists of Indonesian and Malaysian.
NOTE: This figure uses a different data source than figure 2; therefore, estimates are not directly comparable to the estimates in figure 2. The status dropout rate is the percentage of 16- to 24-year-olds who are not enrolled in school and have not earned a high school credential (either a diploma or an equivalency credential such as a GED certificate). Data are based on sample surveys of persons living in households, noninstitutionalized group quarters (such as college or military housing), and institutionalized group quarters (such as correctional or nursing facilities).
SOURCE: U.S. Department of Commerce, Census Bureau, American Community Survey (ACS), 2014. See *Digest of Education Statistics 2015*, table 219.80.

Among Asian youth, the total high school status dropout rate was 2.5 percent in 2014. Five Asian subgroups had status dropout rates that were higher than the total Asian rate: Burmese (27.5 percent), Nepalese (19.6 percent), Laotian (8.9 percent), Cambodian (8.4 percent), and Hmong (5.8 percent). In addition, the overall status dropout rate for Southeast Asian[3] youth (5.3 percent)

was higher than the total Asian rate. Status dropout rates for Japanese (1.3 percent), Chinese[4] (1.2 percent), and Korean (0.9) youth were lower than the total rate for all Asian youth. Status dropout rates for the remaining Asian subgroups were not measurably different from the total rate for all Asian youth.

Figure 7. Status dropout rates of 16- to 24-year-olds, by race/ethnicity and nativity: 2014

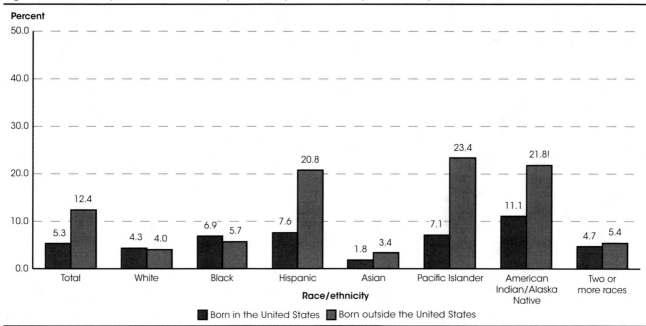

! Interpret data with caution. The coefficient of variation (CV) for this estimate is between 30 and 50 percent.
NOTE: This figure uses a different data source than figure 2; therefore, estimates are not directly comparable to the estimates in figure 2. United States refers to the 50 states, the District of Columbia, Puerto Rico, American Samoa, Guam, the U.S. Virgin Islands, and the Northern Marianas. The status dropout rate is the percentage of 16- to 24-year-olds who are not enrolled in school and have not earned a high school credential (either a diploma or an equivalency credential such as a GED certificate). Data are based on sample surveys of persons living in households and noninstitutionalized group quarters (such as college or military housing). Among those counted in noninstitutionalized group quarters in the American Community Survey, only the residents of military barracks are not included in the civilian noninstitutionalized population in the Current Population Survey. Race categories exclude persons of Hispanic ethnicity.
SOURCE: U.S. Department of Commerce, Census Bureau, American Community Survey (ACS), 2014. See *Digest of Education Statistics 2015*, table 219.80.

Differences in status dropout rates between U.S.- and foreign-born youth living in households and noninstitutionalized group quarters vary by race/ethnicity. In 2014, Hispanic, Asian, and Pacific Islander youth born in the United States had lower status dropout rates than did their counterparts born outside of the United States. The status dropout rate was 7.6 percent for U.S.-born Hispanic youth versus 20.8 percent for foreign-born

Hispanic youth. The status dropout rate was 1.8 percent for U.S.-born Asian youth versus 3.4 percent for their foreign-born peers. The status dropout rate was 7.1 percent for U.S.-born Pacific Islander youth versus 23.4 percent for foreign-born Pacific Islander youth. There were no measurable differences in status dropout rates by nativity for White, Black, and American Indian/Alaska Native youth, or youth of Two or more races.

Endnotes:

[1] In this indicator, status dropout rates are estimated using both the Current Population Survey (CPS) and the American Community Survey (ACS). CPS data have been collected annually for decades, allowing for the analysis of detailed long term trends, or changes over time, for the civilian, noninstitutionalized population. ACS data cover a broader population, including individuals living in institutionalized group quarters (such as adult and juvenile correctional facilities, nursing facilities, and other health care facilities), noninstitutionalized group quarters (such as college and university housing, military quarters, facilities

for workers and religious groups, and temporary shelters for the homeless), and households. The ACS data are available for fewer years than the CPS data, but can be used to provide detail on smaller demographic subgroups.
[2] Consists of the Costa Rican, Guatemalan, Honduran, Nicaraguan, Panamanian, and Salvadoran subgroups and other Central American subgroups not shown separately.
[3] Consists of the Burmese, Cambodian, Hmong, Laotian, Thai, Vietnamese, and Other Southeast Asian (i.e., Indonesian and Malaysian) subgroups.
[4] Includes Taiwanese.

Reference tables: *Digest of Education Statistics 2015*, tables 219.70, 219.75, and 219.80

Related indicators: Educational Attainment of Young Adults, Public High School Graduation Rates

Glossary: Household, Racial/ethnic group, Status dropout rate (Current Population Survey), Status dropout rate (American Community Survey)

This page intentionally left blank.

Young Adults Neither Enrolled in School nor Working

In 2015, some 13 percent of young adults ages 18 to 19 and 17 percent of young adults ages 20 to 24 were neither enrolled in school nor working. In 2015, the percentage of young adults ages 18 to 19 neither enrolled in school nor working was higher for those from poor families (26 percent) than for their peers from nonpoor families (10 percent). The same pattern was observed for young adults ages 20 to 24 (31 percent for those from poor families versus 14 percent for those from nonpoor families).

Young adults who are neither enrolled in school nor working may face limited future prospects. These youth are detached from the core activities of schooling and work, both of which play an important role in one's transition from adolescence to adulthood. Such detachment, particularly if it lasts for several years, hinders a youth's opportunity to build a work history that contributes to future higher wages and employability.[1] There are many reasons why young adults between the ages of 18 and 24 may be neither enrolled in school nor working. They may be seeking but unable to find work or they may have left the workforce or school, either temporarily or permanently, for personal or financial reasons. This indicator provides information on young adults at an age when most are transitioning into postsecondary education or the workforce. This period is critical for young people as they pursue educational and other goals.

Figure 1. Percentage of young adults ages 18 to 24 who were neither enrolled in school nor working, by age group and family poverty status: 2015

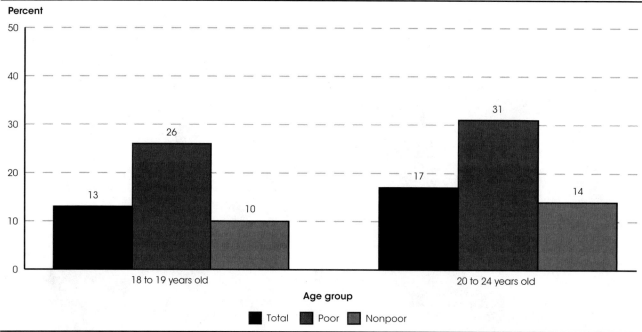

NOTE: *Poor* is defined to include families below the poverty threshold, and *nonpoor* is defined to include families at or above the poverty threshold. For information about how the Census Bureau determines who is in poverty, see http://www.census.gov/hhes/www/poverty/about/overview/measure.html. SOURCE: U.S. Department of Commerce, Census Bureau, Current Population Survey (CPS), Annual Social and Economic Supplement, 2015. See *Digest of Education Statistics 2015*, table 501.30.

In 2015, the percentage of young adults ages 18 to 19 neither enrolled in school nor working was higher for those from poor families (26 percent) than for their peers from nonpoor families (10 percent). The same pattern was observed for young adults ages 20 to 24 (31 percent for those from poor families versus 14 percent for those from nonpoor families). Among young adults from both poor and nonpoor families, the percentage neither enrolled in school nor working was higher for young adults ages 20 to 24 than for young adults ages 18 to 19.

Figure 2. Percentage of young adults ages 18 to 24 who were neither enrolled in school nor working, by age group and race/ethnicity: 2015

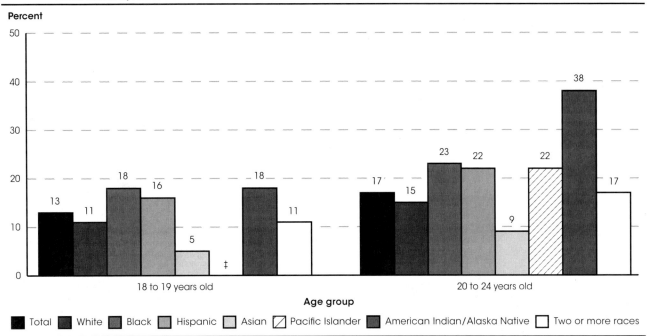

‡ Reporting standards not met (too few cases for a reliable estimate).
NOTE: Race categories exclude persons of Hispanic ethnicity.
SOURCE: U.S. Department of Commerce, Census Bureau, Current Population Survey (CPS), Annual Social and Economic Supplement, 2015. See *Digest of Education Statistics 2015*, table 501.30.

In 2015, the percentage of young adults neither enrolled in school nor working was higher for young adults ages 20 to 24 than for young adults ages 18 to 19, both overall (17 vs. 13 percent) and across most racial/ethnic groups. Among young adults ages 18 to 19, the percentage neither enrolled in school nor working was higher for Black (18 percent) and Hispanic young adults (16 percent) than for White (11 percent) and Asian young adults (5 percent), and the percentage for White young adults was higher than

that for Asian young adults. Among young adults ages 20 to 24, the percentage neither enrolled in school nor working was higher for American Indian/Alaska Native young adults (38 percent) than for any other racial/ethnic group, and lower for Asian young adults (9 percent) than any other racial/ethnic group. The percentage neither enrolled in school nor working was higher for Black (23 percent) and Hispanic (22 percent) young adults than for White young adults (15 percent).

Figure 3. Percentage of young adults ages 20 to 24 who were neither enrolled in school nor working, by educational attainment: 2015

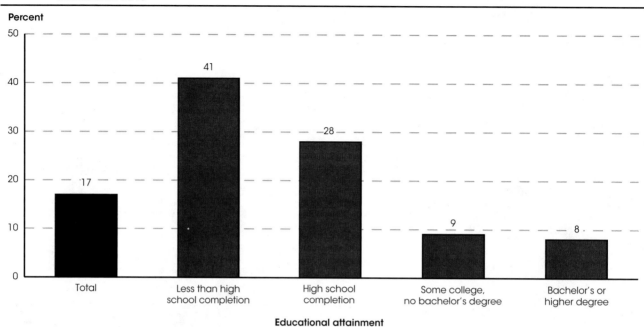

NOTE: High school completion includes equivalency credentials, such as the GED credential. Some college, no bachelor's degree includes persons with no college degree as well as those with an associate's degree.
SOURCE: U.S. Department of Commerce, Census Bureau, Current Population Survey (CPS), Annual Social and Economic Supplement, 2015. See *Digest of Education Statistics 2015*, table 501.30.

In 2015, some 13 percent of young adults ages 18 to 19 and 17 percent of young adults ages 20 to 24 were neither enrolled in school nor working. Among young adults ages 20 to 24, the percentage was highest for those who had not completed high school (41 percent), followed by those who had completed high school only (28 percent) and those who had completed some college (9 percent).

Figure 4. Percentage of young adults ages 20 to 24 who were neither enrolled in school nor working, by sex and educational attainment: 2015

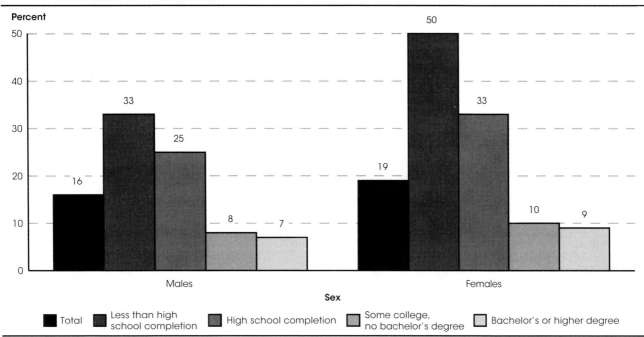

NOTE: High school completion includes equivalency credentials, such as the GED credential. Some college, no bachelor's degree includes persons with no college degree as well as those with an associate's degree.
SOURCE: U.S. Department of Commerce, Census Bureau, Current Population Survey (CPS), Annual Social and Economic Supplement, 2015. See *Digest of Education Statistics 2015*, table 501.30.

In 2015, a higher percentage of females ages 20 to 24 were neither enrolled in school nor working than their male peers (19 vs. 16 percent). A comparable pattern between females and males ages 20 to 24 was also observed at various levels of educational attainment: less than high school completion (50 vs. 33 percent), high school completion only (33 vs. 25 percent), and some college

(10 vs. 8 percent). However, there was no measurable difference by sex among those with a bachelor's or higher degree in the percentage of young adults ages 20 to 24 who were neither enrolled in school nor working. Also, among young adults ages 18 to 19, no such differences by sex were observed overall or by educational attainment.

Endnotes:

[1] Federal Interagency Forum on Child and Family Statistics. (2013). *America's Children: Key National Indicators of Well-Being, 2013*. Washington, DC: U.S. Government Printing Office.

Reference tables: *Digest of Education Statistics 2015*, table 501.30
Related indicators: Employment and Unemployment Rates by Educational Attainment, Immediate College Enrollment Rate

Glossary: Bachelor's degree, College, Educational attainment (Current Population Survey), Enrollment, High school completer, Postsecondary institutions (basic classification by level), Poverty (official measure), Racial/ethnic group

Immediate College Enrollment Rate

The immediate college enrollment rate for high school completers increased from 60 percent in 1990 to 68 percent in 2014. The rate in 2014 for those from high-income families (81 percent) was nearly 29 percentage points higher than the rate for those from low-income families (52 percent). The 2014 gap between those from high- and low-income families did not measurably differ from the corresponding gap in 1990.

Of the 2.9 million high school completers in 2014, some 2.0 million, or 68 percent, enrolled in college by the following October. This rate, known as the *immediate college enrollment rate*, is defined as the annual percentage of high school completers (including GED recipients) ages 16 to 24 who enroll in 2- or 4-year colleges in the fall immediately following high school. The immediate college enrollment rate increased 8 percentage points from 1990 (60 percent) to 2014 (68 percent) and 5 percentage points between 2000 (63 percent) and 2014. The 2014 rate was not significantly different from the corresponding rate in 2013.

Figure 1. Percentage of recent high school completers who were enrolled in 2- or 4-year colleges by the October immediately following high school completion, by level of institution: 1990–2014

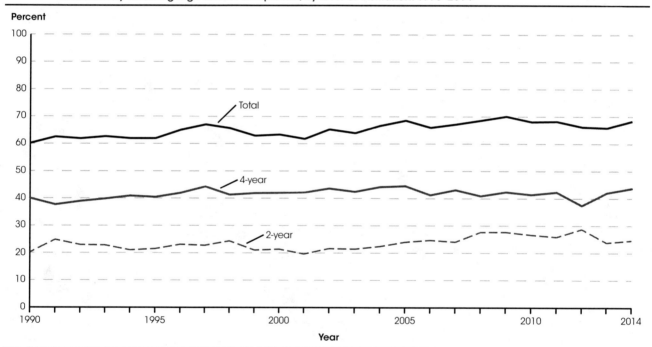

NOTE: Includes individuals ages 16 to 24 who graduated from high school or completed a GED during the calendar year.
SOURCE: U.S. Department of Commerce, Census Bureau, Current Population Survey (CPS), October Supplement, 1990–2014. See *Digest of Education Statistics 2015*, table 302.10.

The immediate college enrollment rate at 4-year colleges (44 percent) was higher than the rate at 2-year colleges (25 percent) in 2014, and has been each year since 1990. The immediate college enrollment rate of high school completers at 2-year colleges increased from 1990 (20 percent) to 2014 (25 percent); however, the rate in 2014 was not measurably different from the rate in 2000 and 2013. At 4-year colleges, the immediate college enrollment rate in 2014 (44 percent) was not measurably different from the rate in 1990, 2000, and 2013.

Figure 2. Percentage of recent high school completers who were enrolled in 2- or 4-year colleges by the October immediately following high school completion, by sex: 1990–2014

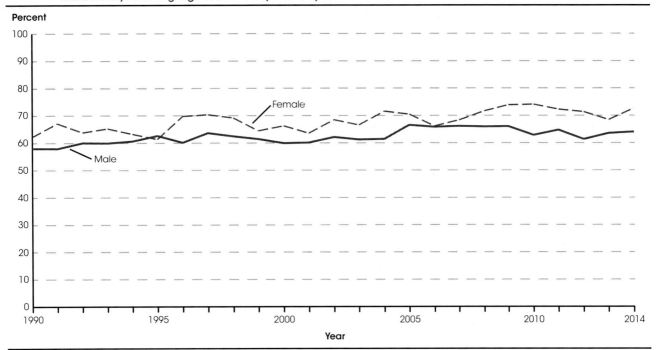

NOTE: Includes individuals ages 16 to 24 who graduated from high school or completed a GED during the calendar year.
SOURCE: U.S. Department of Commerce, Census Bureau, Current Population Survey (CPS), October Supplement, 1990–2014. See *Digest of Education Statistics 2015*, table 302.10.

In 2014, the immediate college enrollment rate for female high school completers (73 percent) was higher than the corresponding rate for males (64 percent). This pattern between males and females was also observed at 2-year colleges. The immediate college enrollment rate for female high school completers increased from 1990 (62 percent) to 2014 (73 percent); it also increased from 2000 (66 percent) to 2014. The rate for female high school completers in 2014 was not measurably different than the rate in 2013. The rate for male high school completers in 2014 (64 percent) was not measurably different from the corresponding rate in 1990, 2000, and 2013.

Figure 3. Percentage of recent high school completers who were enrolled in 2- or 4-year colleges by the October immediately following high school completion, by family income: 1990–2014

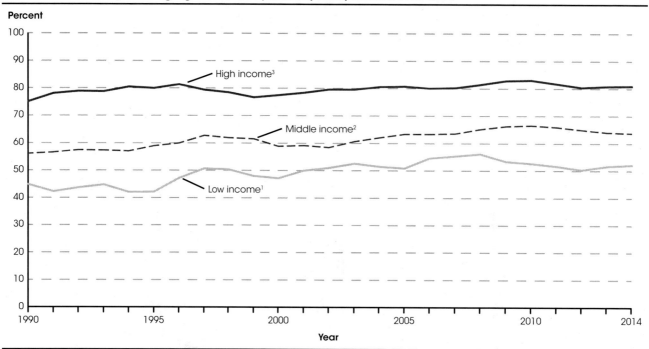

[1] Low income refers to the bottom 20 percent of all family incomes.
[2] Middle income refers to the 60 percent in between the bottom 20 percent and the top 20 percent of all family incomes.
[3] High income refers to the top 20 percent of all family incomes.
NOTE: Includes individuals ages 16 to 24 who graduated from high school or completed a GED during the calendar year. Due to some short-term data fluctuations associated with small sample sizes, percentages for income groups were calculated based on 3-year moving averages, except in 2014, when estimates were calculated based on a 2-year moving average.
SOURCE: U.S. Department of Commerce, Census Bureau, Current Population Survey (CPS), October Supplement, 1990–2014. See *Digest of Education Statistics 2015*, table 302.30.

In each year from 1990 to 2014, the immediate college enrollment rate for high school completers from high-income families was higher than the rates for their peers from middle- and low-income families; the rate for high school completers from middle-income families was also higher than that for their peers from low-income families. In 2014, the immediate college enrollment rate for high school completers from high-income families (81 percent) was 17 percentage points higher than the rate for those from middle-income families (64 percent) and 29 percentage points higher than the rate for those from low-income families (52 percent).[1] Also, the immediate college enrollment rate for high school completers from

middle-income families in 2014 was also higher than that for high school completers from low-income families.

In 2014, the gap between the immediate college enrollment rates of high school completers from high- and middle-income families, as well as the gap between high school completers from high- and low-income families, were not measurably different from the corresponding gaps in 1990 and 2000. Similarly, the gap between the immediate college enrollment rates of high school completers from middle- and low-income families in 2014 was not measurably different from the corresponding gap in 1990 and 2000.

Figure 4. Percentage of recent high school completers who were enrolled in 2- or 4-year colleges by the October immediately following high school completion, by race/ethnicity: 1990–2014

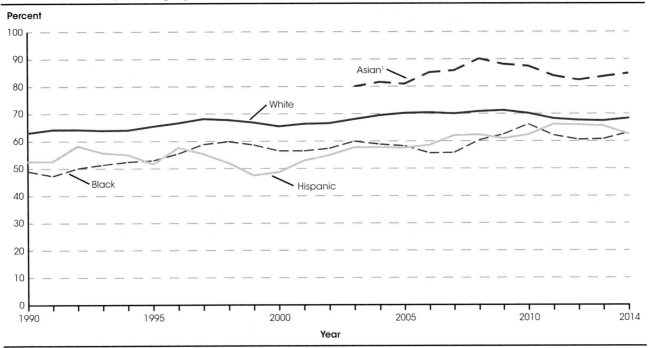

[1] Separate data on Asian high school completers have been collected since 2003.
NOTE: Includes individuals ages 16 to 24 who graduated from high school or completed a GED during the calendar year. Due to some short-term data fluctuations associated with small sample sizes, percentages for racial/ethnic groups were calculated based on 3-year moving averages, except in 2014, when estimates were calculated based on a 2-year moving average. For the data for Asian high school completers, the moving average for 2003 reflects an average of 2003 and 2004. From 2003 onward, data for White, Black, and Asian high school completers exclude persons identifying themselves as of Two or more races. Prior to 2003, each respondent could select only a single race category, and the "Two or more races" category was not reported. Race categories exclude persons of Hispanic ethnicity.
SOURCE: U.S. Department of Commerce, Census Bureau, Current Population Survey (CPS), October Supplement, 1990–2014. See *Digest of Education Statistics 2015*, table 302.20.

In 2014, the immediate college enrollment rate for White high school completers (68 percent) was not measurably different from the rates for Black (63 percent) and Hispanic (62 percent) high school completers, even though the rate for White high school completers has been higher than the rates for Black and Hispanic high school completers in most years since 1990. The immediate college enrollment rate in 1990 was 63 percent for White students, 49 percent for Black students, and 52 percent for Hispanic students. For Asian high school completers, the immediate college enrollment rate (85 percent) was higher than the rates for White, Black, and Hispanic high

school completers in 2014. The rate for Asian high school completers was also higher than the rates for their peers in each year since 2003, when the collection of separate data on Asian high school completers began.[2]

Between 1990 and 2014, the immediate college enrollment rate increased for White (from 63 to 68 percent) and Black (from 49 to 63 percent) high school completers. In contrast, the immediate college enrollment rate for Hispanic high school completers did not change measurably between 1990 and 2014.

Endnotes:
[1] Due to some short-term data fluctuations associated with small sample sizes, estimates for the income groups and racial/ethnic groups were calculated based on 3-year moving averages, except in 2014, when estimates were calculated based on a 2-year moving average. Additionally,

for the data for Asian high school completers, the moving average for 2003 reflects an average of 2003 and 2004.
[2] Prior to 2003, data were collected for the combined race category of Asian/Pacific Islander.

Reference tables: *Digest of Education Statistics 2015*, tables 302.10, 302.20, and 302.30
Related indicators: Undergraduate Enrollment, Public High School Graduation Rates, Status Dropout Rates

Glossary: College, Enrollment, High school completer, Postsecondary institutions (basic classification by level), Racial/ethnic group

College Participation Rates

Although the college enrollment rate increased between 2004 and 2014 for Hispanic young adults (25 vs. 35 percent), it did not measurably differ between 2004 and 2014 for young adults who were White, Black, Asian, Pacific Islander, American Indian/Alaska Native, and of Two or more races.

The college participation rate has increased over the past two decades. Different factors, such as changes in the labor market and, more recently, the economic downturn, have contributed to this increase.[1] In this indicator, the college participation rate, or the college enrollment rate, is defined as the percentage of 18- to 24-year-olds (the traditional college-age population) enrolled in 2- or 4-year degree-granting postsecondary institutions.

Figure 1. Enrollment rates of 18- to 24-year-olds in postsecondary degree-granting institutions, by level of institution: 1990–2014

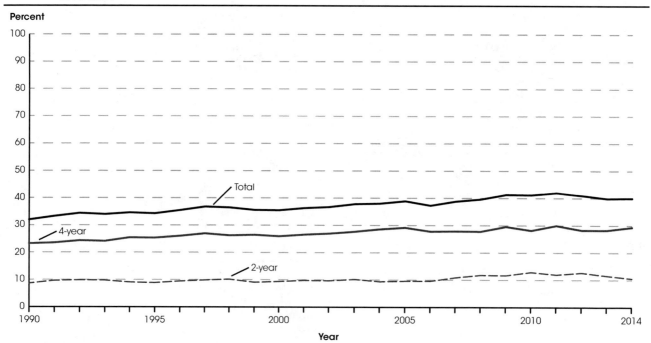

NOTE: Data are based on sample surveys of the civilian noninstitutionalized population.
SOURCE: U.S. Department of Commerce, Census Bureau, Current Population Survey (CPS), October, 1990–2014. See *Digest of Education Statistics 2015*, table 302.60.

The overall college enrollment rate increased from 32 percent in 1990 to 40 percent in 2014. More recently, from 2004 to 2014, the total college enrollment rate increased by 2 percentage points. In 2014, the college enrollment rate at 4-year colleges was 29 percent compared with 11 percent at 2-year colleges.

Figure 2. Enrollment rates of 18- to 24-year-olds in postsecondary degree-granting institutions, by race/ethnicity: 1990–2014

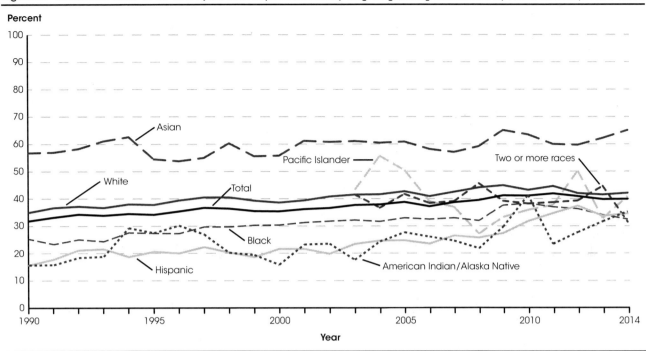

NOTE: Data are based on sample surveys of the civilian noninstitutionalized population. Prior to 2003, data for individual race categories include persons of Two or more races and data for Asians include Pacific Islanders. Race categories exclude persons of Hispanic ethnicity.
SOURCE: U.S. Department of Commerce, Census Bureau, Current Population Survey (CPS), October, 1990–2014. See *Digest of Education Statistics 2015*, table 302.60.

From 1990 to 2014, the college enrollment rate increased for young adults who were White (from 35 to 42 percent), Black (from 25 to 33 percent), Hispanic (from 16 to 35 percent), Asian (from 57 to 65 percent), and American Indian/Alaska Native (from 16 to 35 percent). Although the college enrollment rate increased between 2004 and 2014 for Hispanic young adults (25 vs. 35 percent), it did not measurably differ between 2004 to 2014 for young adults who were White, Black, Asian, Pacific Islander, American Indian/Alaska Native, and of Two or more races.

In 2014, the college enrollment rate was higher for Asian young adults (65 percent) than for young adults

who were White (42 percent), Black (33 percent), and Hispanic (35 percent)—a pattern that has held for the past two decades. The 2014 college enrollment rate was also higher for Asian young adults than for young adults who were Pacific Islander (41 percent), American Indian/Alaska Native (35 percent), and of Two or more races (32 percent). In addition, the college enrollment rate for White young adults was higher than the rates for young adults who were Black, Hispanic, and of Two or more races. The 2014 college enrollment rates for young adults who were Black, Hispanic, Pacific Islander, American Indian/Alaska Native, and of Two or more races were not measurably different from each other.

Figure 3. Enrollment rates of 18- to 24-year-olds in postsecondary degree-granting institutions, by sex and race/ethnicity: 1990 and 2014

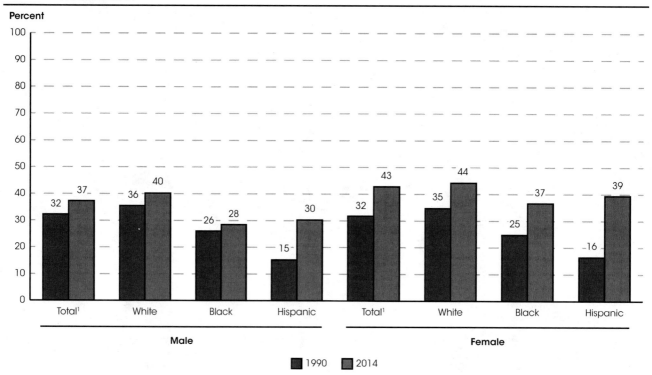

[1] Includes other racial/ethnic groups not shown separately.
NOTE: Data are based on sample surveys of the civilian noninstitutionalized population. In 2014, White and Black data exclude persons identifying as Two or more races. Race categories exclude persons of Hispanic ethnicity.
SOURCE: U.S. Department of Commerce, Census Bureau, Current Population Survey (CPS), October, 1990 and 2014. See *Digest of Education Statistics 2015*, table 302.60.

The college enrollment rate for females was higher in 2014 (43 percent) than in 1990 (32 percent). White (44 vs. 35 percent), Black (37 vs. 25 percent), and Hispanic (39 vs. 16 percent) females all had higher college enrollment rates in 2014 than in 1990. The college enrollment rate for males was also higher in 2014 (37 percent) than in 1990 (32 percent). White (40 vs. 36 percent) and Hispanic (30 vs. 15 percent) males had higher college enrollment rates in 2014 than in 1990. However, the college enrollment rate for Black males in 2014 was not measurably different from the rate in 1990.

Figure 4.   Enrollment rates of 18- to 24-year-olds in postsecondary degree-granting institutions, by race/ethnicity and sex: 1990 and 2014

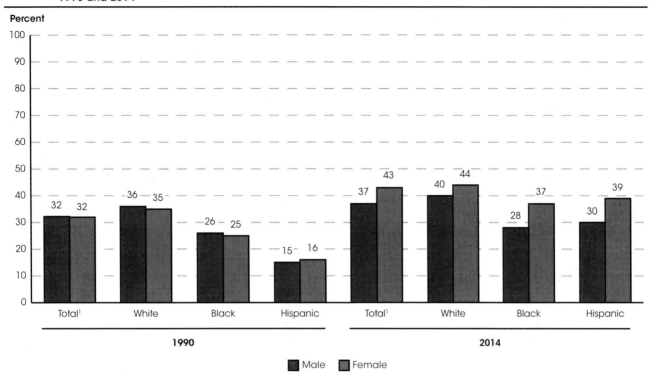

¹ Includes other racial/ethnic groups not shown separately.
NOTE: Data are based on sample surveys of the civilian noninstitutionalized population. In 2014, White and Black data exclude persons identifying as Two or more races. Race categories exclude persons of Hispanic ethnicity.
SOURCE: U.S. Department of Commerce, Census Bureau, Current Population Survey (CPS), October, 1990 and 2014. See *Digest of Education Statistics 2015*, table 302.60.

In 2014, higher percentages of females than of males overall (43 vs. 37 percent), as well as within the White (44 vs. 40 percent), Black (37 vs. 28 percent), and Hispanic (39 vs. 30 percent) subgroups, were enrolled in college. In 1990, however, there was no measurable difference between female and male college enrollment rates overall, nor were there measurable differences between female and male college enrollment rates within the White, Black, and Hispanic subgroups.

Endnotes:
[1] Fry, R. (2009). *College Enrollment Hits All Time High, Fueled by Community College Surge.* Washington, DC: Pew Research Center.

Reference tables: *Digest of Education Statistics 2015*, table 302.60
Related indicators: Undergraduate Enrollment, Immediate College Enrollment Rate

Glossary: College, Enrollment, Postsecondary institutions (basic classification by level), Racial/ethnic group

The indicators in this chapter of *The Condition of Education* examine features of postsecondary education, many of which parallel those presented in the previous chapter on elementary and secondary education. The indicators describe characteristics of postsecondary students, postsecondary programs and courses of study, finance and resources, and postsecondary completions.

Postsecondary education is characterized by diversity both in the types of institutions and in the characteristics of students. Postsecondary institutions vary by the types of degrees awarded, control (public or private), and whether they are operated on a nonprofit or for-profit basis. In addition, postsecondary institutions have distinctly different missions and provide students with a wide range of learning environments.

This chapter's indicators, as well as additional indicators on postsecondary education, are available at *The Condition of Education* website: http://nces.ed.gov/programs/coe.

Chapter 4

Postsecondary Education

Characteristics of Degree-Granting Postsecondary Institutions

In 2014–15, some 29 percent of 4-year institutions had open admissions policies (accepted all applicants), an additional 28 percent accepted three-quarters or more of their applicants, 30 percent accepted from one-half to less than three-quarters of their applicants, and 13 percent accepted less than one-half of their applicants.

In 2014–15, there were 4,207 degree-granting institutions with first-year undergraduates, including 2,603 4-year institutions offering programs at the bachelor's or higher degree level and 1,604 2-year institutions offering associate's degrees. Comparisons by institutional level (i.e., between 2-year and 4-year institutions) may be limited because of different institutional missions. The instructional missions of 2-year institutions generally focus on student instruction and related activities that often include providing a range of career-oriented programs at the certificate and associate's degree levels and preparing students for transfer to 4-year institutions.

Four-year institutions tend to have a broad range of instructional programs at the undergraduate level leading to bachelor's degrees. Many 4-year institutions offer graduate level programs as well, and some 4-year institutions have a strong research focus. These institutions may be governed by publicly appointed or elected officials, with major support from public funds (public control), or by privately elected or appointed officials, with major support from private sources (private control). Private institutions may be operated on a nonprofit or for-profit basis. All institutions in this analysis enroll first-year undergraduates in degree-granting programs.

Figure 1. Number of degree-granting institutions with first-year undergraduates, by level and control of institution: Academic years 2000–01 and 2014–15

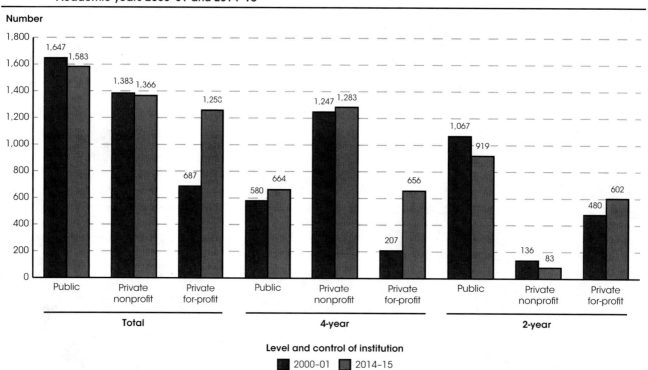

NOTE: Degree-granting institutions grant associate's or higher degrees and participate in Title IV federal financial aid programs. Excludes institutions not enrolling any first-time degree/certificate-seeking undergraduates.
SOURCE: U.S. Department of Education, National Center for Education Statistics, Integrated Postsecondary Education Data System (IPEDS), Fall 2000, Institutional Characteristics component; and Winter 2014–15, Admissions component. See *Digest of Education Statistics 2015*, table 305.30.

In 2014–15, the number of private nonprofit institutions (1,366) was 1 percent lower than in 2000–01 (1,383), and the number of public institutions (1,583) was 4 percent lower than in 2000–01 (1,647). In contrast, the number of private for-profit institutions nearly doubled (from 687 to 1,258) between 2000–01 and 2014–15. The number of public 4-year institutions increased by 14 percent from 580 institutions to 664 institutions between 2000–01 and 2014–15. During the same time period, the number of public 2-year institutions decreased by 14 percent from 1,067 to 919 institutions. Between 2013–14 and 2014–15 the number of public 4-year institutions

increased by 2 percent from 651 to 664 institutions, whereas the number of public 2-year institutions decreased by 2 percent from 933 to 919 institutions. The number of private for-profit 4-year institutions increased by 217 percent from 207 to 656 institutions between 2000–01 and 2014–15. During the same time period, the number of private for-profit 2-year institutions increased by 25 percent from 480 to 602 institutions. However, between 2013–14 and 2014–15 the number of private for-profit 4-year institutions decreased by 6 percent from 701 to 656 institutions and the number of private for-profit 2-year institutions decreased from 644 to 602 institutions.

Figure 2. Percentage distribution of application acceptance rates at 4-year degree-granting institutions with first-year undergraduates, by control of institution: Academic year 2014–15

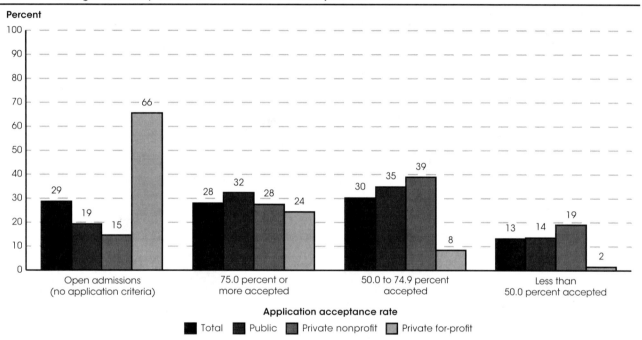

NOTE: Degree-granting institutions grant associate's or higher degrees and participate in Title IV federal financial aid programs. Excludes institutions not enrolling any first-time degree/certificate-seeking undergraduates. Although rounded numbers are displayed, the figures are based on unrounded estimates. Detail may not sum to totals because of rounding.
SOURCE: U.S. Department of Education, National Center for Education Statistics, Integrated Postsecondary Education Data System (IPEDS), Winter 2014–15, Admissions component. See *Digest of Education Statistics 2015*, table 305.40.

In 2014–15, approximately 29 percent of 4-year institutions with first-year undergraduates had open admissions policies (accepted all applicants). A higher percentage of private for-profit 4-year institutions (66 percent) than private nonprofit (15 percent) and public (19 percent) 4-year institutions had open admissions policies in 2014–15. In 2014–15, a higher percentage of public and private for-profit 4-year institutions reported having open admissions policies than in 2013–14. In

2013–14, some 18 percent of public institutions and 65 percent of private for-profit institutions had open admissions policies. While 29 percent of all 4-year institutions had open admissions policies in 2014–15, another 28 percent accepted three-quarters or more of their applicants, 30 percent accepted from one-half to less than three-quarters of their applicants, and 13 percent accepted less than one-half of their applicants.

Figure 3. Percentage distribution of application acceptance rates at 2-year degree-granting institutions with first-year undergraduates, by control of institution: Academic year 2014–15

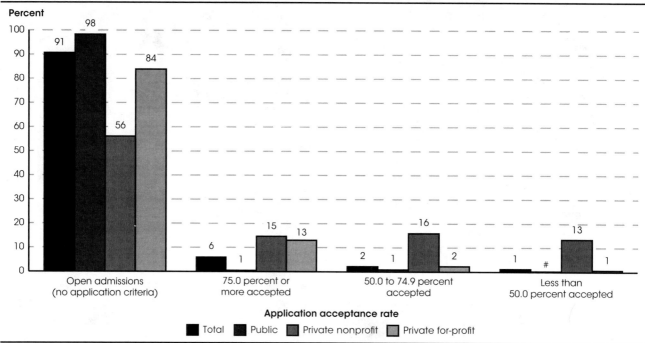

Rounds to zero.
NOTE: Degree-granting institutions grant associate's or higher degrees and participate in Title IV federal financial aid programs. Excludes institutions not enrolling any first-time degree/certificate-seeking undergraduates. Although rounded numbers are displayed, the figures are based on unrounded estimates. Detail may not sum to totals because of rounding.
SOURCE: U.S. Department of Education, National Center for Education Statistics, Integrated Postsecondary Education Data System (IPEDS), Winter 2014–15, Admissions component. See *Digest of Education Statistics 2015*, table 305.40.

In contrast with 4-year institutions, a majority of 2-year institutions (91 percent) had open admissions policies in 2014–15. Open admissions policies were in operation at 98 percent of public 2-year institutions and 84 percent of private for-profit 2-year institutions compared to 56 percent of private nonprofit 2-year institutions.

Although a majority of 2-year institutions had open admissions policies in 2014–15, an additional 6 percent of 2-year institutions accepted three-quarters or more of their applicants, 2 percent accepted from one-half to less than three-quarters of their applicants, and 1 percent accepted less than one-half of their applicants.

Figure 4. Percentage of 4-year degree-granting institutions with first-year undergraduates using various admissions requirements, by control of institution: Academic year 2014–15

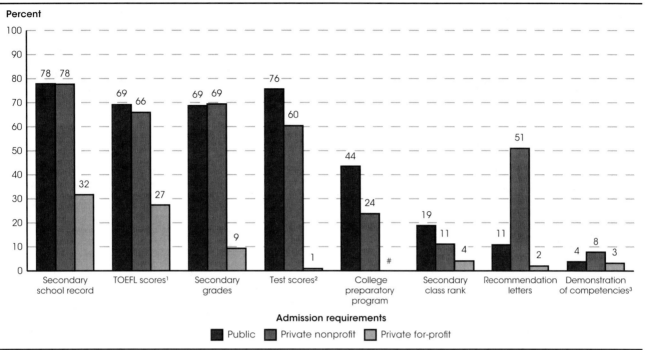

Rounds to zero.
[1] Test of English as a Foreign Language.
[2] Includes SAT, ACT, and other admission tests.
[3] Formal demonstration of competencies (e.g., portfolios, certificates of mastery, assessment instruments).
NOTE: Degree-granting institutions grant associate's or higher degrees and participate in Title IV federal financial aid programs. Excludes institutions not enrolling any first-time degree/certificate-seeking undergraduates. Although rounded numbers are displayed, the figures are based on unrounded estimates.
SOURCE: U.S. Department of Education, National Center for Education Statistics, Integrated Postsecondary Education Data System (IPEDS), Winter 2014–15, Admissions component. See *Digest of Education Statistics 2015*, table 305.30.

In 2014–15, some 71 percent of 4-year institutions had admission requirements for applicants. Admission requirements include the submission of information such as secondary school administrative records, Test of English as a Foreign Language (TOEFL) scores, secondary school grades, admission test (such as the SAT or ACT) scores, recommendations, and college preparatory program information. Reflecting the high percentage of institutions with open admissions policies, a lower percentage of private for-profit 4-year institutions had admission requirements than public and private nonprofit 4-year institutions (33 percent versus 81 and 85 percent, respectively). Among 4-year institutions, the percentages of public and private nonprofit institutions that required secondary school records for admission (both 78 percent) were more than twice the percentage of private for-profit institutions requiring them (32 percent). The percentages of public and private nonprofit 4-year institutions that

required TOEFL scores (69 and 66 percent, respectively) were more than twice the percentage of private for-profit 4-year institutions requiring them (27 percent). Among 4-year institutions, the percentages of public and private nonprofit institutions that required secondary grades (both 69 percent) were more than 7 times the percentage of private for-profit 4-year institutions requiring them (9 percent). Among 4-year institutions, 76 percent of public institutions required admission tests such as the SAT or ACT, compared with 60 percent of private nonprofit and 1 percent of private for-profit institutions. Among 4-year institutions, 44 percent of public institutions required college preparatory program information compared with 24 percent of private nonprofit institutions. In 2014–15, recommendation letters were required by 11 percent of public 4-year institutions, 51 percent of private nonprofit institutions, and 2 percent of private for-profit institutions.

Reference tables: *Digest of Education Statistics 2014*, table 305.30; *Digest of Education Statistics 2015*, tables 305.30 and 305.40

Related indicators: Undergraduate Enrollment, Postbaccalaureate Enrollment, Postsecondary Institution Revenues, Postsecondary Institution Expenses, Characteristics of Postsecondary Faculty, Community Colleges [*The Condition of Education 2008 Special Analysis*]

Glossary: Associate's degree, Bachelor's degree, Degree-granting institution, For-profit institution, Nonprofit institution, Postsecondary education, Postsecondary institutions (basic classification by level), Private institution, Public school or institution, Undergraduate students

Characteristics of Postsecondary Students

Some 10.6 million undergraduate students attended 4-year institutions in fall 2014, while 6.7 million attended 2-year institutions. Some 77 percent of undergraduate students at 4-year institutions attended full time, compared with 40 percent at 2-year institutions.

In fall 2014, there were 17.3 million undergraduate students and 2.9 million postbaccalaureate (graduate) students attending degree-granting postsecondary institutions in the United States. These institutions include 4-year institutions that primarily award bachelor's or higher degrees, and 2-year institutions that award associate's degrees and certificates and offer courses that may be creditable toward a bachelor's degree to be earned at a 4-year institution. Some 10.6 million undergraduate students (61 percent) attended 4-year institutions, while 6.7 million (39 percent) attended 2-year institutions. Of the undergraduate students at 4-year institutions, 8.1 million (77 percent) attended full time. Of the undergraduate students at 2-year institutions, 2.7 million (40 percent) attended full-time and 4.1 million (60 percent) attended part-time.

Figure 1. Percentage of full-time undergraduate enrollment in degree-granting postsecondary institutions, by institutional level and control and student age: Fall 2013

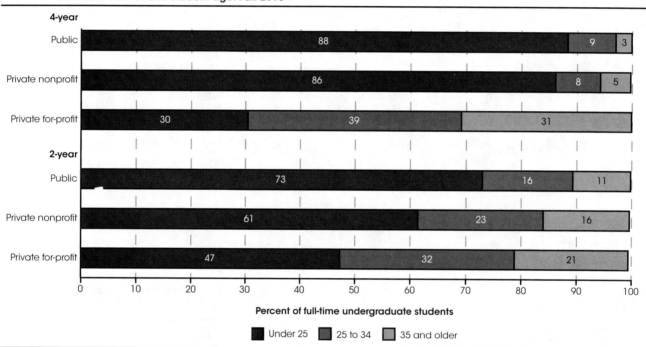

NOTE: Degree-granting institutions grant associate's or higher degrees and participate in Title IV federal financial aid programs. Detail may not sum to totals because of rounding and the exclusion of students whose age was unknown.
SOURCE: U.S. Department of Education, National Center for Education Statistics, Integrated Postsecondary Education Data System (IPEDS), Spring 2014, Enrollment component. See *Digest of Education Statistics 2014*, table 303.50.

In fall 2013, a higher percentage of full-time undergraduate students attending public and private nonprofit 4-year institutions were young adults (i.e., under the age of 25) than at comparable 2-year institutions. At public and private nonprofit 4-year institutions, most of the full-time undergraduates (88 and 86 percent, respectively) were young adults. At private for-profit 4-year institutions, however, just 30 percent of full-time students were young adults.

Of the full-time undergraduate students enrolled at public 2-year institutions in 2013, some 73 percent were young adults, 16 percent were ages 25–34, and 11 percent were age 35 and older. At private nonprofit 2-year institutions, 61 percent of full-time students were young adults, 23 percent were ages 25–34, and 16 percent were age 35 and older. At private for-profit 2-year institutions, 47 percent of full-time students were young adults, 32 percent were ages 25–34, and 21 percent were age 35 and older.

Figure 2. Percentage of part-time undergraduate enrollment in degree-granting postsecondary institutions, by institutional level and control and student age: Fall 2013

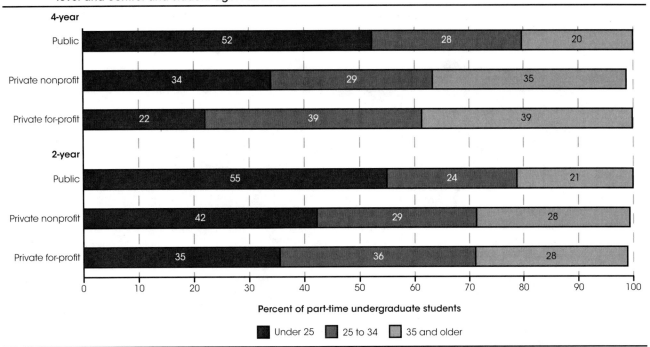

Percent of part-time undergraduate students

■ Under 25　■ 25 to 34　■ 35 and older

NOTE: Degree-granting institutions grant associate's or higher degrees and participate in Title IV federal financial aid programs. Detail may not sum to totals because of rounding and the exclusion of students whose age was unknown.
SOURCE: U.S. Department of Education, National Center for Education Statistics, Integrated Postsecondary Education Data System (IPEDS), Spring 2014, Enrollment component. See *Digest of Education Statistics 2014*, table 303.50.

In contrast to the pattern among full-time students, in fall 2013 a lower percentage of part-time undergraduate students attending public and private nonprofit 4-year institutions were young adults than at comparable 2-year institutions. Young adults made up 52 percent of part-time undergraduates attending public 4-year institutions, 34 percent attending private nonprofit institutions, and 22 percent attending private for-profit institutions. Students ages 25–34 and students age 35 and older accounted for nearly half of the part-time enrollment at public 4-year institutions, nearly two-thirds of the part-time enrollment at private nonprofit 4-year institutions,

and over three-quarters of the part-time enrollment at private for-profit 4-year institutions.

Of part-time students enrolled at public 2-year institutions in 2013, some 55 percent were young adults, 24 percent were ages 25–34, and 21 percent were age 35 and older. At private nonprofit 2-year institutions, 42 percent of part-time students were young adults, 29 percent were age 25–34, and 28 percent were age 35 and older. At private for-profit 2-year institutions, 35 percent of part-time students were young adults, 36 percent were ages 25–34, and 28 percent were age 35 and older.

Figure 3. Percentage distribution of U.S. resident undergraduate enrollment in degree-granting postsecondary institutions, by institutional level and control and student race/ethnicity: Fall 2014

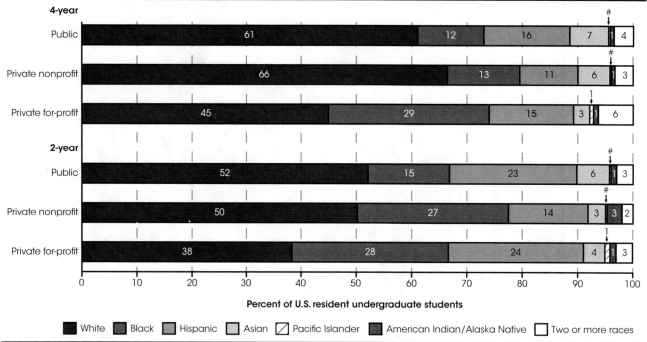

Percent of U.S. resident undergraduate students

Legend: White | Black | Hispanic | Asian | Pacific Islander | American Indian/Alaska Native | Two or more races

Rounds to zero.
NOTE: Degree-granting institutions grant associate's or higher degrees and participate in Title IV federal financial aid programs. Race categories exclude persons of Hispanic ethnicity. Detail may not sum to totals because of rounding.
SOURCE: U.S. Department of Education, National Center for Education Statistics, Integrated Postsecondary Education Data System (IPEDS), Spring 2015, Fall Enrollment component. See *Digest of Education Statistics 2015*, table 306.50.

Attendance patterns for undergraduate students differed by race/ethnicity in fall 2014. Sixty-six percent of undergraduate students (full- and part-time) at private nonprofit 4-year institutions in 2014 were White, which was higher than the percentage of White students at public 4-year institutions (61 percent) and at private for-profit 4-year institutions (45 percent). A higher percentage of the students at private for-profit 4-year institutions were Black (29 percent) than at private nonprofit 4-year institutions (13 percent) and public 4-year institutions (12 percent). A higher percentage of the students at public and private for-profit 4-year institutions were Hispanic (16 and 15 percent, respectively) than at private nonprofit 4-year institutions (11 percent). The percentage of undergraduate students at public 4-year institutions who were Asian (7 percent) was higher than the percentages at private nonprofit institutions (6 percent) and at private for-profit institutions (3 percent).

In 2014, the percentages of both White and Asian undergraduate students at public 2-year institutions (52 and 6 percent, respectively) were higher than the percentages at private nonprofit 2-year institutions (50 and 3 percent, respectively) and at private for-profit 2-year institutions (38 and 4 percent, respectively). In contrast, the percentage of students at private for-profit 2-year institutions who were Black (28 percent) was higher than the percentages at private nonprofit 2-year institutions (27 percent) and at public 2-year institutions (15 percent). The percentage of students at private for-profit 2-year institutions who were Hispanic (24 percent) was higher than the percentages at public 2-year institutions (23 percent) and at private nonprofit 2-year institutions (14 percent).

Figure 4. Percentage of full-time and part-time postbaccalaureate enrollment in degree-granting postsecondary institutions, by institutional control and student age: Fall 2013

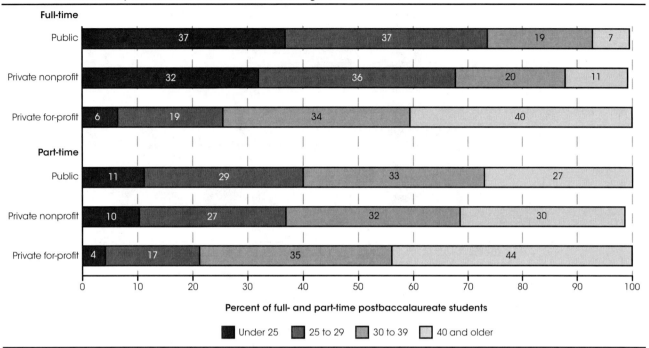

Percent of full- and part-time postbaccalaureate students

■ Under 25   ■ 25 to 29   ■ 30 to 39   □ 40 and older

NOTE: Degree-granting institutions grant associate's or higher degrees and participate in Title IV federal financial aid programs. Detail may not sum to totals because of rounding and the exclusion of students whose age was unknown.
SOURCE: U.S. Department of Education, National Center for Education Statistics, Integrated Postsecondary Education Data System (IPEDS), Spring 2014, Enrollment component. See *Digest of Education Statistics 2014*, table 303.50.

In fall 2013, some 48 percent of graduate students attended public institutions, 42 percent attended private nonprofit institutions, and 10 percent attended private for-profit institutions. In 2013, the majority of full-time graduate students at public institutions were young adults (37 percent) and adults ages 25–29 (37 percent); the same was true at private nonprofit institutions (32 percent were young adults and 36 percent were adults ages 25–29). In

contrast, full-time students at private for-profit institutions were older: 34 percent were ages 30–39 and 40 percent were age 40 and older. Among part-time graduate students, adults age 30 and older comprised 79 percent of the students at private for-profit institutions, 62 percent at private nonprofit institutions, and 60 percent at public institutions.

Figure 5.   Percentage distribution of U.S. resident postbaccalaureate enrollment in degree-granting postsecondary institutions, by institutional control and student race/ethnicity: Fall 2014

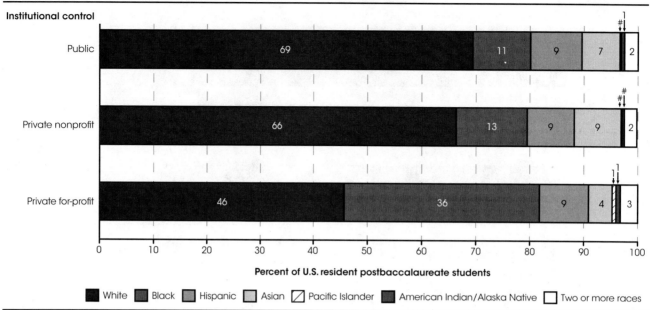

Percent of U.S. resident postbaccalaureate students

Rounds to zero.
NOTE: Degree-granting institutions grant associate's or higher degrees and participate in Title IV federal financial aid programs. Race categories exclude persons of Hispanic ethnicity. Detail may not sum to totals because of rounding.
SOURCE: U.S. Department of Education, National Center for Education Statistics, Integrated Postsecondary Education Data System (IPEDS), Spring 2015, Fall Enrollment component. See *Digest of Education Statistics 2015*, table 306.50.

Attendance patterns for graduate students also differed by race/ethnicity. At public institutions in fall 2014, some 69 percent of graduate students were White, compared with 66 percent at private nonprofit institutions and 46 percent at private for-profit institutions. Thirty-six percent of graduate students at private for-profit institutions were Black, compared with 13 percent at private nonprofit institutions and 11 percent at public institutions. Hispanic students accounted for 9 percent of graduate enrollment across all institutional controls. Asian students accounted for 9 percent of graduate enrollment at private nonprofit institutions, 7 percent at public institutions, and 4 percent at private for-profit institutions.

Figure 6. Percentage of 16- to 24-year-old college students who were employed, by attendance status and hours worked per week: October 2000 through October 2014

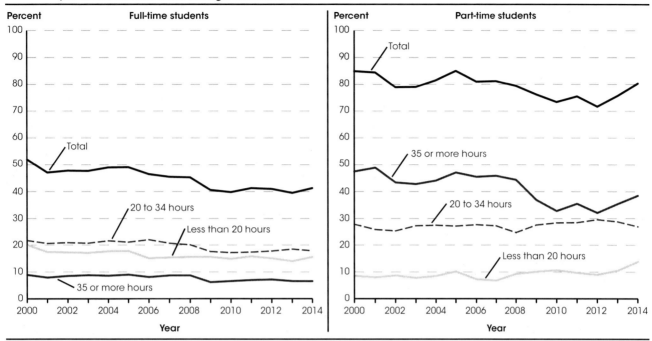

NOTE: Students were classified as full-time if they were taking at least 12 hours of undergraduate classes (or at least 9 hours of graduate classes) during an average school week and as part-time if they were taking fewer hours.
SOURCE: U.S. Department of Commerce, Census Bureau, Current Population Survey (CPS), October 2000 through October 2014. See *Digest of Education Statistics 2015*, table 503.20.

Based on the Current Population Survey, 41 percent of full-time college students 16 to 24 years old and 80 percent of part-time college students 16 to 24 years old were employed in October 2014. The percentage of students who worked 35 or more hours per week declined from 9 percent in 2000 to 7 percent in 2014 for full-time students and from 47 to 39 percent for part-time students. The percentage of full-time students who worked 20 to 34 hours per week declined from 22 percent in 2000 to

18 percent in 2014, while the percentage of part-time students who worked 20 to 34 hours per week was not measurably different in 2014 (27 percent) than it was in 2000. The percentage of full-time students who worked less than 20 hours per week declined from 20 percent in 2000 to 16 percent in 2014. In contrast, the percentage of part-time students who worked less than 20 hours per week increased from 9 percent in 2000 to 14 percent in 2014.

Reference tables: *Digest of Education Statistics 2014,* table 303.50; *Digest of Education Statistics 2015*, tables 303.60, 306.50, and 503.20

Related indicators: Undergraduate Enrollment, Postbaccalaureate Enrollment, Community College [*The Condition of Education 2008 Spotlight*]

Glossary: College, Control of institutions, Employment status, Enrollment, For-profit institution, Full-time enrollment, Nonprofit institution, Part-time enrollment, Postbaccalaureate enrollment, Postsecondary institutions (basic classification by level), Private institution, Public school or institution, Racial/ethnic group, Undergraduate students

Characteristics of Postsecondary Faculty

From fall 1993 to fall 2013, the number of full-time faculty at degree-granting postsecondary institutions increased by 45 percent, while the number of part-time faculty increased by 104 percent. As a result of the faster increase in the number of part-time faculty, the percentage of all faculty who were part time increased from 40 to 49 percent during this period.

In fall 2013, there were 1.5 million faculty at degree-granting postsecondary institutions: 51 percent were full time, and 49 percent were part time. Faculty include professors, associate professors, assistant professors, instructors, lecturers, assisting professors, adjunct professors, and interim professors.

Figure 1. Number of faculty in degree-granting postsecondary institutions, by employment status: Selected years, fall 1993 through fall 2013

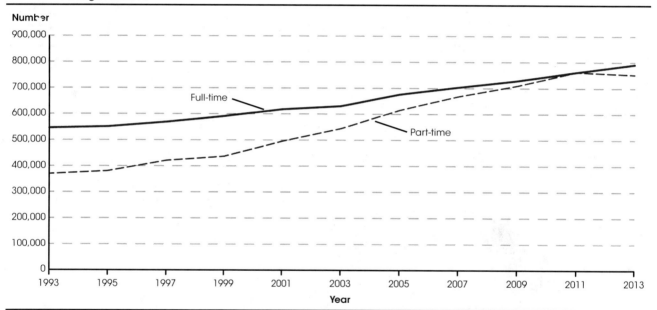

NOTE: Includes faculty members with the title of professor, associate professor, assistant professor, instructor, lecturer, assisting professor, adjunct professor, or interim professor (or the equivalent). Excludes graduate students with titles such as graduate or teaching fellow who assist senior faculty. Degree-granting institutions grant associate's or higher degrees and participate in Title IV federal financial aid programs. Beginning in 2007, data include institutions with fewer than 15 full-time employees; these institutions did not report staff data prior to 2007.
SOURCE: U.S. Department of Education, National Center for Education Statistics, Integrated Postsecondary Education Data System (IPEDS), "Fall Staff Survey" (IPEDS-S:93–99); IPEDS Winter 2001–02 through Winter 2011–12, Human Resources component, Fall Staff section; IPEDS Spring 2014, Human Resources component, Fall Staff section. See *Digest of Education Statistics 2014*, table 315.10.

From fall 1993 to fall 2013, the total number of faculty at degree-granting postsecondary institutions increased by 69 percent (from 915,500 to 1.5 million). The number of full-time faculty increased by 45 percent (from 545,700 to 791,400) over this time period, compared with an increase of 104 percent (from 369,800 to 752,700) in the number of part-time faculty. As a result of the faster increase in the number of part-time faculty, the percentage of all faculty who were part time increased from 40 to 49 percent during this period. Additionally, the percentage of all faculty who were female increased from 39 percent in 1993 to 49 percent in 2013.

Although the number of faculty increased at institutions of each control type (i.e., public, private nonprofit,

and private for-profit) from fall 1993 to fall 2013, the percentage increases in faculty were smaller for public institutions and private nonprofit institutions than for private for-profit institutions. During this period, the number of faculty increased by 49 percent (from 650,400 to 967,700) at public institutions, by 77 percent (from 254,100 to 448,700) at private nonprofit institutions, and by 1,070 percent (from 10,900 to 127,600) at private for-profit institutions. Despite the faster growth in the number of faculty at private for-profit institutions over this period, only 8 percent of all faculty were employed by private for-profit institutions in 2013, while 63 percent were employed by public institutions and 29 percent by private nonprofit institutions.

Figure 2. Percentage distribution of full-time instructional faculty in degree-granting postsecondary institutions, by academic rank, selected race/ethnicity, and sex: Fall 2013

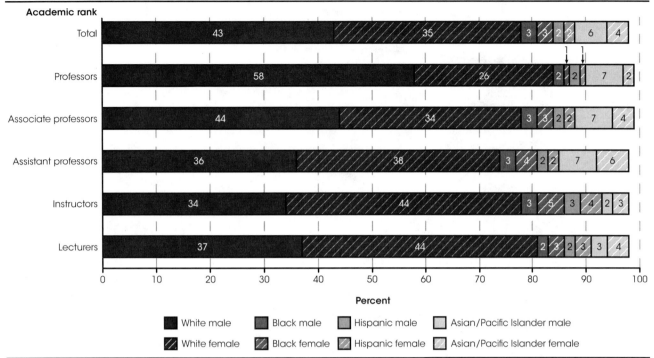

NOTE: Degree-granting institutions grant associate's or higher degrees and participate in Title IV federal financial aid programs. Race categories exclude persons of Hispanic ethnicity. Estimates are based on full-time faculty whose race/ethnicity was known. Detail may not sum to 100 percent because data on some racial/ethnic groups are not shown.
SOURCE: U.S. Department of Education, National Center for Education Statistics, Integrated Postsecondary Education Data System (IPEDS), IPEDS Spring 2014, Human Resources component, Fall Staff section. See *Digest of Education Statistics 2014*, table 315.20.

In fall 2013, of all full-time faculty at degree-granting postsecondary institutions, 43 percent were White males, 35 percent were White females, 3 percent were Black males, 3 percent were Black females, 2 percent were Hispanic males, 2 percent were Hispanic females, 6 percent were Asian/Pacific Islander males, and 4 percent were Asian/Pacific Islander females.[1] Making up less than 1 percent each were full-time faculty who were American Indian/Alaska Native and of Two or more races. Among full-time professors, 58 percent were White males, 26 percent were White females, 2 percent were Black males, 1 percent were Black females, 2 percent were Hispanic males, 1 percent were Hispanic females, 7 percent were Asian/Pacific Islander males, and 2 percent were Asian/Pacific Islander females. Making up less than 1 percent each were professors who were American Indian/Alaska Native and of Two or more races.

Figure 3. Average salary of full-time instructional faculty on 9-month contracts in degree-granting postsecondary institutions, by academic rank: Selected years, 1994–95 through 2014–15

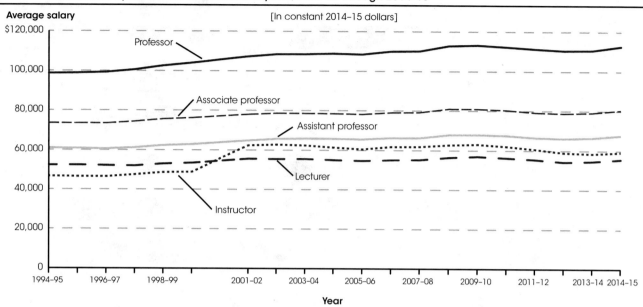

NOTE: Degree-granting institutions grant associate's or higher degrees and participate in Title IV federal financial aid programs. Beginning in 2007, data include institutions with fewer than 15 full-time employees; these institutions did not report staff data prior to 2007. Salaries are reported in constant 2014–15 dollars, based on the Consumer Price Index (CPI). Some data have been revised from previously published figures.
SOURCE: U.S. Department of Education, National Center for Education Statistics, Integrated Postsecondary Education Data System (IPEDS), "Salaries, Tenure, and Fringe Benefits of Full-Time Instructional Faculty Survey" (IPEDS-SA:93–99); and IPEDS, Winter 2001–02 through Winter 2011–12 and Spring 2013 through Spring 2015, Human Resources component, Salaries section. See *Digest of Education Statistics 2015*, table 316.10.

In academic year 2014–15, the average salary for full-time instructional faculty on 9-month contracts at degree-granting postsecondary institutions was $80,200; average salaries ranged from $55,600 for lecturers to $112,700 for professors. The average salary (adjusted for inflation) for all full-time instructional faculty increased by 8 percent from 1994–95 ($75,200) to 2009–10 ($81,500), but was 2 percent lower in 2014–15 ($80,200) than in 2009–10. A similar pattern was observed for faculty at individual academic ranks. The increase between 1994–95 and 2009–10 was 15 percent for professors (from $98,700 to $113,200), 10 percent for associate professors (from $73,500 to $80,900), 11 percent for assistant professors (from $61,000 to $68,000), 35 percent for instructors (from $46,700 to $63,100), and 9 percent for lecturers (from $52,200 to $57,000). The average inflation-adjusted salary for each rank was lower in 2014–15 than in 2009–10. The average salary for instructors was 6 percent

lower in 2014–15 than in 2009–10 and the average salary for lecturers was 2 percent lower, while the averages for faculty at other ranks were less than 1 percent lower.

The average salary for all full-time instructional faculty was higher for males than for females in every year from 1994–95 to 2014–15. In academic year 2014–15, the average salary was $87,200 for males and $71,900 for females. Between 1994–95 and 2014–15, the average salary increased by 8 percent for males and by 11 percent for females, after adjusting for inflation. Due to the faster increase in salary for females, the inflation-adjusted salary gap between male and female instructional faculty overall was slightly lower in 2014–15 than in 1994–95 ($15,200 vs. $15,500). The male-female salary gap for professors, however, increased between 1994–95 and 2014–15 (from $11,800 to $17,600).

Figure 4. Average salary of full-time instructional faculty on 9-month contracts in degree-granting postsecondary institutions, by control and level of institution: 2014–15

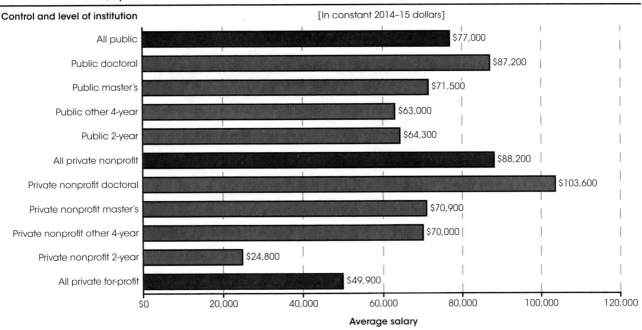

NOTE: Doctoral institutions include institutions that awarded 20 or more doctor's degrees during the previous academic year. Master's institutions include institutions that awarded 20 or more master's degrees, but less than 20 doctor's degrees, during the previous academic year. Degree-granting postsecondary institutions grant associate's or higher degrees and participate in Title IV federal financial aid programs. Salaries are reported in constant 2014–15 dollars, based on the Consumer Price Index (CPI).
SOURCE: U.S. Department of Education, National Center for Education Statistics, Integrated Postsecondary Education Data System (IPEDS), IPEDS Spring 2015, Human Resources component, Salaries section. See *Digest of Education Statistics 2015*, table 316.20.

In academic year 2014–15, the average salary for full-time instructional faculty at private nonprofit institutions ($88,200) was higher than the average salaries for full-time instructional faculty at public institutions ($77,000) and at private for-profit institutions ($49,900). Among the specific types of private nonprofit institutions and public institutions, average salaries for instructional faculty were highest at private nonprofit doctoral institutions ($103,600) and public doctoral institutions ($87,200). Average salaries were lowest for instructional faculty at private nonprofit 2-year institutions ($24,800), public 4-year institutions other than doctoral and master's degree-granting institutions ($63,000), and public 2-year institutions ($64,300). Inflation-adjusted average salaries for instructional faculty were less than 1 percent higher in 2014–15 than in 1999–2000 at public institutions, 9 percent higher at private nonprofit institutions, and 21 percent higher at private for-profit institutions.

In academic year 2013–14, approximately 49 percent of institutions had tenure systems. A tenure system guarantees that professors will not be terminated without just cause after a probationary period. The percentage of institutions with tenure systems ranged from 1 percent at private for-profit institutions to almost 100 percent at public doctoral institutions. Of full-time faculty at institutions with tenure systems, 48 percent had tenure in 2013–14, compared with 54 percent in 1999–2000. From 1999–2000 to 2013–14, the percentage of full-time faculty having tenure decreased by 5 percentage points at public institutions, by 4 percentage points at private nonprofit institutions, and by 58 percentage points at private for-profit institutions. At institutions with tenure systems, the percentage of full-time instructional faculty having tenure was generally higher for males than for females. In 2013–14, some 57 percent of males had tenure, compared with 43 percent of females.

Endnotes:
[1] Percentages are based on full-time faculty whose race/ethnicity was known.

Reference tables: *Digest of Education Statistics 2014*, tables 315.10, 315.20, and 316.80; *Digest of Education Statistics 2015*, tables 316.10 and 316.20
Related indicators: Characteristics of Degree-Granting Postsecondary Institutions, Characteristics of Postsecondary Students

Glossary: Constant dollars, Control of institutions, Degree-granting institution, Doctor's degree, For-profit institution, Nonprofit institution, Postsecondary education, Postsecondary institutions (basic classification by level), Private institution, Public school or institution, Racial/ethnic group, Salary

Undergraduate Degree Fields

From 2003–04 to 2013–14, the number of associate's degrees conferred increased by 51 percent, from 665,300 to over 1 million, and the number of bachelor's degrees conferred increased by 34 percent, from 1.4 million to 1.9 million.

In academic year 2013–14, over 1 million associate's degrees were conferred by Title IV postsecondary institutions, a decrease of less than 1 percent from the previous year. Of the associate's degrees conferred in 2013–14, about two-thirds (67 percent) were concentrated in three fields of study: liberal arts and sciences, general studies, and humanities (35 percent); health professions and related programs (21 percent); and business, management, marketing, and support services

(11 percent). These three fields also accounted for the largest percentage of degrees in 2003–04. In 2013–14, the three next largest percentages of associate's degrees conferred were in the fields of homeland security, law enforcement, and firefighting (5 percent); computer and information sciences and support services (4 percent); and engineering technologies and engineering-related fields[1] (3 percent).

Figure 1. Number of associate's degrees conferred by postsecondary institutions in selected fields of study: Academic years 2003–04 and 2013–14

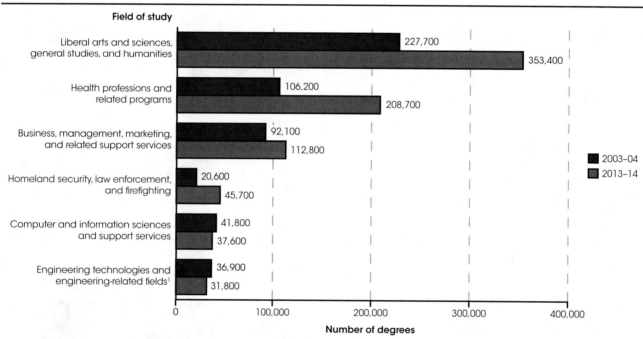

[1] Excludes "Construction trades" and "Mechanic and repair technologies/technicians."
NOTE: The six fields of study shown were the fields in which the largest number of associate's degrees were conferred from the approximately 1,003,400 associate's degrees conferred in 2013–14. Data are for postsecondary institutions participating in Title IV federal financial aid programs. The new Classification of Instructional Programs was initiated in 2009–10. The estimates for 2003–04 have been reclassified when necessary to make them conform to the new taxonomy. The "business, management, marketing, and related support services" field of study does not include personal and culinary services. Some data have been revised from previously published figures.
SOURCE: U.S. Department of Education, National Center for Education Statistics, Integrated Postsecondary Education Data System (IPEDS), Fall 2004 and Fall 2014, Completions component. See *Digest of Education Statistics 2015*, table 321.10.

Between 2003–04 and 2013–14, the number of associate's degrees conferred increased by 338,000 degrees, or 51 percent. Over this time period, the number of associate's degrees conferred in liberal arts and sciences, general studies, and humanities; health professions and related programs; and business, management, marketing, and support services (the three fields of study in which the most degrees were conferred) increased by 55 percent

(from 227,700 to 353,400), 96 percent (from 106,200 to 208,700), and 23 percent (from 92,100 to 112,800), respectively. Of the 20 fields of study in which the greatest number of associate's degrees were conferred in 2013–14, psychology was the field in which there was the largest percentage increase in degrees conferred between 2003–04 and 2013–14 (299 percent, from 1,900 to 7,500 degrees). Additionally, the number of associate's degrees conferred more than doubled over the period in the following fields: social sciences and history (increasing from 6,200 to 16,500, or 165 percent); physical sciences and science technologies (increasing from 2,700 to 6,900, or 158 percent); public administration and social services (increasing from 3,700 to 8,900, or 139 percent); homeland security, law enforcement, and firefighting (increasing from 20,600 to 45,700, or 122 percent); and communication, journalism, and related programs (increasing from 2,400 to 4,900, or 102 percent).

In 2013–14, the three fields in which the greatest number of associate's degrees were conferred overall—liberal arts and sciences, general studies, and humanities; health professions and related programs; and business, management, marketing, and support services—were also the three fields in which the most degrees were conferred across the following racial/ethnic groups: White, Black, Hispanic, Asian, Pacific Islander, American Indian/Alaska Native, Two or more races, and Nonresident alien. The fields in which the fourth and fifth most associate's degrees were conferred overall (homeland security, law enforcement, and firefighting; and computer and information sciences and support services, respectively) were the same as the fields in which the fourth and fifth most degrees were conferred to White (24,900 and 23,000, respectively), Black (7,800 and 6,100, respectively), and Pacific Islander students (200 and 100, respectively), as well as students of Two or more races (900 and 800, respectively). For Hispanic students, the field in which the fourth most associate's degrees were conferred in 2013–14 was homeland security, law enforcement, and firefighting, and the field in which the fifth most were conferred was multi/interdisciplinary studies. For Asian students, the field in which the fourth most associate's degrees were conferred was multi/interdisciplinary studies, and the field in which the fifth most were conferred was computer and information sciences and support services. For American Indian/Alaska Native students, the field in which the fourth most associate's degrees were conferred was education, and the field in which the fifth most were conferred was homeland security, law enforcement, and firefighting.

Figure 2. Number of bachelor's degrees conferred by postsecondary institutions in selected fields of study: Academic years 2003-04 and 2013-14

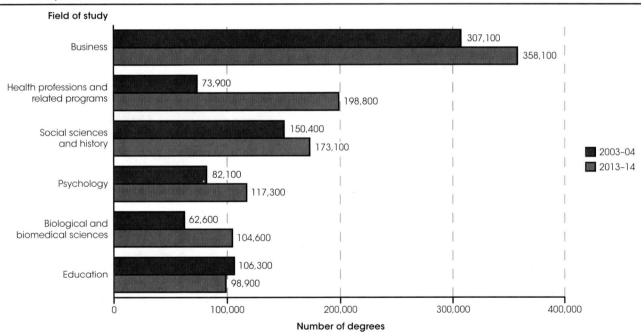

NOTE: The six fields of study shown were the fields in which the largest number of bachelor's degrees were conferred from the approximately 1,869,800 bachelor's degrees conferred in 2013-14. Data are for postsecondary institutions participating in Title IV federal financial aid programs. The new Classification of Instructional Programs was initiated in 2009-10. The estimates for 2003-04 have been reclassified when necessary to make them conform to the new taxonomy. The "business" field of study includes business, management, marketing, and related support services, as well as personal and culinary services. Some data have been revised from previously published figures.
SOURCE: U.S. Department of Education, National Center for Education Statistics, Integrated Postsecondary Education Data System (IPEDS), Fall 2004 and Fall 2014, Completions component. See *Digest of Education Statistics 2015,* table 322.10.

Approximately 1.9 million bachelor's degrees were conferred by Title IV postsecondary institutions in 2013–14. The fields in which the three largest percentages of bachelor's degrees were conferred in 2013–14 were business[2] (19 percent), health professions and related programs (11 percent), and social sciences and history (9 percent). The fields in which the three next largest percentages of bachelor's degrees were conferred in 2013–14 were psychology (6 percent), biological and biomedical sciences (6 percent), and education (5 percent).

The number of bachelor's degrees conferred overall increased by 470,000 degrees, or 34 percent, between 2003–04 and 2013–14. The three fields of study in which the most bachelor's degrees were conferred—business, health professions and related programs, and social sciences and history—had increases during this period of 17 percent (from 307,100 to 358,100), 169 percent (from 73,900 to 198,800), and 15 percent (from 150,400 to 173,100), respectively. In addition to health professions and related programs, of the 20 fields of study in which the most bachelor's degrees were conferred in 2013–14, the next largest percentage increases between 2003–04 and 2013–14 occurred in homeland security, law enforcement, and firefighting (122 percent, from 28,200 to 62,400); and parks, recreation, leisure, and fitness studies (108 percent, from 22,200 to 46,000).

In 2013–14, the three fields of study in which the most bachelor's degrees were conferred overall (business, health professions and related programs, and social sciences and history) were also the three fields in which the most bachelor's degrees were conferred in six racial/ethnic groups: White, Black, Hispanic, Pacific Islander, and American Indian/Alaska Native students and students of Two or more races. The three fields in which Asian students received the most bachelor's degrees were business (25,300), biological and biomedical sciences (16,500), and health professions and related programs (14,700). The field in which the fourth most bachelor's degrees were conferred in 2013–14 was psychology for Black (14,200), Hispanic (17,100), and Pacific Islander (300) students and students of Two or more races (3,500). For White students as well as American Indian/Alaska Native students, the field in which the fourth most bachelor's degrees were conferred was education (78,700 and 700, respectively). The field in which Asian students received the fourth most bachelor's degrees was social sciences and history (11,900).

Figure 3. Number of bachelor's degrees conferred by postsecondary institutions in selected fields of study, by sex: Academic year 2013–14

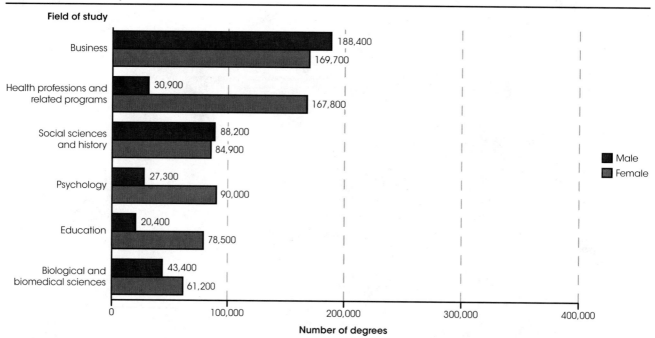

NOTE: The six fields of study shown were the fields in which the largest number of bachelor's degrees were conferred from the approximately 1,869,800 bachelor's degrees conferred in 2013-14. Data are for postsecondary institutions participating in Title IV federal financial aid programs. The "business" field of study includes business, management, marketing, and related support services, as well as personal and culinary services.
SOURCE: U.S. Department of Education, National Center for Education Statistics, Integrated Postsecondary Education Data System (IPEDS), Fall 2014, Completions component. See *Digest of Education Statistics 2015*, tables 322.40 and 322.50.

Some 1.1 million bachelor's degrees were conferred to females in 2013–14, an increase of 1 percent from the previous year. Of the six fields in which the most bachelor's degrees were conferred in 2013–14, females were conferred the majority of degrees in the following four fields: health professions and related programs (167,800 vs. 30,900 for males), education (78,500 vs. 20,400 for males), psychology (90,000 vs. 27,300 for males), and biological and biomedical sciences (61,200 vs. 43,400 for males). Approximately 801,700 bachelor's degrees were conferred to males in 2013–14, and males received the majority of the degrees conferred in business (188,400 vs. 169,700 for females) and social sciences and history (88,200 vs. 84,900 for females).

Endnotes:

[1] Excludes "Construction trades" and "Mechanic and repair technologies/technicians."

[2] For bachelor's degrees, the "business" field of study includes business, management, marketing, and related support services, as well as personal and culinary services. This differs from the "business, management, marketing, and support services" field of study for associate's degrees, which does not include personal and culinary services.

Reference tables: *Digest of Education Statistics 2015*, tables 321.10, 321.30, 322.10, 322.30, 322.40, and 322.50

Related indicators: Annual Earnings of Young Adults, Employment and Unemployment Rates by Educational Attainment, Graduate Degree Fields, Degrees Conferred by Public and Private Institutions

Glossary: Associate's degree, Bachelor's degree, Classification of Instructional Programs (CIP), Racial/ethnic group

Graduate Degree Fields

Between academic years 2003–04 and 2013–14, the number of master's degrees conferred increased by 34 percent, from 564,300 to 754,500, and the number of doctor's degrees conferred increased by 41 percent, from 126,100 to 177,600.

The number of master's degrees conferred by postsecondary institutions increased by less than 1 percent between academic years 2012–13 and 2013–14 (from 751,700 to 754,500 degrees). Of the 754,500 master's degrees conferred in 2013–14, nearly half were concentrated in two fields: business (25 percent) and education (20 percent). The three fields in which the next largest percentages of master's degrees were conferred

were health professions and related programs (13 percent), public administration and social services (6 percent), and engineering (6 percent). Not only did these five fields account for the largest percentages of master's degrees conferred in 2013–14, they also accounted for the largest percentages conferred in 2003–04 (one decade earlier) and 2012–13 (one year earlier).

Figure 1. Number of master's degrees conferred by postsecondary institutions in selected fields of study: Academic years 2003–04 and 2013–14

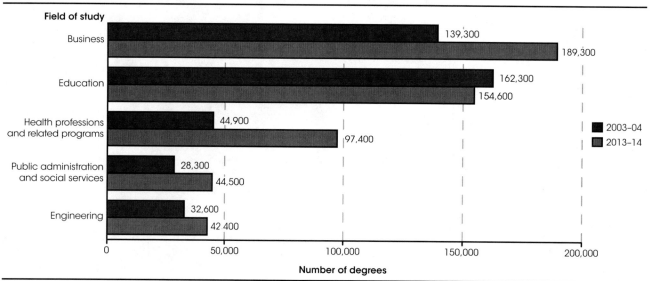

NOTE: The five fields of study shown were the fields in which the largest number of master's degrees were conferred from the 754,500 master's degrees conferred in 2013–14. Data are for postsecondary institutions participating in Title IV federal financial aid programs. The new Classification of Instructional Programs was initiated in 2009–10. The estimates for 2003–04 have been reclassified when necessary to make them conform to the new taxonomy. "Business" includes Business, management, marketing, and related support services and Personal and culinary services.
SOURCE: U.S. Department of Education, National Center for Education Statistics, Integrated Postsecondary Education Data System (IPEDS), Fall 2004 and Fall 2014, Completions component. See *Digest of Education Statistics 2015*, table 323.10.

Between 2003–04 and 2013–14, the number of master's degrees conferred increased by 190,200, reflecting an increase of 34 percent. In 2013–14, the three degree fields in which the most master's degrees were conferred were business (189,300), education (154,600), and health professions and related programs (97,400). The number of business degrees conferred increased by less than 1 percent from 2012–13, and the number of education degrees conferred decreased by 6 percent. All of the 20 largest degree fields in 2013–14 had increases compared to 2003–04, except the field of education. The largest percentage increase in the number of master's degrees conferred between 2003–04 and 2013–14 was in the field of homeland security, law enforcement, and firefighting (150 percent, from 3,700 to 9,300 degrees).

The next largest percentage increase was in the field of parks, recreation, leisure, and fitness studies (138 percent, from 3,200 to 7,600 degrees). Of the 20 fields in which the most master's degrees were conferred in 2013–14, English language and literature/letters was the field in which there was the smallest percentage increase in the master's degrees conferred between 2003–04 and 2013–14 (17 percent, from 8,000 to 9,300 degrees).

In 2013–14, all racial/ethnic groups conferred the most master's degrees in the same top three degree fields (business, education, and health professions and related programs); however, not all were ranked within the same order. The largest numbers of master's degrees conferred were in business, education, and health professions and related programs. The distribution of graduates earning degrees in science, technology, engineering, and mathematics (STEM) fields differed from the overall distribution of master's degrees by race/ethnicity. The percentage of Asian/Pacific Islander graduates earning STEM master's degrees (15 percent) was higher than the percentage of Asian/Pacific Islander graduates earning master's degrees in all fields (7 percent). In contrast, the percentage of White (67 percent), Black (8 percent), and Hispanic (8 percent) graduates earning STEM degrees was lower than the percentage of these graduates earning master's degrees overall (68 percent, 14 percent, and 9 percent, respectively).

The number of doctor's degrees conferred by postsecondary institutions increased by 1 percent between 2012–13 and 2013–14 (from 175,000 to 177,600 degrees). The percentages of doctor's degrees conferred in health professions and related programs (38 percent) and legal professions and studies (25 percent) combined made up almost two-thirds of the 177,600 doctor's degrees conferred in 2013–14. The three fields in which the next largest percentages of doctor's degrees in were conferred in 2013–14 were education (6 percent), engineering (6 percent), and biological and biomedical sciences (5 percent). These fields were the same fields in which the largest percentages of doctor's degrees were conferred in each year during the past decade.

Figure 2. Number of doctor's degrees conferred by postsecondary institutions in selected fields of study: Academic years 2003–04 and 2013–14

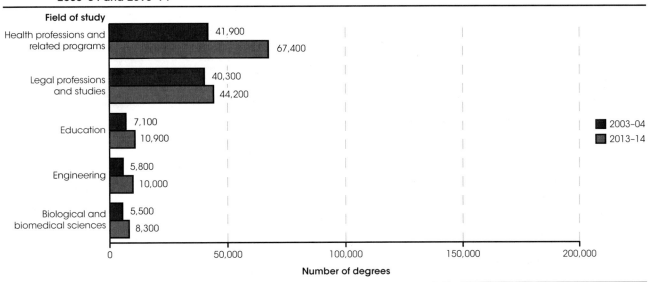

NOTE: The five fields of study were the fields in which the largest number of doctor's degrees were conferred from the 177,600 doctor's degrees conferred in 2013–14. Data are for postsecondary institutions participating in Title IV federal financial aid programs. The new Classification of Instructional Programs was initiated in 2009–10. The estimates for 2003–04 have been reclassified when necessary to make them conform to the new taxonomy.
SOURCE: U.S. Department of Education, National Center for Education Statistics, Integrated Postsecondary Education Data System (IPEDS), Fall 2004 and Fall 2014, Completions component. See *Digest of Education Statistics 2015*, table 324.10.

Between 2003–04 and 2013–14, the number of doctor's degrees conferred increased from 126,100 to 177,600, reflecting an increase of 41 percent. Health professions and related programs, and legal professions and studies were the fields in which the most doctor's degrees were conferred. The number of degrees conferred in those fields increased by 61 percent (from 41,900 to 67,400 degrees) and 10 percent (from 40,300 to 44,200 degrees), respectively, over the period. All of the 20 largest fields in 2013–14 showed increases compared to 2003–04. Among these fields, the field of computer and information sciences had the largest percentage increase in the number of doctor's degrees conferred between 2003–04 and 2013–14 (118 percent, from 900 to 2,000 degrees). The next largest percentage increase during the period was in the field of business (105 percent, from 1,500 to 3,000 degrees).

Among all racial/ethnic groups in 2013–14, the most doctor's degrees were conferred in the same two degree

fields; however, not all ranked in the same order. The largest numbers of doctor's degrees conferred were in health professions and related programs, and legal professions and studies. As with master's degrees, the distribution of graduates earning doctor's degrees in STEM fields differed from the overall distribution of doctor's degrees by race/ethnicity. The percentage of White graduates earning STEM doctor's degrees (75 percent) was higher than their percentage of all doctor's degree recipients (70 percent). The percentage of Black graduates receiving doctor's degrees in STEM fields (5 percent) was lower than their percentage among all doctor's degree recipients (8 percent), while the percentage Hispanic STEM recipients (6 percent) and Asian/Pacific Islander STEM recipients (12 percent) were one percent or less different compared to their overall percentages among doctor's degree recipients.

Figure 3. Number of master's and doctor's degrees conferred by postsecondary institutions, by level of degree and sex: Academic years 2003-04 and 2013-14

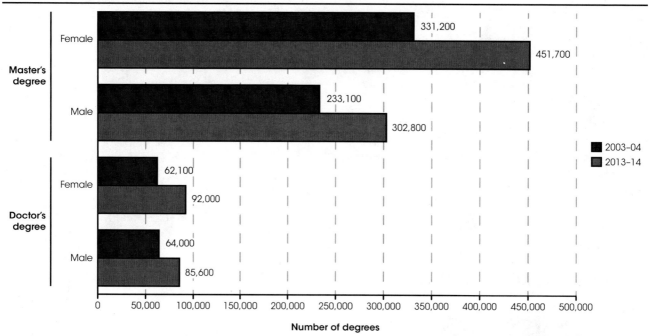

NOTE: Data are for postsecondary institutions participating in Title IV federal financial aid programs.
SOURCE: U.S. Department of Education, National Center for Education Statistics, Integrated Postsecondary Education Data System (IPEDS), Fall 2004 and Fall 2014, Completions component. See *Digest of Education Statistics 2015*, tables 323.20 and 324.20.

More master's degrees were conferred to females than males in 2013–14 (451,700 vs. 302,800 degrees), as well as in nearly the past decade. Between 2003–04 and 2013–14, the number of master's degrees conferred to females increased by 120,500, reflecting an increase of 36 percent. Over the same period, the number of master's degrees conferred to males increased by 69,800, reflecting an increase of 30 percent. The number of master's degrees conferred between academic years 2012–13 and 2013–14 increased by less than one-half of 1 percent for both females and males.

Females earned more doctor's degrees than males in 2013–14 (92,000 vs. 85,600 degrees) as well as in every year since 2005–06. In contrast, males earned more doctor's degrees than females in 2003–04 (64,000 vs. 62,100 degrees). Between 2003–04 and 2013–14, the number of doctor's degrees conferred to females increased by 29,900, reflecting an increase of 48 percent. The number of doctor's degrees conferred to males increased by 21,600 between 2003–04 and 2013–14, reflecting an increase of 34 percent. Between academic years 2012–13 and 2013–14, the number of doctor's degrees conferred to females increased by 2 percent, and the number conferred to males increased by 1 percent.

Reference tables: *Digest of Education Statistics 2015*, tables 318.45, 323.10, 323.20, 323.30, 324.10, 324.20, and 324.25
Related indicators: Annual Earnings of Young Adults, Employment and Unemployment Rates by Educational Attainment, Undergraduate Degree Fields, Degrees Conferred by Public and Private Institutions

Glossary: Classification of Instructional Programs (CIP), Doctor's degree, Master's degree, Racial/ethnic group, STEM fields

This page intentionally left blank.

Undergraduate Retention and Graduation Rates

About 60 percent of students who began seeking a bachelor's degree at a 4-year institution in fall 2008 completed that degree within 6 years; the graduation rate was higher for females than males (62 percent vs. 57 percent).

Figure 1. Percentage of first-time, full-time degree-seeking undergraduates retained at 2- and 4-year degree-granting institutions, by institution level, control of institution, and acceptance rate: 2013 to 2014

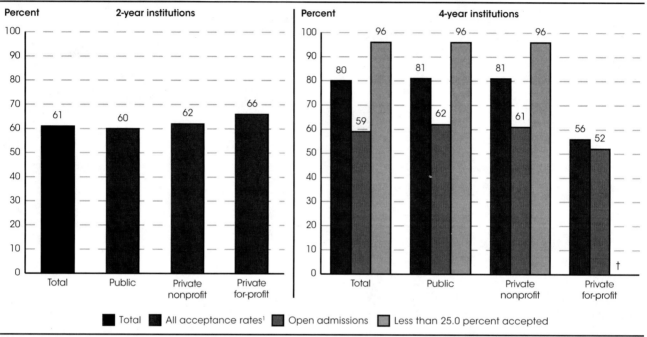

† Not applicable.
[1] Includes institutions that have an open admission policy, institutions that have various applicant acceptance rates, and institutions for which no acceptance rate information is available.
NOTE: Degree-granting institutions grant associate's or higher degrees and participate in Title IV federal financial aid programs. Retained first-time undergraduates are those who returned to the institutions to continue their studies the following fall.
SOURCE: U.S. Department of Education, National Center for Education Statistics, Integrated Postsecondary Education Data System (IPEDS), Spring 2015, Fall Enrollment component; and Fall 2013, Institutional Characteristics component. See *Digest of Education Statistics 2015*, table 326.30.

The retention rate (i.e., the percentage of students returning the following fall) among first-time, full-time degree-seeking students who enrolled at 4-year degree-granting institutions in 2013 was 80 percent. At public and private nonprofit 4-year institutions, retention rates were generally higher at more selective institutions. At public 4-year institutions, the overall retention rate was 81 percent; at the least selective institutions (those with open admissions) the retention rate was 62 percent, while at the most selective institutions (those that accept less than 25 percent of applicants) the retention rate was

96 percent. The overall retention rate was 81 percent at private nonprofit 4-year institutions (61 percent at the least selective institutions and 96 percent at the most selective). The overall retention rate for students at private for-profit 4-year institutions was 56 percent, and retention rates varied according to institutional selectivity as well. At 2-year institutions, the overall retention rate for students was 61 percent; at this institution level, the retention rate for private for-profit institutions (66 percent) was higher than for private nonprofit institutions (62 percent) and public institutions (60 percent).

The 1990 Student Right-to-Know Act requires postsecondary institutions to report the percentage of students who complete their program within 150 percent of the normal time for completion (e.g., within 6 years for students pursuing a bachelor's degree). The graduation rates in this indicator are calculated accordingly. Students who transfer without completing a degree and then complete a degree at another institution are not included as completers in the calculation of these rates.

Figure 2. Graduation rate (within 6 years) from first institution attended for first-time, full-time bachelor's degree-seeking students at 4-year postsecondary institutions, by control of institution and sex: Cohort entry year 2008

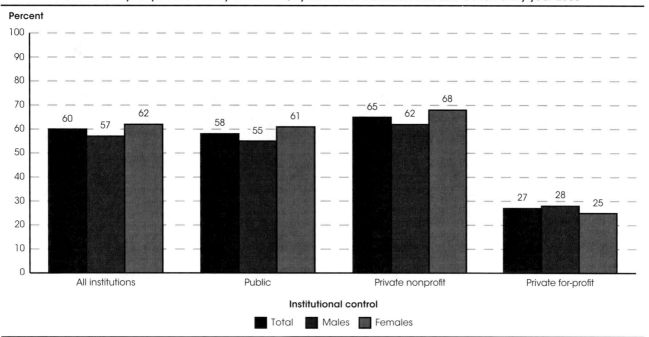

NOTE: Data are for 4-year degree-granting postsecondary institutions participating in Title IV federal financial aid programs. Graduation rates include students receiving bachelor's degrees from their initial institution of attendance only.
SOURCE: U.S. Department of Education, National Center for Education Statistics, Integrated Postsecondary Education Data System (IPEDS), Winter 2014–15 Graduation Rates component. See *Digest of Education Statistics 2015*, table 326.10.

The 6-year graduation rate for first-time, full-time undergraduate students who began their pursuit of a bachelor's degree at a 4-year degree-granting institution in fall 2008 was 60 percent. That is, 60 percent of first-time, full-time students who began seeking a bachelor's degree at a 4-year institution in fall 2008 completed the degree at that institution by 2014. The 6-year graduation rate was 58 percent at public institutions, 65 percent at private nonprofit institutions, and 27 percent at private for-profit institutions. The 6-year graduation rate was 57 percent for males and 62 percent for females; it was higher for females than for males at both public (61 vs. 55 percent) and private nonprofit institutions (68 vs. 62 percent). However, at private for-profit institutions, males had a higher 6-year graduation rate than females (28 vs. 25 percent).

Figure 3. Graduation rate (within 6 years) from first institution attended for first-time, full-time bachelor's degree-seeking students at 4-year postsecondary institutions, by acceptance rate of institution: Cohort entry year 2008

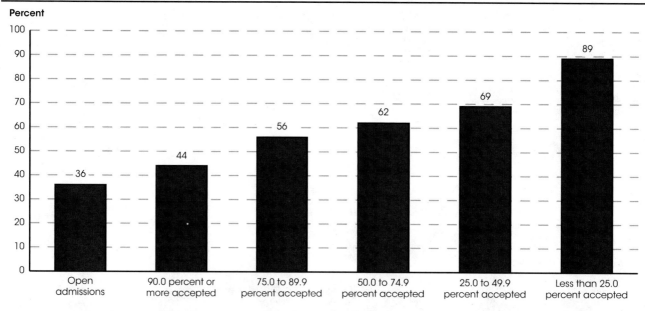

Percent

Acceptance rate of institution

NOTE: Data are for 4-year degree-granting postsecondary institutions participating in Title IV federal financial aid programs. Graduation rates include students receiving bachelor's degrees from their initial institutions of attendance only.
SOURCE: U.S. Department of Education, National Center for Education Statistics, Integrated Postsecondary Education Data System (IPEDS), Winter 2014–15 Graduation Rates component and Fall 2013, Institutional Characteristics component. See *Digest of Education Statistics 2015*, table 326.10.

Six-year graduation rates for first-time, full-time students who began seeking a bachelor's degree in fall 2008 varied according to institutional selectivity. In particular, 6-year graduation rates were highest at postsecondary degree-granting institutions that were the most selective (i.e., had the lowest admissions acceptance rates), and were lowest at institutions that were the least selective (i.e., had open admissions policies). For example, at 4-year institutions with open admissions policies, 36 percent of students completed a bachelor's degree within 6 years. At 4-year institutions where the acceptance rate was less than 25 percent of applicants, the 6-year graduation rate was 89 percent.

Between 2009 and 2014, the overall 6-year graduation rate for first-time, full-time students who began seeking

a bachelor's degree at 4-year degree-granting institutions increased by 2 percentage points, from 58 percent (for students who began their studies in 2003 and graduated within 6 years) to 60 percent (for students who began their studies in 2008 and graduated within 6 years). During this period, 6-year graduation rates were higher in 2014 than in 2009 at both public institutions (58 percent vs. 56 percent) and private for-profit institutions (27 percent vs. 24 percent), but did not change significantly for private nonprofit institutions (where the rates were both around 65 percent). In addition, 6-year graduation rates increased for both males (from 55 percent to 57 percent) and females (from 60 percent to 62 percent) during this period.

Figure 4. Graduation rate within 150 percent of normal time from first institution attended for first-time, full-time degree/certificate-seeking students at 2-year postsecondary institutions, by control of institution and sex: Cohort entry year 2011

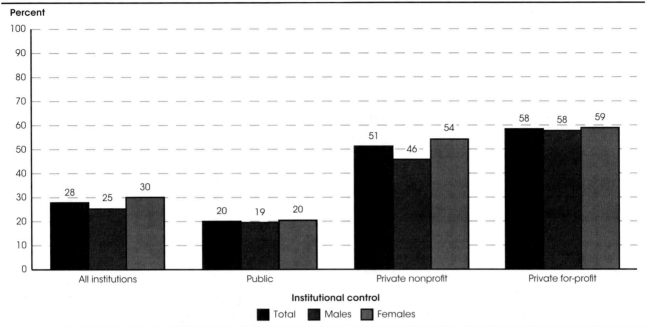

NOTE: Data are for 2-year degree-granting postsecondary institutions participating in Title IV federal financial aid programs. Graduation rates include students receiving associate's degrees or certificates from their initial institutions of attendance only. An example of completing a credential within 150 percent of the normal time required to do so is taking 3 years to complete a 2-year degree.
SOURCE: U.S. Department of Education, National Center for Education Statistics, Integrated Postsecondary Education Data System (IPEDS), Winter 2014–15 Graduation Rates component. See *Digest of Education Statistics 2015*, table 326.20.

At 2-year degree-granting institutions, 28 percent of first-time, full-time undergraduate students who began their pursuit of a certificate or associate's degree in fall 2011 attained it within 150 percent of the normal time required to do so (an example of completing a credential within 150 percent of the normal time is taking 3 years to complete a 2-year degree). This graduation rate was 20 percent at public 2-year institutions, 51 percent at private nonprofit 2-year institutions, and 58 percent at private for-profit 2-year institutions. At 2-year institutions overall, as well as at public, private nonprofit, and private for-profit 2-year institutions, the graduation rates were higher for females than for males. At private nonprofit 2-year institutions, for example, 54 percent of females versus 46 percent of males who began pursuing a certificate or associate's degree in 2011 completed it within 150 percent of the normal time required.

Reference tables: *Digest of Education Statistics 2015*, tables 326.10, 326.20, and 326.30
Related indicators: Educational Attainment of Young Adults

Glossary: Associate's degree, Bachelor's degree, Certificate, Degree-granting institution, For-profit institution, Full-time enrollment, Nonprofit institution, Postsecondary education, Postsecondary institutions (basic classification by level), Private institution, Public school or institution, Undergraduate students

Degrees Conferred by Public and Private Institutions

The number of postsecondary degrees conferred at each degree level increased between 2003–04 and 2013–14. The number of certificates below the associate's degree level awarded during this period increased by 41 percent, the number of associate's degrees increased by 51 percent, the number of bachelor's degrees increased by 34 percent, the number of master's degrees increased by 34 percent, and the number of doctor's degrees increased by 41 percent.

Table 1. Number of degrees conferred by postsecondary institutions and percentage change, by control of institution and level of degree: Academic years 1993–94, 2003–04, and 2013–14

Level of degree and academic year	Total	Public	Private		
			Total	Nonprofit	For-profit
Sub-associate certificates					
1993–94	—	—	—	—	—
2003–04	687,787	364,053	323,734	35,316	288,418
2013–14	969,353	576,258	393,095	30,730	362,365
Percent change from 1993–94 to 2003–04	†	†	†	†	†
Percent change from 2003–04 to 2013–14	40.9	58.3	21.4	-13.0	25.6
Associate's					
1993–94	530,632	444,373	86,259	48,493	37,766
2003–04	665,301	524,875	140,426	45,759	94,667
2013–14	1,003,364	793,180	210,184	53,127	157,057
Percent change from 1993–94 to 2003–04	25.4	18.1	62.8	-5.6	150.7
Percent change from 2003–04 to 2013–14	50.8	51.1	49.7	16.1	65.9
Bachelor's					
1993–94	1,169,275	789,148	380,127	371,561	8,566
2003–04	1,399,542	905,718	493,824	451,518	42,306
2013–14	1,869,814	1,186,397	683,417	544,213	139,204
Percent change from 1993–94 to 2003–04	19.7	14.8	29.9	21.5	393.9
Percent change from 2003–04 to 2013–14	33.6	31.0	38.4	20.5	229.0
Master's					
1993–94	393,037	221,428	171,609	168,718	2,891
2003–04	564,272	285,138	279,134	250,894	28,240
2013–14	754,475	346,101	408,374	333,580	74,794
Percent change from 1993–94 to 2003–04	43.6	28.8	62.7	48.7	876.8
Percent change from 2003–04 to 2013–14	33.7	21.4	46.3	33.0	164.9
Doctor's[1]					
1993–94	112,636	58,366	54,270	53,502	768
2003–04	126,087	64,205	61,882	60,447	1,435
2013–14	177,580	88,904	88,676	80,894	7,782
Percent change from 1993–94 to 2003–04	11.9	10.0	14.0	13.0	86.8
Percent change from 2003–04 to 2013–14	40.8	38.5	43.3	33.8	442.3

— Not available.
† Not applicable.
[1] Includes Ph.D., Ed.D., and comparable degrees at the doctoral level. Includes most degrees formerly classified as first-professional, such as M.D., D.D.S., and law degrees.
NOTE: Data are for postsecondary institutions participating in Title IV federal financial aid programs. Data for associate's degrees and higher awards are for degree-granting institutions.
SOURCE: U.S. Department of Education, National Center for Education Statistics, Integrated Postsecondary Education Data System (IPEDS), "Completions Survey" (IPEDS-C:93); and Fall 2004 and Fall 2014, Completions component. See *Digest of Education Statistics 2015*, table 318.40.

The number of postsecondary degrees conferred at each degree level increased between 2003–04 and 2013–14. The number of certificates below the associate's degree level awarded during this period increased by 41 percent, the number of associate's degrees increased by 51 percent, the number of bachelor's degrees increased by 34 percent, the number of master's degrees increased by 34 percent, and the number of doctor's degrees increased by 41 percent. From 2012–13 to 2013–14, institutions conferred more certificates and bachelor's, master's, and doctor's degrees, but fewer associate's degrees. Over this time, the total number of bachelor's degrees increased by 1.6 percent and the number of doctor's degrees increased by 1.5 percent. The number of certificates and master's degrees both increased by less than one half of one percent, while the number of associate's degrees conferred decreased by less than one half of one percent.

At all levels except master's degrees, the percentage increases from 2003–04 to 2013–14 were greater than the percentage increases from 1993–94 to 2003–04.[1] For example, the total number of bachelor's degrees conferred increased by 34 percent from 2003–04 to 2013–14,

compared with 20 percent from 1993–94 to 2003–04. However, rates of increase in these two periods differed by institutional control. Public institutions had greater percentage increases from 2003–04 to 2013–14 than from 1993–94 to 2003–04 across all levels of degrees except master's degrees. Private nonprofit institutions had greater percentage increases from 2003–04 to 2013–14 than from 1993–94 to 2003–04 across associate's and doctor's degrees; for bachelor's and master's degrees, the percentage increase was greater in the earlier period than the later one. Private for-profit institutions experienced smaller percentage increases from 2003–04 to 2013–14 than from 1993–94 to 2003–04 across all degrees except doctor's.

Figure 1. Percentage distribution of certificates and associate's degrees conferred by postsecondary institutions, by control of institution: Academic years 2003-04 and 2013-14

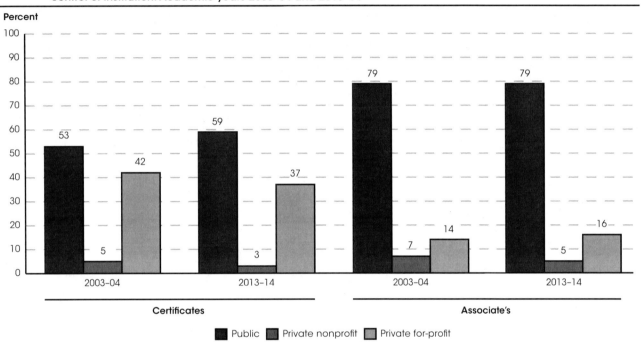

NOTE: Data are for postsecondary institutions participating in Title IV federal financial aid programs. Data for associate's degrees are for degree-granting institutions. Detail may not sum to totals because of rounding.
SOURCE: U.S. Department of Education, National Center for Education Statistics, Integrated Postsecondary Education Data System (IPEDS), Fall 2004 and Fall 2014, Completions component. See *Digest of Education Statistics 2015*, table 318.40.

From 2003–04 to 2013–14, the number of certificates awarded by public institutions increased by 58 percent (from 364,000 to 576,000), and the number awarded by private for-profit institutions increased by 26 percent (from 288,000 to 362,000). However, the number of certificates awarded by private nonprofit institutions decreased by 13 percent (from 35,000 to 31,000). Due to these changes, the share of all certificates conferred by public institutions was higher in 2013–14 than in 2003–04 (a change from 53 to 59 percent), while the shares conferred by private nonprofit institutions and private for-profit institutions were lower in 2013–14 than in 2003–04 (a change from 5 to 3 percent for private nonprofit institutions and from 42 to 37 percent for private for-profit institutions).

The number of associate's degrees awarded from 2003–04 to 2013–14 increased by 51 percent for public institutions (from 525,000 to 793,000), by 16 percent for private nonprofit institutions (from 46,000 to 53,000), and by 66 percent for private for-profit institutions (from 95,000 to 157,000). Due to these changes, the share of all associate's degrees conferred by private for-profit institutions increased from 14 percent in 2003–04 to 16 percent in 2013–14. Additionally, the share of associate's degrees conferred by public institutions was the same in 2003–04 and 2013–14 (79 percent), and the share conferred by private nonprofit institutions decreased from 7 to 5 percent.

Figure 2. Percentage distribution of bachelor's, master's, and doctor's degrees conferred by postsecondary institutions, by control of institution: Academic years 2003-04 and 2013-14

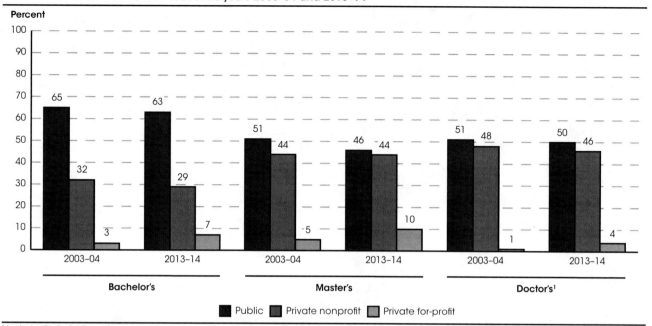

[1] Includes Ph.D., Ed.D., and comparable degrees at the doctoral level. Includes most degrees formerly classified as first-professional, such as M.D., D.D.S., and law degrees.
NOTE: Data are for postsecondary institutions participating in Title IV federal financial aid programs. Data are for degree-granting institutions. Detail may not sum to totals because of rounding.
SOURCE: U.S. Department of Education, National Center for Education Statistics, Integrated Postsecondary Education Data System (IPEDS), Fall 2004 and Fall 2014, Completions component. See *Digest of Education Statistics 2015*, table 318.40.

From 2003–04 to 2013–14, the number of bachelor's degrees awarded by public institutions increased by 31 percent (from 906,000 to 1.2 million), the number awarded by private nonprofit institutions increased by 21 percent (from 452,000 to 544,000), and the number awarded by private for-profit institutions increased by 229 percent (from 42,000 to 139,000). As a result, between 2003–04 and 2013–14, the shares of all bachelor's degrees conferred by public institutions and private nonprofit institutions decreased from 65 to 63 percent and from 32 to 29 percent, respectively, while the share conferred by private for-profit institutions increased from 3 to 7 percent.

The number of master's degrees awarded by public institutions increased by 21 percent (from 285,000 to 346,000) from 2003–04 to 2013–14, yet the percentage of all master's degrees conferred by these institutions declined from 51 to 46 percent. Although the number of master's degrees conferred by private nonprofit institutions increased by 33 percent (from 251,000 to 334,000) from

2003–04 to 2013–14, the percentage of all master's degrees conferred by these institutions was the same in both years (44 percent). In contrast, the number of master's degrees conferred by private for-profit institutions increased by 165 percent (from 28,000 to 75,000) from 2003–04 to 2013–14, resulting in an increase in these institutions' share of total master's degrees conferred, from 5 to 10 percent.

From 2003–04 to 2013–14, the number of doctor's degrees conferred increased by 38 percent at public institutions (from 64,000 to 89,000), by 34 percent at private nonprofit institutions (from 60,000 to 81,000), and by 442 percent at private for-profit institutions (from 1,400 to 7,800). At both public institutions and private nonprofit institutions, the share of all doctor's degrees conferred decreased from 2003–04 to 2013–14 (from 51 to 50 percent and from 48 to 46 percent, respectively), while private for-profit institutions' share increased (from 1 to 4 percent).

Endnotes:
[1] The number of sub-associate certificates conferred in 1993–94 is not available; therefore, certificates are not included in these comparisons.

Reference tables: *Digest of Education Statistics 2015*, table 318.40
Related indicators: Undergraduate Degree Fields, Graduate Degree Fields

Glossary: Associate's degree, Bachelor's degree, Certificate, Control of institutions, Doctor's degree, For-profit institution, Master's degree, Nonprofit institution, Private institution, Public school or institution

This page intentionally left blank.

Price of Attending an Undergraduate Institution

The average net price of attendance (total cost minus grant and scholarship aid) for first-time, full-time students in 2013–14 (in constant 2014–15 dollars) was $12,750 at 4-year public institutions, $24,690 at 4-year private nonprofit institutions, and $21,000 at 4-year private for-profit institutions.

Figure 1. Average total cost of attending degree-granting institutions for first-time, full-time students, by level and control of institution and student living arrangement: Academic year 2014–15

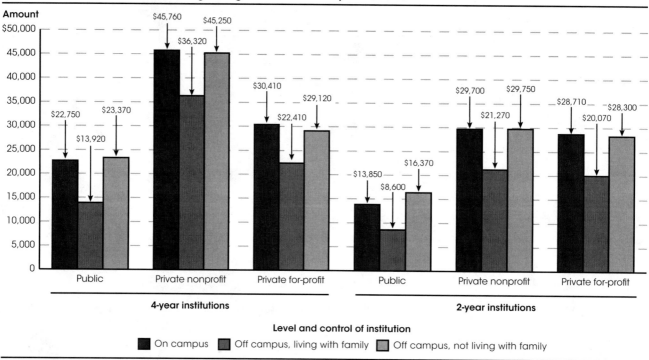

NOTE: The total cost of attending a postsecondary institution includes tuition and required fees, books and supplies, and the average cost for room, board, and other expenses. Tuition and fees at public institutions are the lower of either in-district or in-state tuition and fees. Excludes students who have already attended another postsecondary institution or who began their studies on a part-time basis. Data are weighted by the number of students at the institution receiving Title IV aid. Title IV aid includes grant aid, work-study aid, and loan aid.
SOURCE: U.S. Department of Education, National Center for Education Statistics, Integrated Postsecondary Education Data System (IPEDS), Winter 2014–15, Student Financial Aid component; and Fall 2014, Institutional Characteristics component. See *Digest of Education Statistics 2015*, table 330.40.

The total cost of attending a postsecondary institution includes tuition and required fees, books and supplies, and the average cost for room, board, and other expenses. In academic year 2014–15, the total cost of attendance for first-time, full-time students differed by institution level and control, and by student living arrangement. At 4-year institutions, the average total cost of attendance for students living on campus was $22,750 at public institutions,[1] $45,760 at private nonprofit institutions, and $30,410 at private for-profit institutions. At 2-year institutions, the average total cost of attendance for

students living on campus was $13,850 at public institutions, $29,700 at private nonprofit institutions, and $28,710 at private for-profit institutions. At every level and control of institution, the average total cost of attendance was lowest for students living with family. For example, for students at 2-year public institutions and living with family, the average total cost of attendance was $8,600, compared with $13,850 for students living on campus and $16,370 for students living off campus but not with family.

Figure 2. Average tuition and fees of degree-granting institutions for first-time, full-time students, by level and control of institution: Academic years 2011–12 through 2014–15

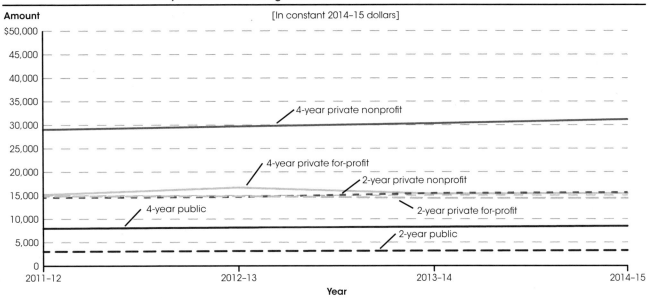

NOTE: Tuition and fees at public institutions are the lower of either in-district or in-state tuition and fees. Excludes students who have already attended another postsecondary institution or who began their studies on a part-time basis. Data are weighted by the number of students at the institution receiving Title IV aid. Title IV aid includes grant aid, work-study aid, and loan aid.
SOURCE: U.S. Department of Education, National Center for Education Statistics, Integrated Postsecondary Education Data System (IPEDS), Winter 2011–12 through Winter 2014–15, Student Financial Aid component; and Fall 2010 through Fall 2014, Institutional Characteristics component. See *Digest of Education Statistics 2015*, table 330.40.

Average undergraduate tuition and fees (in constant 2014–15 dollars) for first-time, full-time students across all 4-year degree-granting postsecondary institutions were higher in 2014–15 than in 2011–12. In 2014–15, 4-year public institutions reported average tuition and fees of $8,440—a 5 percent increase over the 2011–12 amount ($8,010). During this period, 4-year private nonprofit institutions had the largest percentage increase in tuition and fees (7 percent, from $29,050 to $31,180). The tuition and fees at 4-year private for-profit institutions were 2 percent higher in 2014–15 ($15,460) than in 2011–12 ($15,190). In 2014–15, at 2-year public institutions, average undergraduate tuition and fees were $3,270—a 7 percent increase over the 2011–12 amount ($3,060). As with 2-year public institutions, 2-year private nonprofit institutions reported a 7 percent increase in tuition and fees from $14,570 in 2011–12 to $15,630 in 2014–15. In 2014–15, tuition and fees at 2-year private for-profit institutions were 3 percent lower than in 2011–12 ($14,430 versus $14,870).

Many students and their families pay less than the full price of attendance because they receive financial aid to help cover their expenses. The 2013–14 average total cost of attendance (in constant 2014–15 dollars) ranged from a low of $8,530 for students living off campus with their families at 2-year public institutions to a high of $44,680 for students living on campus at 4-year private nonprofit institutions. The primary types of financial aid are grant and scholarship aid, which do not have to be repaid, and loans, which must be repaid. Grant and scholarship aid may be awarded on the basis of financial need, merit, or both, and may include tuition aid from employers. In 2013–14, the average amount of grant and scholarship aid for first-time, full-time students who received Title IV aid[2] was higher for students at private nonprofit institutions than for those at public and private for-profit institutions. Students at 4-year private nonprofit institutions received an average of $19,120 in grant and scholarship aid, compared with $6,840 at 4-year public institutions and $5,350 at 4-year private for-profit institutions.

The net price is the estimate of the actual amount of money that students and their families need to pay in a given year to cover educational expenses. Net price is calculated here as the total cost of attendance minus grant and scholarship aid. Net price provides an indication of what the actual financial burden is upon students and their families.

In 2013–14, the average net price for first-time, full-time students who received Title IV aid (in constant 2014–15 dollars) was lower for students at public institutions

than for those at private nonprofit and private for-profit institutions. The average net price of attendance for first-time, full-time students in 2013–14 was $12,750 at 4-year public institutions, $24,690 at 4-year private nonprofit institutions, and $21,000 at 4-year private for-profit institutions. The average net price of attendance for first-time, full-time students in 2013–14 was $7,100 at 2-year public institutions, $19,040 at 2-year private nonprofit institutions, and $20,170 at 2-year private for-profit institutions.

Figure 3. Average total cost, net price, and grant and scholarship aid for first-time, full-time students paying in-state tuition and receiving aid at 4-year public institutions, by family income level: Academic year 2013–14

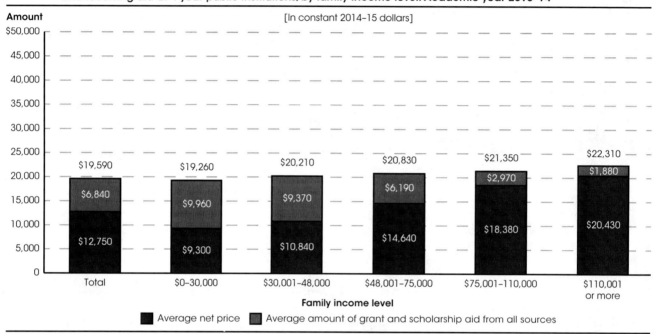

NOTE: Excludes students who previously attended another postsecondary institution or who began their studies on a part-time basis. Net price is calculated here as the total cost of attendance minus grant and scholarship aid. Data are weighted by the number of students at the institution receiving Title IV aid. Includes only first-time, full-time students who paid the in-state or in-district tuition rate and who received Title IV aid. Title IV aid includes grant aid, work-study aid, and loan aid. Detail may not sum to totals because of rounding.
SOURCE: U.S. Department of Education, National Center for Education Statistics, Integrated Postsecondary Education Data System (IPEDS), Winter 2013–14, Student Financial Aid component. See *Digest of Education Statistics 2015*, table 331.30.

The average amount of grant and scholarship aid received and the net price paid (in constant 2014–15 dollars) differed by students' family income level. In general, the lower the income, the greater the total amount of grant and scholarship aid received. For example, at 4-year public institutions, the average amount of grant and scholarship aid received by first-time, full-time students paying

in-state tuition in 2013–14 was highest for those with family incomes of $30,000 or less ($9,960 in aid) and lowest for those with family incomes of $110,001 or more ($1,880 in aid). Accordingly, the lowest average net price ($9,300) was for students with family incomes of $30,000 or less, and the highest average net price ($20,430) was for those with family incomes of $110,001 or more.

Figure 4. Average total cost, net price, and grant and scholarship aid for first-time, full-time students receiving aid at 4-year private nonprofit institutions, by family income level: Academic year 2013-14

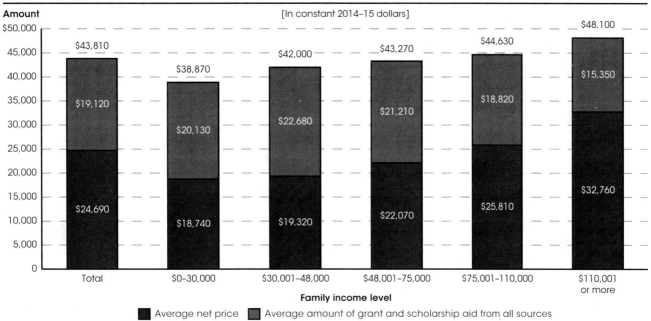

NOTE: Excludes students who previously attended another postsecondary institution or who began their studies on a part-time basis. Net price is calculated here as the total cost of attendance minus grant and scholarship aid. Data are weighted by the number of students at the institution receiving Title IV aid. Includes only first-time, full-time students who received Title IV aid. Title IV aid includes grant aid, work-study aid, and loan aid. Detail may not sum to totals because of rounding.
SOURCE: U.S. Department of Education, National Center for Education Statistics, Integrated Postsecondary Education Data System (IPEDS), Winter 2013–14, Student Financial Aid component. See *Digest of Education Statistics 2015*, table 331.30.

As with 4-year public institutions, the pattern of average net price increasing with family income was also observed at 4-year private nonprofit institutions. However, in 2013–14 the average amount of grant and scholarship aid received (in constant 2014–15 dollars) followed a different pattern. It was highest for students with family incomes between $30,001 and $48,000 ($22,680), followed by those with family incomes between $48,001 and $75,000 ($21,210), those with family incomes of $30,000 or less ($20,130), those with family incomes between $75,001 and $110,000 ($18,820), and those with family incomes of $110,001 or more ($15,350).

Figure 5. Average total cost, net price, and grant and scholarship aid for first-time, full-time students receiving aid at private for-profit 4-year institutions, by family income level: Academic year 2013–14

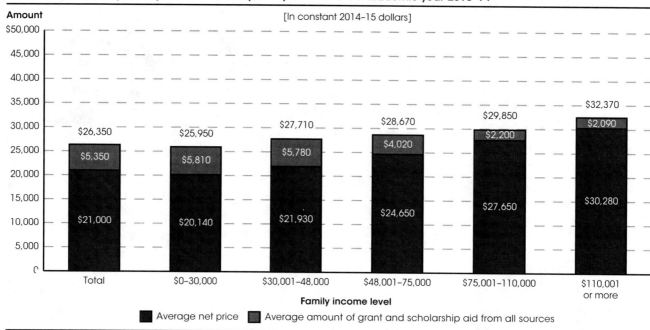

NOTE: Excludes students who previously attended another postsecondary institution or who began their studies on a part-time basis. Net price is calculated here as the total cost of attendance minus grant and scholarship aid. Data are weighted by the number of students at the institution receiving Title IV aid. Includes only first-time, full-time students who received Title IV aid. Title IV aid includes grant aid, work-study aid, and loan aid. Detail may not sum to totals because of rounding.
SOURCE: U.S. Department of Education, National Center for Education Statistics, Integrated Postsecondary Education Data System (IPEDS), Winter 2013–14, Student Financial Aid component. See *Digest of Education Statistics 2015*, table 331.30.

At 4-year private for-profit institutions, the total amount of grant and scholarship aid received (in constant 2014–15 dollars) followed the pattern of 4-year public institutions: the lower the family income level, the greater the total amount of grant and scholarship aid received. The average amount of grant and scholarship aid received by first-time, full-time students in 2013–14 was highest for those with family incomes of $30,000 or less ($5,810), while it was lowest among those with family incomes of $110,001 or more ($2,090). The lowest average net price was for students with family incomes of $30,000 or less ($20,140), and the highest average net price was for those with family incomes of $110,001 or more ($30,280).

In addition to the differences observed for each institution type by family income level, the average amount of grant and scholarship aid received and the average net price of attendance (in constant 2014–15 dollars) also varied by institution control. At each family income level, the average amount of grant and scholarship aid was highest for students at private nonprofit institutions and generally lowest for students at private for-profit institutions; the average net price was generally highest for students at private for-profit institutions and lowest for students at public institutions. The average amount of grant and scholarship aid received by students attending 4-year institutions with family incomes between $30,001 and $48,000 was highest at private nonprofit institutions ($22,680), followed by public institutions ($9,370), and private for-profit institutions ($5,780). The average net price of attending a 4-year private for-profit institution ($21,930) at this income level was higher than the price of attending a 4-year private nonprofit ($19,320) or a 4-year public institution ($10,840).

Endnotes:
[1] All data for public institutions only include students who paid the in-state or in-district tuition and fees.
[2] Title IV aid includes grant aid, work-study aid, and loan aid. All net price and grant and scholarship aid data only include students who received Title IV aid.

Reference tables: *Digest of Education Statistics 2015*, tables 330.40 and 331.30
Related indicators: Loans for Undergraduate Students, Sources of Financial Aid, Financing Postsecondary Education in the United States [*The Condition of Education 2013 Spotlight*]

Glossary: Constant dollars, Control of institutions, Financial aid, For-profit institution, Full-time enrollment, Nonprofit institution, Postsecondary institutions (basic classification by level), Private institution, Public school or institution, Title IV eligible institution, Tuition and fees

This page intentionally left blank.

Loans for Undergraduate Students

In 2013–14, the average annual student loan amount of $7,100 was 23 percent higher than the average of $5,700 in 2005–06 (in constant 2014–15 dollars). For undergraduate students ages 18 to 24 in their 4th year of college or above, the average cumulative amount borrowed was $26,400 in 2011–12.

To help offset the cost of attending a postsecondary institution, Title IV of the Higher Education Act of 1965 authorized several student financial assistance programs—including federal grants, loans, and work study. The largest federal loan program is the William D. Ford Federal Direct Loan Program; the federal government is the lender for this program. Interest on the loans made under the Direct Loan Program may be subsidized, based on need, while the student is in school. Most loans are payable over 10 years, beginning 6 months after the student does one of the following: graduates, drops below half-time enrollment, or withdraws from the academic program.

Figure 1. Average tuition and fees for full-time students at degree-granting postsecondary institutions, by level and control of institution: 2005–06 through 2013–14

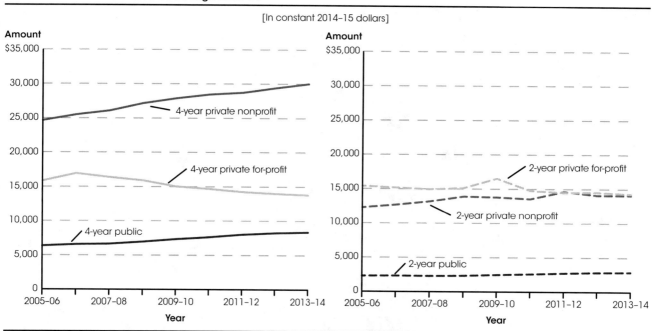

NOTE: Degree-granting institutions grant associate's or higher degrees and participate in Title IV federal financial aid programs. Data on in-state tuition and required fees are used for public institutions. Data for private 2-year colleges must be interpreted with caution because of the low response rate of these institutions. Tuition and fees were weighted by the number of full-time-equivalent undergraduates. Constant dollars based on the Consumer Price Index, prepared by the Bureau of Labor Statistics, U.S. Department of Labor, adjusted to a school-year basis.
SOURCE: U.S. Department of Education, National Center for Education Statistics, Integrated Postsecondary Education Data System (IPEDS), Fall 2005 through Fall 2013, Institutional Characteristics component. See *Digest of Education Statistics 2015*, table 330.10.

Average undergraduate tuition and fees for full-time students across all degree-granting postsecondary institutions in 2013–14 were $11,200—a 23 percent increase over the 2005–06 amount ($9,000).[1] Average tuition and fees at 4-year institutions in 2013–14 were $14,700—a 20 percent increase over the 2005–06 amount ($12,200). Among 4-year institutions, tuition and fees at public institutions had the largest percentage increase (32 percent, from $6,400 to $8,400) between 2005–06 and 2013–14; however, the largest dollar amount increase was at private nonprofit institutions (a $5,400 increase, to $30,000). Tuition and fees at private for-profit 4-year institutions decreased 13 percent between 2005–06 and 2013–14 (from $15,800 to $13,800).

At 2-year institutions, average undergraduate tuition and fees were $3,400 in 2013–14—an 18 percent increase over the 2005–06 amount ($2,900).[1] As with 4-year institutions, the largest percentage increase in tuition and fees among 2-year institutions between 2005–06 and 2013–14 occurred at public institutions (26 percent,

from $2,300 to $2,900), while the largest dollar amount increase was at private nonprofit institutions (a $1,800 increase, from $12,300 to $14,100). The tuition and fees at private for-profit 2-year institutions were 7 percent lower in 2013–14 than in 2005–06 ($14,300 versus $15,400).

Figure 2. Percentage of first-time, full-time students receiving loan aid at degree-granting postsecondary institutions, by level and control of institution: Selected years, 2005–06 through 2013–14

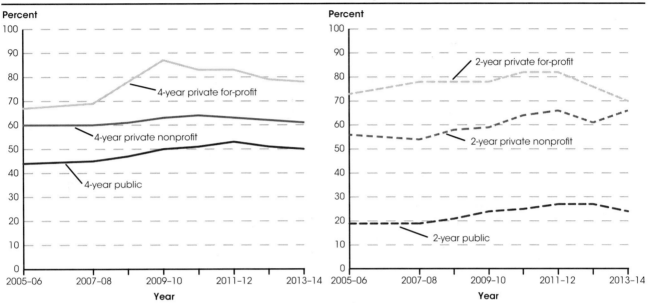

NOTE: Degree-granting institutions grant associate's or higher degrees and participate in Title IV federal financial aid programs. Some data have been revised from previously published figures. Includes only loans made directly to students; does not include Parent Loans for Undergraduate Students (PLUS) and other loans made directly to parents.
SOURCE: U.S. Department of Education, National Center for Education Statistics, Integrated Postsecondary Education Data System (IPEDS), Spring 2006 through Spring 2011 and Winter 2011–12 through Winter 2013–14, Student Financial Aid component. See *Digest of Education Statistics 2015*, table 331.20.

Nearly half (47 percent) of first-time, full-time undergraduate students received loan aid in 2013–14, an increase of 3 percentage points from 2005–06. The percentage of students receiving loan aid was higher in 2013–14 than in 2005–06 for all institution types, except private for-profit 2-year institutions. The largest change among 4-year institutions occurred at private for-profit institutions (11 percentage points), which had a higher percentage of students receiving loan aid in 2013–14 (78 percent) than in 2005–06 (67 percent). Between 2005–06 and 2013–14, the percentage of undergraduates

receiving loans increased from 44 to 50 percent at public 4-year institutions. At private nonprofit 4-year institutions, the percentage of undergraduates receiving loans was higher in 2013–14 (61 percent) than in 2005–06 (60 percent). The percentage of students at 2-year institutions receiving loans between 2005–06 and 2013–14 increased from 19 to 24 percent at public institutions and from 56 to 66 percent at private nonprofit institutions. At private for-profit 2-year institutions, the percentage of undergraduates receiving loans was lower in 2013–14 (70 percent) than in 2005–06 (73 percent).

Figure 3. Average annual loan amounts for first-time, full-time students receiving loan aid at degree-granting postsecondary institutions, by level and control of institution: Selected years, 2005–06 through 2013–14

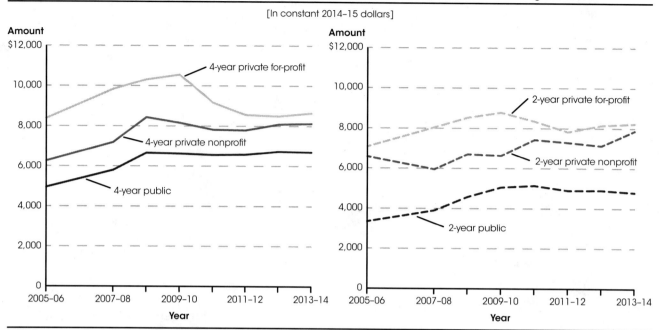

[In constant 2014–15 dollars]

NOTE: Degree-granting institutions grant associate's or higher degrees and participate in Title IV federal financial aid programs. Some data have been revised from previously published figures. Includes only loans made directly to students; does not include Parent Loans for Undergraduate Students (PLUS) and other loans made directly to parents. Constant dollars based on the Consumer Price Index, prepared by the Bureau of Labor Statistics, U.S. Department of Labor, adjusted to a school-year basis.
SOURCE: U.S. Department of Education, National Center for Education Statistics, Integrated Postsecondary Education Data System (IPEDS), Spring 2006 through Spring 2011 and Winter 2011–12 through Winter 2013–14, Student Financial Aid component. See *Digest of Education Statistics 2015*, table 331.20.

As with the percentage of students taking out loans for their education, the average amount of money students borrowed was higher in 2013–14 than in 2005–06. Average annual student loan amounts for first-time, full-time degree/certificate-seeking undergraduate students receiving loan aid were $7,100 in 2013–14, 23 percent higher than in 2005–06 ($5,700).[1] Average loan amounts were higher in 2013–14 than in 2005–06 for all institution types. Among 4-year institutions, the largest percentage increase between 2005–06 and 2013–14 in the average loan amount was at public institutions (35 percent, from $5,000 to $6,700). The average annual loan amount was 30 percent higher at private nonprofit 4-year institutions in 2013–14 ($8,100) than it was in 2005–06 ($6,300); during this period, the average loan amount was 3 percent higher at private for-profit institutions ($8,600 versus $8,400).

Similar to 4-year institutions, the largest percentage increase in the average annual loan amount between 2005–06 and 2013–14 among 2-year institutions was at public institutions (43 percent, from $3,300 to $4,800).[1] The percentage increase at private nonprofit 2-year institutions was 20 percent (from $6,600 to $7,900). At private for-profit institutions, the average annual loan amount was 16 percent higher in 2013–14 ($8,200) than it was in 2005–06 ($7,100). For both 4-year and 2-year institutions, private for-profit institutions had the largest inflation-adjusted average annual student loan amount in 2013–14 ($8,600 for 4-year institutions and $8,200 for 2-year institutions).

Figure 4. Average cumulative amount borrowed for undergraduate students ages 18 to 24 in their 4th (senior) year or above, by control and level of institution: 2011-12

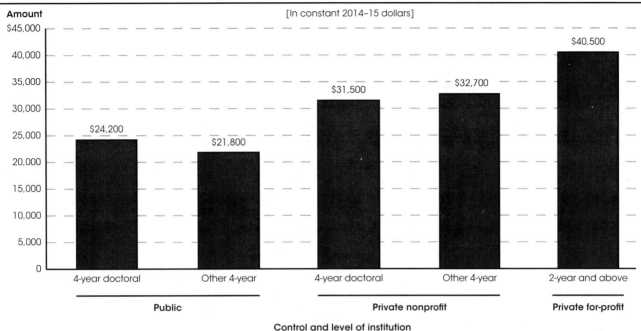

NOTE: Data on public 2-year institutions did not meet reporting standards. Either there were too few cases for a reliable estimate or the coefficient of variation (CV) was 50 percent or greater. Total amount borrowed excludes loans from family and friends. Average loan amounts were calculated only for students who took out a loan. Data exclude Puerto Rico. Some data have been revised from previously published figures. Constant dollars based on the Consumer Price Index, prepared by the Bureau of Labor Statistics, U.S. Department of Labor, adjusted to a school-year basis.
SOURCE: U.S. Department of Education, National Center for Education Statistics, 2011–12 National Postsecondary Student Aid Study (NPSAS:12). See *Digest of Education Statistics 2015*, table 331.95.

For undergraduate students ages 18 to 24 in their 4th year of college and above, the average cumulative amount borrowed was $26,400 in 2011–12.[2] This amount varied by control of institution and level. Students at private for-profit 2-year and above institutions borrowed the most, with a cumulative average of $40,500. Students at other (nondoctoral) public 4-year institutions borrowed the least, with an average cumulative amount of $21,800. Students at public 4-year doctoral institutions borrowed a cumulative average of $24,200, while students at private nonprofit 4-year doctoral institutions borrowed $31,500 and students at other (nondoctoral) private nonprofit 4-year institutions borrowed $32,700.

Endnotes:
[1] Dollar amounts are expressed in constant 2014–15 dollars.
[2] Cumulative amount borrowed excludes loans from family and friends. Average cumulative loan amounts were calculated only for students who took out a loan, and do not include parent PLUS loans. Dollar amounts are expressed in constant 2014–15 dollars.

Reference tables: *Digest of Education Statistics 2015*, tables 330.10, 331.20, and 331.95
Related indicators: Price of Attending an Undergraduate Institution, Sources of Financial Aid, Financing Postsecondary Education in the United States [*The Condition of Education 2013 Spotlight*]

Glossary: Certificate, College, Constant dollars, Control of institutions, Default rate, Doctor's degree, For-profit institution, Full-time enrollment, Nonprofit institution, Postsecondary institutions (basic classification by level), Private institution, Public school or institution, Title IV eligible institution, Tuition and fees, Undergraduate students

Sources of Financial Aid

The percentage of first-time, full-time undergraduate students at 4-year degree-granting postsecondary institutions receiving financial aid was higher in 2013–14 (85 percent) than in 2008–09 (82 percent).

Grants and loans are the major forms of federal financial aid for degree/certificate-seeking undergraduate students. The largest federal grant program available to undergraduate students is the Pell Grant program. In order to qualify for a Pell Grant, a student must demonstrate financial need. Federal loans, on the other hand, are available to all students. In addition to federal financial aid, there are also grants from state and local governments, institutions, and private sources, as well as private loans. In this indicator, student loans include only loans made directly to students; they do not include Parent Loans for Undergraduate Students (PLUS) and other loans made directly to parents.

Figure 1. Percentage of first-time, full-time undergraduate students receiving financial aid at 4-year degree-granting postsecondary institutions, by control of institution: Academic years 2008–09 through 2013–14

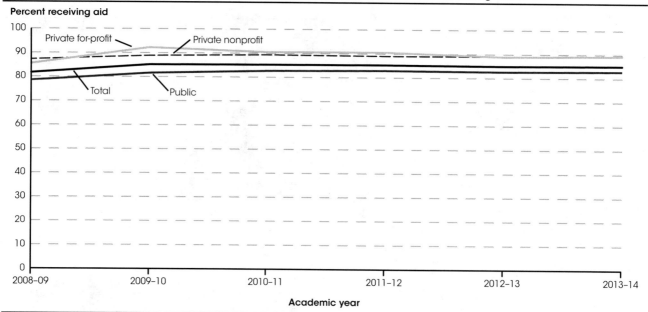

NOTE: Degree-granting institutions grant associate's or higher degrees and participate in Title IV federal financial aid programs. Some data have been revised from previously published figures. Student financial aid includes any Federal Work-Study, loans to students, and grant or scholarship aid from the federal government, state/local government, the institution, and other sources known to the institution. Student loans include only loans made directly to students; they do not include Parent Loans for Undergraduate Students (PLUS) and other loans made directly to parents.
SOURCE: U.S. Department of Education, National Center for Education Statistics, Integrated Postsecondary Education Data System (IPEDS), Spring 2009 through Spring 2011 and Winter 2011–12 through Winter 2013–14, Student Financial Aid component. See *Digest of Education Statistics 2015,* table 331.20.

The percentage of first-time, full-time degree/certificate-seeking undergraduate students at 4-year degree-granting postsecondary institutions receiving any financial aid was higher in 2013–14 (85 percent) than in 2008–09 (82 percent). The percentages of students receiving aid at the different 4-year institutions were also higher in 2013–14 than in 2008–09. In 2013–14, the percentages of students receiving aid at 4-year public institutions (83 percent), 4-year private nonprofit institutions (89 percent), and 4-year private for-profit institutions (89 percent) were higher than they were in 2008–09 (79 percent at public institutions, 87 percent at private nonprofit institutions, and 85 percent at private for-profit institutions).

Figure 2. Percentage of first-time, full-time undergraduate students receiving financial aid at 2-year degree-granting postsecondary institutions, by control of institution: Academic years 2008–09 through 2013–14

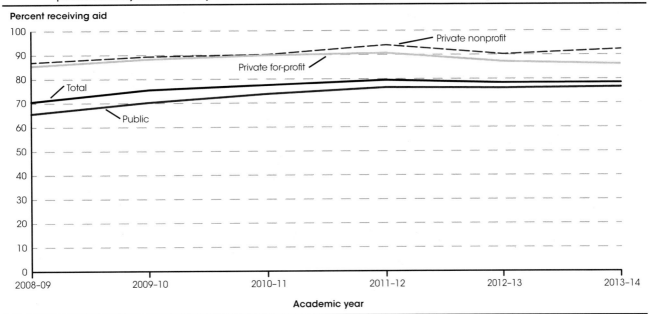

NOTE: Degree-granting institutions grant associate's or higher degrees and participate in Title IV federal financial aid programs. Some data have been revised from previously published figures. Student financial aid includes any Federal Work-Study, loans to students, and grant or scholarship aid from the federal government, state/local government, the institution, and other sources known to the institution. Student loans include only loans made directly to students; they do not include Parent Loans for Undergraduate Students (PLUS) and other loans made directly to parents.
SOURCE: U.S. Department of Education, National Center for Education Statistics, Integrated Postsecondary Education Data System (IPEDS), Spring 2009 through Spring 2011 and Winter 2011–12 through Winter 2013–14, Student Financial Aid component. See *Digest of Education Statistics 2015*, table 331.20.

For 2-year degree-granting postsecondary institutions, the percentage of first-time, full-time degree/certificate-seeking undergraduate students receiving any financial aid increased from 71 percent in 2008–09 to 78 percent in 2013–14. During this time, the percentage of students receiving aid at 2-year public institutions increased from 66 to 77 percent. For students at both 2-year private nonprofit and 2-year private for-profit institutions, the percentage of students receiving aid was also higher in 2013–14 than in 2008–09. In 2013–14, the percentages of students receiving aid at 2-year private nonprofit institutions (92 percent) and 2-year private for-profit institutions (86 percent) were higher than they were in 2008–09 (87 percent at private nonprofit institutions and 85 percent at private for-profit institutions).

Figure 3. Percentage of first-time, full-time undergraduate students receiving financial aid at 4-year degree-granting postsecondary institutions, by type of financial aid and control of institution: Academic year 2013–14

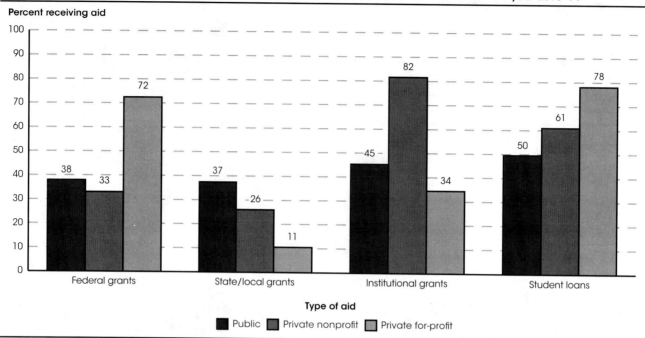

NOTE: Degree-granting institutions grant associate's or higher degrees and participate in Title IV federal financial aid programs. Student financial aid includes any Federal Work-Study, loans to students, and grant or scholarship aid from the federal government, state/local government, the institution, and other sources known to the institution. Student loans include only loans made directly to students; they do not include Parent Loans for Undergraduate Students (PLUS) and other loans made directly to parents.
SOURCE: U.S. Department of Education, National Center for Education Statistics, Integrated Postsecondary Education Data System (IPEDS), Winter 2013–14, Student Financial Aid component. See *Digest of Education Statistics 2015*, table 331.20.

In 2013–14, the percentage of first-time, full-time degree/certificate-seeking undergraduate students receiving federal grants at 4-year institutions was higher at private for-profit institutions (72 percent) than at public institutions (38 percent) and private nonprofit institutions (33 percent). The percentage of students at 4-year institutions receiving state or local grants was higher at public institutions (37 percent) than at private nonprofit institutions (26 percent) and private for-profit

institutions (11 percent). The percentage of students receiving institutional grants was higher at 4-year private nonprofit institutions (82 percent) than at 4-year public institutions (45 percent) and 4-year private for-profit institutions (34 percent). The percentage of students at 4-year institutions receiving student loan aid was 78 percent at private for-profit institutions, 61 percent at private nonprofit institutions, and 50 percent at public institutions.

Figure 4.   Percentage of first-time, full-time undergraduate students receiving financial aid at 2-year degree-granting postsecondary institutions, by type of financial aid and control of institution: Academic year 2013–14

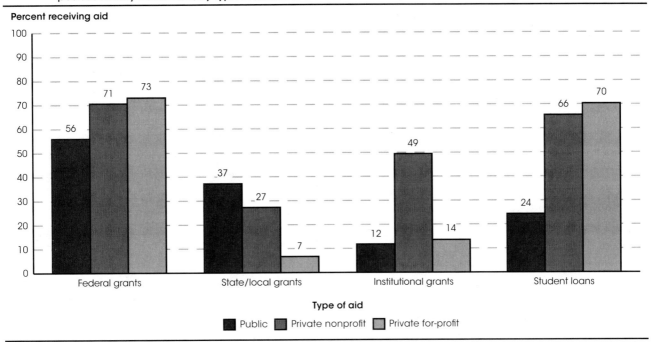

NOTE: Degree-granting institutions grant associate's or higher degrees and participate in Title IV federal financial aid programs. Student financial aid includes any Federal Work-Study, loans to students, and grant or scholarship aid from the federal government, state/local government, the institution, and other sources known to the institution. Student loans include only loans made directly to students; they do not include Parent Loans for Undergraduate Students (PLUS) and other loans made directly to parents.
SOURCE: U.S. Department of Education, National Center for Education Statistics, Integrated Postsecondary Education Data System (IPEDS), Winter 2013–14, Student Financial Aid component. See *Digest of Education Statistics 2015*, table 331.20.

For first-time, full-time degree/certificate-seeking undergraduate students at 2-year institutions in 2013–14, the percentage of students receiving federal grants was higher at private for-profit institutions (73 percent) and private nonprofit institutions (71 percent) than at public institutions (56 percent). A higher percentage of students at 2-year public institutions (37 percent) received state or local grants than students at 2-year private nonprofit institutions (27 percent) and 2-year private for-profit institutions (7 percent). About 49 percent of students at 2-year private nonprofit institutions received institutional grants, compared with 14 percent of students at 2-year private for-profit institutions and 12 percent of students at 2-year public institutions. The percentage of students at 2-year institutions receiving student loan aid was higher at private for-profit institutions (70 percent) and private nonprofit institutions (66 percent) than at public institutions (24 percent).

Figure 5. Average amount of financial aid awarded to first-time, full-time undergraduate students receiving aid at 4-year degree-granting postsecondary institutions, by type of financial aid and control of institution: Academic year 2013–14

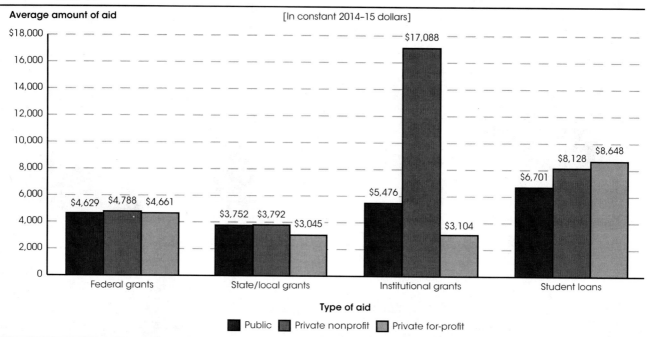

NOTE: Degree-granting institutions grant associate's or higher degrees and participate in Title IV federal financial aid programs. Grant award amounts are in constant 2014–15 dollars, based on the Consumer Price Index (CPI). Student loans include only loans made directly to students; they do not include Parent Loans for Undergraduate Students (PLUS) and other loans made directly to parents.
SOURCE: U.S. Department of Education, National Center for Education Statistics, Integrated Postsecondary Education Data System (IPEDS), Winter 2013–14, Student Financial Aid component. See *Digest of Education Statistics 2015*, table 331.20.

There was variation in the average amounts of federal, state/local, and institutional aid that students received at different types of 4-year institutions in 2013–14. The average federal grant was $4,788 for first-time, full-time students at private nonprofit institutions, $4,661 at private for-profit institutions, and $4,629 at public institutions (reported in constant 2014–15 dollars). The average state or local grant was $3,792 at private nonprofit institutions, $3,752 at public institutions, and $3,045 at private for-profit institutions. There were larger differences by institution control in the average institutional grant awards. The average institutional grant award was higher at private nonprofit institutions ($17,088) than at public institutions ($5,476) and private for-profit institutions ($3,104). The average student loan amount was higher at private for-profit ($8,648) and private nonprofit ($8,128) institutions than at public institutions ($6,701).

Figure 6. Average amount of financial aid awarded to first-time, full-time undergraduate students receiving aid at 2-year degree-granting postsecondary institutions, by type of financial aid and control of institution: Academic year 2013–14

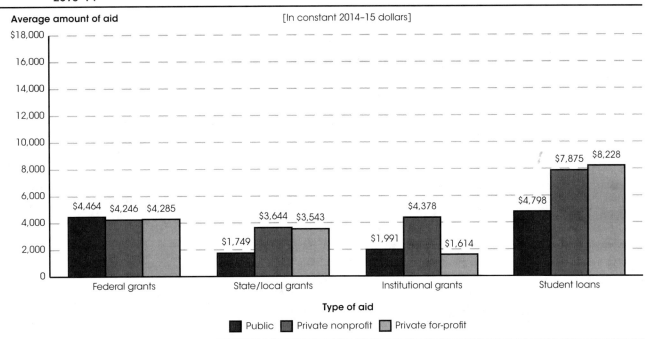

NOTE: Degree-granting institutions grant associate's or higher degrees and participate in Title IV federal financial aid programs. Grant award amounts are in constant 2014–15 dollars, based on the Consumer Price Index (CPI). Student loans include only loans made directly to students; they do not include Parent Loans for Undergraduate Students (PLUS) and other loans made directly to parents.
SOURCE: U.S. Department of Education, National Center for Education Statistics, Integrated Postsecondary Education Data System (IPEDS), Winter 2013–14, Student Financial Aid component. See *Digest of Education Statistics 2015*, table 331.20.

There was variation in the average amounts of aid received by students at different types of 2-year institutions in 2013–14. The average federal grant was $4,464 for first-time, full-time students at public institutions, $4,285 at private for-profit institutions, and $4,246 at private nonprofit institutions (reported in constant 2014–15 dollars). The average state or local grant award was $3,644 at private nonprofit institutions, $3,543 at private for-profit institutions, and $1,749 at public institutions. The average institutional grant award was higher at private nonprofit institutions ($4,378) than at public institutions ($1,991) and private for-profit institutions ($1,614). Similar to 4-year institutions, the average student loan amount at 2-year institutions in 2013–14 was higher at private for-profit ($8,228) and private nonprofit ($7,875) institutions than at public institutions ($4,798).

Reference tables: *Digest of Education Statistics 2015*, table 331.20
Related indicators: Price of Attending an Undergraduate Institution, Loans for Undergraduate Students, Financing Postsecondary Education in the United States [*The Condition of Education 2013 Spotlight*]

Glossary: Certificate, Constant dollars, Control of institutions, Degree-granting institution, Financial aid, For-profit institution, Full-time enrollment, Nonprofit institution, Postsecondary institutions (basic classification by level), Private institution, Public school or institution, Undergraduate students

Postsecondary Institution Revenues

Between 2008–09 and 2013–14, revenues from tuition and fees per full-time-equivalent (FTE) student increased by 17 percent at public institutions (from $5,681 to $6,639, in constant 2014–15 dollars) and by 6 percent at private nonprofit institutions (from $19,206 to $20,293). At private for-profit institutions, revenues from tuition and fees per FTE student were 34 percent higher in 2013–14 than in 2008–09 ($19,480 vs. $14,515).

In academic year 2013–14, total revenues at degree-granting postsecondary institutions in the United States were $605 billion (in current dollars). Total revenues were $353 billion at public institutions, $229 billion at private nonprofit institutions, and $23 billion at private for-profit institutions.

Figure 1. Percentage distribution of total revenues at degree-granting postsecondary institutions, by institutional control and source of funds: 2013–14

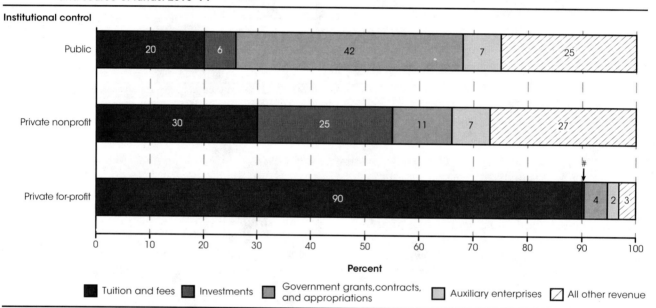

Rounds to zero.
NOTE: Percentages are based on current dollars. Government grants, contracts, and appropriations include revenues from federal, state, and local governments. Private grants and contracts are included in the local government revenue category at public institutions. All other revenue includes gifts, capital or private grants and contracts, auxiliary enterprises, hospital revenue, sales and services of educational activities, and other revenue. Revenue data are not directly comparable across institutional control categories because Pell Grants are included in the federal grant revenues at public institutions but tend to be included in tuition and fees and auxiliary enterprise revenues at private nonprofit and private for-profit institutions. Degree-granting institutions grant associate's or higher degrees and participate in Title IV federal financial aid programs. Detail may not sum to totals because of rounding.
SOURCE: U.S. Department of Education, National Center for Education Statistics, Integrated Postsecondary Education Data System (IPEDS), Spring 2015, Finance component. See *Digest of Education Statistics 2015*, tables 333.10, 333.40, and 333.55.

The primary sources of revenue for all institutions were tuition and fees, investments and government grants, contracts and appropriations, and other unspecified sources. There were notable differences in the percentages from these revenue sources for the different types of institutions. At public institutions the largest percentage of total revenues in 2013–14, at 42 percent, was from government sources (which include federal, state, and local government[1] grants, contracts, and appropriations). At private nonprofit institutions and private for-profit institutions, student tuition and fees constituted the largest percentage of total revenues (30 and 90 percent, respectively). It is important to note that Pell Grants are included in the federal grant revenues at public institutions but tend to be included in tuition and fees and auxiliary enterprise revenues at private nonprofit and private for-profit institutions. Thus, some categories of revenue data are not directly comparable across public, nonprofit, and for-profit institutions.

Investment returns, or investment income, varied by institutional control. Revenues from these investments accounted for 6 percent of total revenues at public institutions, 25 percent of total revenues at private nonprofit institutions, and less than one-half of 1 percent of total revenues at private for-profit institutions.

Figure 2. Revenues from tuition and fees per full-time-equivalent (FTE) student for degree-granting postsecondary institutions, by institutional control: 2008-09 and 2013-14

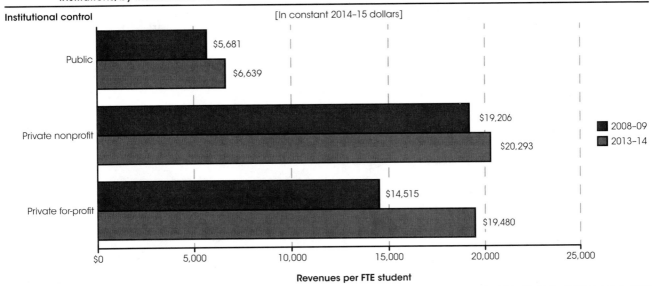

NOTE: Full-time-equivalent (FTE) student includes full-time students plus the full-time equivalent of part-time students. Revenues per FTE student are reported in constant 2014-15 dollars, based on the Consumer Price Index (CPI) adjusted to a school-year basis. Revenue data are not directly comparable across institutional control categories because Pell Grants are included in the federal grant revenues at public institutions but tend to be included in tuition and fees and auxiliary enterprise revenues at private nonprofit and private for-profit institutions. Tuition and fee revenues at public institutions are after deducting discounts and allowances; at private nonprofit institutions and private for-profit institutions, tuition and fee revenues are net of allowances. Degree-granting institutions grant associate's or higher degrees and participate in Title IV federal financial aid programs. Some data have been revised from previously published figures.
SOURCE: U.S. Department of Education, National Center for Education Statistics, Integrated Postsecondary Education Data System (IPEDS), Spring 2010 and Spring 2015, Finance component; and Spring 2009 and 2014 Fall Enrollment component. See *Digest of Education Statistics 2015*, tables 333.10, 333.40, and 333.55.

Between 2008–09 and 2013–14, the percentage change in revenues from tuition and fees per full-time-equivalent (FTE) student varied by institutional control. Revenues per FTE student are reported in constant 2014–15 dollars, based on the Consumer Price Index (CPI). During this period, revenues from tuition and fees per FTE student increased by 17 percent at public institutions (from $5,681 to $6,639) and by 6 percent at private nonprofit institutions (from $19,206 to $20,293). At private for-profit institutions, revenues from tuition and fees were 34 percent higher in 2013–14 ($19,480) than in 2008–09 ($14,515).

Figure 3. Revenues from government grants, contracts, and appropriations per full-time-equivalent (FTE) student for degree-granting postsecondary institutions, by source of funds and institutional control: 2008–09 and 2013–14

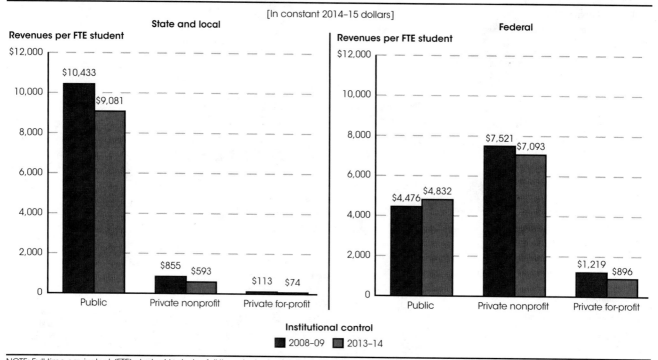

[In constant 2014–15 dollars]

NOTE: Full-time-equivalent (FTE) student includes full-time students plus the full-time equivalent of part-time students. Revenues per FTE student are reported in constant 2014–15 dollars, based on the Consumer Price Index (CPI) adjusted to a school-year basis. Private grants and contracts are included in the local government revenue category at public institutions. Revenue data are not comparable across institutional control categories because Pell Grants are included in the federal grant revenues at public institutions but tend to be included in tuition and fees and auxiliary enterprise revenues at private nonprofit and private for-profit institutions. Degree-granting institutions grant associate's or higher degrees and participate in Title IV federal financial aid programs. Some data have been revised from previously published figures.
SOURCE: U.S. Department of Education, National Center for Education Statistics, Integrated Postsecondary Education Data System (IPEDS), Spring 2010 and Spring 2015, Finance component; and Spring 2009 and 2014 Fall Enrollment component. See *Digest of Education Statistics 2015*, tables 333.10, 333.40, and 333.55.

Total revenues per FTE student from government sources at public institutions decreased by 7 percent from 2008–09 to 2013–14 (from $14,909 to $13,913), by 8 percent at private nonprofit institutions (from $8,376 to $7,685), and by 27 percent at private for-profit institutions (from $1,331 to $970). The percentage change between 2008–09 and 2013–14 in state and local government revenues per FTE student also varied by institutional control. During this period, revenues per FTE student from state and local sources were 13 percent lower at public institutions ($10,433 vs. $9,081), 31 percent lower at private nonprofit institutions ($855 vs. $593), and 34 percent lower at private for-profit institutions ($113 vs. $74).

Revenues from federal sources showed varying patterns of change between 2008–09 and 2013–14 across degree-granting postsecondary institutions. At public institutions, federal revenues per FTE student were 8 percent higher in 2013–14 than in 2008–09 ($4,832 vs. $4,476). At private nonprofit institutions, federal revenues per FTE student was 6 percent lower in 2013–14 ($7,093) than in 2008–09 ($7,521). At private for-profit institutions, revenues per FTE student decreased by 27 percent (from $1,219 to $896).

Endnotes:
[1] Private grants and contracts are included in local government revenues at public institutions.

Reference tables: *Digest of Education Statistics 2015*, tables 333.10, 333.40, and 333.55
Related indicators: Postsecondary Institution Expenses

Glossary: Constant dollars, Consumer Price Index (CPI), Control of institutions, Degree-granting institution, Federal sources (postsecondary degree-granting institutions), For-profit institution, Full-time-equivalent (FTE) enrollment, Nonprofit institution, Postsecondary education, Private institution, Public school or institution, Revenue, Tuition and fees

This page intentionally left blank.

Postsecondary Institution Expenses

In 2013–14, instruction expenses per full-time-equivalent (FTE) student (in constant 2014–15 dollars) was the largest expense category at public institutions ($8,070) and private nonprofit institutions ($17,003). At private for-profit institutions, instruction expenses per FTE student was the second largest expense category ($5,266).

In academic year 2013–14, postsecondary institutions in the United States spent approximately $517 billion (in current dollars). Total expenses were nearly $324 billion at public institutions, $173 billion at private nonprofit institutions, and $21 billion at private for-profit institutions. Some data may not be comparable across institutions by control categories (i.e., public, private nonprofit, and private for-profit) because of differences in accounting standards followed. Comparisons by institutional level (i.e., between 2-year and 4-year institutions) may also be limited because of different institutional missions. The instructional missions of 2-year institutions generally focus on student instruction and related activities that often include providing a range of career-oriented programs at the certificate and associate's

degree levels and preparing students for transfer to 4-year institutions. Four-year institutions tend to have a broad range of instructional programs at the undergraduate level leading to bachelor's degrees. Many 4-year institutions offer graduate-level programs as well. Also, research activities, on-campus student housing, teaching hospitals, and auxiliary enterprises can have a substantial impact on the financial structure of 4-year institutions. In this indicator, expenses are grouped into broad categories, including instruction, research, public service, academic support, student services, institutional support, operation and maintenance of plant, depreciation, scholarships and fellowships, auxiliary enterprises, hospitals, independent operations, interest, and other.

Figure 1. Percentage of total expenses at degree-granting postsecondary institutions, by purpose of expenses and control of institution: 2013–14

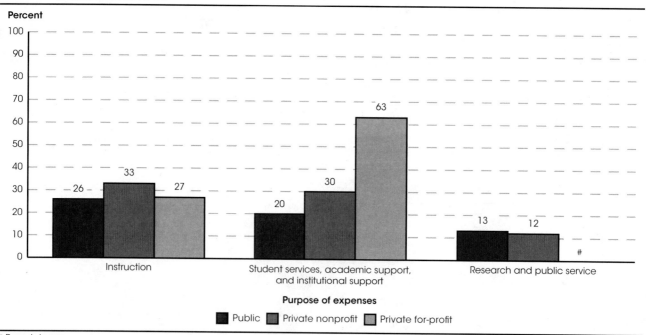

Rounds to zero.
NOTE: Degree-granting institutions grant associate's or higher degrees and participate in Title IV federal financial aid programs.
SOURCE: U.S. Department of Education, National Center for Education Statistics, Integrated Postsecondary Education Data System (IPEDS), Spring 2015, Finance component. See *Digest of Education Statistics 2015*, tables 334.10, 334.30, and 334.50.

Instruction, including faculty salaries and benefits, is the largest single expense category at public and private nonprofit postsecondary institutions. In 2013–14, instruction accounted for 26 percent of total expenses at public institutions, 33 percent of total expenses at private

nonprofit institutions, and 27 percent of total expenses at private for-profit institutions. The largest expense category at private for-profit institutions in that year was for the combined expenses of student services, academic support, and institutional support (63 percent), which includes expenses associated with admissions, student activities, libraries, and administrative and executive activities. By comparison, student services, academic support, and institutional support made up 20 percent of total expenses at public institutions and 30 percent of total expenses at private nonprofit institutions. Combined expenses for research and public service constituted 13 percent and hospitals constituted 11 percent of total expenses at public institutions. At private nonprofit institutions, research and public service combined, hospitals, and auxiliary enterprises (i.e., self-supporting operations, such as residence halls) constituted 12, 10, and 9 percent of total expenses, respectively.

In 2013–14, across all types of postsecondary institutional control, 2-year institutions spent a greater share of their total expenses on instruction than did 4-year institutions. The percentage of total expenses at public institutions for instruction was 35 percent at 2-year institutions, compared with 25 percent at 4-year institutions. At private nonprofit institutions, instruction accounted for 36 percent of total expenses at 2-year institutions and 33 percent at 4-year institutions; at private for-profit institutions, the percentages of total expenses for instruction at 2-year and 4-year institutions were 32 and 25 percent, respectively.

Figure 2. Expenses per full-time-equivalent (FTE) student at degree-granting postsecondary institutions, by purpose of expenses and control of institution: 2013–14

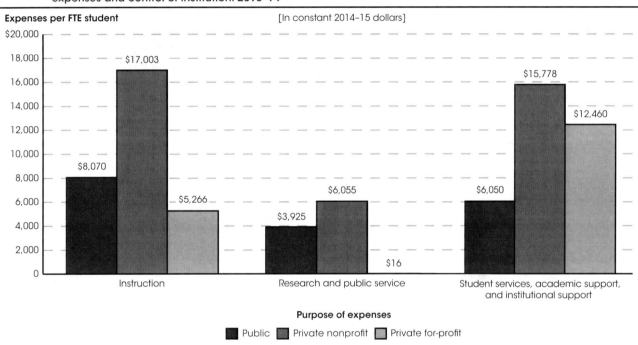

NOTE: Full-time-equivalent (FTE) students include full-time students plus the full-time equivalent of part-time students. Expenditures per FTE student are reported in constant 2014–15 dollars, based on the Consumer Price Index. Degree-granting institutions grant associate's or higher degrees and participate in Title IV federal financial aid programs.
SOURCE: U.S. Department of Education, National Center for Education Statistics, Integrated Postsecondary Education Data System (IPEDS), Spring 2015, Finance component; and Spring 2014 Fall Enrollment component. See *Digest of Education Statistics 2015*, tables 334.10, 334.30, and 334.50.

In 2013–14, total expenses per full-time-equivalent (FTE) student were higher at private nonprofit postsecondary institutions ($51,736) than at public institutions ($30,502) and private for-profit institutions ($19,654). Expenses per FTE student in this indicator are adjusted for inflation using constant 2014–15 dollars, based on the Consumer Price Index (CPI). Private nonprofit institutions spent more than twice as much per FTE student on instruction ($17,003) as public institutions ($8,070) and more than three times as much as private for-profit institutions ($5,266); the amount spent at public institutions was also higher than the amount spent at private for-profit institutions. Expenses per FTE student for research and

public service (such as expenses for public broadcasting and community services) followed the same pattern, with private nonprofit institutions spending more than public institutions ($6,055 vs. $3,925) and private for-profit institutions ($6,055 vs. $16). Similarly, for the combined expenses of student services, academic support, and institutional support, a total of $15,778 per FTE student was spent at private nonprofit institutions, which was higher than the amount spent at private for-profit institutions ($12,460 per FTE student), which was, in turn, higher than the amount spent at public institutions ($6,050 per FTE student).

Figure 3. Expenses per full-time-equivalent (FTE) student for instruction at degree-granting postsecondary institutions, by level and control of institution: 2007–08 and 2013–14

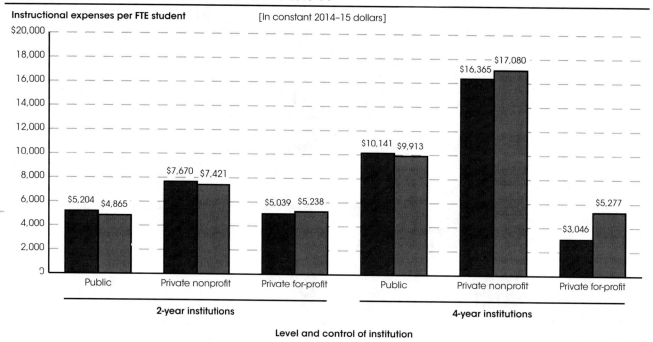

Instructional expenses per FTE student   [In constant 2014–15 dollars]

NOTE: Full-time-equivalent (FTE) students include full-time students plus the full-time equivalent of part-time students. Expenditures per FTE student are reported in constant 2014–15 dollars, based on the Consumer Price Index. Degree-granting institutions grant associate's or higher degrees and participate in Title IV federal financial aid programs.
SOURCE: U.S. Department of Education, National Center for Education Statistics, Integrated Postsecondary Education Data System (IPEDS), Spring 2009 and Spring 2015, Finance component; and Spring 2008 and Spring 2014, Fall Enrollment component. See *Digest of Education Statistics 2015*, tables 334.10, 334.30, and 334.50.

Changes in inflation-adjusted instruction expenses per FTE student between 2007–08 and 2013–14 varied by postsecondary institution control and level. At public 4-year institutions, instruction expenses per FTE student were 2 percent lower in 2013–14 ($9,913) than in 2007–08 ($10,141), and at public 2-year institutions, these expenses were 7 percent lower in 2013–14 ($4,865) than in 2007–08 ($5,204). At private nonprofit 4-year institutions, instruction expenses per FTE student were 4 percent higher in 2013–14 than in 2007–08 ($17,080 vs. $16,365), but at private nonprofit 2-year institutions, they were 3 percent lower in 2013–14 than in 2007–08 ($7,421 vs. $7,670). At private for-profit 4-year institutions, instruction expenses per FTE student were 73 percent higher in 2013–14 than in 2007–08 ($5,277 vs. $3,046), and at private for-profit 2-year institutions, they were 4 percent higher in 2013–14 than in 2007–08 ($5,238 vs. $5,039).

Reference tables: *Digest of Education Statistics 2015*, tables 334.10, 334.30, and 334.50
Related indicators: Postsecondary Institution Revenues

Glossary: Constant dollars, Consumer Price Index (CPI), Control of institutions, For-profit institution, Full-time-equivalent (FTE) enrollment, Nonprofit institution, Postsecondary education, Postsecondary institutions (basic classification by level), Private institution, Public school or institution, Tuition and fees

This page intentionally left blank.

Guide to Sources

National Center for Education Statistics (NCES)

Common Core of Data

The Common Core of Data (CCD) is NCES's primary database on public elementary and secondary education in the United States. It is a comprehensive, annual, national statistical database of all public elementary and secondary schools and school districts containing data designed to be comparable across all states. This database can be used to select samples for other NCES surveys and provide basic information and descriptive statistics on public elementary and secondary schools and schooling in general.

The CCD collects statistical information annually from approximately 100,000 public elementary and secondary schools and approximately 18,000 public school districts (including supervisory unions and regional education service agencies) in the 50 states, the District of Columbia, Department of Defense (DoD) dependents schools, the Bureau of Indian Education (BIE), Puerto Rico, American Samoa, Guam, the Northern Mariana Islands, and the U.S. Virgin Islands. Three categories of information are collected in the CCD survey: general descriptive information on schools and school districts; data on students and staff; and fiscal data. The general school and district descriptive information includes name, address, phone number, and type of locale; the data on students and staff include selected demographic characteristics; and the fiscal data pertain to revenues and current expenditures.

The ED*Facts* data collection system is the primary collection tool for the CCD. NCES works collaboratively with the Department of Education's Performance Information Management Service to develop the CCD collection procedures and data definitions. Coordinators from state education agencies (SEAs) submit the CCD data at different levels (school, agency, and state) to the ED*Facts* collection system. Prior to submitting CCD files to ED*Facts*, SEAs must collect and compile information from their respective local education agencies (LEAs) through established administrative records systems within their state or jurisdiction.

Once SEAs have completed their submissions, the CCD survey staff analyzes and verifies the data for quality assurance. Even though the CCD is a universe collection and thus not subject to sampling errors, nonsampling errors can occur. The two potential sources of nonsampling errors are nonresponse and inaccurate reporting. NCES attempts to minimize nonsampling errors through the use of annual training of SEA coordinators, extensive quality reviews, and survey editing procedures. In addition, each year, SEAs are given the opportunity to revise their state-level aggregates from the previous survey cycle.

The CCD survey consists of five components: The Public Elementary/Secondary School Universe Survey, the Local Education Agency (School District) Universe Survey, the State Nonfiscal Survey of Public Elementary/Secondary Education, the National Public Education Financial Survey (NPEFS), and the School District Finance Survey (F-33).

Public Elementary/Secondary School Universe Survey

The Public Elementary/Secondary School Universe Survey includes all public schools providing education services to prekindergarten, kindergarten, grade 1–12, and ungraded students. For school year (SY) 2013–14, the survey included records for each public elementary and secondary school in the 50 states, the District of Columbia, the DoD dependents schools (overseas and domestic), the Bureau of Indian Education (BIE), Puerto Rico, American Samoa, the Northern Mariana Islands, Guam, and the U.S. Virgin Islands.

The Public Elementary/Secondary School Universe Survey includes data for the following variables: NCES school ID number, state school ID number, name of the school, name of the agency that operates the school, mailing address, physical location address, phone number, school type, operational status, locale code, latitude, longitude, county number, county name, full-time-equivalent (FTE) classroom teacher count, low/high grade span offered, congressional district code, school level, students eligible for free lunch, students eligible for reduced-price lunch, total students eligible for free and reduced-price lunch, and student totals and detail (by grade, by race/ethnicity, and by sex). The survey also contains flags indicating whether a school is Title I eligible, schoolwide Title I eligible, a magnet school, a charter school, a shared-time school, or a BIE school, as well as which grades are offered at the school.

Local Education Agency (School District) Universe

The coverage of the Local Education Agency Universe Survey includes all school districts and administrative units providing education services to prekindergarten, kindergarten, grade 1–12, and ungraded students. The Local Education Agency Universe Survey includes records for the 50 states, the District of Columbia, Puerto Rico, the Bureau of Indian Education (BIE), American Samoa, Guam, the Northern Mariana Islands, the U.S. Virgin Islands, and the DoD dependents schools (overseas and domestic).

The Local Education Agency Universe Survey includes the following variables: NCES agency ID number, state agency ID number, agency name, phone number, mailing address, physical location address, agency type code, supervisory union number, American National Standards

Institute (ANSI) state and county code, county name, core based statistical area (CBSA) code, metropolitan/microplitan code, metropolitan status code, district locale code, congressional district code, operational status code, BIE agency status, low/high grade span offered, agency charter status, number of schools, number of full-time-equivalent teachers, number of ungraded students, number of PK–12 students, number of special education/Individualized Education Program students, number of English language learner students, instructional staff fields, support staff fields, and LEA charter status.

State Nonfiscal Survey of Public Elementary/Secondary Education

The State Nonfiscal Survey of Public Elementary/Secondary Education for the 2013–14 school year provides state-level, aggregate information about students and staff in public elementary and secondary education. It includes data from the 50 states, the District of Columbia, Puerto Rico, the U.S. Virgin Islands, the Northern Mariana Islands, Guam, and American Samoa. The DoD dependents schools (overseas and domestic) and the Bureau of Indian Education are also included in the survey universe. This survey covers public school student membership by grade, race/ethnicity, and state or jurisdiction and covers number of staff in public schools by category and state or jurisdiction. Beginning with the 2006–07 school year, the number of diploma recipients and other high school completers are no longer included in the State Nonfiscal Survey of Public Elementary/Secondary Education file. These data are now published in the public-use CCD State Dropout and Completion Data File.

National Public Education Financial Survey

The purpose of the National Public Education Financial Survey (NPEFS) is to provide district, state, and federal policymakers, researchers, and other interested users with descriptive information about revenues and expenditures for public elementary and secondary education. The data collected are useful to (1) chief officers of state education agencies; (2) policymakers in the executive and legislative branches of federal and state governments; (3) education policy and public policy researchers; and (4) the public, journalists, and others.

Data for NPEFS are collected from state education agencies (SEAs) in the 50 states, the District of Columbia, Puerto Rico, American Samoa, Guam, the Northern Mariana Islands, and the U.S. Virgin Islands. The data file is organized by state or jurisdiction and contains revenue data by funding source; expenditure data by function (the activity being supported by the expenditure) and object (the category of expenditure); average daily attendance data; and total student membership data from the CCD State Nonfiscal Survey of Public Elementary/Secondary Education.

School District Finance Survey

The purpose of the School District Finance Survey (F-33) is to provide finance data for all local education agencies (LEAs) that provide free public elementary and secondary education in the United States. National and state totals are not included (national- and state-level figures are presented, however, in the National Public Education Financial Survey).

NCES partners with the U.S. Census Bureau in the collection of school district finance data. The Census Bureau distributes Census Form F-33, Annual Survey of School System Finances, to all SEAs, and representatives from the SEAs collect and edit data from their LEAs and submit data to the Census Bureau. The Census Bureau then produces two data files: one for distribution and reporting by NCES and the other for distribution and reporting by the Census Bureau.

The files include variables for revenues by source, expenditures by function and object, indebtedness, assets, and student membership counts, as well as identification variables.

Teacher Compensation Survey

The Teacher Compensation Survey (TCS) is a research and development effort designed to assess the feasibility of collecting and publishing teacher-level data from the administrative records residing in state education agencies. Twenty-three states participated in the TCS for school year 2008–09. Participating states provided data on salaries, years of teaching experience, highest degree earned, race/ethnicity, and gender for each public school teacher.

Further information on the nonfiscal CCD data may be obtained from

Patrick Keaton
Administrative Data Division
Elementary and Secondary Branch
National Center for Education Statistics
Potomac Center Plaza
550 12th Street SW
Washington, DC 20202
patrick.keaton@ed.gov
http://nces.ed.gov/ccd

Further information on the fiscal CCD data may be obtained from

Stephen Cornman
Administrative Data Division
Elementary and Secondary Branch
National Center for Education Statistics
Potomac Center Plaza
550 12th Street SW
Washington, DC 20202
stephen.cornman@ed.gov
http://nces.ed.gov/ccd

Early Childhood Longitudinal Study, Kindergarten Class of 2010–11

The Early Childhood Longitudinal Study, Kindergarten Class of 2010–11 (ECLS-K:2011) is providing detailed information on the school achievement and experiences of students throughout their elementary school years. The students participating in the ECLS-K:2011 are being followed longitudinally from the kindergarten year (the 2010–11 school year) through the spring of 2016, when most of them are expected to be in 5th grade. This sample of students is designed to be nationally representative of all students who were enrolled in kindergarten or who were of kindergarten age and being educated in an ungraded classroom or school in the United States in the 2010–11 school year, including those in public and private schools, those who attended full-day and part-day programs, those who were in kindergarten for the first time, and those who were kindergarten repeaters. Students who attended early learning centers or institutions that offered education only through kindergarten are included in the study sample and represented in the cohort.

The ECLS-K:2011 places emphasis on measuring students' experiences within multiple contexts and development in multiple domains. The design of the study includes the collection of information from the students, their parents/guardians, their teachers, and their schools. Information was collected from their before- and after-school care providers in the kindergarten year.

A nationally representative sample of approximately 18,170 children from about 1,310 schools participated in the base-year administration of the ECLS-K:2011 in the 2010–11 school year. The sample included children from different racial/ethnic and socioeconomic backgrounds. Asian/Pacific Islander students were oversampled to ensure that the sample included enough students of this race/ethnicity to make accurate estimates for the group as a whole. Eight data collections have been conducted to date: fall and spring of the children's kindergarten year (the base year), fall 2011 and spring 2012 (the 1st-grade year), fall 2012 and spring 2013 (the 2nd-grade year), spring 2014 (the 3rd-grade year), and spring 2015 (the 4th-grade year). The final data collection is planned for the spring of 2016. Although the study refers to later rounds of data collection by the grade the majority of children are expected to be in (that is, the modal grade for children who were in kindergarten in the 2010–11 school year), children are included in subsequent data collections regardless of their grade level.

A total of approximately 780 of the 1,310 originally sampled schools participated during the base year of the study. This translates to a weighted unit response rate (weighted by the base weight) of 63 percent for the base year. In the base year, the weighted child assessment unit response rate was 87 percent for the fall data collection and 85 percent for the spring collection, and the weighted

parent unit response rate was 74 percent for the fall collection and 67 percent for the spring collection,

Fall and spring data collections were also conducted in the 2011–12 school year, when the majority of the children were in the 1st grade. The fall collection was conducted within a 33 percent subsample of the full base-year sample, and the spring collection was conducted within the full base-year sample. The weighted child assessment unit response rate was 89 percent for the fall data collection and 88 percent for the spring collection, and the weighted parent unit response rate was 87 percent for the fall data collection and 76 percent for the spring data collection.

In the 2012–13 data collection (when the majority of the children were in the 2nd grade) the weighted child assessment unit response rate was 84.0 percent in the fall and 83.4 percent in the spring. Further information on ECLS-K:2011 may be obtained from

Gail Mulligan
Sample Surveys Division
Longitudinal Surveys Branch
National Center for Education Statistics
Potomac Center Plaza
550 12th Street SW
Washington, DC 20202
ecls@ed.gov
http://nces.ed.gov/ecls/kindergarten2011.asp

EDFacts

EDFacts is a centralized data collection through which state education agencies submit K–12 education data to the U.S. Department of Education (ED). All data in EDFacts are organized into "data groups" and reported to ED using defined file specifications. Depending on the data group, state education agencies may submit aggregate counts for the state as a whole or detailed counts for individual schools or school districts. EDFacts does not collect student-level records. The entities that are required to report EDFacts data vary by data group but may include the 50 states, the District of Columbia, the Department of Defense (DoD) dependents schools, the Bureau of Indian Education, Puerto Rico, American Samoa, Guam, the Northern Mariana Islands, and the U.S. Virgin Islands. More information about EDFacts file specifications and data groups can be found at http://www.ed.gov/EDFacts.

EDFacts is a universe collection and is not subject to sampling error, but nonsampling errors such as nonresponse and inaccurate reporting may occur. The U.S. Department of Education attempts to minimize nonsampling errors by training data submission coordinators and reviewing the quality of state data submissions. However, anomalies may still be present in the data.

Differences in state data collection systems may limit the comparability of ED*Facts* data across states and across time. To build ED*Facts* files, state education agencies rely on data that were reported by their schools and school districts. The systems used to collect these data are evolving rapidly and differ from state to state.

In some cases, ED*Facts* data may not align with data reported on state education agency websites. States may update their websites on schedules different from those they use to report data to ED. Furthermore, ED may use methods for protecting the privacy of individuals represented within the data that could be different from the methods used by an individual state.

ED*Facts* firearm incidents data are collected in data group 601 within file 094. ED*Facts* collects this data group on behalf of the Office of Safe and Healthy Students in the Office of Elementary and Secondary Education. The definition for this data group is "The number of incidents involving students who brought or possessed firearms at school." The reporting period is the entire school year. Data group 601 collects separate counts for incidents involving handguns, rifles/shotguns, other firearms, and multiple weapon types. The counts reported here exclude the "other firearms" category. For more information about this data group, please see file specification 094 for the relevant school year, available at http://www2.ed.gov/about/inits/ed/edfacts/file-specifications.html.

For more information about ED*Facts*, contact

ED*Facts*
Administrative Data Division
Elementary/Secondary Branch
National Center for Education Statistics
Potomac Center Plaza
550 12th Street SW
Washington, DC 20202
EDFacts@ed.gov
http://www2.ed.gov/about/inits/ed/edfacts/index.html

Fast Response Survey System

The Fast Response Survey System (FRSS) was established in 1975 to collect issue-oriented data quickly, with a minimal burden on respondents. The FRSS, whose surveys collect and report data on key education issues at the elementary and secondary levels, was designed to meet the data needs of Department of Education analysts, planners, and decisionmakers when information could not be collected quickly through NCES's large recurring surveys. Findings from FRSS surveys have been included in congressional reports, testimony to congressional subcommittees, NCES reports, and other Department of Education reports. The findings are also often used by state and local education officials.

Data collected through FRSS surveys are representative at the national level, drawing from a sample that is appropriate for each study. The FRSS collects data from state education agencies and national samples of other educational organizations and participants, including local education agencies, public and private elementary and secondary schools, elementary and secondary school teachers and principals, and public libraries and school libraries. To ensure a minimal burden on respondents, the surveys are generally limited to three pages of questions, with a response burden of about 30 minutes per respondent. Sample sizes are relatively small (usually about 1,000 to 1,500 respondents per survey) so that data collection can be completed quickly.

Further information on the FRSS may be obtained from

John Ralph
Annual Reports and Information Staff
National Center for Education Statistics
Potomac Center Plaza
550 12th Street SW
Washington, DC 20202
john.ralph@ed.gov
http://nces.ed.gov/surveys/frss

School Safety and Discipline

The FRSS survey "School Safety and Discipline: 2013–14" (FRSS 106, 2014) collected nationally representative data on public school safety and discipline for the 2013–14 school year. The topics covered included specific safety and discipline plans and practices, training for classroom teachers and aides related to school safety and discipline issues, security personnel, frequency of specific discipline problems, and number of incidents of various offenses.

The survey was mailed to approximately 1,600 regular public schools in the 50 states and the District of Columbia. Recipients were informed that the survey was designed to be completed by the person most knowledgeable about safety and discipline at the school. The unweighted survey response rate was 86 percent, and the weighted response rate using the initial base weights was 85 percent. The survey weights were adjusted for questionnaire nonresponse, and the data were then weighted to yield national estimates that represent all eligible regular public schools in the United States. The report *Public School Safety and Discipline: 2013–14* (NCES 2015-051) presents selected findings from the survey.

Further information on this FRSS survey may be obtained from

John Ralph
Annual Reports and Information Staff
National Center for Education Statistics
Potomac Center Plaza
550 12th Street SW
Washington, DC 20202
john.ralph@ed.gov
http://nces.ed.gov/surveys/frss

High School Longitudinal Study of 2009

The High School Longitudinal Study of 2009 (HSLS:09) is a nationally representative, longitudinal study of approximately 21,000 9th-grade students in 944 schools who will be followed through their secondary and postsecondary years. The study focuses on understanding students' trajectories from the beginning of high school into postsecondary education, the workforce, and beyond. The HSLS:09 questionnaire is focused on, but not limited to, information on science, technology, engineering, and mathematics (STEM) education and careers. It is designed to provide data on mathematics and science education, the changing high school environment, and postsecondary education. This study features a new student assessment in algebra skills, reasoning, and problem solving and includes surveys of students, their parents, math and science teachers, and school administrators, as well as a new survey of school counselors.

The HSLS:09 base year took place in the 2009–10 school year, with a randomly selected sample of fall-term 9th-graders in more than 900 public and private high schools that had both a 9th and an 11th grade. Students took a mathematics assessment and survey online. Students' parents, principals, and mathematics and science teachers and the school's lead counselor completed surveys on the phone or online.

The HSLS:09 student questionnaire includes interest and motivation items for measuring key factors predicting choice of postsecondary paths, including majors and eventual careers. This study explores the roles of different factors in the development of a student's commitment to attend college and then take the steps necessary to succeed in college (the right courses, courses in specific sequences, etc.). Questionnaires in this study have asked more questions of students and parents regarding reasons for selecting specific colleges (e.g., academic programs, financial aid and access prices, and campus environment).

The first follow-up of HSLS:09 occurred in the spring of 2012, when most sample members were in the 11th grade. Data files and documentation for the first follow-up were released in fall 2013 and are available on the NCES website.

A between-round postsecondary status update survey took place in the spring of students' expected graduation year (2013). It asked respondents about college applications, acceptances, and rejections, as well as their actual college choices. In the fall of 2013 and the spring of 2014, high school transcripts were collected and coded.

A full second follow-up takes place in 2016, when most sample members are 3 years beyond high school graduation. Additional follow-ups are planned, to at least age 30.

Further information on HSLS:09 may be obtained from

Elise Christopher
Sample Surveys Division
Longitudinal Surveys Branch
National Center for Education Statistics
Potomac Center Plaza
550 12th Street SW
Washington, DC 20202
hsls09@ed.gov
http://nces.ed.gov/surveys/hsls09

High School Transcript Studies

High school transcript studies have been conducted since 1982 in conjunction with major NCES data collections. The studies collect information that is contained in a student's high school record—courses taken while attending secondary school, information on credits earned, when specific courses were taken, and final grades.

A high school transcript study was conducted in 2004 as part of the Education Longitudinal Study of 2002 (ELS:2002/2004). A total of 1,550 schools participated in the request for transcripts, for an unweighted participation rate of approximately 79 percent. Transcript information was received on 14,920 members of the student sample (not just graduates), for an unweighted response rate of 91 percent.

Similar studies were conducted of the coursetaking patterns of 1982, 1987, 1990, 1992, 1994, 1998, 2000, 2005, and 2009 high school graduates. The 1982 data are based on approximately 12,000 transcripts collected by the High School and Beyond Longitudinal Study (HS&B). The 1987 data are based on approximately 25,000 transcripts from 430 schools obtained as part of the 1987 NAEP High School Transcript Study, a scope comparable to that of the NAEP transcript studies conducted in 1990, 1994, 1998, and 2000. The 1992 data are based on approximately 15,000 transcripts collected by the National Education Longitudinal Study of 1988 (NELS:88/92). The 2005 data, from the 2005 NAEP High School Transcript Study, come from a sample of over 26,000 transcripts from 640 public schools and 80 private schools. The 2009 data are from the 2009 NAEP High School Transcript Study, which collected transcripts from a nationally representative sample of 37,700 high school graduates from about 610 public schools and 130 private schools.

Because the 1982 HS&B transcript study used a different method for identifying students with disabilities than was used in NAEP transcript studies after 1982, and in order to make the statistical summaries as comparable as possible, all the counts and percentages in this report are restricted to students whose records indicate that they had not participated in a special education program. This restriction lowers the number of 1990 graduates represented in the tables to 20,870.

Further information on NAEP high school transcript studies may be obtained from

Elise Christopher
Sample Surveys Division
Longitudinal Surveys Branch
National Center for Education Statistics
Potomac Center Plaza
550 12th Street SW
Washington, DC 20202
elise.christopher@ed.gov
http://nces.ed.gov/surveys/hst

Further information on all other high school transcript studies may be obtained from

Carl Schmitt
Administrative Data Division
Elementary and Secondary Branch
National Center for Education Statistics
Potomac Center Plaza
550 12th Street SW
Washington, DC 20202
carl.schmitt@ed.gov
http://nces.ed.gov/surveys/hst

Integrated Postsecondary Education Data System

The Integrated Postsecondary Education Data System (IPEDS) surveys approximately 7,500 postsecondary institutions, including universities and colleges, as well as institutions offering technical and vocational education beyond the high school level. IPEDS, an annual universe collection that began in 1986, replaced the Higher Education General Information Survey (HEGIS). In order to present data in a timely manner, "provisional" IPEDS data are used for the most recent years. These data have been fully reviewed, edited, and imputed, but do not incorporate data revisions submitted by institutions after the close of data collection.

IPEDS consists of interrelated survey components that provide information on postsecondary institutions, student enrollment, programs offered, degrees and certificates conferred, and both the human and financial resources involved in the provision of institutionally based postsecondary education. Prior to 2000, the IPEDS survey had the following subject-matter components: Graduation Rates; Fall Enrollment; Institutional Characteristics; Completions; Salaries, Tenure, and Fringe Benefits of Full-Time Faculty; Fall Staff; Finance; and Academic Libraries (in 2000, the Academic Libraries component became a survey separate from IPEDS). Since 2000, IPEDS survey components occurring in a particular collection year have been organized into three seasonal collection periods: fall, winter, and spring. The Institutional Characteristics and Completions components first took place during the fall 2000 collection; the Employees by Assigned Position (EAP),

Salaries, and Fall Staff components first took place during the winter 2001–02 collection; and the Enrollment, Student Financial Aid, Finance, and Graduation Rates components first took place during the spring 2001 collection. In the winter 2005–06 data collection, the EAP, Fall Staff, and Salaries components were merged into the Human Resources component. During the 2007–08 collection year, the Enrollment component was broken into two separate components: 12-Month Enrollment (taking place in the fall collection) and Fall Enrollment (taking place in the spring collection). In the 2011–12 IPEDS data collection year, the Student Financial Aid component was moved to the winter data collection to aid in the timing of the net price of attendance calculations displayed on the College Navigator (http://nces.ed.gov/collegenavigator). In the 2012–13 IPEDS data collection year, the Human Resources component was moved from the winter data collection to the spring data collection, and in the 2013–14 data collection year, the Graduation Rates and Graduation Rates 200% components were moved from the spring data collection to the winter data collection. Beginning in 2008–09, the first-professional degree category was combined with the doctor's degree category. However, some degrees formerly identified as first-professional that take more than two full-time-equivalent academic years to complete, such as those in Theology (M.Div, M.H.L./Rav), are included in the Master's degree category. Doctor's degrees were broken out into three distinct categories: research/scholarship, professional practice, and other doctor's degrees.

IPEDS race/ethnicity data collection also changed in 2008–09. The "Asian" race category is now separate from a "Native Hawaiian or Other Pacific Islander" category, and a new category of "Two or more races" is added.

The degree-granting institutions portion of IPEDS is a census of colleges that award associate's or higher degrees and are eligible to participate in Title IV financial aid programs. Prior to 1993, data from technical and vocational institutions were collected through a sample survey. Beginning in 1993, all data are gathered in a census of all postsecondary institutions. Beginning in 1997, the survey was restricted to institutions participating in Title IV programs. Tabulations from 1993 forward are based on lists of all institutions and are not subject to sampling errors.

The classification of institutions offering college and university education changed as of 1996. Prior to 1996, institutions that had courses leading to an associate's or higher degree or that had courses accepted for credit toward those degrees were considered higher education institutions. Higher education institutions were accredited by an agency or association that was recognized by the U.S. Department of Education or were recognized directly by the Secretary of Education. The newer standard includes institutions that award associate's or higher degrees and that are eligible to participate in Title IV federal financial aid programs. Presentations that contain any data according to this standard are labeled "degree-granting" institutions. Time-series data presentations may contain data from both series, and they are labeled accordingly. The impact of this change on data collected in 1996 was not large. For example, data on faculty salaries and benefits were only affected to a very small extent. Also, degrees awarded at the bachelor's level or higher were not heavily affected. The largest impact was on private 2-year college enrollment. In contrast, most of the data on public 4-year colleges were affected to a minimal extent. The impact on enrollment in public 2-year colleges was noticeable in certain states, but was relatively small at the national level. Overall, total enrollment for all institutions was about one-half of 1 percent higher in 1996 for degree-granting institutions than for higher education institutions.

Prior to the establishment of IPEDS in 1986, HEGIS acquired and maintained statistical data on the characteristics and operations of institutions of higher education. Implemented in 1966, HEGIS was an annual universe survey of institutions accredited at the college level by an agency recognized by the Secretary of the U.S. Department of Education. These institutions were listed in NCES's *Education Directory, Colleges and Universities.*

HEGIS surveys collected information on institutional characteristics, faculty salaries, finances, enrollment, and degrees. Since these surveys, like IPEDS, were distributed to all higher education institutions, the data presented are not subject to sampling error. However, they are subject to nonsampling error, the sources of which varied with the survey instrument.

The NCES Taskforce for IPEDS Redesign recognized that there were issues related to the consistency of data definitions as well as the accuracy, reliability, and validity of other quality measures within and across surveys. The IPEDS redesign in 2000 provided institution-specific web-based data forms. While the new system shortened data processing time and provided better data consistency, it did not address the accuracy of the data provided by institutions.

Beginning in 2003–04 with the Prior Year Data Revision System, prior-year data have been available to institutions entering current data. This allows institutions to make changes to their prior-year entries either by adjusting the data or by providing missing data. These revisions allow the evaluation of the data's accuracy by looking at the changes made.

NCES conducted a study (NCES 2005-175) of the 2002–03 data that were revised in 2003–04 to determine the accuracy of the imputations, track the institutions that submitted revised data, and analyze the revised data they submitted. When institutions made changes to their data, it was assumed that the revised data were the "true" data. The data were analyzed for the number and type of institutions making changes, the type of changes,

the magnitude of the changes, and the impact on published data.

Because NCES imputes for missing data, imputation procedures were also addressed by the Redesign Taskforce. For the 2003–04 assessment, differences between revised values and values that were imputed in the original files were compared (i.e., revised value minus imputed value). These differences were then used to provide an assessment of the effectiveness of imputation procedures. The size of the differences also provides an indication of the accuracy of imputation procedures. To assess the overall impact of changes on aggregate IPEDS estimates, published tables for each component were reconstructed using the revised 2002–03 data. These reconstructed tables were then compared to the published tables to determine the magnitude of aggregate bias and the direction of this bias.

Since fall 2000 and spring 2001, IPEDS data collections have been web-based. Data have been provided by "keyholders," institutional representatives appointed by campus chief executives, who are responsible for ensuring that survey data submitted by the institution are correct and complete. Because Title IV institutions are the primary focus of IPEDS and because these institutions are required to respond to IPEDS, response rates for Title IV institutions have been high (data on specific components are cited below). More details on the accuracy and reliability of IPEDS data can be found in the *Integrated Postsecondary Education Data System Data Quality Study* (NCES 2005-175).

Further information on IPEDS may be obtained from

Richard Reeves
Administrative Data Division
Postsecondary Branch
National Center for Education Statistics
Potomac Center Plaza
550 12th Street SW
Washington, DC 20202
richard.reeves@ed.gov
http://nces.ed.gov/ipeds

Fall (12-Month Enrollment)

The 12-month period during which data are collected is July 1 through June 30. Data are collected by race/ethnicity, gender, and level of study (undergraduate or postbaccalaureate) and include unduplicated headcounts and instructional activity (contact or credit hours). These data are also used to calculate a full-time-equivalent (FTE) enrollment based on instructional activity. FTE enrollment is useful for gauging the size of the educational enterprise at the institution. Prior to the 2007–08 IPEDS data collection, the data collected in the 12-Month Enrollment component were part of the Fall Enrollment component, which is conducted during the spring data collection period. However, to improve the timeliness of the data, a separate 12-Month

Enrollment survey component was developed in 2007. These data are now collected in the fall for the previous academic year. Of the 7,304 Title IV institutions that were expected to respond to the 12-Month Enrollment component of the fall 2014 data collection, 7,302 responded, for an approximate response rate of 100.0 percent.

Further information on the IPEDS 12-Month Enrollment component may be obtained from

Bao Le
Administrative Data Division
Postsecondary Branch
National Center for Education Statistics
Potomac Center Plaza
550 12th Street SW
Washington, DC 20202
bao.le@ed.gov
http://nces.ed.gov/ipeds

Fall (Completions)

This survey was part of the HEGIS series throughout its existence. However, the degree classification taxonomy was revised in 1970–71, 1982–83, 1991–92, 2002–03, and 2009–10. Collection of degree data has been maintained through IPEDS.

The nonresponse rate does not appear to be a significant source of nonsampling error for this survey. The response rate over the years has been high; for the fall 2014 Completions component, it was about 100.0 percent. Because of the high response rate, there was no need to conduct a nonresponse bias analysis. Imputation methods for the fall 2014 Completions component are discussed in the *2014–15 Integrated Postsecondary Education Data System (IPEDS) Methodology Report* (NCES 2015-098).

The *Integrated Postsecondary Education Data System Data Quality Study* (NCES 2005-175) indicated that most Title IV institutions supplying revised data on completions in 2003–04 were able to supply missing data for the prior year. The small differences between imputed data for the prior year and the revised actual data supplied by the institution indicated that the imputed values produced by NCES were acceptable.

Further information on the IPEDS Completions component may be obtained from

Andrew Mary
Administrative Data Division
Postsecondary Branch
National Center for Education Statistics
Potomac Center Plaza
550 12th Street SW
Washington, DC 20202
andrew.mary@ed.gov
http://nces.ed.gov/ipeds

Fall (Institutional Characteristics)

This survey collects the basic information necessary to classify institutions, including control, level, and types of programs offered, as well as information on tuition, fees, and room and board charges. Beginning in 2000, the survey collected institutional pricing data from institutions with first-time, full-time, degree/certificate-seeking undergraduate students. Unduplicated full-year enrollment counts and instructional activity are now collected in the 12-Month Enrollment survey. Beginning in 2008–09, student financial aid data collected include greater detail. The overall unweighted response rate was 100.0 percent for Title IV degree-granting institutions for 2009 data.

In the fall 2014 data collection, the response rate for the Institutional Characteristics component among all Title IV entities was 100.0 percent: Of the 7,389 Title IV entities expected to respond to this component, all responded.

The *Integrated Postsecondary Education Data System Data Quality Study* (NCES 2005-175) looked at tuition and price in Title IV institutions. Only 8 percent of institutions in 2002–03 and 2003–04 reported the same data to IPEDS and Thomson Peterson consistently across all selected data items. Differences in wordings or survey items may account for some of these inconsistencies.

Further information on the IPEDS Institutional Characteristics component may be obtained from

Moussa Ezzeddine
Chris Cody
Administrative Data Division
Postsecondary Branch
National Center for Education Statistics
Potomac Center Plaza
550 12th Street SW
Washington, DC 20202
moussa.ezzeddine@ed.gov
ccody@air.org
http://nces.ed.gov/ipeds

Winter (Student Financial Aid)

This component was part of the spring data collection from IPEDS data collection years 2000–01 to 2010–11, but it moved to the winter data collection starting with the 2011–12 IPEDS data collection year. This move will aid in the timing of the net price of attendance calculations displayed on College Navigator (http://nces.ed.gov/collegenavigator).

Financial aid data are collected for undergraduate students. Data are collected regarding federal grants, state and local government grants, institutional grants, and loans. The collected data include the number of students receiving each type of financial assistance and the average amount of aid received by type of aid. Beginning in 2008–09, student financial aid data collected includes greater detail on types of aid offered.

In the winter 2014–15 data collection, the Student Financial Aid component collected data about financial aid awarded to undergraduate students, with particular emphasis on full-time, first-time degree/certificate-seeking undergraduate students awarded financial aid for the 2014–15 academic year. In addition, the component collected data on undergraduate and graduate students receiving military service members and veterans benefits. Finally, student counts and awarded aid amounts were collected to calculate the net price of attendance for two subsets of full-time, first-time degree/certificate-seeking undergraduate students: those awarded any grant aid, and those awarded Title IV aid. Of the 7,218 Title IV institutions expected to respond to the Student Financial Aid component, 7,212 Title IV institutions responded, resulting in a response rate that rounded to 100 percent.

Further information on the IPEDS Student Financial Aid component may be obtained from

Chris Cody
Administrative Data Division
Postsecondary Branch
National Center for Education Statistics
Potomac Center Plaza
550 12th Street SW
Washington, DC 20202
ccody@air.org
http://nces.ed.gov/ipeds

Winter (Graduation Rates and Graduation Rates 200 Percent)

In IPEDS data collection years 2012–13 and earlier, the Graduation Rates and 200 Percent Graduation Rates components were collected during the spring collection. In the IPEDS 2013–14 data collection year, however, the Graduation Rates and 200 Percent Graduation Rates collections were moved to the winter data collection.

The 2014–15 Graduation Rates component collected counts of full-time, first-time degree/certificate-seeking undergraduate students beginning their postsecondary education in the specified cohort year and their completion status as of 150 percent of normal program completion time at the same institution where the students started. If 150 percent of normal program completions time extended beyond August 31, 2014, the counts as of that date were collected. Four-year institutions used 2008 as the cohort year, while less-than-4-year institutions used 2011 as the cohort year. Of the 6,433 institutions that were expected to respond to the Graduation Rates component, 6,430 institutions responded, resulting in a response rate that rounded to 100 percent.

The 2014–15 Graduation Rates 200 Percent component was designed to combine information reported in a prior collection via the Graduation Rates component with current information about the same cohort of students. From previously collected data, the following elements were obtained: the number of students entering the institution as full-time, first-time degree/certificate-seeking students in a cohort year; the number of students in this cohort completing within 100 and 150 percent of normal program completion time; and the number of cohort exclusions (such as students who left for military service). Then the count of additional cohort exclusions and additional program completers between 151 and 200 percent of normal program completion time was collected. Four-year institutions reported on bachelor's or equivalent degree-seeking students and used cohort year 2006 as the reference period, while less-than-4-year institutions reported on all students in the cohort and used cohort year 2010 as the reference period. Of the 5,928 institutions that were expected to respond to the Graduation Rates 200 Percent component, 5,926 institutions responded, resulting in a response rate that rounded to 100 percent.

Further information on the IPEDS Graduation Rates and 200 Percent Graduation Rates components may be obtained from

Gigi Jones
Administrative Data Division
Postsecondary Branch
National Center for Education Statistics
Potomac Center Plaza
550 12th Street SW
Washington, DC 20202
gigi.jones@ed.gov
http://nces.ed.gov/ipeds/staff/

Spring (Fall Enrollment)

This survey has been part of the HEGIS and IPEDS series since 1966. Response rates for this survey have been relatively high, generally exceeding 85 percent. Beginning in 2000, with web-based data collection, higher response rates were attained. In the spring 2015 data collection, the Fall Enrollment component covered fall 2014. Of the 7,292 institutions that were expected to respond, 7,284 responded, for a response rate that rounded to 100 percent. Data collection procedures for the Fall Enrollment component of the spring 2015 data collection are presented in *Enrollment and Employees in Postsecondary Institutions, Fall 2014;* and *Financial Statistics and Academic Libraries, Fiscal Year 2014: First Look (Provisional Data)* (NCES 2016-005).

Beginning with the fall 1986 survey and the introduction of IPEDS (see above), the survey was redesigned. The survey allows (in alternating years) for the collection of age and residence data. Beginning in 2000, the survey collected instructional activity and unduplicated headcount data, which are needed to compute a standardized, full-time-equivalent (FTE) enrollment statistic for the entire academic year. As of 2007–08, the timeliness of the instructional activity data has been improved by collecting these data in the fall as part of the 12-Month-Enrollment component instead of in the spring as part of the Fall Enrollment component.

The *Integrated Postsecondary Education Data System Data Quality Study (*NCES 2005-175) showed that public institutions made the majority of changes to enrollment data during the 2004 revision period. The majority of changes were made to unduplicated headcount data, with the net differences between the original data and the revised data at about 1 percent. Part-time students in general and enrollment in private not-for-profit institutions were often underestimated. The fewest changes by institutions were to Classification of Instructional Programs (CIP) code data. (The CIP is a taxonomic coding scheme that contains titles and descriptions of primarily postsecondary instructional programs.)

Further information on the IPEDS Fall Enrollment component may be obtained from

Bao Le
Administrative Data Division
Postsecondary Branch
National Center for Education Statistics
Potomac Center Plaza
550 12th Street SW
Washington, DC 20202
bao.le@ed.gov
http://nces.ed.gov/ipeds

Spring (Finance)

This survey was part of the HEGIS series and has been continued under IPEDS. Substantial changes were made in the financial survey instruments in fiscal year (FY) 1976, FY 1982, FY 1987, FY 1997, and FY 2002. While these changes were significant, considerable effort has been made to present only comparable information on trends and to note inconsistencies. The FY 1976 survey instrument contained numerous revisions to earlier survey forms, which made direct comparisons of line items very difficult. Beginning in FY 1982, Pell Grant data were collected in the categories of federal restricted grant and contract revenues and restricted scholarship and fellowship expenditures. The introduction of IPEDS in the FY 1987 survey included several important changes to the survey instrument and data processing procedures. Beginning in FY 1997, data for private institutions were collected using new financial concepts consistent with Financial Accounting Standards Board (FASB) reporting standards, which provide a more comprehensive view of college finance activities. The data for public institutions

continued to be collected using the older survey form. The data for public and private institutions were no longer comparable and, as a result, no longer presented together in analyses. In FY 2001, public institutions had the option of either continuing to report using Government Accounting Standards Board (GASB) standards or using the new FASB reporting standards. Beginning in FY 2002, public institutions had three options: the original GASB standards, the FASB standards, or the new GASB Statement 35 standards (GASB35).

Possible sources of nonsampling error in the financial statistics include nonresponse, imputation, and misclassification. The unweighted response rate has been about 85 to 90 percent for most of the years of this survey; however, in more recent years, response rates have been much higher because Title IV institutions are required to respond. Beginning with 2002, the IPEDS data collection has been a full-scale web-based collection, which offers features that improve the quality and timeliness of the data. The ability of IPEDS to tailor online data entry forms for each institution based on characteristics such as institutional control, level of institution, and calendar system, and the institutions' ability to submit their data online, are two such features that have improved response.

In the FY 2014 Finance component, of the 7,292 institutions that were expected to respond, 7,284 provided data, resulting in a response rate that rounded to 100 percent. Data collection procedures for the FY 2014 component are discussed in *Enrollment and Employees in Postsecondary Institutions, Fall 2014;* and *Financial Statistics and Academic Libraries, Fiscal Year 2014: First Look (Provisional Data)* (NCES 2016-005).

The *Integrated Postsecondary Education Data System Data Quality Study* (NCES 2005-175) found that only a small percentage (2.9 percent, or 168) of postsecondary institutions either revised 2002–03 data or submitted data for items they previously left unreported. Though relatively few institutions made changes, the changes made were relatively large—greater than 10 percent of the original data. With a few exceptions, these changes, large as they were, did not greatly affect the aggregate totals.

Further information on the IPEDS Finance component may be obtained from

Bao Le
Administrative Data Division
Postsecondary Branch
National Center for Education Statistics
Potomac Center Plaza
550 12th Street SW
Washington, DC 20202
bao.le@ed.gov
http://nces.ed.gov/ipeds

Spring (Human Resources)

The Human Resources component was part of the IPEDS winter data collection from data collection years 2000–01 to 2011–12. For the 2012–13 data collection year, the Human Resources component was moved to the spring 2013 data collection, in order to give institutions more time to prepare their survey responses (the spring and winter collections begin on the same date, but the reporting deadline for the spring collection is several weeks later than the reporting deadline for the winter collection).

IPEDS Collection Years 2012–13 and Later

In 2012–13, new occupational categories replaced the primary function/occupational activity categories previously used in the IPEDS Human Resources component. This change was required in order to align the IPEDS Human Resources categories with the 2010 Standard Occupational Classification (SOC) system. In tandem with the change in 2012–13 from using primary function/occupational activity categories to using the new occupational categories, the sections making up the IPEDS Human Resources component (which previously had been Employees by Assigned Position, Fall Staff, and Salaries) were changed to Full-Time Instructional Staff, Full-time Noninstructional Staff, Salaries, Part-Time Staff, and New Hires.

The webpage "Archived Changes—Changes to IPEDS Data Collections, 2012–13" (https://nces.ed.gov/ipeds/InsidePages/ArchivedChanges?year=2012-13) provides information on the redesigned IPEDS Human Resources component. "Resources for Implementing Changes to the IPEDS Human Resources (HR) Survey Component Due to Updated 2010 Standard Occupational Classification (SOC) System" (https://nces.ed.gov/ipeds/Section/resources_soc) is a webpage containing additional information, including notes comparing the new classifications with the old ("Comparison of New IPEDS Occupational Categories with Previous Categories"), a crosswalk from the new IPEDS occupational categories to the 2010 SOC occupational categories ("New IPEDS Occupational Categories and 2010 SOC"), answers to frequently asked questions, and a link to current IPEDS Human Resources survey screens.

In the 2013–14 collection year, the response rate for the (spring 2014) Human Resources component was 99.9 percent. Data collection procedures for this component are presented in *Enrollment in Postsecondary Institutions, Fall 2013; Financial Statistics, Fiscal Year 2013;* and *Employees in Postsecondary Institutions, Fall 2013: First Look (Provisional Data)* (NCES 2015-012). Of the 7,292 institutions that were expected to respond to the spring 2015 Human Resources component, 7,284 responded, for a response rate that rounded to 100 percent. Data collection procedures for this component are presented in *Enrollment and Employees*

in Postsecondary Institutions, Fall 2014; and *Financial Statistics and Academic Libraries, Fiscal Year 2014: First Look (Provisional Data)* (NCES 2016-005).

IPEDS Collection Years Prior to 2012–13

In collection years before 2001–02, IPEDS conducted a Fall Staff survey and a Salaries survey; in the 2001–02 collection year, the Employees by Assigned Position survey was added to IPEDS. In the 2005–06 collection year, these three surveys became sections of the IPEDS "Human Resources" component.

Data gathered by the Employees by Assigned Position section categorized all employees by full- or part-time status, faculty status, and primary function/occupational activity. Institutions with M.D. or D.O. programs were required to report their medical school employees separately. A response to the EAP was required of all 6,858 Title IV institutions and administrative offices in the United States and other jurisdictions for winter 2008–09, and 6,845, or 99.8 percent unweighted, responded. Of the 6,970 Title IV institutions and administrative offices required to respond to the winter 2009–10 EAP, 6,964, or 99.9 percent, responded. And of the 7,256 Title IV institutions and administrative offices required to respond to the EAP for winter 2010–11, 7,252, or 99.9 percent, responded.

The main functions/occupational activities of the EAP section were primarily instruction, instruction combined with research and/or public service, primarily research, primarily public service, executive/administrative/managerial, other professionals (support/service), graduate assistants, technical and paraprofessionals, clerical and secretarial, skilled crafts, and service/maintenance.

All full-time instructional faculty classified in the EAP full-time non-medical school part as either (1) primarily instruction or (2) instruction combined with research and/or public service were included in the Salaries section, unless they were exempt.

The Fall Staff section categorized all staff on the institution's payroll as of November 1 of the collection year by employment status (full time or part time), primary function/occupational activity, gender, and race/ethnicity. These data elements were collected from degree-granting and non-degree-granting institutions; however, additional data elements were collected from degree-granting institutions and related administrative offices with 15 or more full-time staff. These elements include faculty status, contract length/teaching period, academic rank, salary class intervals, and newly hired full-time permanent staff.

The Fall Staff section, which was required only in odd-numbered reporting years, was not required during the 2008–09 Human Resources data collection. However, of the 6,858 Title IV institutions and administrative offices in the United States and other jurisdictions, 3,295, or 48.0 percent unweighted, did provide data in the Fall Staff section that year. During the 2009–10 Human Resources data collection, when all 6,970 Title IV institutions and administrative offices were required to respond to the Fall Staff section, 6,964, or 99.9 percent, did so. A response to the Fall Staff section of the 2010–11 Human Resources collection was optional, and 3,364 Title IV institutions and administrative offices responded that year (a response rate of 46.3 percent).

The *Integrated Postsecondary Education Data System Data Quality Study* (NCES 2015-012) found that for 2003–04 employee data items, changes were made by 1.2 percent (77) of the institutions that responded. All institutions making changes made changes that resulted in different employee counts. For both institutional and aggregate differences, however, the changes had little impact on the original employee count submissions. A large number of institutions reported different staff data to IPEDS and Thomson Peterson; however, the magnitude of the differences was small—usually no more than 17 faculty members for any faculty variable.

The Salaries section collected data for full-time instructional faculty (except those in medical schools in the EAP section, described above) on the institution's payroll as of November 1 of the collection year by contract length/teaching period, gender, and academic rank. The reporting of data by faculty status in the Salaries section was required from 4-year degree-granting institutions and above only. Salary outlays and fringe benefits were also collected for full-time instructional staff on 9/10- and 11/12-month contracts/teaching periods. This section was applicable to degree-granting institutions unless exempt.

Between 1966–67 and 1985–86, this survey differed from other HEGIS surveys in that imputations were not made for nonrespondents. Thus, there is some possibility that the salary averages presented in this report may differ from the results of a complete enumeration of all colleges and universities. Beginning with the surveys for 1987–88, the IPEDS data tabulation procedures included imputations for survey nonrespondents. The unweighted response rate for the 2008–09 Salaries survey section was 99.9 percent. The response rate for the 2009–10 Salaries section was 100.0 percent (4,453 of the 4,455 required institutions responded), and the response rate for 2010–11 was 99.9 percent (4,561 of the 4,565 required institutions responded). Imputation methods for the 2010–11 Salaries survey section are discussed in *Employees in Postsecondary Institutions, Fall 2010, and Salaries of Full-Time Instructional Staff, 2010–11* (NCES 2012-276).

Although data from this survey are not subject to sampling error, sources of nonsampling error may include computational errors and misclassification in reporting and processing. The electronic reporting system does allow

corrections to prior-year reported or missing data, and this should help with these problems. Also, NCES reviews individual institutions' data for internal and longitudinal consistency and contacts institutions to check inconsistent data.

The *Integrated Postsecondary Education Data System Data Quality Study* (NCES 2015-012) found that only 1.3 percent of the responding Title IV institutions in 2003–04 made changes to their salaries data. The differences between the imputed data and the revised data were small and found to have little impact on the published data.

Further information on the Human Resources component may be obtained from

Moussa Ezzeddine
Administrative Data Division
Postsecondary Branch
National Center for Education Statistics
Potomac Center Plaza
550 12th Street SW
Washington, DC 20202
moussa.ezzeddine@ed.gov
http://nces.ed.gov/ipeds

National Assessment of Educational Progress

The National Assessment of Educational Progress (NAEP) is a series of cross-sectional studies initially implemented in 1969 to assess the educational achievement of U.S. students and monitor changes in those achievements. In the main national NAEP, a nationally representative sample of students is assessed at grades 4, 8, and 12 in various academic subjects.

The assessments are based on frameworks developed by the National Assessment Governing Board (NAGB). Assessment items include both multiple-choice and constructed-response (requiring written answers) items. Results are reported in two ways: by average score and by achievement level. Average scores are reported for the nation, for participating states and jurisdictions, and for subgroups of the population. Percentages of students performing at or above three achievement levels (*Basic, Proficient,* and *Advanced*) are also reported for these groups.

Main NAEP Assessments

From 1990 until 2001, main NAEP was conducted for states and other jurisdictions that chose to participate. In 2002, under the provisions of the No Child Left Behind Act of 2001, all states began to participate in main NAEP, and an aggregate of all state samples replaced the separate national sample. (School district-level assessments—

under the Trial Urban District Assessment [TUDA] program—also began in 2002). Results are available for the mathematics assessments administered in 2000, 2003, 2005, 2007, 2009, 2011, 2013, and 2015. In 2005, NAGB called for the development of a new mathematics framework. The revisions made to the mathematics framework for the 2005 assessment were intended to reflect recent curricular emphases and better assess the specific objectives for students at each grade level.

The revised mathematics framework focuses on two dimensions: mathematical content and cognitive demand. By considering these two dimensions for each item in the assessment, the framework ensures that NAEP assesses an appropriate balance of content, as well as a variety of ways of knowing and doing mathematics.

Since the 2005 changes to the mathematics framework were minimal for grades 4 and 8, comparisons over time can be made between assessments conducted before and after the framework's implementation for these grades. The changes that the 2005 framework made to the grade 12 assessment, however, were too drastic to allow grade 12 results from before and after implementation to be directly compared. These changes included adding more questions on algebra, data analysis, and probability to reflect changes in high school mathematics standards and coursework; merging the measurement and geometry content areas; and changing the reporting scale from 0–500 to 0–300. For more information regarding the 2005 mathematics framework revisions, see http://nces.ed.gov/nationsreportcard/mathematics/frameworkcomparison.asp.

Results are available for the reading assessments administered in 2000, 2002, 2003, 2005, 2007, 2009, 2011, 2013, and 2015. In 2009, a new framework was developed for the 4th-, 8th-, and 12th-grade NAEP reading assessments.

Both a content alignment study and a reading trend or bridge study were conducted to determine if the new assessment was comparable to the prior assessment. Overall, the results of the special analyses suggested that the assessments were similar in terms of their item and scale characteristics and the results they produced for important demographic groups of students. Thus, it was determined that the results of the 2009 reading assessment could still be compared to those from earlier assessment years, thereby maintaining the trend lines first established in 1992. For more information regarding the 2009 reading framework revisions, see http://nces.ed.gov/nationsreportcard/reading/whatmeasure.asp.

In spring 2013, NAEP released results from the NAEP 2012 economics assessment in *The Nation's Report Card: Economics 2012* (NCES 2013-453). First administered in 2006, the NAEP economics assessment measures 12th-graders' understanding of a wide range of topics

in three main content areas: market economy, national economy, and international economy. The 2012 assessment is based on a nationally representative sample of nearly 11,000 12th-graders.

In *The Nation's Report Card: A First Look—2013 Mathematics and Reading* (NCES 2014-451), NAEP released the results of the 2013 mathematics and reading assessments. Results can also be accessed using the interactive graphics and downloadable data available at the new online Nation's Report Card website (http://nationsreportcard.gov/reading_math_2013/#/).

The *Nation's Report Card: A First Look—2013 Mathematics and Reading Trial Urban District Assessment* (NCES 2014-466) provides the results of the 2013 mathematics and reading TUDA, which measured the reading and mathematics progress of 4th- and 8th-graders from 21 urban school districts. Results from the 2013 mathematics and reading TUDA can also be accessed using the interactive graphics and downloadable data available at the online TUDA website (http://nationsreportcard.gov/reading_math_tuda_2013/#/).

The online interactive report *The Nation's Report Card: 2014 U.S. History, Geography, and Civics at Grade 8* (NCES 2015-112) provides grade 8 results for the 2014 NAEP U.S. history, geography, and civics assessments. Trend results for previous assessment years in these three subjects, as well as information on school and student participation rates and sample tasks and student responses, are also presented.

The *Nation's Report Card: 2015 Mathematics and Reading Assessments* (NCES 2015-136) is an online interactive report that presents national and state results for 4th- and 8th-graders on the NAEP 2015 mathematics and reading assessments. The report also presents TUDA results in mathematics and reading for 4th- and 8th-graders.

The online interactive report *The Nation's Report Card: 2015 Mathematics and Reading at Grade 12* (NCES 2016-018) presents grade 12 results from the NAEP 2015 mathematics and reading assessments.

NAEP Long-Term Trend Assessments

In addition to conducting the main assessments, NAEP also conducts the long-term trend assessments. Long-term trend assessments provide an opportunity to observe educational progress in reading and mathematics of 9-, 13-, and 17-year-olds since the early 1970s. The long-term trend reading assessment measures students' reading comprehension skills using an array of passages that vary by text types and length. The assessment was designed to measure students' ability to locate specific information in the text provided; make inferences across a passage to provide an explanation; and identify the main idea in the text.

The NAEP long-term trend assessment in mathematics measures knowledge of mathematical facts; ability to carry out computations using paper and pencil; knowledge of basic formulas, such as those applied in geometric settings; and ability to apply mathematics to skills of daily life, such as those involving time and money.

*The Nation's Report Card: Trends in Academic Progress 2012 (*NCES 2013-456) provides the results of 12 long-term trend reading assessments dating back to 1971 and 11 long-term trend mathematics assessments dating back to 1973.

Further information on NAEP may be obtained from

Daniel McGrath
Assessments Division
Reporting and Dissemination Branch
National Center for Education Statistics
Potomac Center Plaza
550 12th Street SW
Washington, DC 20202
daniel.mcgrath@ed.gov
http://nces.ed.gov/nationsreportcard

National Household Education Surveys Program

The National Household Education Surveys Program (NHES) is a data collection system that is designed to address a wide range of education-related issues. Surveys have been conducted in 1991, 1993, 1995, 1996, 1999, 2001, 2003, 2005, 2007, and 2012. NHES targets specific populations for detailed data collection. It is intended to provide more detailed data on the topics and populations of interest than are collected through supplements to other household surveys.

The topics addressed by NHES:1991 were early childhood education and adult education. About 60,000 households were screened for NHES:1991. In the Early Childhood Education Survey, about 14,000 parents/guardians of 3- to 8-year-olds completed interviews about their children's early educational experiences. Included in this component were participation in nonparental care/education; care arrangements and school; and family, household, and child characteristics. In the NHES:1991 Adult Education Survey, about 9,800 people 16 years of age and older, identified as having participated in an adult education activity in the previous 12 months, were questioned about their activities. Data were collected on programs and up to four courses, including the subject matter, duration, sponsorship, purpose, and cost. Information on the household and the adult's background and current employment was also collected.

In NHES:1993, nearly 64,000 households were screened. Approximately 11,000 parents of 3- to 7-year-olds completed interviews for the School Readiness Survey. Topics included the developmental characteristics of

preschoolers; school adjustment and teacher feedback to parents for kindergartners and primary students; center-based program participation; early school experiences; home activities with family members; and health status. In the School Safety and Discipline Survey, about 12,700 parents of children in grades 3 to 12 and about 6,500 youth in grades 6 to 12 were interviewed about their school experiences. Topics included the school learning environment, discipline policy, safety at school, victimization, the availability and use of alcohol/drugs, and alcohol/drug education. Peer norms for behavior in school and substance use were also included in this topical component. Extensive family and household background information was collected, as well as characteristics of the school attended by the child.

In NHES:1995, the Early Childhood Program Participation Survey and the Adult Education Survey were similar to those fielded in 1991. In the Early Childhood component, about 14,000 parents of children from birth to 3rd grade were interviewed out of 16,000 sampled, for a completion rate of 90.4 percent. In the Adult Education Survey, about 24,000 adults were sampled and 82.3 percent (20,000) completed the interview.

NHES:1996 covered parent and family involvement in education and civic involvement. Data on homeschooling and school choice also were collected. The 1996 survey screened about 56,000 households. For the Parent and Family Involvement in Education Survey, nearly 21,000 parents of children in grades 3 to 12 were interviewed. For the Civic Involvement Survey, about 8,000 youth in grades 6 to 12, about 9,000 parents, and about 2,000 adults were interviewed. The 1996 survey also addressed public library use. Adults in almost 55,000 households were interviewed to support state-level estimates of household public library use.

NHES:1999 collected end-of-decade estimates of key indicators from the surveys conducted throughout the 1990s. Approximately 60,000 households were screened for a total of about 31,000 interviews with parents of children from birth through grade 12 (including about 6,900 infants, toddlers, and preschoolers) and adults age 16 or older not enrolled in grade 12 or below. Key indicators included participation of children in nonparental care and early childhood programs, school experiences, parent/family involvement in education at home and at school, youth community service activities, plans for future education, and adult participation in educational activities and community service.

NHES:2001 included two surveys that were largely repeats of similar surveys included in earlier NHES collections. The Early Childhood Program Participation Survey was similar in content to the Early Childhood Program Participation Survey fielded as part of NHES:1995, and the Adult Education and Lifelong Learning Survey was similar in content to the Adult Education Survey of NHES:1995. The Before- and

After-School Programs and Activities Survey, while containing items fielded in earlier NHES collections, had a number of new items that collected information about what school-age children were doing during the time they spent in child care or in other activities, what parents were looking for in care arrangements and activities, and parent evaluations of care arrangements and activities. Parents of approximately 6,700 children from birth through age 6 who were not yet in kindergarten completed Early Childhood Program Participation Survey interviews. Nearly 10,900 adults completed Adult Education and Lifelong Learning Survey interviews, and parents of nearly 9,600 children in kindergarten through grade 8 completed Before- and After-School Programs and Activities Survey interviews.

NHES:2003 included two surveys: the Parent and Family Involvement in Education Survey and the Adult Education for Work-Related Reasons Survey (the first administration). Whereas previous adult education surveys were more general in scope, this survey had a narrower focus on occupation-related adult education programs. It collected in-depth information about training and education in which adults participated specifically for work-related reasons, either to prepare for work or a career or to maintain or improve work-related skills and knowledge they already had. The Parent and Family Involvement Survey expanded on the first survey fielded on this topic in 1996. In 2003, screeners were completed with 32,050 households. About 12,700 of the 16,000 sampled adults completed the Adult Education for Work-Related Reasons Survey, for a weighted response rate of 76 percent. For the Parent and Family Involvement in Education Survey, interviews were completed by the parents of about 12,400 of the 14,900 sampled children in kindergarten through grade 12, yielding a weighted unit response rate of 83 percent.

NHES:2005 included surveys that covered adult education, early childhood program participation, and after-school programs and activities. Data were collected from about 8,900 adults for the Adult Education Survey, from parents of about 7,200 children for the Early Childhood Program Participation Survey, and from parents of nearly 11,700 children for the After-School Programs and Activities Survey. These surveys were substantially similar to the surveys conducted in 2001, with the exceptions that the Adult Education Survey addressed a new topic—informal learning activities for personal interest—and the Early Childhood Program Participation Survey and After-School Programs and Activities Survey did not collect information about before-school care for school-age children.

NHES:2007 fielded the Parent and Family Involvement in Education Survey and the School Readiness Survey. These surveys were similar in design and content to surveys included in the 2003 and 1993 collections, respectively. New features added to the Parent and Family Involvement Survey were questions about supplemental

education services provided by schools and school districts (including use of and satisfaction with such services), as well as questions that would efficiently identify the school attended by the sampled students. New features added to the School Readiness Survey were questions that collected details about TV programs watched by the sampled children. For the Parent and Family Involvement Survey, interviews were completed with parents of 10,680 sampled children in kindergarten through grade 12, including 10,370 students enrolled in public or private schools and 310 homeschooled children. For the School Readiness Survey, interviews were completed with parents of 2,630 sampled children ages 3 to 6 and not yet in kindergarten. Parents who were interviewed about children in kindergarten through 2nd grade for the Parent and Family Involvement Survey were also asked some questions about these children's school readiness.

The 2007 and earlier administrations of NHES used a random-digit-dial sample of landline phones and computer-assisted telephone interviewing to conduct interviews. However, due to declining response rates for all telephone surveys and the increase in households that only or mostly use a cell phone instead of a landline, the data collection method was changed to an address-based sample survey for NHES:2012. Because of this change in survey mode, readers should use caution when comparing NHES:2012 estimates to those of prior NHES administrations.

NHES:2012 included the Parent and Family Involvement in Education Survey and the Early Childhood Program Participation Survey. The Parent and Family Involvement in Education Survey gathered data on students who were enrolled in kindergarten through grade 12 or who were homeschooled at equivalent grade levels. Survey questions that pertained to students enrolled in kindergarten through grade 12 requested information on various aspects of parent involvement in education (such as help with homework, family activities, and parent involvement at school) and survey questions pertaining to homeschooled students requested information on the student's homeschooling experiences, the sources of the curriculum, and the reasons for homeschooling.

The 2012 Parent and Family Involvement in Education Survey questionnaires were completed for 17,563 (397 homeschooled and 17,166 enrolled) children, for a weighted unit response rate of 78.4 percent. The overall estimated unit response rate (the product of the screener unit response rate of 73.8 percent and the Parent and Family Involvement in Education Survey unit response rate) was 57.8 percent.

The 2012 Early Childhood Program Participation Survey collected data on the early care and education arrangements and early learning of children from irth through the age of 5 who were not yet enrolled in kindergarten. Questionnaires were completed for 7,893 children, for a weighted unit response rate of

78.7 percent. The overall estimated weighted unit response rate (the product of the screener weighted unit response rate of 73.8 percent and the Early Childhood Program Participation Survey unit weighted response rate) was 58.1 percent.

Data for the 2012 NHES Parent and Family Involvement in Education Survey are available in the First Look report, *Parent and Family Involvement in Education, From the National Household Education Surveys Program of 2012* (NCES 2013-028). Data for the 2012 NHES Early Childhood Program Participation Survey are available in the First Look report, *Early Childhood Program Participation, From the National Household Education Surveys Program of 2012* (NCES 2013-029).

Further information on NHES may be obtained from

Andrew Zukerberg
Gail Mulligan
Sample Surveys Division
National Center for Education Statistics
Potomac Center Plaza
550 12th Street SW
Washington, DC 20202
andrew.zukerberg@ed.gov
gail.mulligan@ed.gov
http://nces.ed.gov/nhes

National Postsecondary Student Aid Study

The National Postsecondary Student Aid Study (NPSAS) is a comprehensive nationwide study of how students and their families pay for postsecondary education. Data gathered from the study are used to help guide future federal student financial aid policy. The study covers nationally representative samples of undergraduates, graduates, and first-professional students in the 50 states, the District of Columbia, and Puerto Rico, including students attending less-than-2-year institutions, community colleges, 4-year colleges, and universities. Participants include students who do not receive aid and those who do receive financial aid. Since NPSAS identifies nationally representative samples of student subpopulations of interest to policymakers and obtains baseline data for longitudinal study of these subpopulations, data from the study provide the base-year sample for the Beginning Postsecondary Students (BPS) longitudinal study and the Baccalaureate and Beyond (B&B) longitudinal study.

Originally, NPSAS was conducted every 3 years. Beginning with the 1999–2000 study (NPSAS:2000), NPSAS has been conducted every 4 years. NPSAS:08 included a new set of instrument items to obtain baseline measures of the awareness of two new federal grants introduced in 2006: the Academic Competitiveness Grant (ACG) and the National Science and Mathematics Access to Retain Talent (SMART) grant.

The first NPSAS (NPSAS:87) was conducted during the 1986–87 school year. Data were gathered from about 1,100 colleges, universities, and other postsecondary institutions; 60,000 students; and 14,000 parents. These data provided information on the cost of postsecondary education, the distribution of financial aid, and the characteristics of both aided and nonaided students and their families.

For NPSAS:93, information on 77,000 undergraduates and graduate students enrolled during the school year was collected at 1,000 postsecondary institutions. The sample included students who were enrolled at any time between July 1, 1992, and June 30, 1993. About 66,000 students and a subsample of their parents were interviewed by telephone. NPSAS:96 contained information on more than 48,000 undergraduate and graduate students from about 1,000 postsecondary institutions who were enrolled at any time during the 1995–96 school year. NPSAS:2000 included nearly 62,000 students (50,000 undergraduates and almost 12,000 graduate students) from 1,000 postsecondary institutions. NPSAS:04 collected data on about 80,000 undergraduates and 11,000 graduate students from 1,400 postsecondary institutions. For NPSAS:08, about 114,000 undergraduate students and 14,000 graduate students who were enrolled in postsecondary education during the 2007–08 school year were selected from more than 1,730 postsecondary institutions.

NPSAS:12 sampled about 95,000 undergraduates and 16,000 graduate students from approximately 1,500 postsecondary institutions. Public access to the data is available online through PowerStats (http://nces.ed.gov/datalab/).

Further information on NPSAS may be obtained from

Aurora D'Amico
Tracy Hunt-White
Sample Surveys Division
Longitudinal Surveys Branch
National Center for Education Statistics
Potomac Center Plaza
550 12th Street SW
Washington, DC 20202
aurora.damico@ed.gov
tracy.hunt-white@ed.gov
http://nces.ed.gov/npsas

Principal Follow-up Survey

The Principal Follow-up Survey (PFS), first conducted in school year 2008–09, is a component of the 2011–12 Schools and Staffing Survey (SASS). The 2012–13 PFS was administered in order to provide attrition rates for principals in K–12 public and private schools. The goal was to assess how many principals in the 2011–12 school year still worked as a principal in the same school in the

2012–13 school year, how many had moved to become a principal in another school, and how many no longer worked as a principal. The PFS sample included all schools whose principals had completed SASS principal questionnaires. Schools that had returned a completed 2011–12 SASS principal questionnaire were mailed the PFS form in March 2013.

Further information on the PFS may be obtained from

Isaiah O'Rear
Sample Surveys Division
Cross-Sectional Surveys Branch
National Center for Education Statistics
Potomac Center Plaza
550 12th Street SW
Washington, DC 20202
isaiah.orear@ed.gov
http://nces.ed.gov/surveys/sass/

Private School Universe Survey

The purposes of the Private School Universe Survey (PSS) data collection activities are (1) to build an accurate and complete list of private schools to serve as a sampling frame for NCES sample surveys of private schools and (2) to report data on the total number of private schools, teachers, and students in the survey universe. Begun in 1989 under the U.S. Census Bureau, the PSS has been conducted every 2 years, and data for the 1989–90, 1991–92, 1993–94, 1995–96, 1997–98, 1999–2000, 2001–02, 2003–04, 2005–06, 2007–08, 2009–10, and 2011–12 school years have been released. A *First Look* report on the 2011–12 PSS data, *Characteristics of Private Schools in the United States: Results From the 2011–12 Private School Universe Survey* (NCES 2013-316) was published in July 2013.

The PSS produces data similar to that of the Common Core of Data for public schools, and can be used for public-private comparisons. The data are useful for a variety of policy- and research-relevant issues, such as the growth of religiously affiliated schools, the number of private high school graduates, the length of the school year for various private schools, and the number of private school students and teachers.

The target population for this universe survey is all private schools in the United States that meet the PSS criteria of a private school (i.e., the private school is an institution that provides instruction for any of grades K through 12, has one or more teachers to give instruction, is not administered by a public agency, and is not operated in a private home). The survey universe is composed of schools identified from a variety of sources. The main source is a list frame initially developed for the 1989–90 PSS. The list is updated regularly by matching it with lists provided by nationwide private school associations, state departments of education, and other national guides and

sources that list private schools. The other source is an area frame search in approximately 124 geographic areas, conducted by the U.S. Census Bureau.

Of the 40,302 schools included in the 2009–10 sample, 10,229 were found ineligible for the survey. Those not responding numbered 1,856, and those responding numbered 28,217. The unweighted response rate for the 2009–10 PSS survey was 93.8 percent.

Of the 39,325 schools included in the 2011–12 sample, 10,030 cases were considered as out-of-scope (not eligible for the PSS). A total of 26,983 private schools completed a PSS interview (15.8 percent completed online), while 2,312 schools refused to participate, resulting in an unweighted response rate of 92.1 percent.

Further information on the PSS may be obtained from

Steve Broughman
Sample Surveys Division
Cross-Sectional Surveys Branch
National Center for Education Statistics
Potomac Center Plaza
550 12th Street SW
Washington, DC 20202
stephen.broughman@ed.gov
http://nces.ed.gov/surveys/pss

Projections of Education Statistics

Since 1964, NCES has published projections of key statistics for elementary and secondary schools and institutions of higher education. The latest report is titled *Projections of Education Statistics to 2022* (NCES 2014-051). The *Projections of Education Statistics* series uses projection models for elementary and secondary enrollment, high school graduates, elementary and secondary teachers, expenditures for public elementary and secondary education, enrollment in postsecondary degree-granting institutions, and postsecondary degrees conferred to develop national and state projections. These models are described more fully in the report's appendix on projection methodology.

Differences between the reported and projected values are, of course, almost inevitable. An evaluation of past projections revealed that, at the elementary and secondary level, projections of enrollments have been quite accurate: mean absolute percentage differences for enrollment ranged from 0.3 to 1.3 percent for projections from 1 to 5 years in the future, while those for teachers were less than 3 percent. At the higher education level, projections of enrollment have been fairly accurate: mean absolute percentage differences were 5 percent or less for projections from 1 to 5 years into the future.

Further information on *Projections of Education Statistics* may be obtained from

William Hussar
Annual Reports and Information
National Center for Education Statistics
Potomac Center Plaza
550 12th Street SW
Washington, DC 20202
william.hussar@ed.gov
http://nces.ed.gov/annuals

School Survey on Crime and Safety

The most recent School Survey on Crime and Safety (SSOCS) was conducted by NCES in spring/summer of the 2009–10 school year. SSOCS focuses on incidents of specific crimes/offenses and a variety of specific discipline issues in public schools. It also covers characteristics of school policies, school violence prevention programs and policies, and school characteristics that have been associated with school crime. The survey was conducted with a nationally representative sample of regular public elementary, middle, and high schools in the 50 states and the District of Columbia. Special education, alternative, and vocational schools; schools in the other jurisdictions; and schools that taught only prekindergarten, kindergarten, or adult education were not included in the sample.

The sampling frame for the 2010 SSOCS was constructed from the 2007–08 Public Elementary/Secondary School Universe File of the Common Core of Data, an annual collection of data on all public K–12 schools and school districts. The sample was stratified by instructional level, type of locale (urbanicity), and enrollment size. The sample of schools in each instructional level was allocated to each of the 16 cells formed by the cross-classification of the four categories of enrollment size and four types of locale. The sample was allocated to each subgroup in proportion to the sum of the square roots of the total student enrollment in each school in that stratum. The effective sample size within each stratum was then inflated to account for nonresponse. Once the final sample sizes were determined for each of the 64 strata, the subgroups were sorted by region and racial/ethnic composition of enrollment, and an initial sample of 3,476 schools was selected. Of those schools, 2,648 completed the survey. In February 2010, questionnaires were mailed to school principals, who were asked to complete the survey or to have it completed by the person at the school most knowledgeable about discipline issues.

The next administration of SSOCS occurs in the spring of the 2015–16 school year.

Further information about SSOCS may be obtained from

Rachel Hansen
Sample Surveys Division
Cross-Sectional Surveys Branch
National Center for Education Statistics
Potomac Center Plaza
550 12th Street SW
Washington, DC 20202
rachel.hansen@ed.gov
http://nces.ed.gov/surveys/ssocs

Teacher Follow-up Survey

The Teacher Follow-up Survey (TFS) is a follow-up survey of selected elementary and secondary school teachers who participate in the NCES Schools and Staffing Survey (SASS). Its purpose is to determine how many teachers remain at the same school, move to another school, or leave the profession in the year following a SASS administration. It is administered to elementary and secondary teachers in the 50 states and the District of Columbia. The TFS uses two questionnaires, one for teachers who left teaching since the previous SASS administration and another for those who are still teaching either in the same school as last year or in a different school. The objective of the TFS is to focus on the characteristics of each group in order to answer questions about teacher mobility and attrition.

The 2008–09 TFS is different from any previous TFS administration in that it also serves as the second wave of a longitudinal study of first-year teachers. Because of this, the 2008–09 TFS consists of four questionnaires. Two are for respondents who were first-year public school teachers in the 2007–08 SASS and two are for the remainder of the sample.

The 2012–13 TFS sample was made up of teachers who had taken the 2011–12 SASS survey. The 2012–13 TFS sample contained about 5,800 public school teachers and 1,200 private school teachers. The weighted overall response rate using the initial basic weight for private school teachers was notably low (39.7 percent), resulting in a decision to exclude private school teachers from the 2012–13 TFS data files. The weighted overall response rate for public school teachers was 49.9 percent (50.3 percent for current and 45.6 percent for former teachers). Further information about the 2012–13 TFS, including the analysis of unit nonresponse bias, is available in the First Look report *Teacher Attrition and Mobility: Results From the 2012–13 Teacher Follow-up Survey* (NCES 2014-077).

Further information on the TFS may be obtained from

Isaiah O'Rear
Sample Surveys Division
Cross-Sectional Surveys Branch
National Center for Education Statistics
Potomac Center Plaza
550 12th Street SW
Washington, DC 20202
isaiah.orear@ed.gov
http://nces.ed.gov/surveys/sass/

Other Department of Education Agencies

Office for Civil Rights

Civil Rights Data Collection

The U.S. Department of Education's Office for Civil Rights (OCR) has surveyed the nation's public elementary and secondary schools since 1968. The survey was first known as the OCR Elementary and Secondary School (E&S) Survey; in 2004, it was renamed the Civil Rights Data Collection (CRDC). The survey provides information about the enrollment of students in public schools in every state and about some education services provided to those students. These data are reported by race/ethnicity, sex, and disability.

Data in the survey are collected pursuant to 34 C.F.R. Section 100.6(b) of the Department of Education regulation implementing Title VI of the Civil Rights Act of 1964. The requirements are also incorporated by reference in Department regulations implementing Title IX of the Education Amendments of 1972, Section 504 of the Rehabilitation Act of 1973, and the Age Discrimination Act of 1975. School, district, state, and national data are currently available. Data from individual public schools and districts are used to generate projected national and state data.

The CRDC has generally been conducted biennially in each of the 50 states plus the District of Columbia. The 2009–10 CRDC was collected from a sample of approximately 7,000 school districts and over 72,000 schools in those districts. It was made up of two parts: part 1 contained beginning-of-year "snapshot" data and part 2 contained cumulative, or end-of-year, data.

The 2011–12 CRDC survey, which collected data from approximately 16,500 school districts and 97,000 schools, was the first CRDC survey since 2000 that included data from every public school district and school in the nation. Data from the 2011–12 CRDC are currently available. The 2013–14 CRDC survey also collected information from a universe of every public school district and school in the nation.

Further information on the Civil Rights Data Collection may be obtained from

Office for Civil Rights
U.S. Department of Education
400 Maryland Avenue SW
Washington, DC 20202
OCR@ed.gov
http://www.ed.gov/about/offices/list/ocr/data.html

Office of Special Education Programs

Annual Report to Congress on the Implementation of the Individuals with Disabilities Education Act

The Individuals with Disabilities Education Act (IDEA) is a law ensuring services to children with disabilities throughout the nation. IDEA governs how states and public agencies provide early intervention, special education, and related services to more than 6.5 million eligible infants, toddlers, children, and youth with disabilities.

IDEA, formerly the Education of the Handicapped Act (EHA), requires the Secretary of Education to transmit to Congress annually a report describing the progress made in serving the nation's children with disabilities. This annual report contains information on children served by public schools under the provisions of Part B of IDEA and on children served in state-operated programs for persons with disabilities under Chapter I of the Elementary and Secondary Education Act.

Statistics on children receiving special education and related services in various settings and school personnel providing such services are reported in an annual submission of data to the Office of Special Education Programs (OSEP) by the 50 states, the District of Columbia, the Bureau of Indian Education schools, Puerto Rico, American Samoa, Guam, the Northern Mariana Islands, the U.S. Virgin Islands, the Federated States of Micronesia, Palau, and the Marshall Islands. The child count information is based on the number of children with disabilities receiving special education and related services on December 1 of each year. Count information is available from http://www.ideadata.org.

Since all participants in programs for persons with disabilities are reported to OSEP, the data are not subject to sampling error. However, nonsampling error can arise from a variety of sources. Some states only produce counts of students receiving special education services by disability category because Part B of the EHA requires it. In those states that typically produce counts of students receiving special education services by disability category without regard to EHA requirements, definitions and labeling practices vary.

Further information on this annual report to Congress may be obtained from

Office of Special Education Programs
Office of Special Education and Rehabilitative Services
U.S. Department of Education
400 Maryland Avenue SW
Washington, DC 20202-7100
http://www.ed.gov/about/reports/annual/osep/index.html
http://idea.ed.gov/
http://www.ideadata.org

Other Governmental Agencies and Programs

Bureau of Justice Statistics

National Crime Victimization Survey (NCVS)

The National Crime Victimization Survey (NCVS), administered for the U.S. Bureau of Justice Statistics (BJS) by the U.S. Census Bureau, is the nation's primary source of information on crime and the victims of crime. Initiated in 1972 and redesigned in 1992, the NCVS collects detailed information on the frequency and nature of the crimes of rape, sexual assault, robbery, aggravated and simple assault, theft, household burglary, and motor vehicle theft experienced by Americans and American households each year. The survey measures both crimes reported to police and crimes not reported to the police.

NCVS estimates presented may differ from those in previous published reports. This is because a small number of victimizations, referred to as series victimizations, are included using a new counting strategy. High-frequency repeat victimizations, or series victimizations, are six or more similar but separate victimizations that occur with such frequency that the victim is unable to recall each individual event or describe each event in detail. As part of ongoing research efforts associated with the redesign of the NCVS, BJS investigated ways to include high-frequency repeat victimizations, or series victimizations, in estimates of criminal victimization. Including series victimizations results in more accurate estimates of victimization. BJS has decided to include series victimizations using the victim's estimates of the number of times the victimizations occurred over the past 6 months, capping the number of victimizations within each series at a maximum of 10. This strategy for counting series victimizations balances the desire to estimate national rates and account for the experiences of persons who have been subjected to repeat victimizations against the desire to minimize the estimation errors that can occur when repeat victimizations are reported. Including series victimizations in national rates results in rather large increases in the level of violent victimization; however, trends in violence are generally similar regardless of whether series victimizations are included. For more information on the new counting strategy and supporting research, see *Methods for Counting High-Frequency Repeat*

Victimizations in the National Crime Victimization Survey at http://bjs.ojp.usdoj.gov/content/pub/pdf/mchfrv.pdf.

Readers should note that in 2003, in accordance with changes to the Office of Management and Budget's standards for the classification of federal data on race and ethnicity, the NCVS item on race/ethnicity was modified. A question on Hispanic origin is now followed by a new question on race. The new question about race allows the respondent to choose more than one race and delineates Asian as a separate category from Native Hawaiian or Other Pacific Islander. An analysis conducted by the Demographic Surveys Division at the U.S. Census Bureau showed that the new race question had very little impact on the aggregate racial distribution of the NCVS respondents, with one exception: There was a 1.6 percentage point decrease in the percentage of respondents who reported themselves as White. Due to changes in race/ethnicity categories, comparisons of race/ethnicity across years should be made with caution.

There were changes in the sample design and survey methodology in the 2006 NCVS that may have affected survey estimates. Caution should be used when comparing the 2006 estimates to estimates of other years. Data from 2007 onward are comparable to earlier years. Analyses of the 2007 estimates indicate that the program changes made in 2006 had relatively small effects on NCVS estimates. For more information on the 2006 NCVS data, see *Criminal Victimization, 2006,* at http://bjs.ojp.usdoj.gov/content/pub/pdf/cv06.pdf, the technical notes at http://bjs.ojp.usdoj.gov/content/pub/pdf/cv06tn.pdf, and *Criminal Victimization, 2007,* at http://bjs.ojp.usdoj.gov/content/pub/pdf/cv07.pdf.

The number of NCVS-eligible households in the sample in 2013 was about 107,000. Households were selected using a stratified, multistage cluster design. In the first stage, the primary sampling units (PSUs), consisting of counties or groups of counties, were selected. In the second stage, smaller areas, called Enumeration Districts (EDs), were selected from each sampled PSU. Finally, from selected EDs, clusters of four households, called segments, were selected for interview. At each stage, the selection was done proportionate to population size in order to create a self-weighting sample. The final sample was augmented to account for households constructed after the decennial Census. Within each sampled household, the U.S. Census Bureau interviewer attempts to interview all household members age 12 and older to determine whether they had been victimized by the measured crimes during the 6 months preceding the interview.

The first NCVS interview with a housing unit is conducted in person. Subsequent interviews are conducted by telephone, if possible. About 80,000 persons age 12 and older are interviewed each 6 months. Households remain in the sample for 3 years and are interviewed seven times at 6-month intervals. Since the survey's inception, the initial interview at each sample unit has been used only to bound future interviews to establish a time frame to avoid duplication of crimes uncovered in these subsequent interviews. Beginning in 2006, data from the initial interview have been adjusted to account for the effects of bounding and have been included in the survey estimates. After a household has been interviewed its seventh time, it is replaced by a new sample household. In 2013, the household response rate was about 84 percent and the completion rate for persons within households was about 88 percent. Weights were developed to permit estimates for the total U.S. population 12 years and older.

Further information on the NCVS may be obtained from

Rachel E. Morgan
Victimization Statistics Branch
Bureau of Justice Statistics
rachel.morgan@usdoj.gov
http://www.bjs.gov/

Bureau of Labor Statistics

Consumer Price Indexes

The Consumer Price Index (CPI) represents changes in prices of all goods and services purchased for consumption by urban households. Indexes are available for two population groups: a CPI for All Urban Consumers (CPI-U) and a CPI for Urban Wage Earners and Clerical Workers (CPI-W). Unless otherwise specified, data are adjusted for inflation using the CPI-U. These values are frequently adjusted to a school-year basis by averaging the July through June figures. Price indexes are available for the United States, the four Census regions, size of city, cross-classifications of regions and size classes, and 26 local areas. The major uses of the CPI include as an economic indicator, as a deflator of other economic series, and as a means of adjusting income.

Also available is the Consumer Price Index research series using current methods (CPI-U-RS), which presents an estimate of the CPI-U from 1978 to the present that incorporates most of the improvements that the Bureau of Labor Statistics has made over that time span into the entire series. The historical price index series of the CPI-U does not reflect these changes, though these changes do make the present and future CPI more accurate. The limitations of the CPI-U-RS include considerable uncertainty surrounding the magnitude of the adjustments and the several improvements in the CPI that have not been incorporated into the CPI-U-RS for various reasons. Nonetheless, the CPI-U-RS can serve as a valuable proxy for researchers needing a historical estimate of inflation using current methods.

Further information on consumer price indexes may be obtained from

Bureau of Labor Statistics
U.S. Department of Labor
2 Massachusetts Avenue NE
Washington, DC 20212
http://www.bls.gov/cpi

Employment and Unemployment Surveys

Statistics on the employment and unemployment status of the population and related data are compiled by the Bureau of Labor Statistics (BLS) using data from the Current Population Survey (CPS) (see below) and other surveys. The CPS, a monthly household survey conducted by the U.S. Census Bureau for the Bureau of Labor Statistics, provides a comprehensive body of information on the employment and unemployment experience of the nation's population, classified by age, sex, race, and various other characteristics.

Further information on unemployment surveys may be obtained from

Bureau of Labor Statistics
U.S. Department of Labor
2 Massachusetts Avenue NE
Washington, DC 20212
cpsinfo@bls.gov
http://www.bls.gov/bls/employment.htm

Census Bureau

American Community Survey

The Census Bureau introduced the American Community Survey (ACS) in 1996. Fully implemented in 2005, it provides a large monthly sample of demographic, socioeconomic, and housing data comparable in content to the Long Forms of the Decennial Census up to and including the 2000 long form. Aggregated over time, these data will serve as a replacement for the Long Form of the Decennial Census. The survey includes questions mandated by federal law, federal regulations, and court decisions.

Since 2011, the survey has been mailed to approximately 295,000 addresses in the United States and Puerto Rico each month, or about 3.5 million addresses annually. A larger proportion of addresses in small governmental units (e.g., American Indian reservations, small counties, and towns) also receive the survey. The monthly sample size is designed to approximate the ratio used in the 2000 Census, which requires more intensive distribution in these areas. The ACS covers the U.S. resident population, which includes the entire civilian, noninstitutionalized population; incarcerated persons; institutionalized persons; and the active duty military who are in the United States. In 2006, the ACS began interviewing residents in group quarter facilities. Institutionalized group quarters include adult and juvenile correctional facilities, nursing facilities, and other health care facilities.

Noninstitutionalized group quarters include college and university housing, military barracks, and other noninstitutional facilities such as workers and religious group quarters and temporary shelters for the homeless.

National-level data from the ACS are available from 2000 onward. The ACS produces 1-year estimates for jurisdictions with populations of 65,000 and over and 5-year estimates for jurisdictions with smaller populations. The 2014 1-year estimates used data collected between January 1, 2014, and December 31, 2014, and the 2010–2014 5-year estimates used data collected between January 1, 2010, and December 31, 2014. The ACS produced 3-year estimates (for jurisdictions with populations of 20,000 or over) for the periods 2005–2007, 2006–2008, 2007–2009, 2008–2010, 2009–2011, 2010–2012, and 2011–2013. Three-year estimates for these periods will continue to be available to data users, but no further 3-year estimates will be produced.

Further information about the ACS is available at http://www.census.gov/acs/www/.

Current Population Survey

The Current Population Survey (CPS) is a monthly survey of about 60,000 households conducted by the U.S. Census Bureau for the Bureau of Labor Statistics. The CPS is the primary source of information of labor force statistics for the U.S. noninstitutionalized population (e.g., excludes military personnel and their families living on bases and inmates of correctional institutions). In addition, supplemental questionnaires are used to provide further information about the U.S. population. Specifically, in October, detailed questions regarding school enrollment and school characteristics are asked. In March, detailed questions regarding income are asked.

The current sample design, introduced in July 2001, includes about 72,000 households. Each month about 58,900 of the 72,000 households are eligible for interview, and of those, 7 to 10 percent are not interviewed because of temporary absence or unavailability. Information is obtained each month from those in the household who are 15 years of age and older, and demographic data are collected for children 0–14 years of age. In addition, supplemental questions regarding school enrollment are asked about eligible household members ages 3 and older in the October survey. Prior to July 2001, data were collected in the CPS from about 50,000 dwelling units. The samples are initially selected based on the decennial census files and are periodically updated to reflect new housing construction.

A major redesign of the CPS was implemented in January 1994 to improve the quality of the data collected. Survey questions were revised, new questions were added, and computer-assisted interviewing methods were used for the survey data collection. Further information about the redesign is available in *Current Population Survey,*

October 1995: (School Enrollment Supplement) Technical Documentation at http://www.census.gov/prod/techdoc/cps/cpsoct95.pdf.

Caution should be used when comparing data from 1994 through 2001 with data from 1993 and earlier. Data from 1994 through 2001 reflect 1990 census-based population controls, while data from 1993 and earlier reflect 1980 or earlier census-based population controls. Changes in population controls generally have relatively little impact on summary measures such as means, medians, and percentage distributions. They can have a significant impact on population counts. For example, use of the 1990 census-based population control resulted in about a 1 percent increase in the civilian noninstitutional population and in the number of families and households. Thus, estimates of levels for data collected in 1994 and later years will differ from those for earlier years by more than what could be attributed to actual changes in the population. These differences could be disproportionately greater for certain subpopulation groups than for the total population.

Beginning in 2003, race/ethnicity questions expanded to include information on people of two or more races. Native Hawaiian/Pacific Islander data are collected separately from Asian data. The questions have also been worded to make it clear that self-reported data on race/ethnicity should reflect the race/ethnicity with which the responder identifies, rather than what may be written in official documentation.

The estimation procedure employed for monthly CPS data involves inflating weighted sample results to independent estimates of characteristics of the civilian noninstitutional population in the United States by age, sex, and race. These independent estimates are based on statistics from decennial censuses; statistics on births, deaths, immigration, and emigration; and statistics on the population in the armed services. Generalized standard error tables are provided in the Current Population Reports; methods for deriving standard errors can be found within the CPS technical documentation at http://www.census.gov/programs-surveys/cps/technical-documentation/complete.html. The CPS data are subject to both nonsampling and sampling errors.

Prior to 2009, standard errors were estimated using the generalized variance function. The generalized variance function is a simple model that expressed the variance as a function of the expected value of a survey estimate. Beginning with March 2009 CPS data, standard errors were estimated using replicate weight methodology. Those interested in using CPS household-level supplement replicate weights to calculate variances may refer to *Estimating Current Population Survey (CPS) Household-Level Supplement Variances Using Replicate Weights* at http://thedataweb.rm.census.gov/pub/cps/supps/HH-level_Use_of_the_Public_Use_Replicate_Weight_File.doc.

Further information on the CPS may be obtained from

Education and Social Stratification Branch
Population Division
Census Bureau
U.S. Department of Commerce
4600 Silver Hill Road
Washington, DC 20233
http://www.census.gov/cps

Dropouts

Each October, the Current Population Survey (CPS) includes supplemental questions on the enrollment status of the population ages 3 years and over as part of the monthly basic survey on labor force participation. In addition to gathering the information on school enrollment, with the limitations on accuracy as noted below under "School Enrollment," the survey data permit calculations of dropout rates. Both status and event dropout rates are tabulated from the October CPS. Event rates describe the proportion of students who leave school each year without completing a high school program. Status rates provide cumulative data on dropouts among all young adults within a specified age range. Status rates are higher than event rates because they include all dropouts ages 16 through 24, regardless of when they last attended school.

In addition to other survey limitations, dropout rates may be affected by survey coverage and exclusion of the institutionalized population. The incarcerated population has grown more rapidly and has a higher dropout rate than the general population. Dropout rates for the total population might be higher than those for the noninstitutionalized population if the prison and jail populations were included in the dropout rate calculations. On the other hand, if military personnel, who tend to be high school graduates, were included, it might offset some or all of the impact from the theoretical inclusion of the jail and prison populations.

Another area of concern with tabulations involving young people in household surveys is the relatively low coverage ratio compared to older age groups. CPS undercoverage results from missed housing units and missed people within sample households. Overall CPS undercoverage for October 2014 is estimated to be about 12 percent. CPS coverage varies with age, sex, and race. Generally, coverage is larger for females than for males and larger for non-Blacks than for Blacks. This differential coverage is a general problem for most household-based surveys. Further information on CPS methodology may be found in the technical documentation at http://www.census.gov/cps.

Further information on the calculation of dropouts and dropout rates may be obtained from *Trends in High School Dropout and Completion Rates in the United States: 1972–2012* (NCES 2015-015) at http://nces.ed.gov/pubs2015/2015015.pdf or by contacting

Joel McFarland
Annual Reports and Information Staff
National Center for Education Statistics
Potomac Center Plaza
550 12th Street SW
Washington, DC 20202
joel.mcfarland@ed.gov

Educational Attainment

Reports documenting educational attainment are produced by the Census Bureau using March CPS supplement (Annual Social and Economic Supplement [ASEC]) results. The sample size for the 2014 ASEC supplement (including basic CPS) was about 98,000 addresses; the tables may be downloaded at http://www.census.gov/hhes/socdemo/education/data/cps/2014/tables.html. The sample size for the 2015 ASEC supplement (including basic CPS) was about 100,000 addresses. The results were released in Educational Attainment in the United States: 2015; the tables may be downloaded at http://www.census.gov/hhes/socdemo/education/data/cps/2015/tables.html.

In addition to the general constraints of CPS, some data indicate that the respondents have a tendency to overestimate the educational level of members of their household. Some inaccuracy is due to a lack of the respondent's knowledge of the exact educational attainment of each household member and the hesitancy to acknowledge anything less than a high school education. Another cause of nonsampling variability is the change in the numbers in the armed services over the years.

Further information on educational attainment data from CPS may be obtained from

Education and Social Stratification Branch
Census Bureau
U.S. Department of Commerce
4600 Silver Hill Road
Washington, DC 20233
http://www.census.gov/hhes/socdemo/education

School Enrollment

Each October, the Current Population Survey (CPS) includes supplemental questions on the enrollment status of the population ages 3 years and over. Prior to 2001, the October supplement consisted of approximately 47,000 interviewed households. Beginning with the October 2001 supplement, the sample was expanded by 9,000 to a total of approximately 56,000 interviewed households. The main sources of nonsampling variability in the responses to the supplement are those inherent in the survey instrument. The question of current enrollment may not be answered accurately for various reasons. Some respondents may not know current grade information for every student in the household, a problem especially prevalent for households with members in college or in nursery school. Confusion over college credits or hours taken by a student may make it difficult to determine the year in which the student is enrolled. Problems may occur with the definition of nursery school (a group or class organized to provide educational experiences for children) where respondents' interpretations of "educational experiences" vary.

For the October 2014 basic CPS, the household-level nonresponse rate was 10.56 percent. The person-level nonresponse rate for the school enrollment supplement was an additional 7.8 percent. Since the basic CPS nonresponse rate is a household-level rate and the school enrollment supplement nonresponse rate is a person-level rate, these rates cannot be combined to derive an overall nonresponse rate. Nonresponding households may have fewer persons than interviewed ones, so combining these rates may lead to an overestimate of the true overall nonresponse rate for persons for the school enrollment supplement.

Further information on CPS methodology may be obtained from http://www.census.gov/cps.

Further information on the CPS School Enrollment Supplement may be obtained from

Education and Social Stratification Branch
Census Bureau
U.S. Department of Commerce
4600 Silver Hill Road
Washington, DC 20233
http://www.census.gov/hhes/school/index.html

Decennial Census, Population Estimates, and Population Projections

The decennial census is a universe survey mandated by the U.S. Constitution. It is a questionnaire sent to every household in the country, and it is composed of seven questions about the household and its members (name, sex, age, relationship, Hispanic origin, race, and whether the housing unit is owned or rented). The Census Bureau also produces annual estimates of the resident population by demographic characteristics (age, sex, race, and Hispanic origin) for the nation, states, and counties, as well as national and state projections for the resident population. The reference date for population estimates is July 1 of the given year. With each new issue of July 1 estimates, the Census Bureau revises estimates for each year back to the last census. Previously published estimates are superseded and archived.

Census respondents self-report race and ethnicity. The race questions on the 1990 and 2000 censuses differed in some significant ways. In 1990, the respondent was instructed to select the one race "that the respondent considers himself/herself to be," whereas in 2000, the

respondent could select one or more races that the person considered himself or herself to be. American Indian, Eskimo, and Aleut were three separate race categories in 1990; in 2000, the American Indian and Alaska Native categories were combined, with an option to write in a tribal affiliation. This write-in option was provided only for the American Indian category in 1990. There was a combined Asian and Pacific Islander race category in 1990, but the groups were separated into two categories in 2000.

The census question on ethnicity asks whether the respondent is of Hispanic origin, regardless of the race option(s) selected; thus, persons of Hispanic origin may be of any race. In the 2000 census, respondents were first asked, "Is this person Spanish/Hispanic/Latino?" and then given the following options: No, not Spanish/Hispanic/Latino; Yes, Puerto Rican; Yes, Mexican, Mexican American, Chicano; Yes, Cuban; and Yes, other Spanish/Hispanic/Latino (with space to print the specific group). In the 2010 census, respondents were asked "Is this person of Hispanic, Latino, or Spanish origin?" The options given were No, not of Hispanic, Latino, or Spanish origin; Yes, Mexican, Mexican Am., Chicano; Yes, Puerto Rican; Yes, Cuban; and Yes, another Hispanic, Latino, or Spanish origin—along with instructions to print "Argentinean, Colombian, Dominican, Nicaraguan, Salvadoran, Spaniard, and so on" in a specific box.

The 2000 and 2010 censuses each asked the respondent "What is this person's race?" and allowed the respondent to select one or more options. The options provided were largely the same in both the 2000 and 2010 censuses: White; Black, African American, or Negro; American Indian or Alaska Native (with space to print the name of enrolled or principal tribe); Asian Indian; Japanese; Native Hawaiian; Chinese; Korean; Guamanian or Chamorro; Filipino; Vietnamese; Samoan; Other Asian; Other Pacific Islander; and Some other race. The last three options included space to print the specific race. Two significant differences between the 2000 and 2010 census questions on race were that no race examples were provided for the "Other Asian" and "Other Pacific Islander" responses in 2000, whereas the race examples of "Hmong, Laotian, Thai, Pakistani, Cambodian, and so on" and "Fijian, Tongan, and so on," were provided for the "Other Asian" and "Other Pacific Islander" responses, respectively, in 2010.

The census population estimates program modified the enumerated population from the 2010 census to produce the population estimates base for 2010 and onward. As part of the modification, the Census Bureau recoded the "Some other race" responses from the 2010 census to one or more of the five OMB race categories used in the estimates program (for more information, see http://www.census.gov/popest/methodology/2012-nat-st-co-meth.pdf).

Further information on the decennial census may be obtained from http://www.census.gov.

National Institute on Drug Abuse

Monitoring the Future Survey

The National Institute on Drug Abuse of the U.S. Department of Health and Human Services is the primary supporter of the long-term study entitled "Monitoring the Future: A Continuing Study of American Youth," conducted by the University of Michigan Institute for Social Research. One component of the study deals with student drug abuse. Results of the national sample survey have been published annually since 1975. With the exception of 1975, when about 9,400 students participated in the survey, the annual samples comprise roughly 16,000 students in 150 public and private schools. Students complete self-administered questionnaires given to them in their classrooms by University of Michigan personnel. Each year, 8th-, 10th-, and 12th-graders are surveyed (12th-graders since 1975, and 8th- and 10th-graders since 1991). The 8th- and 10th-grade surveys are anonymous, while the 12th-grade survey is confidential. The 10th-grade samples involve about 17,000 students in 140 schools each year, while the 8th-grade samples have approximately 18,000 students in about 150 schools. In all, approximately 50,000 students from about 420 public and private secondary schools are surveyed annually. Approximately 88.4 percent of 8th-grade students, 87.2 percent of 10th-grade students, and 84.7 percent of 12th-grade students surveyed participated in the study in 2010. Beginning with the class of 1976, a randomly selected sample from each senior class has been followed in the years after high school on a continuing basis.

Understandably, there is some reluctance to admit illegal activities. Also, students who are out of school on the day of the survey are nonrespondents, and the survey does not include high school dropouts. The inclusion of absentees and dropouts would tend to increase the proportion of individuals who had used drugs. A 1983 study found that the inclusion of absentees could increase some of the drug usage estimates by as much as 2.7 percentage points. (Details on that study and its methodology were published in *Drug Use Among American High School Students, College Students, and Other Young Adults,* by L.D. Johnston, P.M. O'Malley, and J.G. Bachman, available from the National Clearinghouse on Drug Abuse Information, 5600 Fishers Lane, Rockville, MD 20857.)

Further information on the Monitoring the Future drug abuse survey may be obtained from

National Institute on Drug Abuse
Division of Epidemiology, Services and
  Prevention Research (DESPR)
6001 Executive Boulevard
Bethesda, MD 20892
mtfinformation@umich.edu
http://www.monitoringthefuture.org

Other Organization Sources

International Association for the Evaluation of Educational Achievement

The International Association for the Evaluation of Educational Achievement (IEA) is composed of governmental research centers and national research institutions around the world whose aim is to investigate education problems common among countries. Since its inception in 1958, the IEA has conducted more than 30 research studies of cross-national achievement. The regular cycle of studies encompasses learning in basic school subjects. Examples are the Trends in International Mathematics and Science Study (TIMSS) and the Progress in International Reading Literacy Study (PIRLS). IEA projects also include studies of particular interest to IEA members, such as the TIMSS 1999 Video Study of Mathematics and Science Teaching, the Civic Education Study, and studies on information technology in education.

The international bodies that coordinate international assessments vary in the labels they apply to participating education systems, most of which are countries. IEA differentiates between IEA members, which IEA refers to as "countries" in all cases, and "benchmarking participants." IEA members include countries such as the United States and Ireland, as well as subnational entities such as England and Scotland (which are both part of the United Kingdom), the Flemish community of Belgium, and Hong Kong (a Special Administrative Region of China). IEA benchmarking participants are all subnational entities and include Canadian provinces, U.S. states, and Dubai in the United Arab Emirates (among others). Benchmarking participants, like the participating countries, are given the opportunity to assess the comparative international standing of their students' achievement and to view their curriculum and instruction in an international context.

Some IEA studies, such as TIMSS and PIRLS, include an assessment portion as well as contextual questionnaires to collect information about students' home and school experiences. The TIMSS and PIRLS scales, including the scale averages and standard deviations, are designed to remain constant from assessment to assessment so that education systems (including countries and subnational education systems) can compare their scores over time, as well as compare their scores directly with the scores of other education systems. Although each scale was created to have a mean of 500 and a standard deviation of 100, the subject matter and the level of difficulty of items necessarily differ by grade, subject, and domain/dimension. Therefore, direct comparisons between scores across grades, subjects, and different domain/dimension types should not be made.

Further information on the International Association for the Evaluation of Educational Achievement may be obtained from http://www.iea.nl.

Trends in International Mathematics and Science Study

The Trends in International Mathematics and Science Study (TIMSS, formerly known as the Third International Mathematics and Science Study) provides data on the mathematics and science achievement of U.S. 4th- and 8th-graders compared with that of their peers in other countries. TIMSS collects information through mathematics and science assessments and questionnaires. The questionnaires request information to help provide a context for student performance. They focus on such topics as students' attitudes and beliefs about learning mathematics and science, what students do as part of their mathematics and science lessons, students' completion of homework, and their lives both in and outside of school; teachers' perceptions of their preparedness for teaching mathematics and science, teaching assignments, class size and organization, instructional content and practices, collaboration with other teachers, and participation in professional development activities; and principals' viewpoints on policy and budget responsibilities, curriculum and instruction issues, and student behavior. The questionnaires also elicit information on the organization of schools and courses. The assessments and questionnaires are designed to specifications in a guiding framework. The TIMSS framework describes the mathematics and science content to be assessed and provides grade-specific objectives, an overview of the assessment design, and guidelines for item development.

TIMSS is on a 4-year cycle. Data collections occurred in 1995, 1999 (8th grade only), 2003, 2007, and 2011. TIMSS 2015 is the sixth administration of TIMSS since 1995. It consists of five assessments: 4th-grade mathematics; numeracy (a less difficult version of 4th-grade mathematics, newly developed for 2015); 8th-grade mathematics; 4th-grade science; and 8th-grade science. In addition to the 4th- and 8th-grade assessments, TIMSS 2015 includes the third administration of TIMSS Advanced since 1995. TIMSS Advanced assesses final-year (12th-grade) secondary students' achievement in advanced mathematics and physics. The study also collects policy-relevant information about students, curriculum emphasis, technology use, and teacher preparation and training.

Progress in International Reading Literacy Study

The Progress in International Reading Literacy Study (PIRLS) provides data on the reading literacy of U.S. 4th-graders compared with that of their peers in other countries. PIRLS is on a 5-year cycle; PIRLS data collections have been conducted in 2001, 2006, and 2011. In 2011, a total of 57 education systems, including 48 IEA members and 9 benchmarking participants, participated in the survey. The next PIRLS data collection is scheduled for 2016. PIRLS collects information through a reading literacy assessment and questionnaires that help to provide a context for student performance. Questionnaires are administered to collect information about students' home and school experiences in learning to read. A student questionnaire addresses students' attitudes towards reading and their reading habits. In addition, questionnaires are given to students' teachers and school principals to gather information about students' school experiences in developing reading literacy. In countries other than the United States, a parent questionnaire is also administered. The assessments and questionnaires are designed to specifications in a guiding framework. The PIRLS framework describes the reading content to be assessed and provides objectives specific to 4th grade, an overview of the assessment design, and guidelines for item development.

TIMSS and PIRLS Sampling and Response Rates

As is done in all participating countries and other education systems, representative samples of students in the United States are selected. The sample design that was employed by TIMSS and PIRLS in 2011 is generally referred to as a two-stage stratified cluster sample. In the first stage of sampling, individual schools were selected with a probability proportionate to size (PPS) approach, which means that the probability is proportional to the estimated number of students enrolled in the target grade. In the second stage of sampling, intact classrooms were selected within sampled schools.

TIMSS and PIRLS guidelines call for a minimum of 150 schools to be sampled, with a minimum of 4,000 students assessed. The basic sample design of one classroom per school was designed to yield a total sample of approximately 4,500 students per population.

About 23,000 students in almost 900 schools across the United States participated in the 2011 TIMSS, joining 600,000 other student participants around the world. Because PIRLS was also administered at grade 4 in spring 2011, TIMSS and PIRLS in the United States were administered in the same schools to the extent feasible. Students took either TIMSS or PIRLS on the day of the assessments. About 13,000 U.S. students participated in PIRLS in 2011, joining 300,000 other student participants around the world. Accommodations were not provided for students with disabilities or students who were unable to read or speak the language of the test. These students were excluded from the sample. The IEA requirement is that the overall exclusion rate, which is composed of exclusions of schools and students, should not exceed more than 5 percent of the national desired target population.

In order to minimize the potential for response biases, the IEA developed participation or response rate standards that apply to all participating education systems and govern whether or not an education system's data are included in the TIMSS or PIRLS international datasets and the way in which its statistics are presented in the international reports. These standards were set using composites of response rates at the school, classroom, and student and teacher levels. Response rates were calculated with and without the inclusion of substitute schools that were selected to replace schools refusing to participate. In TIMSS 2011 at grade 4 in the United States, the weighted school participation rate was 79 percent before the use of substitute schools and 84 percent after the use of replacement schools; the weighted student response rate was 95 percent. In TIMSS 2011 at grade 8 in the United States, the weighted school participation rate was 87 percent before the use of substitute schools and 87 percent after the use of replacement schools; the weighted student response rate was 94 percent. In the 2011 PIRLS administered in the United States, the weighted school participation rate was 80 percent before the use of substitute schools and 85 percent after the use of replacement schools; the weighted student response rate was 96 percent.

Further information on the TIMSS study may be obtained from

Stephen Provasnik
Assessments Division
International Assessment Branch
National Center for Education Statistics
Potomac Center Plaza
550 12th Street SW
Washington, DC 20202
(202) 245-6442
stephen.provasnik@ed.gov
http://nces.ed.gov/timss
http://www.iea.nl/timss_2011.html

Further information on the PIRLS study may be obtained from

Sheila Thompson
Assessments Division
International Assessment Branch
National Center for Education Statistics
Potomac Center Plaza
550 12th Street SW
Washington, DC 20202
(202) 245-8330
sheila.thompson@ed.gov
http://nces.ed.gov/surveys/pirls/
http://www.iea.nl/pirls_2011.html

Organization for Economic Cooperation and Development

The Organization for Economic Cooperation and Development (OECD) publishes analyses of national policies and survey data in education, training, and economics in OECD and partner countries. Newer studies include student survey data on financial literacy and on digital literacy.

Education at a Glance

To highlight current education issues and create a set of comparative education indicators that represent key features of education systems, OECD initiated the Indicators of Education Systems (INES) project and charged the Centre for Educational Research and Innovation (CERI) with developing the cross-national indicators for it. The development of these indicators involved representatives of the OECD countries and the OECD Secretariat. Improvements in data quality and comparability among OECD countries have resulted from the country-to-country interaction sponsored through the INES project. The most recent publication in this series is *Education at a Glance 2015: OECD Indicators*.

Education at a Glance 2015 features data on the 34 OECD countries (Australia, Austria, Belgium, Canada, Chile, the Czech Republic, Denmark, Estonia, Finland, France, Germany, Greece, Hungary, Iceland, Ireland, Israel, Italy, Japan, the Republic of Korea, Luxembourg, Mexico, the Netherlands, New Zealand, Norway, Poland, Portugal, the Slovak Republic, Slovenia, Spain, Sweden, Switzerland, Turkey, the United Kingdom, and the United States) and a number of partner countries, namely, Argentina, Brazil, China, Colombia, Costa Rica, India, Indonesia, Latvia, Lithuania, the Russian Federation, Saudi Arabia, and South Africa.

The *OECD Handbook for Internationally Comparative Education Statistics: Concepts, Standards, Definitions, and Classifications* provides countries with specific guidance on how to prepare information for OECD education surveys; facilitates countries' understanding of OECD indicators and their use in policy analysis; and provides a reference for collecting and assimilating educational data. Chapter 7 of the *OECD Handbook for Internationally Comparative Education Statistics* contains a discussion of data quality issues. Users should examine footnotes carefully to recognize some of the data limitations.

Further information on international education statistics may be obtained from

Andreas Schleicher
Director for the Directorate of Education and Skills
  and Special Advisor on Education Policy
  to the OECD's Secretary General
OECD Directorate for Education and Skills
2, rue André Pascal
75775 Paris CEDEX 16
France
andreas.schleicher@oecd.org
http://www.oecd.org

Program for International Student Assessment

The Program for International Student Assessment (PISA) is a system of international assessments organized by the Organization for Economic Cooperation and Development (OECD), an intergovernmental organization of industrialized countries, that focuses on 15-year-olds' capabilities in reading literacy, mathematics literacy, and science literacy. PISA also includes measures of general, or cross-curricular, competencies such as learning strategies. PISA emphasizes functional skills that students have acquired as they near the end of compulsory schooling.

PISA is a 2-hour paper-and-pencil exam. Assessment items include a combination of multiple-choice questions and open-ended questions that require students to develop their own response. PISA scores are reported on a scale that ranges from 0 to 1,000, with the OECD mean set at 500 and a standard deviation set at 100. In 2012, mathematics, science, and reading literacy were assessed primarily through a paper-and-pencil exam, and problem-solving was administered using a computer-based exam. Education systems could also participate in optional pencil-and-paper financial literacy assessments and computer-based mathematics and reading assessments. In each education system, the assessment is translated into the primary language of instruction; in the United States, all materials are written in English.

To implement PISA, each of the participating education systems scientifically draws a nationally representative sample of 15-year-olds, regardless of grade level. In the United States, about 6,100 students from 161 public and private schools took the PISA 2012 assessment. In the U.S. state education systems, about 1,700 students

at 50 schools in Connecticut, about 1,900 students at 54 schools in Florida, and about 1,700 students at 49 schools in Massachusetts took the 2012 assessment. PISA 2012 was only administered at public schools in the U.S. state education systems.

The intent of PISA reporting is to provide an overall description of performance in reading literacy, mathematics literacy, and science literacy every 3 years, and to provide a more detailed look at each domain in the years when it is the major focus. These cycles will allow education systems to compare changes in trends for each of the three subject areas over time. In the first cycle, PISA 2000, reading literacy was the major focus, occupying roughly two-thirds of assessment time. For 2003, PISA focused on mathematics literacy as well as the ability of students to solve problems in real-life settings. In 2006, PISA focused on science literacy; in 2009, it focused on reading literacy again; and in 2012, it focused on mathematics literacy. PISA 2015 focuses on science, as it did in 2006.

In 2000, 43 education systems participated in PISA. In 2003, 41 education systems participated; in 2006, 57 education systems (30 OECD member countries and 27 nonmember countries or education systems) participated; and in 2009, 65 education systems (34 OECD member countries and 31 nonmember countries or education systems) participated. (An additional nine education systems administered PISA 2009 in 2010.) In PISA 2012, the most recent administration for which results are available, 65 education systems (34 OECD member countries and 31 nonmember countries or education systems), as well as the U.S. states of Connecticut, Florida, and Massachusetts, participated. PISA 2015 is assessing students' mathematics, reading, and science literacy in more than 70 countries and educational jurisdictions. The survey also includes a collaborative problem-solving assessment and an optional financial literacy assessment. U.S. 15-year-old students are participating in this optional assessment.

Further information on PISA may be obtained from

Holly Xie
Dana Kelly Springer
Assessments Division
International Assessment Branch
National Center for Education Statistics
Potomac Center Plaza
550 12th Street SW
Washington, DC 20202
holly.xie@ed.gov
dana.kelly@ed.gov
http://nces.ed.gov/surveys/pisa

Glossary

A

Achievement gap Occurs when one group of students outperforms another group, and the difference in average scores for the two groups is statistically significant (that is, larger than the margin of error).

Achievement levels, NAEP Specific achievement levels for each subject area and grade to provide a context for interpreting student performance. At this time they are being used on a trial basis.

> **Basic**—denotes partial mastery of the knowledge and skills that are fundamental for *proficient* work at a given grade.

> **Proficient**—represents solid academic performance. Students reaching this level have demonstrated competency over challenging subject matter.

> **Advanced**—signifies superior performance.

Associate's degree A degree granted for the successful completion of a sub-baccalaureate program of studies, usually requiring at least 2 years (or equivalent) of full-time college-level study. This includes degrees granted in a cooperative or work-study program.

Averaged freshman graduation rate (AFGR) A measure of the percentage of the incoming high school freshman class that graduates 4 years later. It is calculated by taking the number of graduates with a regular diploma and dividing that number by the estimated count of incoming freshman 4 years earlier, as reported through the NCES Common Core of Data (CCD). The estimated count of incoming freshman is the sum of the number of 8th-graders 5 years earlier, the number of 9th-graders 4 years earlier (when current seniors were freshman), and the number of 10th-graders 3 years earlier, divided by 3. The purpose of this averaging is to account for the high rate of grade retention in the freshman year, which adds 9th-grade repeaters from the previous year to the number of students in the incoming freshman class each year. Ungraded students are allocated to individual grades proportional to each state's enrollment in those grades. The AFGR treats students who transfer out of a school or district in the same way as it treats students from that school or district who drop out.

B

Bachelor's degree A degree granted for the successful completion of a baccalaureate program of studies, usually requiring at least 4 years (or equivalent) of full-time college-level study. This includes degrees granted in a cooperative or work-study program.

C

Capital outlay Funds for the acquisition of land and buildings; building construction, remodeling, and additions; the initial installation or extension of service systems and other built-in equipment; and site improvement. The category also encompasses architectural and engineering services including the development of blueprints.

Catholic school A private school over which a Roman Catholic church group exercises some control or provides some form of subsidy. Catholic schools for the most part include those operated or supported by a parish, a group of parishes, a diocese, or a Catholic religious order.

Certificate A formal award certifying the satisfactory completion of a postsecondary education program. Certificates can be awarded at any level of postsecondary education and include awards below the associate's degree level.

Charter school A school providing free public elementary and/or secondary education to eligible students under a specific charter granted by the state legislature or other appropriate authority, and designated by such authority to be a charter school.

Classification of Instructional Programs (CIP) The CIP is a taxonomic coding scheme that contains titles and descriptions of primarily postsecondary instructional programs. It was developed to facilitate NCES' collection and reporting of postsecondary degree completions by major field of study using standard classifications that capture the majority of reportable program activity. It was originally published in 1980 and was revised in 1985, 1990, 2000, and 2010.

College A postsecondary school that offers general or liberal arts education, usually leading to an associate's, bachelor's, master's, or doctor's degree. Junior colleges and community colleges are included under this terminology.

Combined school A school that encompasses instruction at both the elementary and the secondary levels; includes schools starting with grade 6 or below and ending with grade 9 or above.

Constant dollars Dollar amounts that have been adjusted by means of price and cost indexes to eliminate inflationary factors and allow direct comparison across years.

Consumer Price Index (CPI) This price index measures the average change in the cost of a fixed market basket of goods and services purchased by consumers. Indexes vary for specific areas or regions, periods of time, major groups of consumer expenditures, and population groups. The CPI reflects spending patterns for two population groups: (1) all urban consumers and urban wage earners and (2) clerical workers. CPIs are calculated for both the calendar year and the school year using the U.S. All Items CPI for All Urban Consumers (CPI-U). The calendar year CPI is the same as the annual CPI-U. The school year CPI is calculated by adding the monthly CPI-U figures, beginning with July of the first year and ending with June of the following year, and then dividing that figure by 12.

Control of institutions A classification of institutions of elementary/secondary or postsecondary education by whether the institution is operated by publicly elected or appointed officials and derives its primary support from public funds (public control) or is operated by privately elected or appointed officials and derives its major source of funds from private sources (private control).

Current expenditures (elementary/secondary) The expenditures for operating local public schools, excluding capital outlay and interest on school debt. These expenditures include such items as salaries for school personnel, benefits, student transportation, school books and materials, and energy costs. Beginning in 1980–81, expenditures for state administration are excluded.

    Instruction expenditures Includes expenditures for activities related to the interaction between teacher and students. Includes salaries and benefits for teachers and instructional aides, textbooks, supplies, and purchased services such as instruction via television, webinars, and other online instruction. Also included are tuition expenditures to other local education agencies.

    Administration expenditures Includes expenditures for school administration (i.e., the office of the principal, full-time department chairpersons, and graduation expenses), general administration (the superintendent and board of education and their immediate staff), and other support services expenditures.

    Transportation Includes expenditures for vehicle operation, monitoring, and vehicle servicing and maintenance.

    Food services Includes all expenditures associated with providing food to students and staff in a school or school district. The services include preparing and serving regular and incidental meals or snacks in connection with school activities, as well as the delivery of food to schools.

    Enterprise operations Includes expenditures for activities that are financed, at least in part, by user charges, similar to a private business. These include operations funded by sales of products or services, together with amounts for direct program support made by state education agencies for local school districts.

D

Default rate The percentage of loans that are in delinquency and have not been repaid according to the terms of the loan. According to the federal government,

a federal student loan is in default if there has been no payment on the loan in 270 days. The Department of Education calculates a *3-year cohort* default rate, which is the percentage of students who entered repayment in a given fiscal year (from October 1 to September 30) and then defaulted within the following 2 fiscal years. For example, the *3-year cohort* default rate for fiscal year (FY) 2009 is the percentage of borrowers who entered repayment during FY 2009 (any time from October 1, 2008, through September 30, 2009) and who defaulted by the end of FY 2011 (September 30, 2011).

Degree-granting institutions Postsecondary institutions that are eligible for Title IV federal financial aid programs and grant an associate's or higher degree. For an institution to be eligible to participate in Title IV financial aid programs it must offer a program of at least 300 clock hours in length, have accreditation recognized by the U.S. Department of Education, have been in business for at least 2 years, and have signed a participation agreement with the Department.

Disabilities, children with Those children evaluated as having any of the following impairments and who, by reason thereof, receive special education and related services under the Individuals with Disabilities Education Act (IDEA) according to an Individualized Education Program (IEP), Individualized Family Service Plan (IFSP), or a services plan. There are local variations in the determination of disability conditions, and not all states use all reporting categories.

    Autism Having a developmental disability significantly affecting verbal and nonverbal communication and social interaction, generally evident before age 3, that adversely affects educational performance. Other characteristics often associated with autism are engagement in repetitive activities and stereotyped movements, resistance to environmental change or change in daily routines, and unusual responses to sensory experiences. A child is not considered autistic if the child's educational performance is adversely affected primarily because of an emotional disturbance.

    Deaf-blindness Having concomitant hearing and visual impairments which cause such severe communication and other developmental and educational problems that the student cannot be accommodated in special education programs solely for deaf or blind students.

    Developmental delay Having developmental delays, as defined at the state level, and as measured by appropriate diagnostic instruments and procedures in one or more of the following cognitive areas: physical development, cognitive development, communication development, social or emotional development, or adaptive development. Applies only to 3- through 9-year-old children.

Emotional disturbance Exhibiting one or more of the following characteristics over a long period of time, to a marked degree, and adversely affecting educational performance: an inability to learn which cannot be explained by intellectual, sensory, or health factors; an inability to build or maintain satisfactory interpersonal relationships with peers and teachers; inappropriate types of behavior or feelings under normal circumstances; a general pervasive mood of unhappiness or depression; or a tendency to develop physical symptoms or fears associated with personal or school problems. This term does not include children who are socially maladjusted, unless they also display one or more of the listed characteristics.

Hearing impairment Having a hearing impairment, whether permanent or fluctuating, which adversely affects the student's educational performance. It also includes a hearing impairment which is so severe that the student is impaired in processing linguistic information through hearing (with or without amplification) and which adversely affects educational performance.

Intellectual disability Having significantly subaverage general intellectual functioning, existing concurrently with defects in adaptive behavior and manifested during the developmental period, which adversely affects the child's educational performance.

Multiple disabilities Having concomitant impairments (such as intellectually disabled-blind, intellectually disabled-orthopedically impaired, etc.), the combination of which causes such severe educational problems that the student cannot be accommodated in special education programs solely for one of the impairments. Term does not include deaf-blind students.

Orthopedic impairment Having a severe orthopedic impairment which adversely affects a student's educational performance. The term includes impairment resulting from congenital anomaly, disease, or other causes.

Other health impairment Having limited strength, vitality, or alertness due to chronic or acute health problems, such as a heart condition, tuberculosis, rheumatic fever, nephritis, asthma, sickle cell anemia, hemophilia, epilepsy, lead poisoning, leukemia, or diabetes which adversely affect the student's educational performance.

Specific learning disability Having a disorder in one or more of the basic psychological processes involved in understanding or in using spoken or written language, which may manifest itself in an imperfect ability to listen, think, speak, read, write, spell, or do mathematical calculations. The term includes such conditions as perceptual disabilities, brain injury, minimal brain dysfunction, dyslexia, and developmental aphasia. The term does not include children who have learning problems which are primarily the result of visual, hearing, motor, or intellectual disabilities, or of environmental, cultural, or economic disadvantage.

Speech or language impairment Having a communication disorder, such as stuttering, impaired articulation, language impairment, or voice impairment, which adversely affects the student's educational performance.

Traumatic brain injury Having an acquired injury to the brain caused by an external physical force, resulting in total or partial functional disability or psychosocial impairment or both, that adversely affects the student's educational performance. The term applies to open or closed head injuries resulting in impairments in one or more areas, such as cognition; language; memory; attention; reasoning; abstract thinking; judgment; problem-solving; sensory, perceptual, and motor abilities; psychosocial behavior; physical functions; information processing; and speech. The term does not apply to brain injuries that are congenital or degenerative or to brain injuries induced by birth trauma.

Visual impairment Having a visual impairment which, even with correction, adversely affects the student's educational performance. The term includes partially seeing and blind children.

Distance education Education that uses one or more technologies to deliver instruction to students who are separated from the instructor and to support regular and substantive interaction between the students and the instructor synchronously or asynchronously. Technologies used for instruction may include the following: Internet; one-way and two-way transmissions through open broadcasts, closed circuit, cable, microwave, broadband lines, fiber optics, and satellite or wireless communication devices; audio conferencing; and DVDs and CD-ROMs, if used in a course in conjunction with the technologies listed above.

Doctor's degree The highest award a student can earn for graduate study. Includes such degrees as the Doctor of Education (Ed.D.); the Doctor of Juridical Science (S.J.D.); the Doctor of Public Health (Dr.P.H.); and the Doctor of Philosophy (Ph.D.) in any field, such as agronomy, food technology, education, engineering, public administration, ophthalmology, or radiology. The doctor's degree classification encompasses three main subcategories—research/scholarship degrees, professional practice degrees, and other degrees—which are described below.

Doctor's degree—research/scholarship A Ph.D. or other doctor's degree that requires advanced work beyond the master's level, including the preparation and defense of a dissertation based on original research, or the planning and execution of an original project demonstrating substantial artistic or scholarly achievement. Examples of this type of degree may include the following and others, as designated by the awarding institution: the Ed.D. (in education), D.M.A. (in musical arts), D.B.A. (in business administration), D.Sc. (in science), D.A. (in arts), or D.M (in medicine).

Doctor's degree—professional practice A doctor's degree that is conferred upon completion of a program providing the knowledge and skills for the recognition, credential, or license required for professional practice. The degree is awarded after a period of study such that the total time to the degree, including both preprofessional and professional preparation, equals at least 6 full-time-equivalent academic years. Some doctor's degrees of this type were formerly classified as first-professional degrees. Examples of this type of degree may include the following and others, as designated by the awarding institution: the D.C. or D.C.M. (in chiropractic); D.D.S. or D.M.D. (in dentistry); L.L.B. or J.D. (in law); M.D. (in medicine); O.D. (in optometry); D.O. (in osteopathic medicine); Pharm.D. (in pharmacy); D.P.M., Pod.D., or D.P. (in podiatry); or D.V.M. (in veterinary medicine).

Doctor's degree—other A doctor's degree that does not meet the definition of either a doctor's degree—research/scholarship or a doctor's degree—professional practice.

E

Educational attainment The highest grade of regular school attended and completed.

Educational attainment (Current Population Survey) This measure uses March CPS data to estimate the percentage of civilian, noninstitutionalized people who have achieved certain levels of educational attainment. Estimates of educational attainment do not differentiate between those who graduated from public schools, those who graduated from private schools, and those who earned a GED; these estimates also include individuals who earned their credential or completed their highest level of education outside of the United States.

1972–1991 During this period, an individual's educational attainment was considered to be his or her last fully completed year of school. Individuals who completed 12 years of schooling were deemed to be high school graduates, as were those who began but did not complete the first year of college. Respondents who completed 16 or more years of schooling were counted as college graduates.

1992–present Beginning in 1992, CPS asked respondents to report their highest level of school

completed or their highest degree received. This change means that some data collected before 1992 are not strictly comparable with data collected from 1992 onward and that care must be taken when making comparisons across years. The revised survey question emphasizes credentials received rather than the last grade level attended or completed. The new categories include the following:

- High school graduate, high school diploma, or the equivalent (e.g., GED)
- Some college but no degree
- Associate's degree in college, occupational/vocational program
- Associate's degree in college, academic program (e.g., A.A., A.S., A.A.S.)
- Bachelor's degree (e.g., B.A., A.B., B.S.)
- Master's degree (e.g., M.A., M.S., M.Eng., M.Ed., M.S.W., M.B.A.)
- Professional school degree (e.g., M.D., D.D.S., D.V.M., LL.B., J.D.)
- Doctor's degree (e.g., Ph.D., Ed.D.)

Elementary school A school classified as elementary by state and local practice and composed of any span of grades not above grade 8.

Employment status A classification of individuals as employed (either full or part time), unemployed (looking for work or on layoff), or not in the labor force (due to being retired, having unpaid employment, or some other reason).

English language learner (ELL) An individual who, due to any of the reasons listed below, has sufficient difficulty speaking, reading, writing, or understanding the English language to be denied the opportunity to learn successfully in classrooms where the language of instruction is English or to participate fully in the larger U.S. society. Such an individual (1) was not born in the United States or has a native language other than English; (2) comes from environments where a language other than English is dominant; or (3) is an American Indian or Alaska Native and comes from environments where a language other than English has had a significant impact on the individual's level of English language proficiency.

Enrollment The total number of students registered in a given school unit at a given time, generally in the fall of a year. At the postsecondary level, separate counts are also available for full-time and part-time students, as well as full-time-equivalent enrollment. See also Full-time enrollment, Full-time-equivalent (FTE) enrollment, and Part-time enrollment.

Glossary

Expenditures, Total For elementary/secondary schools, these include all charges for current outlays plus capital outlays and interest on school debt. For degree-granting institutions, these include current outlays plus capital outlays. For government, these include charges net of recoveries and other correcting transactions other than for retirement of debt, investment in securities, extension of credit, or as agency transactions. Government expenditures include only external transactions, such as the provision of perquisites or other payments in kind. Aggregates for groups of governments exclude intergovernmental transactions among the governments.

Expenditures per pupil Charges incurred for a particular period of time divided by a student unit of measure, such as average daily attendance or fall enrollment.

F

Federal sources (postsecondary degree-granting institutions) Includes federal appropriations, grants, and contracts, and federally funded research and development centers (FFRDCs). Federally subsidized student loans are not included.

Financial aid Grants, loans, assistantships, scholarships, fellowships, tuition waivers, tuition discounts, veteran's benefits, employer aid (tuition reimbursement), and other monies (other than from relatives or friends) provided to students to help them meet expenses. Except where designated, includes Title IV subsidized and unsubsidized loans made directly to students.

For-profit institution A private institution in which the individual(s) or agency in control receives compensation other than wages, rent, or other expenses for the assumption of risk.

Free or reduced-price lunch See National School Lunch Program.

Full-time enrollment The number of students enrolled in postsecondary education courses with total credit load equal to at least 75 percent of the normal full-time course load. At the undergraduate level, full-time enrollment typically includes students who have a credit load of 12 or more semester or quarter credits. At the postbaccalaureate level, full-time enrollment includes students who typically have a credit load of 9 or more semester or quarter credits, as well as other students who are considered full time by their institutions.

Full-time-equivalent (FTE) enrollment For postsecondary institutions, enrollment of full-time students, plus the full-time equivalent of part-time students. The full-time equivalent of the part-time students is estimated using different factors depending on the type and control of institution and level of student.

G

Geographic region One of the four regions of the United States used by the U.S. Census Bureau, as follows:

Northeast	Midwest
Connecticut (CT)	Illinois (IL)
Maine (ME)	Indiana (IN)
Massachusetts (MA)	Iowa (IA)
New Hampshire (NH)	Kansas (KS)
New Jersey (NJ)	Michigan (MI)
New York (NY)	Minnesota (MN)
Pennsylvania (PA)	Missouri (MO)
Rhode Island (RI)	Nebraska (NE)
Vermont (VT)	North Dakota (ND)
	Ohio (OH)
	South Dakota (SD)
	Wisconsin (WI)

South	West
Alabama (AL)	Alaska (AK)
Arkansas (AR)	Arizona (AZ)
Delaware (DE)	California (CA)
District of Columbia (DC)	Colorado (CO)
Florida (FL)	Hawaii (HI)
Georgia (GA)	Idaho (ID)
Kentucky (KY)	Montana (MT)
Louisiana (LA)	Nevada (NV)
Maryland (MD)	New Mexico (NM)
Mississippi (MS)	Oregon (OR)
North Carolina (NC)	Utah (UT)
Oklahoma (OK)	Washington (WA)
South Carolina (SC)	Wyoming (WY)
Tennessee (TN)	
Texas (TX)	
Virginia (VA)	
West Virginia (WV)	

Gross domestic product (GDP) The total national output of goods and services valued at market prices. GDP can be viewed in terms of expenditure categories which include purchases of goods and services by consumers and government, gross private domestic investment, and net exports of goods and services. The goods and services included are largely those bought for final use (excluding illegal transactions) in the market economy. A number of inclusions, however, represent imputed values, the most important of which is rental value of owner-occupied housing.

H

High school completer An individual who has been awarded a high school diploma or an equivalent credential, including a GED certificate.

Glossary

High school diploma A formal document regulated by the state certifying the successful completion of a prescribed secondary school program of studies. In some states or communities, high school diplomas are differentiated by type, such as an academic diploma, a general diploma, or a vocational diploma.

Household All the people who occupy a housing unit. A house, an apartment, a mobile home, a group of rooms, or a single room is regarded as a housing unit when it is occupied or intended for occupancy as separate living quarters, that is, when the occupants do not live and eat with any other people in the structure, and there is direct access from the outside or through a common hall.

I

Individuals with Disabilities Education Act (IDEA) IDEA is a federal law enacted in 1990 and reauthorized in 1997 and 2004. IDEA requires services to children with disabilities throughout the nation. IDEA governs how states and public agencies provide early intervention, special education, and related services to eligible infants, toddlers, children, and youth with disabilities. Infants and toddlers with disabilities (birth–age 2) and their families receive early intervention services under IDEA, Part C. Children and youth (ages 3–21) receive special education and related services under IDEA, Part B.

Interest on debt Includes expenditures for long-term debt service interest payments (i.e., those longer than 1 year).

International Standard Classification of Education (ISCED) Used to compare educational systems in different countries. ISCED is the standard used by many countries to report education statistics to the United Nations Educational, Scientific, and Cultural Organization (UNESCO) and the Organization for Economic Cooperation and Development (OECD). ISCED was revised in 2011.

> **ISCED 2011** ISCED 2011 divides educational systems into the following nine categories, based on eight levels of education.

> **ISCED Level 0** Education preceding the first level (early childhood education) includes early childhood programs that target children below the age of entry into primary education.

> > **ISCED Level 01** Early childhood educational development programs are generally designed for children younger than 3 years.

> > **ISCED Level 02** Pre-primary education preceding the first level usually begins at age 3, 4, or 5 (sometimes earlier) and lasts from 1 to 3 years, when it is provided. In the United States, this level includes nursery school and kindergarten.

> **ISCED Level 1** Education at the first level (primary or elementary education) usually begins at age 5, 6, or 7 and continues for about 4 to 6 years. For the United States, the first level starts with 1st grade and ends with 6th grade.

> **ISCED Level 2** Education at the second level (lower secondary education) typically begins at about age 11 or 12 and continues for about 2 to 6 years. For the United States, the second level starts with 7th grade and typically ends with 9th grade. Education at the lower secondary level continues the basic programs of the first level, although teaching is typically more subject focused, often using more specialized teachers who conduct classes in their field of specialization. The main criterion for distinguishing lower secondary education from primary education is whether programs begin to be organized in a more subject-oriented pattern, using more specialized teachers conducting classes in their field of specialization. If there is no clear breakpoint for this organizational change, lower secondary education is considered to begin at the end of 6 years of primary education. In countries with no clear division between lower secondary and upper secondary education, and where lower secondary education lasts for more than 3 years, only the first 3 years following primary education are counted as lower secondary education.

> **ISCED Level 3** Education at the third level (upper secondary education) typically begins at age 15 or 16 and lasts for approximately 3 years. In the United States, the third level starts with 10th grade and ends with 12th grade. Upper secondary education is the final stage of secondary education in most OECD countries. Instruction is often organized along subject-matter lines, in contrast to the lower secondary level, and teachers typically must have a higher level, or more subject-specific, qualification. There are substantial differences in the typical duration of programs both across and between countries, ranging from 2 to 5 years of schooling. The main criteria for classifications are (1) national boundaries between lower and upper secondary education and (2) admission into educational programs, which usually requires the completion of lower secondary education or a combination of basic education and life experience that demonstrates the ability to handle the subject matter in upper secondary schools. Includes programs designed to review the content of third level programs, such as preparatory courses for tertiary education entrance examinations, and programs leading to a qualification equivalent to upper secondary general education.

ISCED Level 4 Education at the fourth level (postsecondary nontertiary education) straddles the boundary between secondary and postsecondary education. This program of study, which is primarily vocational in nature, is generally taken after the completion of secondary school and typically lasts from 6 months to 2 years. Although the content of these programs may not be significantly more advanced than upper secondary programs, these programs serve to broaden the knowledge of participants who have already gained an upper secondary qualification.

ISCED Level 5 Education at the fifth level (short-cycle tertiary education) is noticeably more complex than in upper secondary programs giving access to this level. Content at the fifth level is usually practically based, occupationally specific, and prepare students to enter the labor market. However, the fifth level may also provide a pathway to other tertiary education programs (the sixth or seventh level). Short cycle-tertiary programs last for at least 2 years, and usually for no more than 3. In the United States, this level includes associate's degrees.

ISCED Level 6 Education at the sixth level (bachelor's or equivalent level) is longer and usually more theoretically oriented than programs at the fifth level, but may include practical components. Entry into these programs normally requires the completion of a third or fourth level program. They typically have a duration of 3 to 4 years of full-time study. Programs at the sixth level do not necessarily require the preparation of a substantive thesis or dissertation.

ISCED Level 7 Education at the seventh level (master's or equivalent level) has significantly more complex and specialized content than programs at the sixth level. The content at the seventh level is often designed to provide participants with advanced academic and/or professional knowledge, skills, and competencies, leading to a second degree or equivalent qualification. Programs at this level may have a substantial research component but do not yet lead to the award of a doctoral qualification. In the United States, this level includes professional degrees such as J.D., M.D., and D.D.S., as well as master degrees.

ISCED Level 8 Education at the eighth level (doctoral or equivalent level) is provided in graduate and professional schools that generally require a university degree or diploma as a minimum condition for admission. Programs at this level lead to the award of an advanced, postgraduate degree, such as a Ph.D. The theoretical duration of these programs is 3 years of full-time enrollment in most countries (for a cumulative total of at least 7 years at the tertiary level), although the length of the actual enrollment is often longer. Programs at this level are devoted to advanced study and original research.

ISCED 1997 ISCED 1997 divides educational systems into the following seven categories, based on six levels of education.

ISCED Level 0 Education preceding the first level (early childhood education) usually begins at age 3, 4, or 5 (sometimes earlier) and lasts from 1 to 3 years, when it is provided. In the United States, this level includes nursery school and kindergarten.

ISCED Level 1 Education at the first level (primary or elementary education) usually begins at age 5, 6, or 7 and continues for about 4 to 6 years. For the United States, the first level starts with 1st grade and ends with 6th grade.

ISCED Level 2 Education at the second level (lower secondary education) typically begins at about age 11 or 12 and continues for about 2 to 6 years. For the United States, the second level starts with 7th grade and typically ends with 9th grade. Education at the lower secondary level continues the basic programs of the first level, although teaching is typically more subject focused, often using more specialized teachers who conduct classes in their field of specialization. The main criterion for distinguishing lower secondary education from primary education is whether programs begin to be organized in a more subject-oriented pattern, using more specialized teachers conducting classes in their field of specialization. If there is no clear breakpoint for this organizational change, lower secondary education is considered to begin at the end of 6 years of primary education. In countries with no clear division between lower secondary and upper secondary education, and where lower secondary education lasts for more than 3 years, only the first 3 years following primary education are counted as lower secondary education.

ISCED Level 3 Education at the third level (upper secondary education) typically begins at age 15 or 16 and lasts for approximately 3 years. In the United States, the third level starts with 10th grade and ends with 12th grade. Upper secondary education is the final stage of secondary education in most OECD countries. Instruction is often organized along subject-matter lines, in contrast to the lower secondary level, and teachers typically must have a higher level, or more subject-specific, qualification. There are substantial differences in the typical duration of programs both across and between countries, ranging from 2 to 5 years of schooling. The main criteria for classifications are (1) national boundaries between lower and upper secondary education and (2) admission into educational programs, which usually requires the completion of lower secondary education or a combination of basic education and life experience that demonstrates the ability to handle the subject matter in upper secondary schools.

ISCED Level 4 Education at the fourth level (postsecondary nontertiary education) straddles the boundary between secondary and postsecondary education. This program of study, which is primarily vocational in nature, is generally taken after the completion of secondary school and typically lasts from 6 months to 2 years. Although the content of these programs may not be significantly more advanced than upper secondary programs, these programs serve to broaden the knowledge of participants who have already gained an upper secondary qualification.

ISCED Level 5 Education at the fifth level (first stage of tertiary education) includes programs with more advanced content than those offered at the two previous levels. Entry into programs at the fifth level normally requires successful completion of either of the two previous levels.

> ***ISCED Level 5A*** Tertiary-type A programs provide an education that is largely theoretical and is intended to provide sufficient qualifications for gaining entry into advanced research programs and professions with high skill requirements. Entry into these programs normally requires the successful completion of an upper secondary education; admission is competitive in most cases. The minimum cumulative theoretical duration at this level is 3 years of full-time enrollment. In the United States, tertiary-type A programs include first university programs that last approximately 4 years and lead to the award of a bachelor's degree and second university programs that lead to a master's degree or a first-professional degree such as an M.D., a J.D., or a D.V.M.

> ***ISCED Level 5B*** Tertiary-type B programs are typically shorter than tertiary-type A programs and focus on practical, technical, or occupational skills for direct entry into the labor market, although they may cover some theoretical foundations in the respective programs. They have a minimum duration of 2 years of full-time enrollment at the tertiary level. In the United States, such programs are often provided at community colleges and lead to an associate's degree.

ISCED Level 6 Education at the sixth level (advanced research qualification) is provided in graduate and professional schools that generally require a university degree or diploma as a minimum condition for admission. Programs at this level lead to the award of an advanced, postgraduate degree, such as a Ph.D. The theoretical duration of these programs is 3 years of full-time enrollment in most countries (for a cumulative total of at least 7 years at levels five and six), although the length of the actual enrollment is often longer. Programs at this level are devoted to advanced study and original research.

L

Locale codes A classification system to describe a type of location. The "Metro-Centric" locale codes, developed in the 1980s, classified all schools and school districts based on their county's proximity to a Metropolitan Statistical Area (MSA) and their specific location's population size and density. In 2006, the "Urban-Centric" locale codes were introduced. These locale codes are based on an address's proximity to an urbanized area. For more information see http://nces.ed.gov/ccd/rural_locales.asp.

Pre-2006 Metro-Centric Locale Codes

> ***Large City:*** A central city of a consolidated metropolitan statistical area (CMSA) or MSA, with the city having a population greater than or equal to 250,000.

> ***Mid-size City:*** A central city of a CMSA or MSA, with the city having a population less than 250,000.

> ***Urban Fringe of a Large City:*** Any territory within a CMSA or MSA of a Large City and defined as urban by the Census Bureau.

> ***Urban Fringe of a Mid-size City:*** Any territory within a CMSA or MSA of a Mid-size City and defined as urban by the Census Bureau.

> ***Large Town:*** An incorporated place or Census-designated place with a population greater than or equal to 25,000 and located outside a CMSA or MSA.

> ***Small Town:*** An incorporated place or Census-designated place with a population less than 25,000 and greater than or equal to 2,500 and located outside a CMSA or MSA.

> ***Rural, Outside MSA:*** Any territory designated as rural by the Census Bureau that is outside a CMSA or MSA of a Large or Mid-size City.

> ***Rural, Inside MSA:*** Any territory designated as rural by the Census Bureau that is within a CMSA or MSA of a Large or Mid-size City.

Glossary

2006 Urban-Centric Locale Codes

City, Large: Territory inside an urbanized area and inside a principal city with population of 250,000 or more.

City, Mid-size: Territory inside an urbanized area and inside a principal city with population less than 250,000 and greater than or equal to 100,000.

City, Small: Territory inside an urbanized area and inside a principal city with population less than 100,000.

Suburb, Large: Territory outside a principal city and inside an urbanized area with population of 250,000 or more.

Suburb, Mid-size: Territory outside a principal city and inside an urbanized area with population less than 250,000 and greater than or equal to 100,000.

Suburb, Small: Territory outside a principal city and inside an urbanized area with population less than 100,000.

Town, Fringe: Territory inside an urban cluster that is less than or equal to 10 miles from an urbanized area.

Town, Distant: Territory inside an urban cluster that is more than 10 miles and less than or equal to 35 miles from an urbanized area.

Town, Remote: Territory inside an urban cluster that is more than 35 miles from an urbanized area.

Rural, Fringe: Census-defined rural territory that is less than or equal to 5 miles from an urbanized area, as well as rural territory that is less than or equal to 2.5 miles from an urban cluster.

Rural, Distant: Census-defined rural territory that is more than 5 miles but less than or equal to 25 miles from an urbanized area, as well as rural territory that is more than 2.5 miles but less than or equal to 10 miles from an urban cluster.

Rural, Remote: Census-defined rural territory that is more than 25 miles from an urbanized area and is also more than 10 miles from an urban cluster.

M

Master's degree A degree awarded for successful completion of a program generally requiring 1 or 2 years of full-time college-level study beyond the bachelor's degree. One type of master's degree, including the Master of Arts degree, or M.A., and the Master of Science degree, or M.S., is awarded in the liberal arts and sciences for advanced scholarship in a subject field or discipline and demonstrated ability to perform scholarly research. A second type of master's degree is awarded for the completion of a professionally oriented program, for example, an M.Ed. in education, an M.B.A. in business administration, an M.F.A. in fine arts, an M.M. in music, an M.S.W. in social work, and an M.P.A. in public administration. Some master's degrees—such as divinity degrees (M.Div. or M.H.L./Rav), which were formerly classified as "first-professional"—may require more than 2 years of full-time study beyond the bachelor's degree.

Median earnings The amount which divides the income distribution into two equal groups, half having income above that amount and half having income below that amount. Earnings include all wage and salary income. Unlike mean earnings, median earnings either do not change or change very little in response to extreme observations.

N

National School Lunch Program Established by President Truman in 1946, the program is a federally assisted meal program operated in public and private nonprofit schools and residential child care centers. To be eligible for free lunch, a student must be from a household with an income at or below 130 percent of the federal poverty guideline; to be eligible for reduced-price lunch, a student must be from a household with an income between 130 percent and 185 percent of the federal poverty guideline.

Nonprofit institution A private institution in which the individual(s) or agency in control receives no compensation other than wages, rent, or other expenses for the assumption of risk. Nonprofit institutions may be either independent nonprofit (i.e., having no religious affiliation) or religiously affiliated.

Nonsectarian school Nonsectarian schools do not have a religious orientation or purpose and are categorized as regular, special program emphasis, or special education schools. See also Regular school.

O

Organization for Economic Cooperation and Development (OECD) An intergovernmental organization of industrialized countries that serves as a forum for member countries to cooperate in research and policy development on social and economic topics of common interest. In addition to member countries, partner countries contribute to the OECD's work in a sustained and comprehensive manner.

Other religious school Other religious schools have a religious orientation or purpose, but are not Roman Catholic. Other religious schools are categorized according to religious association membership as Conservative Christian, other affiliated, or unaffiliated.

P

Part-time enrollment The number of students enrolled in postsecondary education courses with a total credit load less than 75 percent of the normal full-time credit load. At the undergraduate level, part-time enrollment typically includes students who have a credit load of less than 12 semester or quarter credits. At the postbaccalaureate level, part-time enrollment typically includes students who have a credit load of less than 9 semester or quarter credits.

Postbaccalaureate enrollment The number of students working towards advanced degrees and of students enrolled in graduate-level classes but not enrolled in degree programs.

Postsecondary education The provision of formal instructional programs with a curriculum designed primarily for students who have completed the requirements for a high school diploma or equivalent. This includes programs of an academic, vocational, and continuing professional education purpose, and excludes avocational and adult basic education programs.

Postsecondary institutions (basic classification by level)

4-year institution An institution offering at least a 4-year program of college-level studies wholly or principally creditable toward a baccalaureate degree.

2-year institution An institution offering at least a 2-year program of college-level studies which terminates in an associate degree or is principally creditable toward a baccalaureate degree. Data prior to 1996 include some institutions that have a less-than-2-year program, but were designated as institutions of higher education in the Higher Education General Information Survey.

Less-than-2-year institution An institution that offers programs of less than 2 years' duration below the baccalaureate level. Includes occupational and vocational schools with programs that do not exceed 1,800 contact hours.

Poverty (official measure) The U.S. Census Bureau uses a set of money income thresholds that vary by family size and composition. A family, along with each individual in it, is considered poor if the family's total income is less than that family's threshold. The poverty thresholds do not vary geographically and are adjusted annually for inflation using the Consumer Price Index. The official poverty definition counts money income before taxes and does not include capital gains and noncash benefits (such as public housing, Medicaid, and food stamps).

Prekindergarten Preprimary education for children typically ages 3–4 who have not yet entered kindergarten. It may offer a program of general education or special education and may be part of a collaborative effort with Head Start.

Preschool An instructional program enrolling children generally younger than 5 years of age and organized to provide children with educational experiences under professionally qualified teachers during the year or years immediately preceding kindergarten (or prior to entry into elementary school when there is no kindergarten). See also Prekindergarten.

Private institution An institution that is controlled by an individual or agency other than a state, a subdivision of a state, or the federal government, which is usually supported primarily by other than public funds, and the operation of whose program rests with other than publicly elected or appointed officials.

Private nonprofit institution An institution in which the individual(s) or agency in control receives no compensation other than wages, rent, or other expenses for the assumption of risk. These include both independent nonprofit institutions and those affiliated with a religious organization.

Private for-profit institution An institution in which the individual(s) or agency in control receives compensation other than wages, rent, or other expenses for the assumption of risk (e.g., proprietary schools).

Private school Private elementary/secondary schools surveyed by the Private School Universe Survey (PSS) are assigned to one of three major categories (Catholic, other religious, or nonsectarian) and, within each major category, one of three subcategories based on the school's religious affiliation provided by respondents.

Catholic Schools categorized according to governance, provided by Catholic school respondents, into parochial, diocesan, and private schools.

Other religious Schools that have a religious orientation or purpose but are not Roman Catholic. Other religious schools are categorized according to religious association membership, provided by respondents, into Conservative Christian, other affiliated, and unaffiliated schools. Conservative Christian schools are those "Other religious" schools with membership in at least one of four associations: Accelerated Christian Education, American Association of Christian Schools, Association of Christian Schools International, and Oral Roberts University Education Fellowship. Affiliated schools are those "Other religious" schools not classified as Conservative Christian with membership in at least 1 of 11 associations—Association of Christian Teachers and Schools, Christian Schools International, Evangelical Lutheran Education Association, Friends

Council on Education, General Conference of the Seventh-Day Adventist Church, Islamic School League of America, National Association of Episcopal Schools, National Christian School Association, National Society for Hebrew Day Schools, Solomon Schechter Day Schools, and Southern Baptist Association of Christian Schools—or indicating membership in "other religious school associations." Unaffiliated schools are those "Other religious" schools that have a religious orientation or purpose but are not classified as Conservative Christian or affiliated.

Nonsectarian Schools that do not have a religious orientation or purpose and are categorized according to program emphasis, provided by respondents, into regular, special emphasis, and special education schools. Regular schools are those that have a regular elementary/secondary or early childhood program emphasis. Special emphasis schools are those that have a Montessori, vocational/technical, alternative, or special program emphasis. Special education schools are those that have a special education program emphasis.

Property tax The sum of money collected from a tax levied against the value of property.

Proprietary (for profit) institution A private institution in which the individual(s) or agency in control receives compensation other than wages, rent, or other expenses for the assumption of risk.

Public school or institution A school or institution controlled and operated by publicly elected or appointed officials and deriving its primary support from public funds.

Pupil/teacher ratio The enrollment of pupils at a given period of time, divided by the full-time-equivalent number of classroom teachers serving these pupils during the same period.

Purchasing Power Parity (PPP) indexes PPP exchange rates, or indexes, are the currency exchange rates that equalize the purchasing power of different currencies, meaning that when a given sum of money is converted into different currencies at the PPP exchange rates, it will buy the same basket of goods and services in all countries. PPP indexes are the rates of currency conversion that eliminate the difference in price levels among countries. Thus, when expenditures on gross domestic product (GDP) for different countries are converted into a common currency by means of PPP indexes, they are expressed at the same set of international prices, so that comparisons among countries reflect only differences in the volume of goods and services purchased.

R

Racial/ethnic group Classification indicating general racial or ethnic heritage. Race/ethnicity data are based on the *Hispanic* ethnic category and the race categories listed below (five single-race categories, plus the *Two or more races* category). Race categories exclude persons of Hispanic ethnicity unless otherwise noted.

White A person having origins in any of the original peoples of Europe, the Middle East, or North Africa.

Black or African American A person having origins in any of the black racial groups of Africa. Used interchangeably with the shortened term *Black*.

Hispanic or Latino A person of Cuban, Mexican, Puerto Rican, South or Central American, or other Spanish culture or origin, regardless of race. Used interchangeably with the shortened term *Hispanic*.

Asian A person having origins in any of the original peoples of the Far East, Southeast Asia, or the Indian subcontinent, including, for example, Cambodia, China, India, Japan, Korea, Malaysia, Pakistan, the Philippine Islands, Thailand, and Vietnam. Prior to 2010–11, the Common Core of Data (CCD) combined Asian and Pacific Islander categories.

Native Hawaiian or Other Pacific Islander A person having origins in any of the original peoples of Hawaii, Guam, Samoa, or other Pacific Islands. Prior to 2010–11, the Common Core of Data (CCD) combined Asian and Pacific Islander categories. Used interchangeably with the shortened term *Pacific Islander*.

American Indian or Alaska Native A person having origins in any of the original peoples of North and South America (including Central America), and who maintains tribal affiliation or community attachment.

Two or more races A person identifying himself or herself as of two or more of the following race groups: White, Black, Asian, Native Hawaiian or Other Pacific Islander, or American Indian or Alaska Native. Some, but not all, reporting districts use this category. "Two or more races" was introduced in the 2000 Census and became a regular category for data collection in the Current Population Survey in 2003. The category is sometimes excluded from a historical series of data with constant categories. It is sometimes included within the category "Other."

Regular school A public elementary/secondary or charter school providing instruction and education services that does not focus primarily on special education, vocational/technical education, or alternative education.

Revenue All funds received from external sources, net of refunds, and correcting transactions. Noncash transactions, such as receipt of services, commodities, or other receipts in kind are excluded, as are funds received from the issuance of debt, liquidation of investments, and nonroutine sale of property.

S

Salary The total amount regularly paid or stipulated to be paid to an individual, before deductions, for personal services rendered while on the payroll of a business or organization.

School district An education agency at the local level that exists primarily to operate public schools or to contract for public school services. Synonyms are "local basic administrative unit" and "local education agency."

Secondary school A school comprising any span of grades beginning with the next grade following an elementary or middle school (usually 7, 8, or 9) and ending with or below grade 12. Both junior high schools and senior high schools are included.

Socioeconomic status (SES) The SES index is a composite of often equally weighted, standardized components, such as father's education, mother's education, family income, father's occupation, and household items. The terms high, middle, and low SES refer to ranges of the weighted SES composite index distribution.

Status dropout rate (Current Population Survey) The percentage of civilian, noninstitutionalized young people ages 16–24 who are not in school and have not earned a high school credential (either a diploma or equivalency credential such as a GED certificate). The numerator of the status dropout rate for a given year is the number of individuals ages 16–24 who, as of October of that year, have not completed a high school credential and are not currently enrolled in school. The denominator is the total number of individuals ages 16–24 in the United States in October of that year. Status dropout rates count the following individuals as dropouts: those who never attended school and immigrants who did not complete the equivalent of a high school education in their home country.

Status dropout rate (American Community Survey) Similar to the status dropout rate (Current Population Survey), except that institutionalized persons, incarcerated persons, and active duty military personnel living in barracks in the United States may be included in this calculation.

STEM fields Science, Technology, Engineering, and Mathematics (STEM) fields of study that are considered to be of particular relevance to advanced societies. For the purposes of *The Condition of Education 2016*, STEM fields include agriculture and natural resources, architecture, biology and biomedical sciences, computer and information sciences, engineering and engineering technologies, health studies, mathematics and statistics, and physical and social sciences. STEM occupations include computer scientists and mathematicians; engineers and architects; life, physical, and social scientists; medical professionals; and managers of STEM activities.

Student membership Student membership is an annual headcount of students enrolled in school on October 1 or the school day closest to that date. The Common Core of Data (CCD) allows a student to be reported for only a single school or agency. For example, a vocational school (identified as a "shared time" school) may provide classes for students from a number of districts and show no membership.

T

Title IV eligible institution A postsecondary institution that meets the criteria for participating in federal student financial aid programs. An eligible institution must be any of the following: (1) an institution of higher education (with public or private, nonprofit control), (2) a proprietary institution (with private for-profit control), and (3) a postsecondary vocational institution (with public or private, nonprofit control). In addition, it must have acceptable legal authorization, acceptable accreditation and admission standards, eligible academic program(s), administrative capability, and financial responsibility.

Traditional public school Publicly funded schools other than public charter schools. See also Public school or institution and Charter school.

Tuition and fees A payment or charge for instruction or compensation for services, privileges, or the use of equipment, books, or other goods. Tuition may be charged per term, per course, or per credit.

U

Undergraduate students Students registered at an institution of postsecondary education who are working in a baccalaureate degree program or other formal program below the baccalaureate, such as an associate's degree, vocational, or technical program.